Trade and Industrial Development in Africa

The book is a product of the Guy Mhone conference on 'Rethinking Trade and Development in Africa'.

Trade and Industrial Development in Africa

Rethinking Strategy and Policy

Edited by
Theresa Moyo

CODESRIA
Council for the Development of Social Science Research in Africa
DAKAR

© CODESRIA 2014
Council for the Development of Social Science Research in Africa
Avenue Cheikh Anta Diop, Angle Canal IV
BP 3304 Dakar, 18524, Senegal
Website: www.codesria.org

ISBN: 978-2-86978-571-7

Typesetting: Daouda Thiam
Cover Design: Ibrahima Fofana

Distributed in Africa by CODESRIA
Distributed elsewhere by African Books Collective, Oxford, UK
Website: www.africanbookscollective.com

The Council for the Development of Social Science Research in Africa (CODESRIA) is an independent organisation whose principal objectives are to facilitate research, promote research-based publishing and create multiple forums geared towards the exchange of views and information among African researchers. All these are aimed at reducing the fragmentation of research in the continent through the creation of thematic research networks that cut across linguistic and regional boundaries.

CODESRIA publishes *Africa Development*, the longest standing Africa based social science journal; *Afrika Zamani*, a journal of history; the *African Sociological Review*; the *African Journal of International Affairs*; *Africa Review of Books* and the *Journal of Higher Education in Africa*. The Council also co-publishes the *Africa Media Review*; *Identity, Culture and Politics: An Afro-Asian Dialogue*; *The African Anthropologist* and the *Afro-Arab Selections for Social Sciences*. The results of its research and other activities are also disseminated through its Working Paper Series, Green Book Series, Monograph Series, Book Series, Policy Briefs and the CODESRIA Bulletin. Select CODESRIA publications are also accessible online at www.codesria.org.

CODESRIA would like to express its gratitude to the Swedish International Development Cooperation Agency (SIDA), the International Development Research Centre (IDRC), the Ford Foundation, the Carnegie Corporation of New York (CCNY), the Norwegian Agency for Development Cooperation (NORAD), the Danish Agency for International Development (DANIDA), the French Ministry of Cooperation, the United Nations Development Programme (UNDP), the Netherlands Ministry of Foreign Affairs, the Rockefeller Foundation, the Open Society Foundations (OSFs), TrustAfrica, UNESCO, UN Women, the African Capacity Building Foundation (ACBF) and the Government of Senegal for supporting its research, training and publication programmes.

Contents

PART ONE

Trade and Industrial Policy in Africa:
Theoretical Debates and Experiences from Developing Regions

PART TWO
Trade and Industrial Policy: International and Regional Context

PART THREE
Intellectual Property Rights, Technology Transfer and Culture Policy

PART FOUR
Institutional Dimensions of Trade and Industrial Policy

Abbreviations

ACP	African, Caribbean and Pacific Countries
AfDB	African Development Bank
APEC	Asia Pacific Economic Cooperation
AU	African Union
ASYCUDA	Automated Systems for Customs Data
BDC	Botswana Development Corporation
BEDIA	Botswana Export Development and Investment Agency
BIS	Basic Industry Strategy
CAADP	Comprehensive African Agriculture Development Programme
CEDA	Citizen Entrepreneurial Development Agency
CERs	Certified Emissions Reduction
CDM	Clean Development Mechanism
CFA	Cameroonian Francs
CPI	Corruption Perception Index
CODESRIA	Council for the Development of Social Science Research in Africa
COMESA	Common Market for Eastern and Southern Africa
EAC	East African Community
ECA	Economic Commission for Africa
ECOWAS	Economic Community of West African States
EDF	European Development Fund
EOI	Export-Oriented Industrialisation
EPAs	Economic Partnership Agreements
EU	European Union
FDI	Foreign Direct Investment
FTA	Free Trade Area
GDP	Gross Domestic Product
GHGs	Green House Gases
HHD	High Human Development

HIPC	Highly Indebted Poor Countries
HIV/AIDS	Human Immuno-deficiency Virus/Acquired Immune Deficiency Syndrome
HPAEs	High Performing Asian Economies
ICI	Investment Climate Index
ICOR	Incremental Capital Output Ratio
IDDA	Industrial Development Decade for Africa
IDS	Institute of Development Studies
IMF	International Monetary Fund
IP	Intellectual Property
IPCC	Intergovernmental Panel on Climate Change
ISI	Import Substitution Industrialization
KP	Kyoto Protocol
LDCs	Least Developed Countries
LHD	Low Human Development
MDGs	Millennium Development Goals
MHD	Medium Human Development
MMD	Movement for Multi-Party Democracy
MVA	Manufacturing Value Added
NAMB	National Agricultural Marketing Board
NCZ	Nitrogen Chemicals of Zambia
NEPAD	New Partnership for African Development
NERP	National Economic Recovery Programme
OPEC	Organisation of Oil Exporting Countries
PANAFTEL	Pan African Telecommunications Network
RASCOM	Regional African Satellite Communications
RECs	Regional Economic Communities
SACU	South African Customs Union
SADC	Southern Africa Development Community
SAP	Structural Adjustment Programme
SEA	South East Asia
SIA	Sustainability Impact Assessment
SMEs	Small to Medium Enterprises
SSA	Sub-Saharan Africa
SSATP	Sub-Saharan African Transport Policy Programme
TAH	Trans African Highway
TBT	Technical Barriers to Trade

TDCA	Trade, Development and Cooperation Agreement
TI	Transparency International
TIPAZ	Inter State Transit Agreement for Central African Countries
TNC	Transnational Corporation
TRIPs	Trade Related Aspects of Intellectual Property Rights
TT	Technology Transfer
UDI	Unilateral Declaration of Independence
UNCTAD	United Nations Commission on Trade and Development
UNECA	United Nations Economic Commission for Africa
UNESCO	United Nations Educational and Scientific Convention
UNFCCC	United Nations Framework Convention on Climate Change
UNIDO	United Nations Industrial Development Organization
UNIP	United National Independent Party
WAC	West African Community
WDI	World Development Indicators
WTO	World Trade Organization
ZAMEFA	Zambia Metal Fabrications Limited
ZCCM	Zambia Consolidated Copper Mines
ZK	Zambian Kwacha
ZPA	Zambia Privatization Agency

Tables

Boxes

Figures

Acknowledgement

The editor would like to thank the Executive Secretariat of CODESRIA for all the support provided throughout the writing and publication process of this book. In particular, Ebrima Sall the Executive Secretary, Carlos Cardoso and Mame Sokhna Thiaré Touré at the Research Programme, and Alexander Bangirana and Chifaou Amzat at the Publications and Dissemination Programme. Without your sterling input and support, it would not have been possible to complete the book. The editor also wishes to acknowledge and appreciate Adebayo Olukoshi, CODESRIA's former Executive Secretary, for his scientific input during the Guy Mhone International Conference on 'Rethinking Trade and Development in Africa'. The papers which were presented at that conference formed the basis for writing this book.

Theresa Moyo
Editor

Contributors

Adewole Musiliu Adeolu is a Lecturer in the Department of Economics and Development Studies at the College of Business and Social Sciences, Covenant University, Ota, Ogun State, Nigeria.

Oluyele Akinkugbe is a Professor in the Department of Economics and Economic History, Rhodes University, Grahamstown, South Africa.

Euston Chiputa is the Head, Department of History, School of Humanities and Social Sciences, University of Zambia, Lusaka.

Anthony I. Monye-Emina lectures in the Department of Economics and Statistics, University of Benin, Nigeria.

Stephen M. Kapunda is a Professor in the Department of Economics, University of Botswana.

Theresa Moyo is a Senior Lecturer on the Master of Development Programme and Acting Director of the Turfloop Graduate School of Leadership, University of Limpopo, South Africa.

Sunday Aninpah Khan is a Lecturer in the Faculty of Economics and Management, University of Yaounde II, Cameroon.

Godwell Nhamo is Chair of the Business and Climate Change unit of the Centre for Corporate Citizenship at UNISA, South Africa.

Aderibigbe S. Olomola is a Research Professor and Director of the Agriculture and Rural Development Department, Nigerian Institute of Social and Economic Research (NISER), Ibadan, Nigeria.

Patrick Juvet G. Lowe is a Professor in the Faculty of Law and Political Sciences, University of Dschang, Cameroon.

Ntangsi Max Memfih is a Lecturer in the Department of Economics and Management, Faculty of Social and Management Sciences, University of Buea, Cameroon.

E. S. Nwauche is an Associate Professor of Law at the Rivers State University, Port Harcourt, and Director Centre for African Legal Studies, Port Harcourt, Rivers State, Nigeria.

Howard Stein is a Professor at the Centre for Afro-American and African Studies, University of Michigan, United States of America.

Foreword

Aderibigbe S. Olomola

The subject of trade and industrial development in Africa is a topical issue. In an attempt to enhance their benefits from their rich natural and human resource base, many African countries have shifted from the dominant strategy of Import Substitution Industrialization (ISI) of the 1960s and 1970s to Western-backed market-oriented reforms of trade liberalization. Those reforms were expected to improve the competitiveness of industry, among other sectors, improve export performance and the overall balance of payments, and ultimately increase economic growth as measured by the Gross Domestic Product (GDP). It has been acknowledged that, indeed, economic reforms have led to an increase in economic growth. In the last seven years, Africa has experienced strong economic growth, averaging about 6.5 per cent per annum between 2002 and 2007. The growth has largely been attributed to strong demand for Africa's primary commodity exports and also the macroeconomic reforms which most countries implemented since the 1990s. It was also achieved as a result of increases in productivity and domestic investment and remittances from Africans living in the diaspora.

Yet despite the unprecedented growth performance, the impact of trade and industry on development has been limited. This is despite the continent's endowment with vast human, mineral and natural resources. Most countries on the continent are classified in the United Nations Human Development Report (2007/2008) under the Low Human Development (LHD) category. They are also listed under the High Human Poverty Index (HPI) group. Countries such as South Africa, Botswana, Morocco, Maurititus and Namibia which are among the few African countries classified in the Medium Human Development (MHD) category, are cited among the most unequal societies on the continent, with Gini coefficient values (notwithstanding the weakness of the coefficient as a measure of inequality) of above 0.6 in 2007 (UN Human Development Report, 2007/2008). Furthermore, and notwithstanding the controversy regarding the UN Millennium Development Goals (MDGs), according to the United

Nations (2007), progress on the MDGs has been slower in Africa than any other region.

The agenda of Africa's development has been at the centre of the activism of the Council for the Development of Social Science Research in Africa (CODESRIA), a continental think-tank whose work is widely recognized across the globe. In 2008, CODESRIA held a conference in honour of the late Professor Guy Mhone, an African scholar whose works championed African liberation and freedom from the yoke of capitalist bondage and exploitation of the continent. Scholars from across Africa, as well as from other regions outside the continent, converged to deliberate on re-thinking African trade and industry policy for development. A number of papers were presented. They covered a number of topics which ranged from theoretical debates on the link between trade and industry policy and development to empirical analyses on country experiences with different trade and industry policy scenarios. Highlights of the papers are presented below.

Theresa Moyo summarizes the debates on trade and industrial policy and its implications for Africa's development. The paper reviews the historical evolution of trade and industry in Africa and also presents the theoretical relationship between trade, industry and development. An empirical review of the evidence in the context of Africa and also in the case of selected East and South Asian economies is presented for the purpose of identifying policies that have worked to transform those economies from developing to developed country-status (notwithstanding, of course, some of the controversies around definitions of development). Based on some of the debates on re-thinking Africa's development, the paper argues that trade policy in the context of the trade liberalization model, and trade based on commodity exports, has failed to deliver development in SSA. It proposes that a developmental trade and industry policy has to be based on a developmental paradigm that is contextualized within the continent; and that Africa can draw lessons from the experiences of some countries in Asia where the state played an activist role at the early stages of their industrialization. Finally, the paper proposes what should be the key components of such a developmental trade and industry framework.

Anthony Monye-Emina examines Nigeria's trade and industrial performance in the dispensation of the Structural Adjustment Programme (SAP). He argues that, while policy reconsideration was desirable in the wake of macroeconomic disturbances of the early 1980s, the programme of reform under the SAP did not do much to lift the fortune of the economy in terms of trade and industrial development. The country seemed to fare better under the regulated regime. In his opinion, Nigeria's experience with the SAP raises fundamental questions about the propriety of the theoretical basis and elements of the policy as it concerns trade and industrial development, given Nigeria's peculiar characteristics. He concludes that the 'visible' hand of government is still desirable, to some extent, in regulating the flow of trade and in industrial development.

Stephen Kapunda presents a comparative study of Botswana and Tanzania in the context of trade, industrial policy and development in the era of globalization in Africa. He examines globalization and regional challenges and opportunities in industrial policy, development and trade in Africa focusing on similar and dissimilar experiences of the two countries. The paper identifies some positive as well as negative impact of globalization. Botswana and Tanzania and other African countries should take advantage of the opportunities arising from the positive impact of globalization. However, they should counter the negative impact of globalization effects which arise from unregulated free trade and unfair competition. He advocates that the state should effectively implement competition policy, appropriate industrial policy, protect infant and strategic industries, plan and establish long-run intermediate and capital goods industries which ensure economic independence. This requires prudent use of resources like minerals as the case of Botswana and domestic savings in addition to foreign investment.

Euston Chiputa presents a comparative study of India and Zambia, two countries which in 1991 were almost at a similar level in terms of development and over the period 1991-1992, decided to embark on market reforms. He analyses the different trajectories followed by the two countries even though both were implementing reforms which targeted, among others, the trade and industry sectors. Chiputa argues that India was more successful than Zambia in designing and implementing policies which promoted the development of these sectors. A number of factors accounted for India's success. India's internally-generated policies were considered to be more effective in stimulating local supply responses than Zambia's externally-determined reforms which were designed by the World Bank and the International Monetary Fund (IMF). The author argues that Zambia's reforms tended to accentuate the macroeconomic, social and political challenges facing the country; that trade liberalization created competition for local industry which did not have the capacity or resources to compete; that reform-induced inflationary spirals also raised the cost of doing business and led to de-industrialization rather than the expansion of industry. Chiputa also argues that an important success factor in the case of India was that, over time, it managed to build a strong indigenous base prior to reforms as compared to Zambia where state policies actually stifled the development of such a base. Consequently, when foreign firms closed down or left the country, the impact on local industry was more severe than in the case of India where the indigenous industry base was more established. Another significant factor with regard to India's success was the drive to develop the capital goods industrial base consisting of capital and machine tool factories, whereas Zambia's industrial development policy was said to be skewed towards the production of consumer goods. Chiputa's paper emphasizes the critical role which the state can play in developing policies and strategies which promote indegenous participation in industry and building of a strong production base founded on locally-driven policies and priorities.

Oluyele Akinkugbe presents the findings of an econometric study on facilitating the production and export of manufactured goods within the framework of a comparative study of Africa and Asia/Pacific. He uses panel data to analyse empirically, how key aspects of the familiar Singapore issues – the facilitation of production and international exchange of goods and services – impact on output and export of manufactures in Africa and South-east Asia. Pooled, cross-country, annual time series data for the period 1995 – 2006 for 20 selected African countries and 10 countries in the Asia Pacific Economic Cooperation (APEC) regional grouping were used to examine the nature of the relationship between selected indicators of conducive industrial environment and trade facilitation – taxes on exports (an indication of restrictive trade policy regime); number of start-up procedures to register a business (to measure the stringency of, transparency and stability of local regulations); a measure of international linkages; infrastructure development; corruption perception index; e-commerce; the transparency and ease of enforcement of environmental regulation of industries and trade, etc – and export of manufactured goods from Africa and the Asia Pacific region. The conjecture is that policy-regime improvements and conscious efforts at removing all forms of constraints to the production and free flow of goods could lead to enhanced international exchanges and the ease of linking up with the global value chain – attainment of global competitiveness in Africa and the APEC region. Our recommendation is that governments in different African countries will need to rededicate attention to ways of achieving acceptable standards, if not best practices, in facilitating industrial and trade expansion. Reform policies and programmes have to be targeted at the different indicators for Africa to be globally competitive in manufactured goods export, if it is to escape the commodity export dilemma that has plagued the continent's development far too long.

Sunday Khan examines China's role in Africa in general and more specifically, in Cameroon. The objective of the paper is to examine the nature of trade (exports and imports) relations between China and Cameroon and how this has modified Cameroon's trade configuration and the potential impact on various stakeholders in the country. Khan indicates that over the last few years, China's share of the Cameroonian market has been increasing rapidly although European countries still remain the country's major trading partners. The country has reaped some benefits as a result of China's growing role in the country – for example, Chinese companies have contributed to infrastructure development. Cheap imports of consumer and producer goods have reduced domestic costs of production for some businesses. However, there are some concerns which arise from the negative impact of cheap imports on the competitiveness of local industry. The author argues that the emergence of China as regards its trade with Cameroon is gradually changing the latter's trade configuration where it is expected that, eventually, China might replace the EU as the country's main import source. That poses new challenges for Cameroon because cheap Chinese imports are already threatening locally manufactured goods than is the case with goods from Europe which are more expensive and therefore allow some market space for local industry. Trade with China presents both opportunities and challenges, and it is advisable for Cameroon (and other African countries) to systematically and regularly assess the nature and impact on their economies in view of maximizing the benefits and reducing the risks. Else, Chinese aid and infrastructural projects will overshadow other potentially damaging economic interactions with China, especially the effect of cheap imports on the industrialization process.

Ntangsi Max Memfih analyses trade facilitation and its implications for intra-African trade within a globalized economy. He is motivated by a realization that most analyses on trade issues seem to focus more on policy and less so on natural barriers to trade. His paper provides evidence to show that natural barriers in most African countries are more important sources of trade cost than trade policy, and thus are contributing significantly to the sluggish response to intra-African trade liberalization. Drawing on a study by the World Trade Organisation (WTO) in 2004, he contends that for the majority of sub-Saharan African countries, the transport cost incidence for exports is five times higher than the tariff cost incidence. This demonstrates that tariffs, quotas and other trade policies constitute only part of the overall cost of trade and that efforts to improve customs procedures, minimize the trade distorting impact of standards and reduce transport costs may have higher payoff than reciprocal reductions in overt trade policy barriers, because logistical, institutional and regulatory barriers are often more costly and generate no offsetting revenue (World Bank 2005). Memfih also argues that if other constraints, such as market information and reliable utilities such as electricity and telecommunications, could be quantified, the implicit taxation of exporters associated with transaction costs would be even higher. Therefore, while trade policy reforms are important to improve incentives and encourage efficiency, they would be more effective if transaction costs resulting from natural barriers are also lowered. These are all tied in what is generally referred to as trade facilitation. This has become prominent among WTO issues because the international business community is increasingly demanding for greater transparency, efficiency, and procedural uniformity of cross-border transportation of goods; as well as the need for an efficient legal redress mechanism, proper co-ordination between customs and other inspection agencies, use of modern customs techniques and improvement of transit regimes.

Aderibigbe Olomola addresses the critical issue of the EU-Africa Economic Partnership Agreements (EPAs) with a focus on the risks, rewards and requisites for agricultural trade and African development. He argues that the free trade model in agriculture under the EU-Africa EPA is flawed. It can be a major cause of hunger and poverty in the continent if it is not carefully addressed. The EPA is a source of possible destruction of domestic industries on account of influx of cheap imports from the EU. It is therefore critical for African states to identify the types of adjustments which will possibly yield desired outcomes given the level of development and available resources. Thus, the paper seeks to (i) determine the potential impacts of the EU-Africa EPAs, through a critical review of contemporary literature on this subject, (ii) examine the risks and challenges of agricultural FTAs, (iii) undertake a comparative analysis of the approaches to agricultural liberalization in EU FTAs in selected countries with a view to drawing lessons for successful EU-Africa EPAs, and (iv) proffer a configuration of agricultural liberalization for EU-Africa EPAs that will ensure a 'win-win' paradigm of agricultural trade and genuine partnership for African development.

Olomola analyses the structure of agricultural liberalization in the context of the EU-Africa EPAs including the key issues in the basic trade in food and agricultural products under an EPA. He makes a number of recommendations to address the issues, especially in terms of (i) meeting the challenge of reciprocity, (ii) preference erosion, (iii) costs associated with EU food safety standards, (iv) increased competitiveness,(v) production of higher value-added products, (vi) coping with increasingly differentiated EU markets, (vii) rules of origin, (viii) safeguard measures, (ix) food security clause, (x) MDGs clause, and (xi) improved regional trade and agricultural development. The paper concludes that changes in the EPAs will be required in several areas especially in terms of (i) doing away with arbitrary time frames and setting realistic time that reflects the pace of development in Africa, (ii) reviewing the rules of origin and the demand for reciprocity, (iii) providing concrete assurance to address resulting revenue losses by African countries, (iv) supporting regional initiatives aimed at developing African agriculture, and (v) ensuring that African countries are not constrained in attaining the MDGs. Moreover, the agricultural sector should be regarded as a sensitive sector and should be exempted from any rule of reciprocity.

Godwell Nhamo introduces climate change into the trade and industry debate. His paper focuses on carbon trade, an issue which has arisen from concerns over the impact of industrial and other pollution on the environment. He argues that international trade within the confines of climate change and global warming is certainly a confirmed twenty-first Century Agenda. After the ratification of the Kyoto Protocol (KP) and its market-based cooperation mechanisms in 2005, and the subsequent debates and gatherings looking beyond the 2012 KP mandate, African governments must be seriously concerned about the implications of these developments. He indicates that one of the cooperation mechanisms in which greenhouse gases (GHGs) will be reduced from the atmosphere through the KP is the Clean Development Mechanism (CDM). The CDM permits developed countries to invest in projects that reduce GHGs in developing countries and earn carbon credits or carbon offsets. The CDM is documented as one of the new investment avenues in developing countries with huge amounts of foreign direct investment (FDI) that were predicted to start flowing since 2006 to 2012.It is the foundation of the CDM that most developing nations, including many from Africa have questioned as providing an uneven trading platform in terms of the carbon credits. Indeed, it has been a contested terrain. Nhamo's paper addresses the following twin objectives: (1) to continuously raise awareness around the KP and post-KP carbon trade facilitation; and (2) to keep on interrogating the impacts of the proposed post-KP trade mechanisms on Africa's development. The paper strongly argues for a vigilant African continent that sees itself with an increasing and irreversible, pro-active, and participatory role regarding the post-KP trade mechanisms. The main argument is to have African countries speak with one true voice for the benefit of fair trade mechanisms within the new KP as well as confirming African countries' status as collaborative partners in the processes.

Patrick Juvet Lowe writes on intellectual property (IP) and technology transfer (TT) towards African countries. He questions international law on these issues as to whether it is a beneficial policy or not. He explains that, although technology transfer has been consecrated by the TRIPS Agreement of the WTO as a real obligation for developed countries towards developing and Least Developed Countries, however, the practice contradicts this obligation radically. He argues that it seems that Africa is still far from benefiting from the IP international legislation on technology transfer. The paper explores the reasons for such a dichotomy. The author contends that the gap may not only be a matter of legislation versus reality, but also the extent to which mechanisms exist and function in order to make IP and TT transfers to Africa possible. Lowe emphasizes that issues of IP and TT are an integral part of the industry and trade agenda and the fact that Africa so far has not benefited much from such transfers should not be blamed on law alone, but rather on its implementation. He recommends that Africa should increase its representation on bodies that are dealing with IP and TT issues at the continental and international levels, coupled with what he terms a 'voluntarist' approach of development and technology transfer at national levels.

Nwauche examines the UNESCO Convention for the Protection and Promotion of the Diversity of Cultural Expressions with respect to its implications for African trade and culture policy. He explains that the Convention seeks to protect and promote the diversity of cultural expressions within territories of member states against the sweeping tide of globalization (Articles 5 & 6), noting that the Treaty is protectionist and, to a large extent, potentially in conflict with the free trade ethos of the WTO. As the international community grapples with whether to recognize culture as an exception within the WTO framework or to recognize parallel trade regimes in the world, it is important to interrogate what the Treaty portends for Africa. His paper raises a number of questions that are relevant for the future of trade and culture policy in Africa. He seeks to find out what exactly the UNESCO Treaty means for the trade and culture policy of African countries within the framework of the NEPAD and the AU, and for sub-regional economic groupings such as SADC, ECOWAS and others. The paper also examines the obligations for African States with respect to adoption of proactive measures to protect and promote 'cultural religious and linguistic communities' within their competence. Nwauche also asks if there is protection of cultural expressions such as folklore and traditional knowledge compatible with the Convention. Finally, he assesses the lessons of regime shifting in international economic relations should Africa imbibe.

Howard Stein examines institutional dimensions of trade and industry policy in Africa. He starts by highlighting the stark contrast between Southeast Asian (SEA) and sub-Sahara African (SSA) in terms of trade and industry performance. He argues that a central element of the changes in SEA was the ability to expand and structurally transform the industrial sector. In contrast, SSA has largely de-industrialized and continues to rely heavily on the primary product exports with consequences to the terms of trade and the standard of living. The paper proposes an institutional theoretical framework for understanding the nature of industrial policy and applies it to contrast the experience of the two regions. Stein argues that, in Africa, while there were weaknesses with the industry put in place after independence, instead of building on the accumulated knowledge and capacities, structural adjustment battered industry, leaving the countries increasingly reliant on resource exports. As a result, African economies have been subject to the vicissitudes of commodity prices with implications to the terms of trade and the standard of living. The paper proposes an institutional theoretical framework for understanding the nature of industrial policy and applies it to contrast the experience of the two regions with some examples taken from Kenya and Malaysia. The paper concludes that development is a dynamic process that requires the institutional and structural transformation of economies. Based on the experience of Asia, a state-led approach to transforming economies through industrial policy interventions is still relevant even while recognising the role of markets as complementary strategies.

Adewole Musiliu Adeolu also examines the institutional foundation of trade and industrial policies in Africa. By developing a model of institutions where the objective function of the ruling elites is the maximization of the relative share of total wealth, and by extension control over the larger society, he predicts the sub-optimal supply of public goods required to facilitate the process of large-scale industrial development and significant success in growth-promoting exports of manufactures and capital goods. The important public goods under-supplied include human and physical capital as well as investment in R & D activities. The author therefore concludes that the mere switch from the protectionist policies of the 1960s through the 1980s to the more open and outward oriented strategies of the 1990s, have not produced the expected results because the underlying institutional cause of underdevelopment is yet to be addressed.

Introduction

Theresa Moyo

The subject of trade and industrial development in Africa is a topical issue which has been debated since the 1960s and 70s. That is because African states recognize the importance of industry and trade as important strategies to achieve growth and development. This is evident in national development plans and strategies. At the continental level, trade and industry issues have been prioritized in key policy documents such as the Lagos Plan of Action, the United Nations Industrial Organization (UNIDO) Industrial Development Decade for Africa (IDDA) and, more recently, the New Partnership for Africa's Development (NEPAD), the Africa Productive Capacity Initiative (APCI) and the African Union's Action Plan for Accelerated Industrialization of Africa (APFAIDA). The experience of industrialized economies and also emerging economies such as China, India and Brazil, as well as a number of countries in East and South Asia (Singapore, Republic of Korea, Malaysia and Taiwan), among others, clearly demonstrate that trade and industry are fundamental to growing an economy, creating jobs, diversifying the economy and creating backward and forward linkages which provide dynamic opportunities for further growth and expansion. Despite recognizing this potential, industry is not developed in many African countries.

This volume calls for a rethinking of trade and industry for Africa's development. That call arises because despite introducing plans at national, regional and continental levels, Africa's industry and trade performance has been poor. Although a number of countries have experienced high rates of growth since the 1990s, their industry base largely consists of consumer goods manufacturing or light industries. Most of the continent still produces and exports primary commodities and imports manufactured goods. A number of factors explain this situation. These include, but are not limited to, the lack of technological capacity required for industry development; inadequate skills or limited human resource capacity; failure on the part of African states to implement some of the industry development plans which have been formulated at national and regional levels; and, lack of infrastructure (Tribe 2002; Chang 2003; Kieh 2008 and UNCTAD 2010). A very serious challenge is also posed by the new trading and international environment under the World Trade Organization (WTO) which has ushered in a new era of market-based trade and industry policies. Although many least developed countries have embraced the WTO, many of them are very critical of the reforms which it has advocated since its inception in 1994. For example, in order to achieve the WTO's goal of free trade, member countries have entered into agreements in which they commit to reduce tariffs and non-tariff barriers to trade. Compliance with these agreements has effectively reduced the policy space available for African states particularly in terms of promoting industry development. UNCTAD (2010) notes that the shrinking of industrial policy space under emerging and current trade rules is evident in the following areas: the imposition of tariff cuts under the emerging, but not yet finalized, non-agricultural market access (NAMA) negotiations; the replacement of preferential trade agreements with reciprocal economic partnership agreements in conformity with WTO rules, regulations on subsidies imposed under the Subsidies and Countervailing Measures Agreement, the Uruguay Round Agreement on Trade-Related Investment Measures (TRIMs) and the Agreement on Trade-Related Aspects of Intellectual Property Rights (TRIPS). As a result of WTO rules, it is now more difficult to nurture local infant industries through subsidies. However, it is still permissible to use subsidies to promote innovation and regional development and to achieve environmental goals.

Ironically, as argued by Thilwall (2007), most of the industrialized countries used protectionist policies when they first started to build their industries. In addition, they are still protecting their markets through subsidies to their farmers and local industries. Chiang (2003), Kieh (2008) and Kohl (2008), among others, review the success of several countries from East and South Asia and argue that their states used interventionist trade and industry policies to support and nurture their growth.

A number of authors have also argued that, trade liberalization, for example, has led to the de-industrialization of Africa because many companies were ill-prepared for external competition. (Bennel 1998; Tribe 2002; Shafaeddin 2005; and UNCTAD 2010). Chiputa and Kapinda, writing about the experiences of Zambia, Botswana and Tanzania, respectively, also present similar arguments.

It may be instructive at this point to explain what trade policy and industrial policy are. Dicken (2007) presents a very detailed definition of each. He explains that trade policy traditionally consisted of the use of tariff and non-tariff barriers (NTBs). Tariffs refer to those taxes which are levied on the value of imports. These effectively increase the price which a domestic consumer has to pay for the imported good. Tariffs are typically used as an instrument to protect domestic industries whilst, at the same time, allowing the import of industrial goods. NBTs include, but are not limited to, import quotas, import licenses, import surcharges, rules of origin anti-dumping measures, special labelling and packaging regulations, health and safety regulations, subsidies to domestic producers of import-competing goods and awarding of government contracts only to domestic producers. These measures were used to protect domestic industries from external competition. Trade policy also consists of policies towards the promotion of export growth or expansion. These include financial and fiscal incentives to export producers, export credits and guarantees, setting of export targets, establishment of export processing or free trade zones and imposing embargoes on strategic exports.

Industrial policies refer to those policies which regulate and stimulate industry formation and growth. They can be general (applicable to all industry) or they can be selective (i.e., targeted to a few sectors or firms). The range of industrial policies include, but are not limited to, investment incentives (which may be capital and/or tax-related), subsidies, preferential state procurement, technology policies, policies to encourage industrial restructuring, competition policies, mergers and acquisition policies, state ownership of production assets, health and environmental protection regulations.

Under the WTO, the use of most of the policies has been curtailed or restricted as part of the mechanism to liberalize or free trade.

Liberalization of the international trading regime is also embodied in Economic Partnership Agreements (EPAs) which have now replaced the non-reciprocal, development-oriented preferential trading arrangements that existed between the EU and African, Caribbean and Pacific (ACP) countries under the Cotonou and Lomé accords. EPAs were signed between the EU and 79 ACP countries in 2008. EPAs were designed to liberalize trade between the EU and ACP countries and they were also part of the strategies to comply with the new rules of the WTO. On paper, they were also supposed to alleviate poverty in ACP nations by promoting economic growth. Many developing member countries of the EPAs have been and are still critical of the agreements primarily because they are compelled to liberalize their trade even though, in most instances, their local manufacturing industries are not adequately prepared to face international competition. They are viewed as an attempt to force ACP countries to open up their struggling markets to European industrial (and some agricultural) exports and to foreign investment, targeted especially at the agricultural, forestry and mining sectors, all of which are likely to aggravate deforestation and food security concerns. Equally important is their concern about what they consider to be loss of sovereignity and policy space in that they can no longer use trade policies such as tariff barriers, export restrictions and investment regulations, for example, to promote equitable, local and sustainable economic development and also to protect their natural resources. Under EPAs, the use of export taxes is being scrapped. Export taxes have historically been used as a means to support local infant industries, generate value-added by promoting the local processing of raw materials into industrial goods and raise government revenues as happened in countries such as China, India and Brazil that could play an important strategic role in Africa's industrialization.There are strong concerns that the EPAs will undermine the integration efforts of ACP countries. This is particularly evident in the case of Eastern and Southern Africa, where countries belonging to COMESA, SADC and EAC are now split up between the two artificially created EPA blocs (ESA and SADC7).

An overview of trade and industrial performance in Africa is presented in order to provide the context for the volume. Although there has been some growth in recent years, the share of African trade in global trade is still relatively small compared to other regions in the world. UNECA (2010) observes that Africa continued to play a marginal role in world trade in 2009, with about a 3.4 per cent share of global merchandise trade and an insignificant share in trade in services. Commodities continue to be the major exports, most of which are destined to industrialized countries. Exports also still largely consist of commodities, also widely destined for industrialized country markets although, in more recent years, some of these exports now target the South-East Asia and Brazil markets. The narrow range of export markets and also the narrow range of exports add to the vulnerability of export earnings due to volatility in those markets. The report also notes that intra-African trade continued to be minimal, at less than 10 per cent of total trade in 2009.

According to UNCTAD (2008:54-56), the shares of African countries' manufacturing exports to GDP over the last 25 years have remained very small for most countries. It also observes that Africa has made marginal progress in terms of increasing its exports of manufactured products, even after trade liberalization. The Commission notes that over the period 2000-2006, Africa had the lowest share of all developing regions. Over the same period, manufacturing export shares of total merchandise exports in East Asia, South Asia and Latin America were 92 per cent, 56 per cent and 54.5 per cent, respectively. The Commission attributes the low level of manufacturing exports to low manufacturing production, noting that from 1965 to 2005, sub-Saharan Africa's manufacturing value added did not improve from its original value of 15 per cent of GDP in the 1960s. From the 1990s onwards, the ratio of MVA to GDP has been declining, except for a few countries such as South Africa, Tunisia, Algeria, Libya, Morocco and Egypt. UNCTAD also argues that Africa has failed to take advantage of new export opportunities because of three key factors. A major constraint is that Africa has not invested heavily in manufacturing industry because the resources required are deemed to very high. Another constraint has been the limited technological capacity which is also a very critical element for successful industrialization. Another factor relates to the comparative advantage which Africa has in producing primary commodities due to the abundance of labour and natural resources. Unfortunately, for years, African countries have been encouraged to embrace the comparative advantage principle and even after realizing how it disadvantages them in global markets, many countries have failed to shift from that focus towards manufactured exports. That is the challenge which Africa has to deal with in its quest for a more developmental trade and industry policy for the continent's development.

Whereas the position of the continent in global trade remains marginal, these positive trends are likely to be adversely influenced by the current global economic downturn. In 2007, African total merchandise trade (exports plus imports) amounted to over $782 billion, accounting for 2.7 per cent of world trade. In terms of the trade growth rate, 30 African countries performed above the world average of 9.26 per cent in 1997-2007. Equatorial Guinea registered the highest average growth rate (36 %), followed by Chad (29 %), the Sudan and Angola (22 %), and Mozambique (18 %). In contrast, Eritrea and Zimbabwe registered negative growth rates (-0.85 %) and (-0.24 %), respectively (UNECA 2009).

The African Development Bank (2008) observes that there is a genuine concern that Africa's share of global trade remains marginalized, amounting to only 3.1 per cent of total global trade in 2007. Intra-Africa trade has also lagged behind, with both imports and exports a little over 9 per cent of total trade. The cause of Africa's sluggish trade performance can be attributed to various reasons from domestic policies to high trade restrictions in developed countries. The report also notes that although most African countries have undertaken extensive trade liberalization –

and most can be said to have had open economies since the mid- to late 1990s – export performance following trade liberalization has been weak in terms of increased export volumes, increased export/GDP ratios and diversification in high-value agricultural exports and manufactures. Table 1.1 presents current and projected trends in export performance over the period 2006-2010. A sharp decline from 52.2 per cent in 2008 to 35.7 per cent in 2009 is predicted for oil exporters. Oil exporters (excluding Nigeria) have an even more drastic fall from 70.2 per cent in 2008 to 46.3 per cent in 2009. Middle and low-income countries will also experience some decline although of a smaller magnitude than oil exporters. The reason could be the lower degree of integration into the world system in the case of most countries under this category. Evidence from the IMF (2009) also indicates that despite a sustained positive growth, Africa still accounts for a negligible 3 per cent of world total exports. Exports increased by 15.6 per cent between 2006 and 2007 compared to an average growth rate of 20 per cent in the previous four years. African exports are highly undiversified with crude oil and minerals contributing about 70 per cent, and agriculture and manufacturing about 30 per cent. On the other hand, Africa's share in world imports was about 2.5 per cent in 2007 and imports grew by 24 per cent in the same year. Imports were mainly concentrated in manufactured goods.

Lack of export diversification exposes the continent to severely adverse terms-of trade shocks such as the one gripping the world economy today. Indeed, the prospects for trade growth in the medium term remain bleak in view of the current financial crisis and falling commodity prices. Sixty per cent of the top ten African exporters are oil-exporting countries and the ten top exporters accounted for 81.5 per cent of African exports in 2007. The major trading partners of African countries are North America and the EU, with a cumulative share of exports of over 61 per cent in 2000. Asia is gradually becoming a major trading partner with African countries. In 2005-2007, African exports to Asia grew by nearly 50 per cent (UNECA 2007). About 78 per cent of these exports were fuels and mining products. With regard to the export sector, primary products still dominate Africa's exports; although there has been an upward trend in manufactured exports, particularly in countries like Cameroon, Egypt, Madagascar, Mauritius, Morocco, Kenya, Seychelles and Zambia. However, for most African countries, the volume of manufactured exports is said to have declined. The UNECA report also points out that high technology exports account for only four per cent of manufactured exports from Africa as compared to 32 per cent in East Asia and a developing country average of 23 per cent (UNECA 2007).

Despite the importance of industry in the context of sustainable development in Africa, Africa's share of world manufacturing output declined from 0.9 per cent to a lower figure of 0.8 per cent over the two decades spanning 1980-2001. Within Africa, the distribution of manufacturing activity is highly skewed with just one country, South Africa, accounting for 27.3 per cent of total Manufacturing Value Added (MVA) in sub-Saharan Africa and registering significant growth over the past two decades. Thus, for most countries of Africa, there has been a loss in their share of global manufacturing output (UNECA 2006). In 2007, intra-Africa trade remained low; despite the positive trends in export growth at the continental level, less than 10 per cent of total merchandise exports were destined to African countries.

Table 0.1: Africa: Trends in exports of goods and services 2006-2010

	2006	2010	2008	2009	2010
Oil exporting countries	51.4	51.5	52.2	35.7	37.5
Oil exporting countries (excluding Nigeria)	65.1	67	70.2	46.3	47.9
Middle-income countries	32	33.7	37.1	36.5	37.4
Middle-income countries (excluding South Africa)	51.3	52.1	49.9	44.9	46.3
Low-income countries	24.9	24.9	24.2	20.9	20.8
Fragile countries (incl. Zimbabwe)	41.6	44.8	43	32.9	33.1
Sub-Saharan Africa	37.9	38.9	40.8	32.1	33.1
CFA Franc Zone	44.4	44.1	45.1	35.4	37.3
EAC	21.7	21.9	22.9	21.5	20.1
SADC	36.8	39.8	43.9	35.8	36.6
SACU	31.2	32.9	36.3	35.8	36.8
COMESA	43.8	47.1	49	30.3	30.8

Source: International Monetary Fund (IMF) 2009. Regional Economic Outlook: Sub-Saharan Africa, p. 80.

This low-level of intra-Africa trade illustrates the weakness of continental integration, highlighting the urgency with which regional economic communities (RECs) should deal with the obstacles, both in terms of policy and investment. West Africa appears to be the most inte-grated sub-region in terms of intra-regional trade 1996-2006 (UNECA 2006).

It is clear from the above that the African trade structure has remained undiversified in terms of products and destination of exports. However, since 2005, Asia is emerging as a new and important trade partner for Africa. This trend is likely to continue given that the increasing presence of Asia in Africa is being reinforced through development cooperation and trade frameworks. Of concern to Africa's long-term development prospects is the emerging picture that, like the old traditional partners, the trade with Asia is also being focused on extraction of fuels and mining products. Failure to tackle high trade costs due to poor infrastructure and inefficient trade facilitation continue to make African producers and exporters prefer to trade with the rest of the world. This has been the case despite the huge potential for developing competitive industries on the continent.

The stagnation of Africa's industry and the continued focus on primary commodity exports has its foundations in the history of colonialism and imperialist exploitation of the continent's resources. Although most of the continent has achieved political independence and self-rule, economic emancipation remains an illusion. Globalization has introduced new rules and processes of production and exchange which reinforce and perpetuate the notion of free trade and comparative advantage which shaped Africa's specialization in primary goods exports. Africa has been under pressure to liberalize trade and open up its markets to Northern goods and services even when countries were not ready for external competition. Consequently, despite the opportunities which globalization could offer, market reforms in some cases crippled local industry, largely because local companies had not achieved a level of competitiveness that could match the international market. According to the UNECA (2008), several structural constraints continue to limit trade performance in Africa. These include lack of diversification, existence of supply side constraints, and low levels of sub-regional and continental trade integration. As trade liberalization progresses, it is argued that artificial barriers such as tariffs are becoming less important, leaving natural barriers such as infrastructure related to ports, transport, and border posts, among others, as the most binding constraints to trade. Ports in Africa are said to be besieged by huge inefficiencies. These bottle-necks impose high transaction costs which affect the competitiveness of African economies, lowering trade performance (African Development Bank 2007).

Africa's dependence on primary exports to countries of the North contributed to its vulnerability to the global economic crisis which started in 2009. GDP growth, export volumes and earnings were negatively affected by declining demand in the United States and Europe where the recession originated. Africa's exports tend to be concentrated in commodities, with oil, metals and minerals and agricultural commodities the most notable. Due to falling demand in Europe, the United States of America and China, Africa's export performance was forecast to decline over the period 2008 to 2009, with a slight improvement in 2010. Falling commodity prices of export goods from Africa and the rising import costs of intermediate goods worsened the balance of trade. Page (2009) argues that the impact of the recession on industry depends on the degree of diversification of a country's production base and also the extent to which there is concentration in terms of destination of the final product. A country like Mauritius, with an export structure which is highly concentrated in just two product lines – apparel (50 % of total exports) and food products (29 %) – was more vulnerable than South Africa which has a more diversified industry base. Tunisia and Morocco have been negatively affected due to the concentration of their exports in high income markets. For example, two sectors, apparel and electrical machinery accounted for about half of all their exports and mostly these target advanced country markets. Ghana and the Cote d'Ivoire, both major exporters of food and wood products which together account for more than 60 per cent of total manufactured exports have about 80 per cent of the exports are concentrated in high income markets. Other examples are the apparel exports from Kenya and manufactured goods from Uganda. Vulnerability is high because of their high level of concentration ratios in advanced markets (90 %). Evidence from the IMF (2009) shows that the global crisis which started in 2009 has adversely affected those countries which are highly dependent on natural resources such as copper, diamonds, timber, platinum. The Bank of Zambia (2009) reported that the fall in copper prices led to a drop in export receipts.

Africa's vulnerability arises from the fact that the average export-to-GDP ratio for the continent is 35 per cent. Around 69 per cent of the exports are destined for advanced economies; about 30 per cent to the Euro area alone. Exports from Africa to the US and Europe started to fall as a result of the downturn in these economies. Wolfgang Schneider-Barthold (2010:1) argues that industrialization in Africa has failed and he attributes the failure to the strategies of donors in the North and also the African power elites whose preference for large-scale, multinational enterprises tend to be capital-intensive. He postulates that:

The policies of these powerful elites have historically marginalized small-scale and micro-enterprises where large numbers of the population derive their sustainance. With minimal capital and maximum labour input, limited and mostly handed-down commercial and technical knowledge, without experience in company management and marketing, using easily procurable tools and locally available raw materials, and adapting to the low educational level of their workers as well as patchy infrastructures, these businesses produced goods and provided services for the local people in town and country. However, most of the new governments did not recognise and promote these activities as the starting point for development. Instead, they saw them as being backward and subjected them to discrimination and marginalization (Wolfgang 2010:1).

Since 2000, the globalization of world production has gathered new strength, pushing further to the periphery of the world economy those countries that have not developed the capacity to compete strongly in the world market or participate effectively in the new global economic order which is characterized by interdependent production structures cutting across national boundaries. In response to growing world economic recovery, increasing privatization of public enterprises, emerging financial markets, and a wide range of incentives provided to private investment, there has been a massive surge in private capital flows, which would mainly benefit countries with attractive investment environment and markets. African countries have not benefited as other developing countries have. UNIDO (2009) points out that although there are trade preferences which developing countries could have taken advantage of, many of them are ill-equipped to benefit from such opportunities largely because of weak infrastructure, lack of productive capacities and the inability to meet product specifications and increasingly stringent requirements in terms of quality, safety, and health. They also lack the capacity to produce goods that can compete in terms of quantity, quality, timely delivery and price in export markets. These and other developments are evidently fraught with innumerable challenges and concerns with great opportunities of far-reaching consequences that African countries must effectively manage if they are to mobilize fully their resources for development, and reverse the present tendency of marginalization in the world economy. This is not, however, an easy task knowing the serious obstacles that African countries face in their drive to meet the challenges of domestic development, including the reorganization and transformation of their economic structures. World trade is more and more globalized, reinforced by the fact that it increased more rapidly than world production, through the creation of the World Trade Organization and conclusion of the Uruguay Round. This liberalization of world trade will be an opportunity for African states in as much as they carry out reforms intended to transform their competitive base.

The volume proposes some alternative strategies and policies which are necessary for trade and industry to grow and to contribute to the development aspirations of African states. It calls for a developmental trade and industry policy which fundamentally must be people-centred. African states should invest time, energy and resources to develop policies which seek to meet the aspirations and priorities of the African people. Historically, a centralized, top-down approach has dictated policy and served the interests of ruling elites and the foreign interests who were the actual architects of the policies. Consequently, poor producers are not only economically disadvantaged but often are politically powerless, and when their interests are pitted against those of more powerful actors, they frequently lose. They are often marginalized from trade opportunities due lack of political power and voice, lack of access to public services, trade information, lack of information and understanding of customs procedures and processes, lack of access to trade finance, the challenge of poor trade logistics and infrastructure and the lack of skills with regard to procedures and modalities required in the export of goods and services. African states therefore need to develop strategies that also expand opportunities for the poor and marginalized producers in agriculture and the small-scale industry sector.

In a continent which has labour in abundance, it will be inevitable to develop industry policies which are complemented by intensive skills and capacity building investments. This should promote industry development which will be able to absorb much of that labour. Rethinking industry policy in Africa essentially means moving away from those models which are based on low wages policies. It must be based on recognition of fundamental human and worker rights and the principle of decent work. When governments develop incentive packages to attract foreign direct investment, domestic policies should seek to promote job creation, protect the rights of workers, and of women who are often exploited particularly in export processing zones. A development-oriented industry policy should use local resources in mining, agriculture, forestry and fisheries, among others to promote inter-sectoral linkages, for example, the creation of agro-processing industries. Trade policy will have to be sensitive to strategic sectors such as agriculture in order to ensure food security and also in cognizance of the dependence of millions of people on agriculture for livelihoods, jobs and income. The challenge of inadequate and poor industry and trade infrastructure in Africa calls for massive investments and commitment to implement infrastructure development programmes. Although the New Partnership for African Development (NEPAD) has been criticized for its neo-liberal framework, it has some very useful proposals with regard to industry and trade development and these are ideas which African Heads of State should seriously follow through. As Box 1.1 shows, at the continental level, NEPAD calls for the promotion of intra-African trade by reducing trade barriers among member states, reducing transaction costs and promoting and improvement of regional trade agreements, among other measures.

At the international level, it calls on African Heads of State to implement strategies to enhance market access for African goods and services into markets of the North and other regions. It also highlights the need to build capacity for member states to engage in trade negotiations, particularly as regards the rules and regulations of the WTO. NEPAD rightly encourages African countries to actively participate in the world trading system based on terms and conditions that take into account the concerns, needs and interests of the region.

Beyond strengthening physical infrastructure, governments also need to undertake improvements in the regulatory environment and in the conditions for cross-border facilitation. Simplifying and reducing documentation requirements and formalities, lowering the level of fees and charges for importation and exportation, expediting the release and clearance of goods from customs custody, enhancing transparency and predictability of trade-related regulations and fees, and improving border agency coordination (both within and across countries) will lower the transaction costs for trade.

One of the challenges of moving towards alternative strategies lies in the heavy dependence of a number of African governments on Western countries for budgetary support. Dependence can be reduced by improving the rate of GDP growth and improving the administration and collection of tax revenue and, more importantly, in re-prioritizing expenditure allocations in a manner which promotes industry and trade infrastructure development.

Box 0.1: New Partnership for African Development Proposals for Trade
Promotion

At the African level: Promote intra-African trade with the aim of sourcing within Africa, imports formerly sourced from other parts of the world; Create marketing mechanisms and institutions to develop marketing strategies for African products; Publicise African exporting and importing companies and their products, through trade fairs; Reduce the cost of transactions and operations; Promote and improve regional trade agreements, foster interregional trade liberalisation, and harmonise rules of origin, tariffs and product standards Reduce export taxes. At the international level: Negotiate measures and agreements to facilitate market access for African products to the world market; Encourage foreign direct investment; Assist in capacity-building in the private sector, as well as strengthening country and sub-regional capacity in trade negotiations, implementing the rules and regulations of the WTO, and identifying and exploiting new trading opportunities that emerge from the evolving multilateral trading system; The African heads of state must ensure active participation in the world trading system, which has been managed under the auspices of the WTO since 1995. If a new round of multilateral trade negotiations is started, it must recognise and provide for the African continent's special concerns, needs and interests in future WTO rules.

Source: New Partnership for African Development (NEPAD) Section 169.

It must be emphasized that a development-oriented trade policy has to prioritize the concerns, needs and interests of Africa. Wholesale market-based approaches to trade based on comparative advantage, trade liberalization and foreign direct investment, as some aspects of the NEPAD propose, unfortunately, have failed to ensure that Africa's interests are put at the forefront of negotiations with WTO. Re-thinking trade for development fundamentally implies that negotiations on trade at regional and international levels must be cast in the framework of advancing the interests of African people. Section 171 of the document also contains some useful strategies which should be implemented. It calls for 'renewed political action by African countries to intensify and deepen the different integration initiatives on the continent. To this end, consideration should be given to: (1) a discretionary preferential trade system for intra-African trade; (2) the alignment of domestic and regional trade and industrial policy objectives, thereby increasing the potential for intra-regional trade critical to the sustainability of regional economic arrangements'. Trade policy should address the challenges posed by the standards and quality rules in WTO, for instance, the WTO Technical Barriers to Trade Agreement and the Sanitary and Phytosanitary standards which are widely perceived in Africa to have become 'de facto' trade obstacles for developing countries. 'Aid for Trade' emerged from the WTO Doha negotiation process when in their Hong Kong Declaration of 2005, trade ministers called on bilateral and multilateral donors to increase resources Africa to improve its trade. They endorsed the enhancing of the Integrated Framework for Trade-Related Assistance to least developed countries (UNIDO 2009:92). The Aid for Trade strategies should aim to help developing countries to build the supply-side capacity and trade-related infrastructure that they need to assist them to implement and benefit from WTO Agreements and, more broadly, to expand their trade. The initiative is to develop trade-related infrastructure such as trade facilitation, transport, port and quality infrastructure.

Standards set by the WTO are generally considered stringent. African countries therefore need to improve their ability to meet sanitary and phytosanitary standards through better laboratories, standards, and negotiation of mutual recognition agreements, and rich countries need to reduce the degree of cascading tariffs in agricultural processing and move toward the imposition of transparent ad-valorem tariffs. Capacity building in terms of negotiation with WTO and other international trade agencies is also critical. Training is still necessary to develop the negotiation skills of government officials on trade-related issues in the context of international agreements.

There is need to develop infrastructure for the development of industry clusters which are geared to trade. Spatial industrial policies are necessary to provide a framework of such cluster zones. The main benefit of such clusters is that they provide a clear focus for government investments and institutional reforms designed to encourage the location of firms in a specific locality. Yet, many such zones in Africa have failed to attract a sufficient number of firms to realize cluster economies and, in many cases, they offer excessive subsidies to the few firms that they succeed in attracting. In a bid to attract foreign investors to these zones, governments have offered incentives which have failed to protect the rights of workers. Consequently, zones have been notorious for the low wages and poor working conditions for workers. Recognizing the importance of industry clusters and export zones, a new approach will be necessary to ensure that countries benefit from the economies of scale which they offer whilst at the same time, the cluster offer opportunities for decent work.

A developmental trade policy has to promote trade amongst African countries through, for example, intra-regional trade. Although there are regional trading blocs such as COMESA, SADC, ECOWAS and the WAC, the volume of trade among African countries is still small as compared to that between Africa and US and Europe. Removal of barriers to the free movement of people and goods within the region will also open up more opportunities for intra-African trade.

Intellectual property rights are a part of the multilateral framework for trade. Yusuf and others (2003) advocate for the stronger protection of Africa's intellectual property rights in order to encourage innovation. They also call for increased investments in skills and provision of a competitive business environment that encourages innovation. Several of the region's more advanced countries can hope to stimulate technological advances if they better protect intellectual property and pay more attention to competition. Stronger copyright laws, provided they can be enforced, may yield some significant gains for domestic software industries as well as the arts and music sectors. Environmental concerns and considerations have to be taken into account in the context of achieving sustainable environment in Africa. Industrialization in the context of sustainable use of resources poses challenges for the continent in terms of technological adaptation, investment in environmentally friendly consumption, production and trading strategies. Policies are necessary to promote ecologically sustainable industrial development especially those that promote cleaner production technologies and reduction of waste during the production process.

African states can learn some important lessons from the experience of some East Asian countries which have made in-roads in terms of industry development and trade. The United Nations Economic Commission for Africa (UNECA 2008) highlights the factors behind the success of those countries with regard to their industrialization and trade performance. The Commission explains that it was the strategic development vision in East Asia which enabled state authorities to make the necessary choices in terms of investment, financing, subsidies and the provision of institutional support to specific sectors. Accordingly, trade policies were integrated into overall development strategies, but while the dynamism of these strategies in East Asia drove their trade policies, those policies remained passive in Africa. In East Asia, trade-policy tools ranging from tariff and non-tariff barriers, export subsidies and credits to exchange rate policies were used to address development priorities and options. The Commission also argues that building a dense and multi-layered network of institutions makes it possible for growth dynamics to be stabilized and deepened. Sectoral policies then help to strengthen and consolidate the factors leading to growth. Industrial, agricultural or macroeconomic policies help in long-term institution-building that can lead to economic development and improve the competitiveness of national economies. Trade policies are no exception to this rule and must be closely integrated into the process of accelerating growth and improving the national position in the global economy. For this reason, trade policies cannot be analyzed or pursued in isolation from development options and strategies; they form the basic elements of any development strategy and therefore strengthen development options and choices. Trade policy dynamics follow, and must be integrated into the dynamics and evolution of overall development options. From this perspective, trade policies help to reinforce the institutional fabric necessary for countries to develop.

In Africa, the experience of Mauritius is cited in the literature as a success story. The country used to be a poor, sugar-dependent nation but has now diversified its economy in which manufacturing and tourism are now the major sectors. Some of the policies which the government implemented included the introduction of an effective system of tax incentives to manufacturing businesses, protection of existing import-substitution industries, duty-free imports for export firms. The government also created an environment which promoted the growth of investments in service industries such as finance and information and telecommunications technologies. Government spending on skills development and infrastructure also increased. Efforts to fight corruption were intensified in order to enhance the attractiveness of the country to investors.

The failure of trade and industry to develop in most of the African continent calls into question the policies and strategies which have been implemented in the past. Although most countries have shifted from the Import-Substitution Industrialization (ISI) strategy towards and export-oriented approach within the framework of free trade, Africa's trade performance lags behind that of other regions. Industry development is still small and consequently, primary commodities still constitute the greater proportion of the exports from the continent. Although globalization has opened up many opportunities for developing countries to trade, it is only those countries which are able to compete on the international market that can benefit from trade. In that regard, Africa faces many challenges. Its industry sector is not competitive due to obstacles such as high transaction costs due to poorly developed infrastructure and other logistical constraints and a regulatory environment which is inimical to business development and particularly indigenous enterprises. Even for those countries which have demonstrated capacity to increase their exports, access into developed country markets remains a challenge due to protectionist policies adopted by those countries.

UNCTAD´s Least Developed Countries Report (2006) argues that the development of domestic productive capacities and concomitant expansion of productive employment opportunities is the key to sustained economic growth and poverty reduction in the least developed countries (LDCs). Defining productive capacities as

> the productive resources, entrepreneurial capabilities and production linkages which together determine the capacity of a country to produce goods and services and enable it to grow and develop,

the Report shows that the core processes through which productive capacities develop – capital accumulation, technological progress and structural change – have been very weak in most LDCs. Consequently, labour productivity is low and underemployment is rampant. This has contributed to the persistence of poverty in the developing countries.

UNCTAD (2008:53) also argues that any trade and development strategy should attempt to increase manufacturing exports. This is based on the following key factors. Firstly, that trade in manufactured products has played a central role in the successful development of other regions and Africa can learn from those lessons. Secondly, manufacturing would promote export diversification, something which would reduce Africa's current vulnerability due to the dominance of primary commodities in its exports. Thirdly, the export of high-value manufactured products would increase foreign exchange earnings and government revenues which, if channelled into development, could improve the development of the continent. Finally, UNCTAD argues that the large size of external markets could also help Africa's firms to realize economies of scale which are necessary to become internationally competitive. The Commission emphasizes that increasing manufacturing exports is necessary to maintain industrial growth, expand employment opportunities and diversify exports. (UNCTAD 2008:54).

The experience of countries in East Asia demonstrates that it is possible to industrialize and to increase the export of high-value manufactured goods and to use the proceeds of such exports to finance social and economic development. Such a strategy calls for a greater role of the state in terms of investing in industry infrastructure and providing the necessary incentives that can stimulate the growth of that sector. The lesson for

Africa is that, contrary to the dictates of the 'free-market' model, the state has an important role to play in facilitating, planning and financing industry and trade development and in ensuring that proceeds are invested in development that benefits the people. There is controversy about the extent of state intervention in the economy – raising the question of what should be the nature and scope of intervention. The failure of state-owned enterprises in Africa is well known and the author is not advocating for a similar type of state intervention in the economy. Rather, the emphasis should be on the leading role the state should play in terms of engaging local and international investors, identifying opportunities for industrial development and supporting the emergence and growth of industry through infrastructure development, a conducive policy environment and supporting industry linkages which promote learning. The state should also play a critical role in the area of human resource development, so as to develop the technical capacity required for industrialization by investing heavily in science and engineering education and other technical-related areas which are vital for building an industry base.

Examples of how the state can guide the industrialization drive are provided by the experience of Mauritius and Botswana, two countries which have made some progress in terms of diversifying their economies and developing an industry base.

Mauritius has used government policies and strategies to diversity a monocultural economy which for over 50 years had depended on sugar production and export. It had benefited from preferential access with Europe, an arrangement which guaranteed Mauritius sugar prices which were 100 to 200 per cent higher than world price. As the agreement was phased out in 2009, the government's strategy for diversification included development of export-processing zones, duty-free industrialization areas, tax incentives to businesses. It also promoted its services and telecommunications sector.

Since 1997, Botswana has been diversifying its industry base in order to reduce dependence on diamonds. The industrialization drive has been based on value-added industries in the cattle sector (meat and hides). The government has also promoted the growth of textiles, motor vehicle assembly, electronics, garments and jewellery industries. Policies to attract foreign investment have been promoted particularly for those investors who can manufacture. For instance, in the diamond sector, a Belgian-based diamond company called Eurostar Diamond Traders constructed a new diamond cutting and polishing factory. In Namibia, an Israeli-owned diamond polishing factory was opened; and when it started, it hired 550 workers.

Another important aspect of that developmental role is for the state to use its capacity to engage in cooperation arrangements with other countries, particularly the emerging industrialized countries of East Asia and Latin America and to forge partnerships which promote bilateral and multilateral agreements on foreign investment, aid, technical support, creation of joint ventures and technological diffusion.

Re-thinking trade and industry for Africa's development, therefore, calls for a shift from the current dominant model of primary exports towards more high-value manufactured exports. Such a shift requires strong leadership whereby the state assumes a lead role in terms of planning, designing and implementing industry development policies and strategies which will improve the performance of the local manufacturing sector and also increase growth of manufactured exports. A developmental trade and industry framework fundamentally calls for a people-oriented and people-centred approach where, for example, industry should be developed in such a way that it maximises absorption of the abundant labour resources which characterize the African continent. Strategies to enhance the quality of that labour input are critical because the nature of industrialization requires labour with technical competencies and skills. It should also make use of the mineral and land resources which are abundant in Africa. Investing in the development of institutions will be vital in order to build state capacity for policy development and implementation with regard to promoting industry and trade development. Africa should also strengthen existing institutions such as regional bodies in order to promote intra-African trade. In view of the challenges of market access in international markets, Africa should also intensify its efforts to increase both the volumes and quality of intra-African trade by strengthening regional integration and also improving transport and other logistical infrastructure. African countries should also strengthen their united voice which is critical for negotiations with the WTO, in particular the Doha Development Round which holds promise for enhancing development in much of the developing world.

In the last 10 years, some African countries have increased their cooperation with other developing countries in the South. The role of China, India, Brazil, the Republic of Korea, Turkey and Malaysia in terms of trade and foreign investment in Africa has increased. Brazil has actively invested in Lusophone countries. India has made some notable investments in Nigeria and the Sudan, Mali and Senegal. The role of these countries in Africa has increased. New trading, investment and finance relationships between Africa and Southern partners present an opportunity for Africa.

They also enhance its bargaining power in multilateral negoatiations, diversification of the export base and, therefore, reduce vulnerability to country-specific external shocks.

The Republic of Korea has provided aid to countries such as Angola, Liberia, Senegal, Egypt and Tanzania, among others. Turkey has supported Sudan, Somalia, Mauritania and Ethiopia. China has invested in infrastructure in many countries on the continent. According to UNCTAD (2006), thirty-five African countries have benefited from Chinese infrastructure finance. The report also notes that Southern partners provide more support to the infrastructure and production sectors of African economies than traditional donors who tended to focus on social sectors. Over the period 2002-2007, 54 per cent of China's support to Africa went to infrastructure and public works. Key sectors which benefited included electricity, transport, ICT and water. A notable feature of the cooperation with Southern partners has been the diffusion of technology and transfer of skills. For example, the RoK's Korean Overseas Volunteers (KOVs) Programme is said to have despatched 938 KOVs to Africa between 1990 and 2008. These volunteers have provided training and capacity building to a number of African countries. Brazil has also implemented a Technology Transfer Programme through the Brazilian Technology Cooperation Agency.

At the same time, however, there are challenges which Africa has to deal with. For example, questions have been raised about the focus of the investments of some of these countries in Africa's natural resources and whether in fact, these new investment and trading relationships are not actually reinforcing the same exploitative relationships which Africa has experienced with some countries in the North. These issues are explored in greater detail in the book. UNCTAD (2010) raises the concern that the rise of the large developing country partners in the global market for light manufactured goods may have a harmful effect on sub-Saharan Africa's manufacturing exports

There are also concerns that Africa's growing trade relations with the large developing country partners is reinforcing the region's dependence on commodity exports, thereby inhibiting and delaying structural transformation. Further, the growing demand for commodities has led to a declining trend in the manufactures commodities terms of trade in favour of commodities. Given the growing need for commodities by emerging economies, it is likely that the current terms of trade reversal may be more than a transient phenomenon. This implies that Africa's industrial development will need to ride against the market tide. Its industrial development will need to proceed, despite rising global prices for its primary commodities and lowering prices for its manufactures. State intervention will be necessary to defy the market from pulling private-sector activity towards low value-added commodities and away from high value-added industry. Industrial policy in Africa is hence necessary to effect a structural transformation that the free market on its own may not command.

FDI to Africa from developing countries tends to be concentrated in the natural resource sector. Other investment is in transport, telecommunications, finance and light industry.

Aid from Southern partners has little or no policy conditions. Rather, it uses non-policy conditions such as access to natural resources or purchase of goods and services provided by firms in the donor country.

Although there are many potential benefits, there are also some potential risks such as:

i.   Reduction in environmental quality;

ii.   Weakening of governance;

iii. Replication of Africa's trade and investment relationship with Northern countries.

Despite the threats, cooperation with Southern partners should be pursued because it also offers some opportunities and real possibilities for industry development in the continent.

This chapter presents the context for trade and industry in Africa in terms of their contribution to growth and development. It also discusses the factors that constrain the growth of the sector. Arguments in favour of industrialization are presented. The chapter concludes by reviewing some strategies that have been proposed in favour of a more development-oriented industry and trade policy.

The various chapters presented in the book address the issues raised above. They all agree that there is need to rethink policy and strategy in order to achieve industrial development in Africa. There is no unique solution or answer as countries are different. While Africa can draw lessons from other regions which have successfully industrialized, the book argues that policies and strategies will have to be adapted to country-specific situations and circumstances. However, there are certain common and fundamental issues. These include the critical role which the state should play in developing clear policies and strategies which promote industrial development, its role in financing infrastructure, in supporting the development of innovation, technology and expertise required for such development. African states should also take advantage of Southern

Cooperation, but ensure that the new partnerships and agreements which they enter into do not replicate the exploitative and unequal relationships which they have or continue to experience with some Northern partners. All this calls for a research and needs-based industry development agenda. They should also continue to negotiate with the North in order to create a more equitable international trading and financial system which works to their benefit.

The rest of the volume is structured as follows:

Part One Trade and Industrial Policy in Africa: Theoretical Debates and Experiences From Developing Regions

The section consists of five chapters which focus on the theoretical dimensions of trade and industry and its role in development. It also reviews the experiences of Nigeria, Botswana, Tanzania, Zambia and India with structural adjustment programmes. The case of Cameroun examines the role of China on the country's industry.

Part Two Trade and industry policy: international and regional context

Three chapters examine trade and industry policy within an international and regional context. EU-Africa Economic Partnership Agreements are reviewed with a focus on their implications for agricultural development and food security in Africa. The section also reviews the challenges of trade facilitation and their impact on intra-African trade. A comparative analysis is made with regard to facilitation of production and export of manufactured goods in Africa and Asia/Pacific. The implications of climate change and carbon trade on Africa's development are also analysed.

Part Three Intellectual property rights, technology transfer and culture policy

The WTO entails an agreement on Intellectual Property Rights (IPRs). The section discusses the key provisions of the agreement particularly with respect to technology transfer to African countries. It reviews the challenge of implementing the agreement and ensuring that technology transfer does in fact takes place. The section also discusses the UNESCO Convention for the Protection and Promotion of the Diversity of Cultural Expressions: Implications for African trade and culture policy.

Part Four Institutional dimensions of trade and industrial policy

The last section of the volume presents the institutional dimensions of trade and industry policy. An institutional framework is proposed.

Finally, the book ends with some conclusions and recommendations.

References

Arndt, 1987, 'Industrial Policy in East Asia' in *Industry and Development* (22), Pp. 1-66.

African Development Bank, 2009a, *African Economic Outlook.*

African Development Bank, 2008, *The Economic Development in Africa Report*, 2008: Export Performance following Trade.

African Development Bank, 2007, Africa Competitiveness Report 2007, *Response to the Economic Impact of the Financial Crisis*, Tunis, March 2009.

Bennel, P., 1998, 'Fighting for Survival: Manufacturing Industry and Adjustment in sub-Saharan Africa', *Journal of International Development*, 4 (1): 83-114.

Chang-Ha-Joon, 2008, 'The East Asian Development Experience', in *Rethinking Development Economics*, Anthem Press.

Dicken, P., 2007, *Global Shift: Mapping the Changing Contours of the World Economy*, 5th ed. Sage Publications.

IMF Regional Economic Outlook for sub-Saharan Africa, October 2008.

G.J. McCord, Sachs and W. Woo., 2005. 'Understanding African poverty: beyond the Washington Consensus to the Millennium Development Goals approach', in Teunissen, J. and A. Akkerman, (eds.) *Africa in the World Economy: The National, Regional and International Challenges*, FONDAD, The Hague: 23-45

Held, D et al., 2008, *Global Transformations: Politics, Economics and Culture*, Polity Press.

Kieh, K.G, 2008, *Africa and the New Globalisation*, Ashgate Publishing Company.

Kohli, A., 2004, *State-directed Development: Political Power and Industrialisation in the Global Periphery*, Cambridge University Press.

Krumm, K. and Kharas, H., 2004, *A Trade Policy Agenda for Shared Growth: East Asia Integrates*, World Bank and Oxford Press, World Bank, Pp. 39-171.

Morrissey, O. and Filatotchev, I., 2000, 'Globalization and Trade: The Implications for Exports from Marginalized Economies', *Journal of Development Studies*, Vol. 37, No. 2, pp. 1–12.

Mutume, G., 2004, 'Against odds: Africa strives to rebuild its domestic industries' *Africa Renewal*, Vol. 18 No 3. Oct. 2004.

Tribe, M., 2002, 'An Overview of Manufacturing Development in sub-Saharan Africa' in Belshaw and Livingstone, Chapter 15.

UNIDO, 2004, *Industrial Development Report.*

UNCTAD, 2006, *Least Developed Countries Report*, Geneva.

UNCTAD, 2008, *Trade and Development Report*, Geneva.

UNCTAD, 2008, *Economic Development in Africa*, Geneva.

UNCTAD, 2009, *Economic Development Report in Africa*, Geneva.

UNDP, 2009, 'The Economic Crisis is in Africa', www.undp.org/economic_crisis/africa/html retrieved on 2009/07/07

UNECA, 2006, *African Regional Implementation Review for the Commission on Sustainable Development* (CSD-14:iv), pp. 2-44.

UNIDO, 2009, *Industrial Development Report*, United Nations, New York. pp 80-200.

UNIDO, 2004, *Industrial Development Report*, pp. 5-16.

World Bank, 2008, *World Development Indicators.*

Wolfgang Schneider-Barthold, 2010, 'Africa's Aborted Industrialisation: Modernisation Strategies Impede Organic Industrial Growth', *Development and Cooperation* (No 1, January/February 2002, pp 15-17 accessed 13 May 2010 from www.inwent.org

PART ONE

Trade and Industrial Policy in Africa: Theoretical Debates and Experiences from Developing Regions

1

The Case for a Developmental Trade and Industrial Policy for Africa

Theresa Moyo

Introduction

The quest for a developmental trade and industrial policy for Africa arises out of deep concern and frustration at the failure of the trade and industry policies which have been pursued over the last two decades. According to an ECA report (2007), despite notable economic recovery in Africa in the last five years or so, the continent still faces important challenges in attaining its development goals. It explains that the high level of commodity dependence has contributed to the volatility of growth which has in turn retarded progress towards achieving the Millennium Development Goals (MDGs). Oil prices, which have been increasing into 2008, have also added pressure that threatens price stability in oil-importing countries.

This chapter reviews the evidence on the performance of Africa in trade and industry and analyses the extent to which it has been developmental. It argues that the developmental impact of trade is limited due to the slow pace of industrialization and the many constraints which hamper industrial development on the continent. Africa's trade continues to be dictated by the neo-liberal agenda which has seen the continent become a net exporter of primary commodities and an importer of manufactured goods from Northern countries. With the unfavourable terms of trade which are inherent in such a pattern, it is argued that it will be difficult for the continent to eradicate poverty, unemployment and achieve development even though the rate of economic growth (as measured by the Gross Domestic Product) has improved in the last few years, largely due to increased volumes of exports. The chapter also argues that without a clearly defined 'Afro-centric' definition and conceptualization of development, it will not be feasible to define a developmental trade and industrial policy. It also presents the many obstacles and constraints which are making it difficult for the continent to industrialise to a scale which would make it possible to reverse the historically-determined patterns of specialization. Without a solid industrial base, it will be difficult to achieve development through trade particularly as Africa is increasingly being integrated into the global economy. Based on these discussions, the chapter suggests some important components which could contribute towards a more developmental trade and industry policy for the continent.

Trade, Industry and Development: Theoretical Perspectives

The importance of trade and industry in the economic growth and development of a country is widely accepted in both developed as well as developing countries. The experience of the developed countries provides evidence of this as illustrated in various United Nations Industrial Organization (UNIDO) and United Nations Conference on Trade and Development (UNCTAD) reports. The interrelation between trade and industry determines the extent to which a country may benefit from trade and therefore enhance its prospects for achieving development. One of the reasons why trade has had a limited impact on Africa's development lies in the historically-determined pattern of specialization whereby due to its poorly-developed industrial base, the continent has largely been an exporter of primary commodities. In sharp contrast, developed countries have specialized in the export of manufactured or processed goods which have a higher value and so, the balance of trade has been more favourable to them. Thus, the depth of industrial development ultimately determines the extent to which a country can reap benefits from trade. In this regard, therefore, the quest for a developmental trade and industry policy for Africa rests on, among other things, the extent to which the continent is able to develop an industrial base which is capable of reversing the historically-determined comparative advantages so that the continent moves towards production of high-value-adding goods which have potential for better terms of trade. Development goes beyond realizing huge trade surpluses; it also includes how governments prioritize development spending and the efficiency with which such resources are utilized in the context of a comprehensive national development framework.

Historically, Africa has engaged in trade since the colonial era. But due to the unequal and exploitative pattern of trade where Africa was largely a producer of primary raw materials and an importer of finished or manufactured goods, the benefits of trade were minimal. In fact, evidence shows that the balance of payments problems and external indebtedness which many African countries experienced during the 1960s and 1970s were clear indicators that trade was not benefiting the region. Trade policy was dictated by what neo-classical theory referred to as the Ricardian theory of comparative advantage where it was argued that a country had to specialize in the production and export of those goods for which it had a relative comparative advantage (in terms of costs), over its trading partners. In the case of Africa, with its rich natural resource base, coupled with its abundant labour, it was relatively cheaper to export raw agricultural commodities and minerals and to import what was more expensive for it to produce (for example, machinery, equipment and manufactured inputs). Terms of trade on the international market were always such that primary commodities fetched lower prices than the manufactured imports from Northern countries.

In the period that immediately followed political independence (1960s and 1970s), many countries sought to address balance of payments problems and rising debts by embarking on strategies to reduce their dependence on imports. Historically, developing countries adopted inward-looking trade policies. These were characterized by tariffs and quantitative restrictions which were designed to protect import-competing sectors. The import-substitution industrialization (ISI) model was a dominant industrialization strategy which many African countries adopted in the immediate post-independence period in the 1960s. It was adopted as a way to break the economy's dependence on the vagaries of global primary commodity markets. Kirkpatrick et al (2002:68) argue that industrialization is a necessary but not a sufficient condition for the rapid and sustained development of low-income countries. They define industrialization as 'the development of a modern manufacturing sector alongside the transformation and modernization of the agricultural sector, the development of efficient infrastructural facilities, the creation of indigenous technological capabilities, including human capital formation, and the creation of an income distribution profile consistent with the achievement of agreed development objectives'. Their arguments in favour of promoting the manufacturing sector are that it is an 'engine of growth', that it leads to a rapid productivity growth, that it yields dynamic returns to scale and leads to rapid technological change. In their view, the question for developing countries is 'not whether but how to industrialise'.

The ISI model has largely been viewed as a failure due to what Little (1970) refers to as 'misguided government intervention in factor and product markets'. Other authors argued that the ISI strategy helped to develop the technological capabilities, internal and external economies of scale, inter-industry linkages and infrastructure which provided the basis for the expansion of manufactured goods exports. It has also been pointed out that, although East Asian countries pursued the Export-Oriented Industrialization (EOI) strategy, they did not abandon the ISI. The EOI strategy derives from neoclassical theories of international trade, specifically the Ricardian theory of comparative advantage. Institutions like the World Bank were more in favour of the EOI strategy, arguing that it was superior to the ISI strategy. The superiority of the EOI, it was argued, was due to the neutrality of government interventions in the incentive structure facing manufacturing enterprises (Lall 1991).

With the abandonment of the ISI, the Export-Oriented Industrialization Strategy was adopted. Trade policy was geared towards promotion of exports through, for example, devaluation of currencies and increasing the production of primary commodities. In fact, as a large number of African economies experienced stagnant growth, it was argued that the problem was that of excessive state intervention in the market where it controlled prices to levels that were not viable for producers in most cases. Structural Adjustment Programmes (SAPs) were introduced by the World Bank and the International Monetary Fund (IMF) as a strategy to shift the policy regime from regulated, state interventionist policies towards liberalized, market-driven economies. Trade liberalization was one of the key components of the SAPs. It was argued that in order to improve efficiency and competition, countries had to liberalize their trade sectors, factor and commodity markets. Under the SAPs, trade policy was to reduce or eradicate protection of import substitutes through tariff and non-tariff barriers. A liberal trade policy would lead to trade expansion, which would also lead to improved economic growth and trade revenues which could be channelled towards development. Africa's poor growth performance during the 1970s to mid-1990s period was widely viewed as being attributable to poor trade performance (Sachs and Warner 1997).

The broad liberalization package (which has come to be referred to as the Washington Consensus) emphasized that African countries (and indeed, other developing countries), should pursue a comprehensive package of market reforms. These include the liberalization of trade; factor markets (labour, financial, capital); commodity markets (pricing of goods and services); and, exchange rate markets. Underpinning the strategy was the push for macro-economic stability and minimal government intervention in the economy. The SAP Model has been heavily criticized as one of the stumbling blocks which have impeded Africa's development. Some of the criticisms are that it eroded the policy autonomy of governments, that they opened up trade prematurely and exposed infant industries to external competition when they were not ready. The result was the collapse of industry (notably the textile and footwear industries). The argument is that the SAPs contributed to the 'de-industrialization of Africa'.

One of the major negative consequences of Africa's pursuit of the wholesale liberalization agenda has been the loss of autonomy. Werner Corrales-Leal, Sugathan and Primack (2003) argue that it has led to a large increase in the encroachment of the rules of the multilateral system on domestic economic policy implementation. More specifically, 'it has led to the effective prohibition in the use of many of the tools that had enabled these Asian economies to pursue trade integration in a strategic manner'. Many developing theorists argue that it is this loss of autonomy which makes it difficult for many developing countries to significantly break from the poverty trap. Lall (1991) defines 'successful' industrialization as a process whereby capacity is built and utilized efficiently and growth is sustained over the longer term by increases in productivity and competitiveness, implying a certain efficiency and dynamism in the industrialization process. He postulates that the 'basic building block of industrial success is the attainment of static and dynamic efficiency at firm level'. Specifically,

i.   Firms have to invest time and effort to learn new skills for static efficiency;

ii.   The acquisition of skills is key;

iii. Dynamic efficiency calls for adaptation to change, improved productivity, performance and innovation;

iv.   At the national level, industrial performance is determined by incentives, capabilities and   institutions to deal with market failure.

According to Lall, successful industrialization is thus characterized by direct but selective government intervention and growing local content in physical, human and technological inputs. He also adds that, economic progress requires that a country moves successfully to higher productivity sectors; that the country must, while exploiting existing productive capabilities, endeavour to become competitive in new lines of production i.e. create new comparative advantages. He explains that this process of structural transformation, both internal and external, requires new investment in plant and technology and the acquisition of necessary skills. The country has to invest in technology and build the capacity for innovativeness. It should also promote research and development and improve science and engineering education. All these investments are geared towards 'creation of new comparative advantages'.

UNCTAD (1996:123) advises that countries must develop competitive/ dynamic positions in order to increase their share of the market for a dynamic product. The notion of industrialization is seen to focus on 'acquisition of international competitiveness by enterprises'. This calls for an industrial strategy where the country moves to higher productivity sectors (productivity being a function of human and social capital, skills, knowledge intensity and cultural transformation). The challenge for developing economies is that the new trading system and its rules ensure that developing countries continue to specialize in non-dynamic, low-technology manufacturing activities. The underlying theoretical paradigm does not appear to be helping Africa to achieve development. That is why a shift in thinking is imperative.

Defining Development: The Debate

Development as a concept has been widely debated and discussed in empirical literature. Although the development discourse emerged due to the dissatisfaction with the more 'economistic', 'GDP-centred' approach which considered development as being synonymous with growth in GDP, there are divergent opinions as to its precise meaning. In this chapter, we argue that the key towards defining and adopting a developmental trade and industrial policy for Africa lies in articulating and understanding the concept of development within the African context. It emphasizes that in terms of sequencing, Africa should forge a common vision of the kind of development paradigm it wishes to pursue. Next would be to develop trade and industrial policies which are instrumental in achieving that common vision. What unfortunately has happened, partly due to colonial domination, but also due to challenges and obstacles faced by the continent, is that it has been difficult for the continent to move towards its own unique, original and home-grown development framework. Instead, since the attainment of independence, development on the continent appears to have been externally determined (from the state interventionist approaches of the early years of independence to the adoption of Structural Adjustment Programmes (SAPs) in the 1980s and 1990s and, currently, in the era of globalization, the acceptance of the notion of integrating African economies into the 'world economy.' As the evidence shows, these 'development experiences' may have improved gross domestic product and export volumes, but have not actually delivered development to the mass of the population on the continent. It is the disillusionment with this poor record which calls for a re-think in trade and industry policy.

A review of the literature regarding different approaches to development is necessary in the quest for a developmental trade and industry policy for Africa. As argued above, perceptions on development have been evolving over time. Chenery et al (1970), in his basic needs approach, defined development as meeting basic human needs (food, shelter, clothing) and provision of services (water, health and education). Neo-classical theory, building on Adam Smith's 'invisible hand' of the market, assumed that once an economy achieves a high rate of growth in GDP, the population would automatically benefit through the 'trickle down' effect – the notion that development was 'a given'. This theory is the foundation of SAPs which led many African countries to shift from the state-interventionist policies of the immediate post-independence period to policies of trade liberalization, financial sector liberalization, liberalization of factor markets (labour and capital). The United Nations explains that human development is 'about creating an environment in which people can develop their full potential and lead productive, creative lives in accord with their needs and interests and thus about expanding the choices people have to lead lives that they value' (UNDP 2002:9). Human rights are about creating an environment in which people can develop their full potential and lead creative lives by assuring 'the dignity and worth of the human person' and promoting 'social and better standards of life in larger freedom' (UN Declaration of Human Rights).

Sen (1998), the 1998 Nobel Prize Winner for Economics, views development as a process which enhances human capabilities. He noted that development is about enhancing the capacity of an individual to function, to make choices and to live a full and meaningful life. He argues that development has to go beyond the basic needs which go towards satisfying the physical and material needs. Development has a spiritual, intellectual and emotional dimension. It has to guarantee not just the physical and material well-being of the individual, but must allow them to enjoy several freedoms – freedom from hunger, freedom from oppression on the grounds of race, gender, religion, and ethnicity, freedom of expression, freedom of movement, etc. Although Sen focuses on individual freedoms, his analysis is important because of its emphasis on the human rights dimension to development. Zubairu (2005), calls for an alternative development paradigm which moves away from a 'Eurocentric' to an 'Afrocentric' approach. His critique of the 'development' approaches pursued by Africa so far is that they have been basically Eurocentric and mostly crafted to meet the needs of the North and not Africa. He argues that Eurocentric approaches are embodied in the export-oriented development paradigm which most of Africa has pursued for decades; it also embraces the SAPs, PRSPs, dependence on aid and foreign direct investment (FDI) and the integration of Africa into the world economy under the WTO system of trade and finance. Zubairu contends that the approach has not succeeded in bringing about development to the continent. He calls on Africa to consider a more 'Afrocentric' development paradigm. He defines this as a reconstruction of development – that is, 'development should necessarily begin with seeking to understand indigenous cultural conceptions, processes and practices of socio-economic provisioning, that is, to seek to understand how indigenous cultural conceptions regard economic and social processes and how they are mediated and negotiated'. In his opinion, development is a social totality where both social and economic lives are integrated. Consequently, an Afrocentric development framework should embrace, cultural institutional practices, reject a single worldview in preference for plurality of discourses. He believes that in Africa, development appears to be seen more in terms of human dignity particularly within a community, a state of well-being and happiness.'

Ake (1996) seems to concur with Zubairu's analysis. In his view, in the African context, development must first be conceived as rural development, largely because of its strategic position as a source of primary products (agriculture, mining, foodstuffs and labour) and the fact that most of Africa's population resides in that sector. He argues that the fundamental reason for the failure of rural development in Africa is the adoption of an inappropriate development paradigm which focuses almost exclusively on the urban sector and prioritizes urban-based industry over rural communities. He notes that one of the factors behind the success of the East Asian countries lay in their efforts at prioritizing rural development. Ake's argument seems plausible, especially in the context of Zubairu's Afrocentric framework. However, the cost of such a paradigm shift would be immense due to the spatial development implications of 're-engineering the rural sector'. A major cost-benefit analysis would have to be done to determine the feasibility of such a strategy in comparison to an urban-based industry framework which takes advantage of already existing infrastructure and other positive externalities.

Stiglitz (1998), at the 9th Raul Prebische lecture at UNCTAD, was very critical of the neo-liberal policy prescriptions of the Washington Consensus. He called for a 'broad conception of development'. He defined development as 'a transformation of society' – that change was not an end in itself, but a means to other objectives; 'the changes that provide individuals and societies with more control over their own destiny, development that enriches the lives of individuals by widening their horizons and reducing their sense of isolation... change that increases life spans and the vitality of life.' Stiglitz also argued that 'approaching development from the perspective of transforming society has profound implications for what governments and aid agencies do, and how they engage participation and partnership.' He explained that change was about changing ways of thinking; it was about social inclusion, participation and building consensus.

Implications for a Developmental Trade and Industry Framework

What are the implications of these theoretical approaches for Africa? They suggest that a developmental trade and industrial policy must fundamentally be embedded within an Afrocentric framework. One expects, for example, that the trading system which emerges from such a framework is such that domestic needs take precedence over requirements of external markets, it must utilize the local resource base (natural and human resources), and in a manner which transforms and sustains local society. A trade policy which impoverishes through exploitation of labour (through, for example, low wage policies, retrenchments, unequal terms of trade, etc.) cannot lead to the transformation of society which Stiglitz (1998) considers to be the meaning of development. From Sen's perspective, it cannot enhance the capabilities of the individual and society to function in the most optimal way, however defined, in their own local contexts. In the same vein, a developmental industry policy necessarily has to be consistent with the defined indigenous developmental framework – is it based on consensus? Who are the ultimate beneficiaries? A labour-intensive industrial strategy seems to be more consistent with development in most of Africa which are labour-surplus economies. It must also promote the use of local resources and promote the processing of those resources in order to improve the revenue from the export of manufactured goods. For too long, Africa has remained a net primary commodity exporter and, due to the unfavourable terms of trade on the international markets, the continent has reeled from balance of payments crises which led to indeb-tedness and increased vulnerability to loss of autonomy in policy making.

To summarize the argument, a developmental trade and industry policy should contribute towards the goal of increasing human dignity, well-being and happiness; it must create a trading system which *transforms* African society towards a high level of *inclusive human development*; it must be a system which is sustainable and rooted in the traditions, cultures and norms of indigenous populations. Africa has yet to define such a development paradigm. That should precede any attempts to enter into the various international trading agreements which should lead to further integration of Africa into the world economy. Clearly, Africa is entering into that engagement rather prematurely because it is in a weaker position and lacks the necessary conditions for it to benefit fully from such integration (given the continuing challenges of governance, lack of infrastructure, the inadequate skills and technological base, etc). It appears the continent has been driven by global imperatives rather than pursuing its own developmental agenda. It has experimented with the import-substitution industrialization Strategy (ISI) of the 1960s and 1970s; state control/mixed economy model that was 'fashionable in the immediate post- independence era'; the World Bank and IMF-designed Structural Adjustment Programmes of the 1980s and 1990s which called for market-led economic reforms which included trade liberalization. Today, although economic growth is improving, the industrial base of most of SSA remains small, and trade structure has not changed fundamentally despite the emergence of a dynamic and competitive global economy in which survival critically depends on a nation's innovative and technological capacity and these require a strong industrial base.

Empirical Evidence on Trade and Industry Policy and its Developmental Impact

The overview presents a summary of the evidence on economic performance in Africa in terms of trade and industry, emphasizing the type of policies which shaped those developments. It also reviews the experiences of some of the East and South Asian countries with regard to their policy approach to industrialization which is internationally acclaimed as one of the most successful in terms of what it achieved over a period of 20 years.

The African Experience

Economic Trends

The report by UNECA (2005) presents a detailed description of the trends in economic growth in Africa. It indicates that between the 1970s and 1980s, growth has been slow and erratic, particularly when compared to other developing regions. This has made it difficult for the continent to eradicate poverty and achieve development. Generally; growth in Africa has been erratic. Per capita growth rates rose from 2 per cent in the early

1960s to nearly 5 per cent by the end of that decade; then fell steadily through the early 1970s; turned negative during the mid-1980s; and then climbed back to around 2 per cent since the mid-1990s. Alemayehu (2000) indicates that over the period 1960-1980, Africa's annual real GDP rate of growth averaged about 4.1 per cent, that it declined over 1980-1993 and it picked up between 1994 and 1995 (2.9 per cent in 1994 and 3.0 per cent in 1995). Two primary factors accounted for Africa's slow growth: a relatively low rate of capital accumulation and a low growth rate of productivity for the investments that are made in the region compared to productivity in other developing regions. By 2005, African growth had rebounded to the levels of the 1960s and with more diversified economies. With the exception of Botswana and Mauritius, growth in the rest of sub-Saharan Africa has been erratic since the 1960s, resulting in the region falling further behind the rest of the developing world and in income levels regressing relative to the levels in 1960.

In 2004, the per capita income for a group of nine African countries had actually regressed relative to the levels in 1960. These include Angola, Central African Republic, Comoros, Madagascar, Niger, Senegal, Sierra Leone, Democratic Republic of Congo and Zambia. In the same year (2004), the per capita incomes of 13 middle income African countries were several-fold higher than the 1960 levels. Although these countries together are home to 13 per cent of Africa's population, they account for a combined total of 66 per cent of all incomes earned in the region. Alemayehu (2000) argues that Zambia's and Cote d'Ivoire's per capita incomes have hardly progressed beyond their 1960 levels . Somalia and Liberia, too, have lost significant ground in income levels compared to the early 1960s.

Trade and Development

According to UNCTAD's (2003) report on economic development in Africa, trade performance in Africa has been bleak despite growth in exports. Africa's share in world trade has been falling consistently since 1980 and the continent remains heavily dependent on the export of a few primary commodities, most of which have suffered a decline in prices leading to large terms-of-trade losses . Trade policy has evolved from the ISI strategies of the 1960s and 1970s towards more export orientation. Due to the poor performance of SSA economies in the 1980s and 1990s, SAPs were implemented as explained above. The SAP package included the liberalization of trade which was to be achieved by the elimination or reduction of tariff and non-tariff barriers to imports and also included strategies to promote exports (for example, by devaluing currencies).

Michaely (1991:123) argues that it is not automatic that trade liberalization can improve trade performance. He says that in Africa, trade liberalization occurred at a fast pace and it damaged the productive capacity of sectors which were key to development, for example, food processing, clothing, textiles and footwear. Cheaper imports from China, for example, have contributed to the collapse of these industries in Southern and Eastern Africa in particular. Stiglitz (1999:36) also argues that trade liberalization one is not sufficient for developing countries to reap the full benefits from integration into the world economy. He says that a liberalized trade regime would not necessarily on its own place an economy on a 'self-sustained growth path'. Rather, to achieve higher overall growth depends on the composition and structure of exports. He argues that it is those countries which had a greater manufacturing base that appeared to benefit from liberalization. The demise of the clothing and textile industry in countries like Zimbabwe has been cited as an example to illustrate the point. Unlike other developing regions, Africa has by and large not been able to diversify into manufactures or market-dynamic products and has even lost market shares for its traditional exports, the report noted, adding that 'market-oriented policies have not been able to reverse the situation'.

In the case of cotton, the World Bank estimates that in 2002, the world market price would have been more than 25 per cent higher but for the direct support of the US for its cotton producers. Other estimates suggest that in 2002, cotton subsidies by the US and the EU have caused a loss of up to US$300 million in revenue to Africa as a whole, which is more than the total debt relief of US$230 million approved by the World Bank and IMF under the advanced HIPC initiative to nine countries in West and Central Africa in the same year. While trade (merchandise imports plus exports) as a share of GDP for Africa (excluding South Africa and Nigeria) increased from 45 per cent to 50.4 per cent between 1980/1981 and 2000/2001, on the whole, however, Africa's share in world exports fell from about 6 per cent in 1980 to 2 per cent in 2002, and its share of world imports from 4 per cent in 1980 to 2 per cent in 2002. UNCTAD says that this phenomenon has as much to do with the structure of international trade as with the composition of merchandise trade of Africa, the trade policies applied there in the past 20 years, and market access and agricultural policies in industrial countries.

While the structure of developing countries exports has changed significantly over the past two decades – where 70 per cent of these exports are manufactured goods – Africa has hardly benefited from the boom in manufactured exports. Alemayehu (2000:53) indicates that the rate of manufacturing value added dropped from 8 per cent in the 1960s to 5.56 per cent in the 1970s and had dropped to 0.25 per cent in the 1980s. Manufactured exports fell drastically and Africa's share in world exports declined from 1.12 per cent in 1970 to 0.60 per cent in 1975. The share for SSA fell from 0.6 per cent in 1970 to 0.3 per cent in 1995. He explains that the reasons for the poor performance include the lack of adequate foreign exchange to import industrial inputs and also infrastructural constraints which impacted negatively on the availability of raw material supplies. The overall contribution of the manufacturing industry was relatively low compared to other developing regions. Africa is still the least industrialized region in the world. Its share in world merchandise exports fell from 6.3 per cent in 1980 to 2.2 per cent in 2000 in value terms. Similarly, its share of total developing country merchandise exports fell to almost 8 per cent in 2000, while its share in manufactures remained at below one per cent.

By comparison, Asia's share of global merchandise exports increased from 18 per cent in 1980 to 22 per cent in 2000, while its share of total developing country merchandise exports increased from almost 60 per cent to 72 per cent over the same period. Similarly, its share in global manufactures trade increased threefold, reaching 21.5 per cent in 2000. Even though Africa has remained commodity-dependent, it has fallen behind other regions in the world in exports of non-fuel primary commodities. The report said that these trends indicate that most African countries have been losing market shares in commodity exports to other developing countries, while at the same time most have been unable to diversify into manufactured exports. UNCTAD notes that a major explanation for the poor economic performance of the region in the past two decades is a significant loss of resources due to adverse terms of trade. The World Bank suggests that the cumulative loss resulting from adverse terms of trade over a period of almost three decades (1970-1997) for African non-oil-exporting countries (excluding South Africa) amounted to 119 per cent of combined GDP of these countries in 1997, 51 per cent of cumulative net resource flows, and 68 per cent of net resource transfers to the region. UNCTAD research indicates that if sub-Saharan Africa's terms of trade had remained at 1980 levels, the share of the sub-continent in world exports would have been double its current level. Coffee and sugar producing countries would have earned an additional US$19 billion and US$1.4 billion respectively, and West African cotton-producing countries would have earned an additional US$1 billion if prices for these products during 1999-2002 had remained at 1998 levels, the report said.

Furthermore, terms-of-trade losses have also contributed to the debt overhang of African countries. According to the IMF, 'almost all countries hit hardest by falling commodity prices are also among the world's poorest. All but two (Brazil and Chile) are classified as low-income countries by the World Bank; over half are [in] sub-Saharan Africa; and sixteen are Heavily Indebted Poor Countries.' Another contributory factor is the low rate of domestic investment. Estimates show that average gross domestic fixed investment for the continent was only 20 per cent in the 2000-2003 period. Out of 46 countries with adequate data, only nine (Chad, Lesotho, Mauritania, Angola, Sao Tome and Principe, Mozambique, Seychelles and Gabon) achieved investment rates of above 25 per cent of GDP during 2000-2003. Reasons for the poor investment performance range from the high cost of doing business in Africa (as perceived by investors), the inadequate infrastructure, the weak regulatory environment for business, and the lack of local capacity in terms of technical skills and know-how. Low rates of investment also explain the slow pace of industrial development in SSA countries. The World Bank (2006) reports that although Africa represents only 10 per cent of the global population, yet it is home to 30 per cent of the world's poor. Similarly, although per capita incomes for Africa and East Asia were virtually the same in 1960, by the end of the 20th century, sub-Saharan Africa's per capita income – even after adjusting for differences in purchasing power – was less than one-fourth of East Asia's.

The UNDP (2005) argues that despite the recent improvements in the rates of economic, these rates still fall short of the threshold required to accelerate poverty alleviation and achieve development. On a medium-term basis, only four countries (Equatorial Guinea, Chad, Angola and Mozambique) met the 7 per cent growth threshold. It adds that very few African countries have been able to sustain sufficiently high economic growth rates, which largely explains the slow progress in social development. The UNDP (2006) indicates that most of the SSA countries fall in the Low Human Development Group of countries with Human Development Indices (HDI) falling below 0.5 as compared to ratios of above 0.8 for developed countries and the few oil-producing African countries. Only a few SSA countries such as Uganda, Botswana, Kenya, South Africa and Swaziland fell within the Medium Human Development Group (MHD). Part of the reason for the poor performance in terms of development is the fact that growth has not been accompanied by job creation. Labour statistics presented by the ECA (2005), indicate that the industrial work force did not increase significantly during the past few years despite a steady growth in industrial production. This is attributed to the growing dominance of capital-intensive industries as most of new investments in the industrial sector in African countries are absorbed by the mining and energy sector. Furthermore, labour-intensive industries in Africa, such as textiles and clothing, are no longer competitive on both foreign and domestic markets after the admission of China to WTO. The African labour force was estimated at 380 million in 2005, with about 20 per cent in the industrial sector.

Also significant is the fact that growth has concentrated in capital-intensive sectors such as oil and mining and the shift from agriculture into industry without necessarily absorbing the surplus labour from the rural sectors. It is such economic stagnation that has led these countries to embark on structural reforms most of which aim to increase exports, restore macroeconomic stability and resolve the poverty and unemployment which continue to plague their economies. Trade policies of the Northern countries have undermined Africa's trade performance. Studies by UNECA (2006) point out that market access remains a problem for African exports, as most of the tariff peaks are in agriculture, including processed products. For example, coffee beans and final processed coffee are subject to tariffs of 7.3 per cent and 12.1 per cent respectively in the EU, 0.1 per cent and 10.1 per cent in the US and 6 per cent and 18.8 per cent in Japan.

Industry Development

The development of industry in Africa has been slow and it remains a challenge. UNIDO (2005) indicates that the manufacturing sector accounted for only 12.1 per cent of GDP, down from an average of 14 per cent over 2000-2004. The underdevelopment of the manufacturing sector largely explains the limited contribution of industry to GDP growth. Countries with the most diversified economies on the continent (Egypt, Morocco, South Africa and Tunisia) continue to focus on traditional industries, such as food processing and textiles, except for South Africa, which is more industrialized than any other African country. There has been recently a gradual shift towards more capital-intensive industries in Tunisia, such as electrical and electronics industries, while the textiles and clothing sector is experiencing continued decline in its importance in all African economies. In the oil-producing countries, there has also been gradual production development in intermediate and oil-based industries, particularly chemicals, petrochemicals, fertilizers, plastics, and energy-intensive industries. Exports of industrial goods are still dominated by mining and crude oil. In oil-producing countries, there has been a gradual production development in intermediate and oil-based industries especially chemicals, petrochemicals, fertilizers, plastics and energy-intensive industries.

In spite of the observable trends towards a re-orientation in industrial development strategies and policies in many African countries, an effective and early realization of the target growth rate of 8 per cent per annum that was set in IDDA II for the manufacturing sector is hardly in sight, given the entrenched structural rigidities, weak inter-industry and inter-sectoral linkages, technological backwardness and poor institutional and physical infrastructure in the region. The investment needs for rehabilitation, infrastructural development and capital deepening in Africa have never been greater. The continued reliance on raw material exports is a major contributory factor. Inadequate public sector investments into infrastructural development, the lack of skills and dependence on foreign direct investment to invest in industry development are also key factors. The UNECA (2004) observes that, 'mid-way through the second Industrial Development Decade for Africa (IDDA-II), there is little or no indication of the structural transformation of the manufacturing sector in most countries of sub-Saharan Africa. The sector continues to be characterized by structural weaknesses such as low productivity, under-utilization of capacity and inadequate industrial investments; acute dependence on external sources of raw materials, technology and other essential inputs; and obsolete machinery and ill-maintained equipment. With the liberalization of trade, the sector also faces problems of intense competition from cheap imports from relatively technologically better-off developing countries, especially those of South-East Asia, which are making rapid inroads into the African market for basic consumer goods'.

The current multilateral trading system poses serious challenges for Africa with regard to the availability of space for more autonomous policy-making based on unique situations and realities which prevail in each country. The developmental dimension of the multilateral trade rules in the context of the WTO system appears limited and, in fact, threatened. Trade rules were not designed with developmental issues in mind. The move to the 'single-undertaking' – that all members had to undertake obligations in all areas of rules – regardless of their level of development, makes it difficult for developing economies to compete in global markets. The institutionalization of the idea of restricting governments' access to the use of many active policies which were used by early industrializers in East and South Asia in the 1960s and 70s also limits the policy space for African countries. Furthermore, the inclusion of intellectual property rights, investment measures, health and food safety measures into the package of multilateral rules have serious cost implications in terms of compliance and some of these standards are effectively barring African products from markets of the North (Third World Network 2000).

The East and South Asian Experience: What are the Lessons?

East and South Asia (for example, South Korea, Taiwan, Singapore, Thailand, Hong Kong) which have been cited as successes in terms of their performance in trade and industry followed a more strategic path of trade integration. The strategy was founded on government policy interventions in the economy especially on the supply side. Some authors argue that it was under that global environment of relative policy autonomy that the early 'Asian Tigers' developed. Their success was due to the active intervention of their governments in the economy. They used traditional active industrial policies and technology-related approaches to improve supply-side constraints. This led to an improvement in their competitiveness. Instead of a comprehensive trade liberalization strategy, they employed a strategic approach to trade integration. They took some policies from the trade liberalization package to advantage and left out those policies which were deemed to be inappropriate for their situations. The experience of those countries highlight the significance of the role played by government through activist intervention policies. These included, among others to be discussed in the below, selective and targeted import controls, tariff protection to selected infant industries, targeted subsidies and incentives. They also included extensive investments in human capital development which led to improvements in labour productivity. Chowdhury and Islam (1993:13) argue that the superlative growth of the four East Asian Newly Industrialising Economies (NIEs) has been accompanied by extensive changes in the structures of their production. They observe that by 1986, Korea, Malaysia, Singapore and Taiwan had a greater share of production in industry than the average for the matured industrial market economies. They also argue that it was the rapid growth in manufacturing which provided the impetus for structural change. Another important factor was the rapid improvement in human capital. Most important was the central role played by the state through the development of a clear strategic framework for trade and industry. Those strategies were also implemented to a large extent.

In the short term, there was heavy and direct government intervention initially to protect local industry through tariff protection. Other strategies were directed towards promoting productive investment, investing in human and technological capability of domestic firms, specific targeted interventions to promote growth of small to medium-sized firms. There were strategic efforts to link TNCs with local firms in order to promote skills and technology transfer. The governments also introduced policies to promote export growth. Chowdry and Islam (1993) describe in detail, some of the strategic interventions which those countries made. The countries faced a challenge of low growth in the 1960s. They lacked the natural resources and their domestic markets were small. But in just two decades, they managed to raise their savings ratios from below 10 per cent to above 30 per cent. Income per capita grew at an average annual growth rate of around 7 per cent from 1960. The structure of their production changed such that the share of manufacturing in GDP more than doubled to a level where the sector contributed 30 per cent or more to their GDP. The share of manufacturing to total exports increased to 30 per cent as compared to 20 per cent in 1960. They achieved macroeconomic stability, with inflation rates falling to single-digit levels by the end of 1989. The economies operated at near-full employment during most of the 1971 to 1989 period. The application of rapid, labour-intensive technologies and methods to manufacture exports contributed to job creation. Growth was also followed by sustained reduction in poverty and inequality. Income inequality as measured by the Gini coefficient (though an imperfect measure), was reduced to a level where in 1981, Hong Kong, Korea, Singapore, and Taiwan had a Gini index of below 0.4 (indicating a relatively low rate of inequality). For most of SSA, the ratio was above 0.6 in 1980. Hughes (1989) dubbed these economies as 'leaders in social development'.

What were the critical success factors? These included change in the structure of industry. The share of more complex activities like iron and steel products, machinery and transport equipment in manufacturing value-added increased. The importance of food, beverage and tobacco declined in the share of MVA. Industry was transformed from light and basic manufacturing towards high quality, high value and fashion items through an extensive diversification programme. The governments adopted market policies but were also actively involved through, for example, providing infrastructural support. More importantly, in the early stages, they protected their infant industries through tariffs and non-tariff barriers, gave export incentives and subsidies to lower production costs. These were eventually reduced and later completely removed once the domestic firms were able to compete. Singapore and South Korea pursued intensive and active industrial restructuring programmes which helped to shift manufacturing to more sophisticated activities. South Korea achieved what some refer to as 'spectacular industrialisation'. Since the 1960s, it started industrialization using ISI strategy. This led to a rapid growth in production as entrepreneurs moved to take advantage of attractive conditions with low risks. Initially, there were high levels of protection with no overseas competition for the protected industries. Production was based on delivery of low-level goods using unskilled labour. With time, they moved to higher-level goods (production of refrigerators, intermediate goods) Demand for larger markets increased and they moved towards export-orientation. At that stage, they overhauled the incentive system, reduced protection of domestic industries and increased the export of manufactured goods.

Korea introduced an industrial restructuring programme which shifted emphasis from labour-intensive to heavy and capital-intensive activities. Priority activities included steel and non-ferrous metals, chemicals, petrochemicals, machinery, shipbuilding and electronic industrial equipment. Industrial restructuring was coupled with Research and Development (R&D) and human resource development programmes. Evidence from UNIDO (1986) shows that the share of manufacturing in GDP soared and that Manufacturing Value Added (MVA) increased 340 times in 20 years. It developed a policy package with the following features:

i.   Tax exemptions for technology and development funds;

ii.   Strong export subsidies;

iii.   Quantitative and tariff restrictions on exports;

iv.   Targeted and subsidized credit;

v.   Programmes to link conglomerates in heavy industries through, for example, providing financing and protected markets; and,

vi.   Reduced their dependence on FDI and forced them into export markets.

Korea is said to have 25 times higher R&D by industry as a proportion of GDP than Mexico which has the same size of manufacturing value-added. Chowdry provides evidence that the index of production of fabricated metal products, machinery and basic metal industry rose from 2.5 (1980=100) in 1965 to 226.5 in 1984; that Korea became an efficient producer of steel and leading producer of consumer electronics and automobiles.

Singapore initiated its industrial restructuring program in the 1970s. The government set up the Economic Development Board which laid out priorities for industry. The aim of the programme was to shift manufacturing activities towards certain 'priority' industries which are more skill and technology-intensive. State intervention was in form of:

i. Laying down of priorities for industrial activities;

ii. Development of policies to channel both domestic and foreign investment to priority industries;

iii. Launch of a five-year technology plan for the development of key sectors (1991);

iv. Launch of a sector-specific policy package;

v. Channelling more than half of the natural savings into public institutions such as the Central Provident Fund and using them to invest in industrial development;

vi. Doubling of S&T expenditure to US$ 4 billion over 5 years (30 per cent was for strategic industry (1997);

vii. Making substantial investments in shipbuilding and iron and steel and using selective grants and loan schemes to support private industries;

viii. Providing industrial infrastructure support;

ix. Pursuing a high wage policy to discourage labour-intensive activities;

x. Providing tax incentives to attract FDI;

xi. Creating competence in new technology;

xii. Increasing spending on research and development and investments in science and engineering training;

xiii. Improving patenting and copyright laws so as to encourage innovation and transfer of technology;

xiv. Providing export financing; and

xv. Establishing EPZs to attract FDI in textiles, agro-food and consumer electronics.

Singapore's industrial restructuring programme was introduced in 1979 and it used capital-intensive methods where resources were shifted towards more skill and technology-intensive activities, microprocessors and other sophisticated electronic products. The government also stepped up its R&D and HRD programme, improved the patent system and tightened copyright laws in order to encourage innovation and the transfer of technology. In labour-abundant economies as is the case with most African countries, it would appear that the Singapore model of course would not be the most appropriate. However, by investing extensively in skills development, labour can be absorbed into industry development. This has to be a priority in national development planning and budgeting processes.

Chowdry and Islam (1993:98) provide evidence to show that in 1983, the Singapore government either wholly or partially owned 450 companies involving US$2.4 billion paid-up capital and US$18.2 billion in fixed assets, and it employed 5 per cent of the total labour force. They quote Mr Lee Kuan Yew, the former Prime Minister and architect of modern Singapore who said,

> In the early stages, when you try to bring up a very low level of economy to catch up with others, the government must be an activist, and a catalyst to growth. But once the business gets going, they would become too complex and specialized for any government to be involved. Hence private entrepreneurs and companies must be encouraged to take over.

The Singapore model was, indeed, successful in terms of industry development in the country and in improving export performance, economic growth and development (through government's social spending). However, its emphasis on capital-intensive production would not be suitable for Africa where unemployment is high. As a result of the programme, the electronics industry increased its MVA by four times between1965-1985. It also increased production of industrial chemicals and communication equipment.

Malaysia, Thailand and China (sometimes referred to as the 'mature Asian Tigers') implemented strategies to spread the developmental impacts of technological and trade interactions. Some of the strategies which they undertook included designing impressive programmes to foster the creation of inter-firm linkages between TNC affiliates and local SMEs. These programmes succeeded in increasing internal economic multipliers. They also improved technological capabilities of local enterprises, created jobs and enhanced export capacity. Taiwan had a mix of trade and credit policies for upgrading the technological base of its predominantly SME industry base. It also encouraged industries into skill and technology-intensive activities and had selective use of FDI. China introduced the Production Networks for Exports (PNE) in the 1980s. It developed a network of suppliers, promoted training collaboration between TNCs and local enterprises and focused on light industrial products, textiles, machines and electronic goods for export (involving over 200 rural export enterprises). In Malaysia, the Vendor Support programme was established in 1988, the programme is a comprehensive approach to upgrading local supplier capabilities. The package includes:

- Debt financing on a preferential basis to those entrepreneurs involved in the programme;
- Provision of venture capital to local firms;
- Technological assistance via collaboration with the TNCs;
- Industry-led training initiatives.

As reported by the UNDP Human Development Report of 2006, most of these early industrializers fall in the High Human Development Group of countries with HDIs of over 0.9 as compared to most of SSA where indices are below 0.5. The success of the East and South Asian countries should not lead one to overlook some of the negative aspects of their strategies. Although they did much to improve income distribution and overall development, one cannot ignore the fact that their competitiveness was partly achieved through the exploitation of labour as reflected in the low wages and poor working conditions of workers particularly in the Export Processing Zones. These should also offer lessons as the continent strives to develop a more 'developmental' trade and industry policy; that it has to integrate labour standards which are consistent with the continent's developmental agenda. Such a policy has to promote strategies which based on fundamental human rights and also promote the use of labour in the industrialization effort. The World Bank (1993), argued that the growth and development of the high-performing Asian economies (HPAEs) was largely due to 'getting the basics right' – which basics included:

     i. High levels of domestic financial savings and high investment levels;

     ii. Rapidly growing human capital;

     iii. Rapid growth and productivity improvements in agriculture;

     iv. Rapid decline in population growth rates;

     v. A better-educated labour force and a more effective system of public administration.

The Bank argues that it was the 'superior accumulation of human and physical capital, coupled with sound macroeconomic policies which explained the Asian miracle'. The Bank has warned developing counties not to follow the HPAEs (World Bank 1993), that those selective interventions are based on 'too rigorous requirements', that targeted industrial policies (except in Japan), had led to lower rates of growth of productivity than some other industries. It also argues that industrial policy has disappeared from the development agenda even of East Asia. In its place, there has been a shift towards trade liberalization, structural adjustment and stabilization. It barely acknowledges the role of government intervention which had been instrumental in the development of specific industries and development in general. Indeed, the approach used by the East and South Asian economies produced positive results but those interventions were, admittedly, expensive. They depended on the capacity of the state both in financial as well as operational terms (design and monitoring of interventions). It may not be feasible for Africa to pursue similar industrial and trade strategies due to weak fiscal performance. However, given the absolute importance of building a strong industry base, the challenge must be how to mobilize domestic and external resources in order to finance industry development. Trade integration in East and South Asia was linked to a growth pattern which was associated with relevant increases in the employment rate, reduction in poverty levels, and substantial improvements in income distribution.

To summarize, the review of the evidence on the experience of selected countries in East Asia provides a number of lessons for Africa. Firstly, it demonstrates the critical role which the government should play in promoting a development-oriented trade and industry base. As argued by North (1990) and Chang and Rowthorn (1995), 'there is no industrialized country in which the government has not played a central role in promoting and supporting change'. Through appropriate investments, regulations, and policies, the state complements the role of markets. Secondly, it emphasizes that whilst trade liberalization and policies to integrate the economies of developing countries into the global economy indeed provide opportunities for growth, it is important for African economic and development planners to take into account their own local contexts and situations. Thus, it may be necessary in the short-term, to protect sensitive industries whose wholesale liberalization may have serious or negative immediate impact in terms of the country's development. A selective and phased approach to liberalization of such sectors as agriculture, textile industry, and agro-processing industries, for example, is necessary to protect against job losses and also the potential destruction of local industrial initiatives which are not yet ready for external competition in terms of their capacities, efficiencies and production volumes.

Thirdly, the East Asian experience shows that industry development calls for commitment on the part of governments to invest in infrastructure which promotes trade and industry development. This cannot be left to the private sector. Governments also have a role in terms of creating a conducive policy environment which allows for private sector participation in trade and industry. Emphasis must be on promoting indigenous or local private sector, not necessarily to the exclusion of foreign investors. Governments should create environments where joint ventures between foreign and local firms can be established. Such ventures should also include small and medium enterprises which tend to be locally owned. African countries also need to invest much more in human, technological and skills development which are vitally needed for industry development. Strategies to develop a disciplined, hard-working, educated workforce and the promotion of rapid capital accumulation were critical in the trade and industrialization efforts of those countries. In addition, the building of an in-house technological capacity played a critical role. Fourthly, as Soludo and Ogbu (1998) argue, dynamic comparative advantages can be deliberately created. African countries should not confine themselves to traditional exports but also develop new advantages by making appropriate research, technological and capacity investments in manufacturing based on the continent's rich endowment of natural resources in mining and agriculture. The experiences of the East Asian economies emphasize the importance of innovative approaches where developing countries have to derive new national competitive advantages from basic factors of production. UNIDO (1991/1992) advocates a three-pronged strategy: promotion of industries which promote inputs to agriculture; industries that process agricultural commodities; and, industries that are based in indigenous resources (mining, forestry, textiles, leather and footwear, cosmetics, pharmaceuticals, fruit canning, milling and sugar processing, vegetable processing, sea-food processing or canning. The innovative strategies should also promote efforts to develop a disciplined, hard-working, educated workforce and the promotion of rapid capital accumulation that were critical in the trade and industrialization efforts of those countries. In addition, the building of an in-house technological capacity played a critical role.

UNCTAD (2006) points out that LDCs need not just lower tariffs or improve market entry but also enhance supply chain capacities in order to benefit from the global economy through producing and trading competitive goods and services. It puts emphasis on enhancing productive capacities; building effective institutions of state and private sector and increasing investments in infrastructure; improving labour productivity through skills development; supporting small to medium size enterprises and using appropriate trade and industry policies to promote the manufacturing sector. In developing productive capacities, priority should be to link industry development to the natural resources available in the country – for example, to build on agriculture to promote agro-processing industries and the mining sector for minerals processing.

Conclusions and Recommendations

Based on a review of the evidence on the status of trade and industry development in Africa, we conclude that although economic growth and trade performance in Africa has improved in the last few years, the structure of that trade still places Africa in a vulnerable position in the context of the global trading and financial system in which it is increasingly integrating. The continent continues to be a net producer and exporter of raw materials. The pace of industry development is low and this partly explains why its structure of trade has not changed. More importantly, we have argued that the pursuit of trade liberalization policies at a time when the fundamental requirements are not in place (as reflected, for example, in the low productivity levels of industry and the consequent low level of competitiveness, the inadequate human and technological base, among other factors), has retarded rather than facilitated industry development and trade expansion. Consequently, the developmental impact of trade and industry has been limited. This chapter has presented different views on the meaning of development and argued that the definition of a developmental trade and industry policy should be based on a more comprehensive, Afrocentric perspective of development because current approaches, as argued by Zubairu (2005), are Eurocentric in their approach and inappropriate for the continent. We argue that Africa has yet to define that development framework in order to move away from pre-mature integration into the world economy where, as is the case at the moment, the continent is negotiating on an unequal footing with long developed economies of the North. This is an issue where scholars could engage in deeper reflection on whether it is indeed possible for the continent to define and develop policies which lead to the achievement of that Afrocentric development paradigm. Such a paradigm does not and should not necessarily imply that they reject integration into the global economy. It simply suggests the need for consensus building, for clarity of vision, for the laying of the necessary foundation which will ensure that in the long-term, Africa will benefit from global trade through an appropriate industrialization strategy which is based on the resource-base of the continent. We therefore emphasize that a developmental trade and industry agenda critically depends on Africa being able to define and articulate a comprehensive, home-grown development framework in the context of a more Afrocentric development paradigm instead of pursuing externally-designed policies and strategies which have failed.

Sub-Saharan African countries should draw some lessons from the experiences of the East and South Asian countries which embarked on industrialization through export promotion based on an aggressive strategy of industrial development. Contrary to the prescriptions of the SAP model, in the early stages of their industrialization effort, they used state intervention (infrastructural support, tariff and non-tariff protection, linkages between transnational corporations and local enterprises, export incentives, for example) to promote the growth of domestic industry. The major recommendation is that a more developmental trade and industry agenda must be driven by the state as was the case with some countries in

East and South Asia; that industrial policy must advocate a more selective and targeted approach to providing state support and incentives to emerging industry; and that a phased approach within a short, medium to long-term framework would be more ideal than a strategy which embraces wholesale opening up of African markets to external competition when domestic industries are ill-prepared, as was the case with the World Bank and IMF-determined SAP model.

It will be necessary for Africa to enter into extensive dialogue with Northern countries in the context of the Doha Development Round and to try to influence the developmental agenda of the WTO so that it is more favourable to Africa. In addition to the provision of better market access and reduction in subsidies for products competing with African exports, external resources are required to compensate for losses and to fill the resource gap in order to ensure adequate investment in the development of human and physical infrastructure, institution building and diversification.

Africa has to make regional integration work. Through COMESA, SADC, ECOWAS and the EAC, among other groupings, Africa should be promoting regional integration within the continent and also South-South trade. This is not to say they should not trade with the North but rather that trading arrangements with the developed world should be more gradual and only entered into after careful and informed negotiation. At the international level, and as pointed out by Corrales et al (2003), Africa requires more developmental spaces for development policy. Africa has to challenge those aspects of the WTO Agreements which impede the development prospects of developing countries. They need to push for policies which enhance the continent's capacity to diversify production and exports, build supply-side capacity and pursue competiveness. They have to explore the possibilities of influencing the developmental agenda in the S&DT in WTO Agreements as indicated in the Doha Declaration and the Decision on Implementation-related concerns (Paragraph 44 of the Doha Round and paragraph 12 of the later set of agreements). Due to the daunting challenges posed by globalization, there is need for developing countries to adopt a more coordinated approach to negotiate the creation of a more equitable international trading and financial environment. Africa should seek a more unified approach to dealing with the World Trade Organisation (WTO) some of whose trading rules have been criticized for further marginalizing rather than developing Africa. Africa should have a common agenda in negotiating the Economic Partnership Agreements (EPAs) with the European Union instead of what the continent has witnessed as many African nations, through their regional groupings

(SADC, COMESA, EAC, ECOWAS) or even singly (e.g., South Africa). Furthermore, non-tariff measures such as sanitary and phytosanitary technical barriers to trade, requirements and other contingency trade-protection measures should be applied in a manner that does not necessarily hinder the exports of African countries. Such a process would be facilitated by greater liberalization of OECD domestic agricultural markets through a significant reduction, and finally elimination, of massive agricultural subsidies and support for commodities such as cotton, groundnuts and sugar, which are of export interest to Africa.

References

Alemayehu, Makonnen, 2000, *Industrializing Africa: Development Options and Challenges for the 21st Century,* Trenton, NJ: Africa World Press.

Chowdry, A., and Islam, I., 1993, *The Newly Industrialising Economies of East Asia,* New York: Routledge.

Helleiner, G. K., 1995, *Trade, Trade Policy and Industrialisation Reconsidered,* World Development Studies, No 6, Helsinki: WIDER (UNU).

Kirkpatrick, Colin, Clarke, Ron, and Polidano, Charles, 2002, *Handbook of Development Policy and Management.* Cheltenham: Edward Elgar.

Lall, S., 1991, 'Explaining Industrial Success in the Developing World', in Balabubramanam, V. N., and Lall, S., eds, *Current Issues in Developing Economies,* Basingstoke, UK: Macmillan.

McCord, G., Sachs, J.and Woo, W., 2005, 'Understanding African Poverty: Beyond the Washington Consensus to the Millennium Development Goals Approach', in Teunissen, J. and Akkerman, A., eds, *Africa in the World Economy: The National, Regional and International Challenges,* The Hague: FONDAD, 23-45

Nash, J., 1993, 'Trade policy Reform Implementation in Sub-Saharan Africa: How Much Heat and How Much Light?', Mimeo, Washington DC: World Bank.

Sachs, T. D., and Warner, 1997, 'Sources of Slow Growth in African Economies', *Journal of African Economies,* Vol. 6.

Schmitz, H., 1984, 'Industrialization Strategies in Less Developed Countries: Some Lessons of Historical Experience', *Journal of Development Studies,* Vol. 21, No. 1, pp. 1-21.

Sen, A., 1998, *Development as Freedom,* Oxford: Oxford University Press.

Singh, A., 1995, 'The Causes of Fast Economic Growth in East Asia', *UNCTAD Review,* New York.

Soludo, C. and Ogbu, O., 1998, 'The Politics of Trade Policy in Africa', *IDRC Report.* (www.idrc.ca). 5 May 2010.

Stein, H., 1992, 'Deindustrialization Adjustment, the World Bank and the IMF in Africa', *World Development,* Vol. 20, No. 1, pp. 83-95.

Stiglitz, J., 1998, 9th Raul Prebische Lecture, presented at the United Nations Commission on Trade and Development (UNCTAD), Geneva.

UNDP, 2006, *Human Development Report,* New York: United Nations.

UNIDO, 1997, *Industrial Development Decade for Africa (IDDA) II,* Report on the Mid-Term Programme Evaluation, Geneva.

Zubairu, W., 2005, *Re-thinking African Development,* Dakar: CODESRIA.

2

The Theoretical Basis, Elements and Impact of Nigeria's Trade and Industrial Policy under the Structural Adjustment Programme

Anthony Monye-Emina

Introduction

In the second half of 1986, Nigeria made its first attempt in recent years to restructure her economy via the Structural Adjustment Programme. A key component of this programme was the reform of its trade policy. The country's industrial policy was also reformed, as the industry and trade play a crucial role in the economy. Adebiyi (1997) explains the rationale for the trade and industrial policy reform as contained in the SAP in terms of the demonstration effect of the success of export-oriented Asian economies on the other developing countries; deteriorating balance of payments position and pressure from multilateral financial institutions that nations move towards greater reliance on export expansion and liberalized trade policy. On the industrial front, it was necessitated by the persistent conditions of underdevelopment of the sector (Ekuerhare 1996). Prior to this, the Nigerian economy had been heavily dependent on crude petroleum, which dominated the export basket and thus was a major source of foreign exchange as well as government revenue and development capital. It accounted for 90 per cent of foreign exchange earnings and 70 per cent of government revenue. This had an exaggerated effect on the economy. Public expenditure rose considerably in the bid to expand infrastructure and so on. The Import-Substitution-Industrialization Strategy was adopted in the immediate post-independence era to produce items hitherto imported in order to reduce the excessive reliance on external trade and thus save foreign exchange. It however turned out that activities in the sector became a mere assemblage of the imported goods in question. Besides, most of the materials needed in the industries to *produce* these import substitutes were imported (Anyanwu et al 1997). Unfavourable dramatic developments in the international market for crude oil consequent on declining prices in the 1980s precipitated a macroeconomic problem. The economy was afflicted with huge and rising debt, fiscal crisis, increasing unemployment rate, low capacity utilization in manufacturing, shortages of industrial raw materials and spare parts, rising rates of inflation, low purchasing power and rapidly deteriorating living standards. Obviously, the economy was bedevilled by structural distortions, which was described as a case of 'Double-Dutch' disease (Aboyade 1993; Obadan and Ekuerhare 1993).

Government's reaction to this development was slow thus causing further internal and external disequilibrium. It adopted various short-term measures that were inadequate. The debate that ensued laid bare the desirability for policy reform aimed at restructuring the economy in order to avert total collapse. Consequent on this the Structural Adjustment Programme was introduced in the second half of 1986. The propriety of the theoretical basis, elements and impact of this reform, especially as it affects external trade and industry and their implications for the larger Nigerian economy, are in contest. Moreover the country has had to undertake another round of reform by the first quinquennium of this century. This study attempts to make an ex-post evaluation of the reform under the Structural Adjustment Programme, especially as it relates to trade and industrial policy and the implications in Nigeria.

Pre-Structural Adjustment Programme Trade and Industrial Policy in Brief

This section focuses on trade and industrial policy in the era before the introduction of Structural Adjustment Programme. The discussion is, however, preceded by conceptual clarification and the role of trade and industrial policy in economic growth and development.

Conceptual Clarification and the Role of Trade and Industry in Economic Growth

Trade policy refers to a set of measures adopted to influence the direction of flow of a nation's foreign trade. Sahn et al (1997) defined it as measures such as trade taxes and quotas that act in such a way as to change the relative prices of tradable goods. Trade policy *reform* can be seen as involving reduced protection of the domestic market from foreign competition. It involves moves from quantitative to tariff-based import protection as well as reductions in import tariff. The process works in a straightforward way. Given any set of trade policies there exists a set of relative prices and profit abilities resulting from various activities. These provide incentives and determine production and consumption pattern of goods and hence imports and exports. The effects of trade policy reform can be static and dynamic. In the former it involves the reallocation of resources away from protected import-competing sectors to production with comparative advantage and manifests via declining prices and profits in the hitherto protected sector. The dynamic effect gives rise to more open economies and the creation of opportunities to realize economies of scale with greater exposure to technological developments and increased competitive pressures. Common trade policy instruments include foreign exchange rationing, tariff and non-tariff barriers and domestic economic policies that indirectly impact on trade. When trade policy changes it has implication for the flow of trade (Ogiogio 1996; IDS Policy Briefing 2003). Industrial policy, on the other hand, refers to a set of incentives and measures aimed at promoting the growth and development of a country's industrial sector. It represents a deliberate effort by governments to guide the market by coordinating and planning industrial activities. In other words, it involves directing the market through strategic coordination of business investments in order to increase export market shares (Todaro and Smith 2003). Thus there is a close link between trade and industrial policies.

The role that trade and industry play in economic growth and development is well-articulated in the literature. However, there is controversy with regard to the role of trade. The traditional view sees trade as an engine of growth. There are, however, some dissenting views which suggest that trade does not only hinder growth but also perpetuates underdevelopment, especially in poor countries. Kindleberger identifies three distinct and mutually exclusive situations. Trade can serve as a leading, lagging or balancing sector (Iyoha 1998). In other words, trade can promote growth, hinder it or remain neutral. The classical and neoclassical trade theories in particular posit that trade across national boundaries serves as an engine of growth. Meier (1975) argues that trade provides an opportunity to import, among others things, capital goods required for industrial production in the drive for economic growth. Trade also stimulates economic growth via enlargement of consumption capacities and provision of access to scarce resources. It promotes greater local and international equality, equalizes factor prices and raises real income of trading countries. Trade also, via the vent-for-surplus argument, provides opportunity for underutilized resources to expand productive capacity and raise National Income at little or no real cost, thereby also increasing efficiency and productivity. It encourages innovations and invention while also attracting foreign capital. The drive for industrialization is justified on a number of grounds. It solves the problems of underemployment and instability in earnings from export. Socio-economic conditions that are not conducive to growth and development are altered by industrialization, as it effects the fundamental changes required to raise growth potentials. Industrialization leads to improvement in productivity and efficiency of factors of production. The process, above all, is seen by the less developed countries as a necessary strategy and prerequisite for accelerated growth and development (Torado and Smith 2003; Monye-Emina 2007).

Pre-Structural Adjustment Trade and Industrial Policy

At independence, Nigeria inherited a trade policy whose initial objective was to generate revenue for the government. This was, however, reviewed shortly after independence, precisely in 1962, to serve a dual purpose: solve balance of payments problem, and protect domestic industries. The second objective, namely the 'protection of industries', is an aspect of the Import-Substitution-Industrialization Policy which was meant to discourage the importation of consumer goods. Policy instruments that were used in this dispensation include tariffs on imports, export taxes, import regulations, quota, prohibitions and import licensing. Also used were foreign exchange controls, advanced deposit on imports and systems of deferred payments, among others. There were adjustments in tariff rates which were influenced by the extent to which trade policy objectives were achieved and changes in the general macroeconomic objective. In 1983 and 1984, for instance, the general trade and industrial policy aimed to protect local industries, reduce unemployment, generate more revenue from the non-oil sector and boost the use of local inputs. This necessitated a reduction in the tariff rate from between 500 per cent to 5 per cent and also a 20 per cent reduction effected in import duties. This remained so for about three years. Concessionary zero duty to manufacturers was abolished. Duties on machinery and equipment used in agriculture were abolished, while those on selected agricultural products were raised in order to discourage their export. In 1985, advance payment of custom duty was introduced as well as Approved User Scheme while General Concessionary Rates of Duty were eliminated. In addition, tariffs were rationalized and only 20 items were allowed to be imported free as against the case of several commodities (Ogiogio 1996; Egwaikhide 1999). Generally, in this dispensation the policy thrust was protection-inclined.

The pre-adjustment industrial policy predated independence, having been pursued right from 1957. It was a policy of Import-Substitution-Industrialization (ISI) supplemented at some point with export promotion drive. The Import Substitution strategy in particular aimed to discourage the importation of consumer goods while also saving foreign exchange as indicated earlier on. It was hoped that the ISI, if properly conceived and implemented, would stimulate growth and productivity in consumer goods. While the policy aimed to promote import-substitution production activities in the economy, it was framed on the recognition that foreign private investment should be the hub of the process of industrialization. Some of the main features of the policy identified include tax-and-infrastructure measures, and credit and tariff protection incentives. There was a modification of the policy with indigenization exercise via a decree in the early 1970s. The exercise merely delineated areas of operation for foreign investors and also encouraged state joint ventures with them (Ndebbio 1991; Ekuerhare 1996). Again, just like its trade counterpart, the industrial policy preceding SAP was inclined towards protection of infant industries.

Outline/Elements of the Trade and Industrial Policy Reform under Structural Adjustment Programme

Presentation in this section is in dual parts with discussion dwelling on separate issues. The first focuses on the theoretical basis of the entire Structural Adjustment Programme in Nigeria. The theoretical basis and outline/elements of trade and industrial policy reform under the Structural Adjustment Programme is given attention in the succeeding sub-section.

The Theoretical Basis and Elements of Nigeria's Structural Adjustment Programme

The Nigerian variant of the general Structural Adjustment Programme is based on the World Bank/IMF framework and support. The latter's programme aimed at addressing structural disequilibrium in an economy while also altering and realigning aggregate domestic expenditure and production to achieve balances both the sectoral and in the entire macroeconomy. A viable medium-term balance of payments and a stable and high level of economic growth are among the targets of Structural Adjustment (Soludo 1993). The Structural Adjustment Programme has no single theory underlying it both generally and especially for Nigeria and other developing countries; being essentially eclectic. It is, however, the monetary variant of neo-classical economics anchored on the framework of the 'invisible hand' or free market mechanism and *laissez faire*. The free market system, as it were, is adjudged to be more efficient in allocating resources to their best use. It holds that given certain conditions, market equilibrium will correspond to *'pareto optimum'*; that is efficiency in production and consumption. This model sees balance of payments as a monetary phenomenon in which money plays a pivotal role in macroeconomic disturbances and therefore adjustments. In other words, disturbances in the macroeconomy are viewed as indicative of stock disequilibrium between demand and supply in the money market. That is to say, in simple terms, that deficit in the balance of payments is due to expansion of domestic money leack supply. When the resultant excess money abroad, it causes a deficit in the balance of payments (Obadan and Ekuerhare 1993; Soludo 1993).

For Nigeria, the components of the programme included a financial programme to discipline aggregate demand and exchange variations, monitor and discipline resource utilization and borrowing to provide foreign exchange. The main elements of the programme included deregulation of economic activities, liberalization of trade and prices, and reduction in the size of government, among others. Others were reinforcing earlier strong demand management policies and programmes; stimulating domestic production; adoption of a realistic exchange rate policy; withdrawal of subsidy on petroleum products; and, rationalization and privatization of public enterprises. The main thrust of the programme was trade and exchange rate reform. Monetary and fiscal policies were to serve as stabilization instruments (Tallroth 1988; Ekpo 1993; Soludo 1993).

The Theoretical Basis and Elements of Nigeria's Trade and Industrial Policy Reform

Nigeria's trade and industrial policy reform under the Structural Adjustment Programme was founded on classical and neo-classical economic liberalism. Its philosophical underpinning rested upon the assumption that the industrial underdevelopment and the consequent macroeconomic crises that emerged in the 1980s were due to state intervention, regulation and control of economic activities. Thus, the philosophical conception of the Structural Adjustment Programme as it affects trade and industry was such that it was aimed at the elimination of areas of perceived distortions and constraints, and moving the economy on the path of sustainable development in line with the country's natural resources endowment and comparative advantage in external trade. Free market mechanism was thus adopted to encourage private sector activities in industrial enterprise and also restored in economic policy making and management. It reduced state's role in the economy. Local and foreign investors were encouraged, while constraints to the free flow of external trade and payments were reduced considerably (Ekuerhare 1996). As indicated in the preceding sub-section, the main thrust of Nigeria's Structural Adjustment Programme was trade and exchange rate reform. In particular, the elements of the reform as it affected trade and industrial policy aimed at:

i. Deregulation of controls on prices and marketing;

ii. Elimination of import and export license;

iii. Reduction of import prohibited items;

iv. Reform of tariff for a more stable and predictable tariff regime;

v. Introduction of duty or tax concessions, and so on, to encourage non-oil exports and foreign direct investment;

vi. Adoption of market-oriented changes in the foreign exchange system;

vii. Encouraging the development and use of local raw materials;

viii. Encouraging the development and use of local technology;

ix. Maximization of the growth in value-added in manufacturing production;

x. Promotion of export-oriented industries;

xi. Liberalization of controls to allow for greater indigenous and foreign investment;

xii. Elimination of bottlenecks and constraints that hamper industrial development (Ekuerhare 1996; Adebiyi 1997).

The policy instruments put in place in order to achieve these goals saw the abrogation of the import surcharge of 30 per cent; goods on the import prohibition list were reduced; and design of appropriate tariff structure with the tariff rate slashed. As a key element, the exchange rate of the naira was devalued. Exporters were allowed to retain 100 per cent of their earnings; export taxes were eliminated; and the tariff rebate introduced allowed export manufacturers to import raw materials, spare parts and so on duty-free. The Duty-Back Scheme was simplified to facilitate export promotion, and the Manufacturing-In-Bond Scheme was introduced. This allowed manufacturers to export goods and import basic inputs free of stipulated duties. In addition to these, a Refinancing and Rediscounting Facility as well as a Foreign Input Facility were created. In a bid to promote non-oil export, the Nigerian Export-Import Bank was established. Furthermore, Export Processing Zones were established and the ECOWAS trade liberalization policy began to be implemented. In order to successfully implement some of these policies as they related to industrial development, a central agency, Industrial Development and Coordinating Committee, was set up (Ekuerhare 1996; Ogiogio 1996).

According to Ekuerhare (1996), all of these measures were put in place and, in particular, the exchange rate was devalued in order to eliminate commodity-and-factor-price distortions common in the pre-SAP era and which supposedly prevented the efficient allocation of resources. In simple terms, it was meant to reduce the economic costs associated with an over-valued naira. The design of an appropriate tariff was in line with the neo-classical critique of pre-SAP restrictive policy and to allow for liberalization of trade. Maximization of value-added in manufacturing was also to be encouraged.

Evaluation of Trade and Industrial Policy under the Structural Adjustment Programme

Evidently from the foregoing, the Structural Adjustment Programme's trade and industrial policy was outward-looking. However according to Analogbei (2000), trade policy, ex-ante and ex-post reform exhibited common characteristics of being short-term in nature and directed at specific objectives. Obviously, its short-term nature can have implications for general productivity in the economy. There are, however, some pertinent issues in trade and industrial policy reform which need to be given attention before evaluating the impact.

Issues in Trade and Industrial Policy Reform

The major issues in trade and industrial policy reform according to Agosin (see Adebiyi 1997) include the relationships between price stability and trade policy reform; promotion of export and economic growth; export orientation and liberalization of trade; import substitution and industrialization; and, the functions of the exchange rate. The attainment of some degree of general price level stability is a prerequisite for successful reform. The essence is for real exchange rate to serve as signal for rational economic decisions. When prices are not stable, there will be alteration in the incentive structure, that should serve as attraction to entrepreneurs; local and foreign.

The superiority of export-promotion over import-substitution as a growth strategy remains contentious. Export-promotion does encourage economic prosperity because it eases the problem of foreign exchange constraint and also enables indigenous producers to come in contact with new technologies and international business practices. This has the advantage of raising total factor productivity. But according to Adebiyi (1997), Rodrik posits that import-substitution can generate the same result given certain conditions. These are the existence of a large domestic market and local entrepreneurs who are not satisfiers but optimisers. At the same time, the absorptive and adaptive capacity for foreign technology, income and price elasticity of products involved in trade and prevailing conditions in the international market among other factors do swing decisions for or against export-promotion and import-substitution.

As regards export-orientation/promotion versus trade liberalization, evidence is inconclusive as to whether countries with more liberal trade practices have more rapid growth than those whose trade is restrictive. If government intervenes by means of heavy export subsidies without liberalizing trade, economic growth is possible. In addition, the simultaneous adoption of export expansion and liberalization of import to promote economic growth is a subject of debate. It has been pointed out that it could increase internal and external disequilibrium (Goncalves 1988in Adebiyi 1997). Should import-substitution be pursued first in the process of industrialization prior to the production of internationally acceptable goods? This, again, is debatable. On the role of the exchange rate in trade policy reform, its level and stability significantly determine export and import. The challenge is to determine the appropriate level and keep it stable.

Evaluation of SAP Trade and Industrial Policy

The preceding section shows that a country's trade, and in particular industrial development, does not take place in a vacuum. Both are subject to certain conditions referred to as trade and industrial policy. However, the appropriate policy for less developed countries is in controversy according to Todaro (see Dinye and Nyaba 2001). The contention is between free market advocates and trade protectionists. While the former are in favour of an outward-looking, export-oriented trade regime, the latter support an inward-looking arrangement. Both, however, see industrialization as the key to economic prosperity. Nigeria has witnessed a trade and industrial policy trend that is associated with two major macroeconomic regimes: pre and post-economic reform under the Structural Adjustment Programme – with both having varying degrees of effect on the country's fortune. The propriety of the latter is the subject of attention in this section. First it is observed that the theoretical basis of the trade and industrial policy of the Structural Adjustment Programme is rooted in neo-classical economic reasoning which is based on some restrictive conditions/assumptions and the effective operations of the *'invisible hand'* of market forces for efficient allocation of productive resources. Some of the conditions include perfect competition, full general equilibrium, adequate supply of domestic inputs in import-competing industries, stability in the foreign exchange market and the exchange rate, and capacity of the bureaucracy to make policies and so on. These conditions, unfortunately, hardly operate or exist in developing countries especially. In other words, there exist some constraints which make it difficult for these conditions to operate in the economy. In welfare economics' theorizing, in a *'pareto optimal'* world, the introduction of one or more constraints which prevents the attainment of those conditions indicated via a breakdown of one or more of the assumptions will prevent the attainment of 'allocative efficiency'. What therefore exists is a sub-optimal state which may not necessarily be superior to another sub-optimal state, many of which may exist in a system. Nigeria, like other developing countries, has several constraints which prevent the attainment of those identified conditions necessary for the effective operation of the market system. The existence of these constraints therefore suggests that the trade and industrial policy of the Structural Adjustment Programme in Nigeria is a sub-optimal state and, by implication, a second-best programme. As a sub-optimal state it may not necessarily be superior to the pre-SAP policy, another sub-optimal state, and so, as designed and implemented, may not guarantee 'allocative efficiency'.

The view that trade and industrial policy of Structural Adjustment Programme failed to guarantee 'allocative efficiency' with almost disastrous consequence for the economy is supported by the estimated results adapted from an earlier study and presented in this study (Monye-Emina and Odejimi 2007, see Table 2.2 in the Appendix to this chapter). The economy on the whole fared better with the trade and industrial policy that preceded the SAP reform as it impacted positively. The policy under Structural Adjustment Programme adversely affected the macro-economy from the negative result obtained. What appears to be is that the 'liberalized' trade policy in the reform era opened up the economy for import of not only input resources but also finished goods. Indeed, several finished consumable goods visibly flooded the local market. These apparently out-competed local goods with obvious implication for local manufacturing production effort. This development undoubtedly wiped out the gains of the pre-reform trade and industrial policy. The result confirm Moran's position on the positive harmful effect of output and investment of trade and *industrial* policy reform, as may have been witnessed in the SAP period.

One of the goals of the Structural Adjustment Programme was to resolve the persistent deficit in Nigeria's balance of payments position immediately prior to SAP. Unfortunately, this goal is far from being realised even with the introduction of the Structural Adjustment Programme, as the deficit persisted thereafter with the first surplus recorded in 1997 – that is, eleven years after. The goal of diversification of export with a view to minimizing the excessive dependence on crude oil as the main source of foreign exchange earning remained and still remains elusive. Crude oil still dominates the export basket. In other words export diversification through export-promotion industrialization policy has not paid-off. Worse still, the fortune of the industrial sector did not record appreciable improvement. As shown in Table 2.1 in the appendix to this chapter, manufacturing sub-sector capacity utilization did not respond to the *palliatives* of SAP as it remained far below the pre-SAP era on the average. In the pre-SAP era, the average capacity utilisation was 66.7 as against 34.4 in the adjustment period. In other words, in terms of the static and dynamic effects of trade and industrial policy reform, the country was worse off. Local industries hitherto protected witnessed declining fortune and most soon folded up. Exports were marginally stimulated even with reform in exchange rate management. While the economy opened up the more, it did not seem to reap any benefit of opportunity of economies-of-scale as expected through exposure to technological development and pressure from increased competition. Industrial production on the aggregate and capacity utilization in the sector remain below the pre-SAP era. As Analogbei (2000) observed, trade policy, ex-ante and ex-post reform exhibited common characteristics of being short-term and directed at specific objectives. Policy actions that are short-term in nature do not often achieve the desired impact; instead, they tend to have an adverse effect on general productivity in the economy.

Summary and Recommendations

Nigeria has experienced two trade and industrial policy regimes under two different macroeconomic scenarios: that is, pre- and post-structural adjustment. The pre-adjustment trade and industrial policy was regulated and inward-looking with emphasis on import substitution. The structural adjustment policy was liberalized and outward-looking with emphasis on export promotion. The adjustment policy was desirable to address the macroeconomic disturbances that emerged in the wake of the slump in the world market in the early 1980s. The adopted trade and industrial policy, however, failed to yield the desired result trade and industry-wise.

Policy reconsideration is, in this instance, desirable. In the event of reconsideration, policy option should give attention to the need for a negotiated trade relationship with trading partners taking into consideration the country's potentials; natural resources and otherwise. In addition, the industrial policy should consider either of the options of balanced development and local resource-based approaches. The former approach aims to promote greater linkages among the sectors by creating intra-industry and inter-sectional linkages. This has the effect of increasing intra-industry transactions. However, Nigeria has a weak industrial base such that the linkages envisaged may not be possible. The only option in the light of this shortcoming is a local resource-based approach that is slightly modified in its original conception. The original concept seeks industrialization by means of local sourcing of raw materials and/or local substitutes/alternatives for its industries.

Nigeria should also implement the African Productive Capacity Initiative (APCI) which was approved by the African Union in 2004. Former President Obasanjo was the AU chairman then and he actually decided to implement the Cassava Value Chain. But that strategy has not materialized.

The Local Resource-Based Approach proposed here calls for the development of an industrial sector based on the predominantly available natural resources. The process could begin with semi-processing of such natural resources and over time develop it to a fully-processed product. This development should depend largely on a local engineering industry/technology which must be encouraged to evolve for the purpose. Considering that policy actions in Nigeria tend to be short-term and may not have the desired impact, it is necessary to allow policy prescriptions to run the course of time necessary for them to generate the desired effect. Otherwise, the result may be policy inconsistency which can generate instability in the system.

References

Aboyade, O., 1993,   'The Nigerian Perspective on Structural Adjustment', *Economic and Financial Review*, Vol. 31, No. 4.

Adebiyi, S. O., 1997, 'Trade Policy Reform and Economic Performance in Nigeria', *The Nigerian Economic and Financial Review*, Vol. 2, December.

Analogbei, F. C. O., 2000, 'Trade Reforms and Productivity in Nigeria', in Proceedings of the Ninth Conference of the Zonal Research Units of the CBN entitled 'Productivity and Capacity Building in Nigeria', pp. 159–85, Lagos: CBN Press.

Anyanwu, J. C., et al, 1999, *The Structure of Nigerian Economy (1960-1997)*, Onitsha: Joanee Publishers.

Ekpo, A. H., 1993, 'A Re-Examination of the Theory and Philosophy of Structural Adjustment', *The Nigerian Journal of Economic and Social Studies*, Vol. 35, Nos. 1, 2, 3.

Ekuerhare, B. U., 1996, 'Design and Management of Sectoral Policies in Nigeria: Industrial Policy under SAP', in M. I. Obadan and M. A. Iyoha, eds, *Macroeconomic Policy Analysis: Tools, Techniques and Applications to Nigeria*, Ibadan: NCEMA.

Institute of Development Studies, 2003, 'Can Trade Reform Reduce Global Poverty?' *IDS Policy Briefing*, No. 19, August.

Iyoha, M.A., 1998, 'An Econometric Analysis of the Impact of Trade on Economic Growth in ECOWAS Countries', *The Nigerian Economic and Financial Review*, Vol. 3, December. Meier, G. M., 1975, *The International Economics of Development*, New York: Harper and Row.

Monye-Emina, A. I. and Odejimi, D., 2007, 'Trade Policy Reform and Economic Growth in Nigeria', *African Journal of Stability and Development*, Vol. 1, No.2.

Monye-Emina, A. I., 2007, 'Trade Policy, Imported Capital Goods and Manufacturing in Nigeria', *Prajnan; Journal of Social and Management Sciences*, Vol. XXXV, No. 4. Ndebbio, J. E. U., 1991, 'Industrial Development Policies/Incentives and Their Impact on the Nigerian Economy', in Ndebbio, J. E. U. and Ekpo, A. H., eds, *The Nigerian Economy at the Crossroads: Policies and Their Effectiveness*, Calabar: University of Calabar Press.

Obadan, M. I. and Ekuerhare, B. U., 1993, 'The Theoretical Basis of Structural Adjustment: An Appraisal', *The Nigerian Journal of Economic and Social Studies*, Vol. 35, Nos.1, 2&3.

Ogiogio, G. O., 1996, 'Exchange Rate Policy, Trade Policy Reform and the Balance of Payments', in Obadan, M. I., ed., *Macroeconomic Policy Analysis, Tools, Techniques and Applications to Nigeria*, Ibadan: National Centre for Economic Management and Administration.

Sahn, D. E., et al, 1997, *Structural Adjustment Reconsidered: Economic Policy and Poverty in Africa*, Cambridge: Cambridge University Press.

Soludo, C.C., 1993, 'Theoretical Basis for the Structural Adjustment Programme in Nigeria', *The Nigerian Journal of Economic and Social Studies*, Vol. 35, Nos.1, 2, 3.

Tallroth, N. B., 1988, *Structural Adjustment in Nigeria, Finance and Development*, Washington, D. C., International Monetary Fund.

Todaro, M. P. and Smith, S. C., 2003, *Economic Development*, Delhi: Pearson Education (Singapore) Pte. Ltd.

Appendices

Table 2.1: Selected Trade and Industrial Performance Indicators

YEAR	Exports (₦'Million)	Imports (₦'Million)	Trade Balance	Overall BOP Balance	Non-Oil Exports	Manu. (Average Capacity Utilisation
1970	885.4	756.4	129.3	46.5	375.4	NA
1971	1293.4	1078.9	214.5	117.4	340.5	NA
1972	1434.2	990.1	444.1	57.2	258.0	NA
1973	2278.4	1224.8	1053.6	197.5	384.9	NA
1974	5794.8	1737.3	4057.5	3102.2	429.1	NA
1975	4925.5	3721.5	1204.0	157.5	362.4	NA
1976	6751.1	5148.5	1602.6	-339.0	429.5	76.6
1977	7630.7	7093.7	537.0	-527.2	557.9	77.4
1978	6064.4	8211.7	-2147.3	1293.6	662.8	78.7
1979	10836.8	7472.5	3364.3	18689.9	670.0	72.9
1980	14186.7	9095.6	5091.1	2402	554.4	71.5
1981	11023.3	12839.6	-1816.3	3020	342.8	70.1
1982	8206.4	10770.5	-2564.1	203.2	73.3	
1983	7502.5	8903.7	1401.2	301.3	63.6	
1984	9088.0	7178.3	1909.7	354.9	247.4	49.7
1985	11720.8	7062.6	4658.2	349.1	497.1	43.0
1986	8920.6	5983.6	2937.0	-56667.7	552.1	38.3
1987	30360.6	17861.7	12498.9	-18264.8	2152.0	38.8
1988	31192.8	21445.7	9747.1	-20795.0	2757.4	40.4
1989	57971.2	30860.2	27111.0	-22993.5	2954.4	42.4
1990	109886.1	45717.9	64168.2	-5761.9	3259.6	43.8
1991	121535.4	89448.2	24275.0	-15796.6	4677.3	40.3
1992	205611.7	143151.2	244282.9	-99332.8	4227.8	42.0
1993	218770.1	165629.4	12004.6	-39550.7	4991.3	38.1
1994	206059.2	755127.7	43270.4	-42623.3	5349.0	37.2

Table 2.1: (Continued)

1995	950661.4	562626.6	195533.7	-195316.3	23096.1	30.4
1996	1309543.0	845716.6	746916.8	-53152.0	23327.5	29.3
1997	1241662.0	837418.7	395946.1	1076.3	29163.3	32.5
1998	751856.7	837418.7	-85562.0	-220675.1	34070.2	30.4
1999	1188969.0	862515.7	326454.1	-326634.3	19492.9	32.4
2000	1945723.0	1357695.0	982759.4	314139.2	24822.9	34.6
2001	2001230.0	1580527.0	643535.8	24729.9	28008.6	36.1
2002	1882668.0	1956110.0	302141.0	-565353.3	94731.9	42.7
2003	2889846.0	2080235.0	933736.3	-162839.7	94776.4	44.3
2004	4602781.0	1987045.0	2615736.3	1124157.2	113309.4	46.1
2005	6372052.0	2479322.5	3892729.9	1362253.9	105955.8	45.0
2006	5752747.7	2528085.0	3224661.8	1772650.9	133594.9	52.8

Sources: Central Bank of Nigeria Statistical Bulletin and Annual Report and Statement of Accounts, Various Issues.

Table 2.2: Regression Results*

Variables	**1970 – 2003**	**1970 – 1985**	**1986 – 2003**
Constant	0.22 (3.63)	0.11 (12.28)	0.30 (29.08)
DInNrd	0.02 (0.52)	0.02 (2.25)	0.11 (0.76)
DInDop	0.63 (6.90)	0.81 (6.59)	-0.82 (-2.48)
DInHcd	0.14 (2.48)	-0.05 (-2.55)	-0.47 (-4.09)
DInInf	-0.04 (-1.58)	0.01 (0.88)	-0.06 (-1.65)
DInIfd	-0.34 (-4.30)	0.14 (5.12)	-0.57 (-4.59)
DInKst	-0.10 (-2.93)	-0.43 (-8.86)	-0.67 (-4.41)
R^2	0.68	0.98	0.92
Adjusted R^2	0.41	0.96	0.73
F	20.81	40.52	4.92
D. W.	1.70	1.80	2.17

*Adapted from an earlier study (See Monye-Emina and Odejimi 2007).

3

Trade, Industrial Policy and Development in the Era of Globalization in Africa: The Case of Botswana and Tanzania

Stephen M. Kapunda

Introduction

Most African countries are endeavouring to industrialize from either a predominantly agriculture-based or mineral-based economy. Tanzania and Botswana are essentially chosen to represent such African countries. Both countries are members of the Southern African Development Community (SADC) and other regional blocs (Southern Customs Union – SACU and East Africa Community – EAC). Both are attempting to industrialize and trade in regional and global environment. They face stiffer competition and challenges than the more industrialized countries within the regions and elsewhere. At the advent of globalization both countries had to shift their industrial policy strategies from import substitution to export-oriented strategy. They currently face the challenges of industrial policy harmonization within the regions and the incorporation of the 'free trade and comparative advantage doctrine' implied in globalization and originally underlined by Adam Smith and David Ricardo. Whereas Botswana depends heavily on mining (diamond), Tanzania depends heavily on agriculture. However, both economies face the danger of de-industrialization if the negative impact of globalisation and internal problems are not addressed effectively. The manufacturing sector's contribution to gross domestic product (GDP) has been falling since 1980 from about 5 per cent to the current 4 per cent in Botswana; and from about 18 per cent to 9 per cent in the same period in Tanzania. This tendency is not limited to Africa. The challenge is how 'to turn the table of underdevelopment' using heterodox or appropriate trade and industrial policies in Botswana and Tanzania and elsewhere in Africa. This is in line with the late Guy Mhone's views.

The thrust of this chapter is to examine the globalization and regional challenges and opportunities in industrial policy, development and trade in Africa focusing on Botswana and Tanzania and provide policy recommendations, some of which may be relevant to other African countries. The chapter uses a variety of conceptual and empirical literature in addition to personal sources.

Theoretical Framework

This study hinges squarely on the conceptual proposition that theories based on free trade and comparative advantage have significantly influenced industrial policy and development over time. Even the roots of the current globalization process may be traced back to the works of the earliest political economists, Adam Smith and David Ricardo, in the 18th century. Free trade was underlined by Adam Smith against protection and is currently used to discourage government intervention in industrial development mainly in form of tariffs and subsidies. Ricardo's theory of comparative advantage rests on the least opportunity cost analysis. In other words, a country should specialize in producing commodities in which it has least opportunity cost. This theory has been used by opponents of industrialization in Africa to justify the structure of trade where less developed countries (LDCs) produced and continued to produce and export agricultural and mineral (primary) products in exchange for industrial products from the North (Kulindwa and Mbelle 2001: 292).

The theory has also been used by recent economists who are promoting the shift from 'comparative advantages' to 'competitive advantages' without giving Africa the opportunity to protect its infant industries. Extremists include Siebert and Koop (1990). They regard industrial policies and protection of infant industries as counter-competitive and counter-productive. Other scholars like Lall (1994, 2004) and Edigheji (2004), on the other hand, consider industrial policies and infant industries in LDCs to be very crucial to industrial growth. (See also Vickers 2008: 7; and Adongo 2008: 76).

Even when industrialization is considered, the emphasis is on unbalanced growth which considers only small and light consumer industries (as if this was the end of the road). Globalization may have both positive and negative effect on industrial development. On the one hand, free trade opens new opportunities and increased availability of inputs. This is likely to attract new industries and the old ones may expand, resulting in employment creation. On the other hand, the liberalization policies which discourage government subsidies in line with the World Trade Organization (WTO) are likely to be detrimental to small and medium enterprises (SMEs) and light consumer industries.

Regarding intermediate and capital goods industries, private investors, during the globalization era, are likely not to invest in them since their payback periods are relatively long, unless the Botswana and Tanzania governments give them special incentives or form joint-ventures with them.

Trade, Industrial Policy and Development in Sub-Saharan Africa: The Case of Botswana and Tanzania

Sub-Saharan Africa

At independence, mostly in the 1960s, many sub-Saharan African countries viewed industrialization as a positive move to diversify the economy away from the primary sector to the industrial sector and eventually gain 'real economic independence'. The African states inherited the key role of directing the operationalization of trade and industrial policies with various degrees of central planning and protectionism. Tariffs and subsidies were enhanced. The state also participated directly in investment, especially in industry and large-scale agricultural projects. Import substitution industries were established in many African countries to produce for the domestic market and substitute for imports.

In the early 1980s, however, many sub-Saharan African economies faced economic crises because of internal and external factors. Proponents of the Ricardian theory of comparative advantage guided by their 'hidden' agenda took advantage of the situation and tended to discourage African countries from serious industrialization so that they concentrate on agriculture and mining – where 'they have comparative advantage'. Examples include Woods and (1977), quoted in Collier (1999). In the mid-1980s, structural adjustment programmes guided by the International Monetary Fund (IMF) and the World Bank (WB) were introduced into many countries. Market liberalization and reform in line with free trade principles were promoted. The state-led model of development was weakened. The traditional protectionist policies involving tariffs and subsidies were frowned upon to give room for free trade.

Although the failure of the structural adjustment programmes in some countries may be attributed to implementation and internal problems such as corruption, their direct negative impact on industrial development and social services remains pronounced. Consequently, the manufacturing sector's contribution to gross domestic product (GDP) in sub-Saharan Africa has been stagnant at about 17 per cent since the 1980s. In some countries like Tanzania and Zambia, it has declined. This is contrary to the conventional industrial development trends over time (Kapunda 2007). Furthermore, poverty alleviation and inequality have remained major problems in Africa. In line with Guy Mhone's view, an attempt to implement neoliberal economic policies in many ways resulted in negative socio-economic impact which included persistence of poverty and inequality in the affected countries.[1] Globalization may be regarded as an extension of the structural adjustment or reforms. However, it intensifies more the free trade and comparative advantage principles. Even countries which were not involved in the structural adjustment programmes like Botswana are now feeling the negative impact of policies based on globalization as shall be elaborated in the next sections.

Regarding the debate on gains and losses brought about by globalization in less developed countries (LDCs) like Botswana and Tanzania the following examination is in order: Proponents of globalization in general argue that globalization will open markets and opportunities through free trade (Harvey et al 2000; Oosthuizen 2006). The opponents, on the other hand, argue that the expected gains of globalization should not be used to hide its disadvantages (Edigheji 2004:2). This is supported by Kapunda (2006:555) and Satyanarayan (2006) who explain the economic threat of globalization on industries, especially the SMEs in LDCs. Others who warn against globalization include Chachage (2003) and Shivji (2003). A specific example on industrialization is the case of expected reduction and subsequent removal of subsidies on important industries in LDCs like SMEs, strategic and infant industries. This will adversely affect their per-formance. Unless African leaders take a common positive position on unfair competition, industrial development in Africa will remain behind schedule.

In order to underscore the need for industrialization, let us consider CODESRIA's and Amanor-Wilks' (2008)[2] propositions: the industrialized North grew rich basically because of the industrial revolution in Britain. This was quickly imitated in all countries in Western Europe and later in the USA and Japan. Even the more recent experience of South Korea, Thailand, China and India points to the proposition that the value added through manufacturing processes is relatively crucial for sustainable economic growth. The industrialized countries' trade, industrial policy framework and experience suggest that the ideology or theories of free trade and comparative advantage should not be taken on face value. The actual practices of African states should re-interpret the theories seriously to give room for sustainable industrialization and economic independence. Industrial policies based on free trade and comparative advantages should be re-examined.

The Case of Botswana

Since independence in 1966 Botswana's development strategy has been based on the philosophy of free enterprises and a market economy (Narayana et al 2005: 21). However, the government is also active in terms of preparing and implementing 5-year national development plans and guiding policies such as the industrial development policy and competition policy; provision of public good and services; and has the major shares in the dominant mineral resources. Botswana's economy has been propelled by the primary sector (initially, agriculture and currently mining). At independence, the agricultural sector predominantly contributed about 40 per cent to GDP while the mining sector's contribution to GDP was close to zero. Manufacturing was contributing about 6 per cent to GDP. At that time, beef production was the mainstay of the economy in terms of output and export earnings (Kapunda and Akinkugbe 2005: 152). Almost 20 years after independence, Botswana's GDP grew at an average of 15 per cent and was for a long time one of the fastest growing economies of the world (Kapunda and Botlhole 2008). Botswana's successful economic growth and transformation has been attributed to the country's prudent financial management of its dominant mineral resources. Even when many African economies were going through economic crises in the early 1980s, Botswana's economic performance was relatively good. The country, therefore, was not subjected to the World Bank/IMF-supported Structural Adjustment Programmes (SAPs).

On the industrial front, it should be noted that historically, industrial development in Botswana ties squarely with South Africa and Southern African Custom Union (SACU) established in 1910 and revised in 1969. The challenge, however, as will be noted in the subsequent section, is to have appropriate harmonization of industrial policy among SACU members while maintaining national industrial policies and accommodating other global trade agreements. The first national industrial development policy in Botswana was launched in 1984. This was mainly prompted by the increasing need to diversify the economy away from minerals. Although the mineral sector recorded the highest contribution to GDP (52.6 per cent) in 1983/84, the future uncertainty and fluctuations of the sector performance was questionable. The 1984 industrial development policy was based on import-substitution strategy. Despite the questionability of the strategy due to limited domestic demand based on a small population it was appropriate for the then closed economies of the Southern African region. The strategy became an underlying premise of Botswana's industrial policy and subsequent National Development Plans (Republic of Botswana 1998:1). The primary specific objectives of the policy included:

- Creation of productive jobs for citizens;
- Training of citizens for jobs with higher productivity;
- Diversification of the productive sectors of the economy;
- Growth of value added or GDP accruing to Botswana; and
- Dispersion of industrial activities to rural areas.

The second and current Botswana's industrial development policy was crafted in 1998, essentially to respond to the forces of globalization through an export-oriented strategy; and also to promote further economic diversification and employment creation. It was also to re-orient the economy towards the existing SADC and SACU trade and industrial development agreements that provide increased competition for investment and trade opportunities within the region. Additionally, the impact of the decline in the degree of industrial protection against outside competition following the establishment of the World Trade Organization (WTO) and opening of South Africa under the new political dispensation were to be taken on board. So also was the need to promote rapid growth in productivity and efficiency as critical elements of competitiveness in global trade in gold and services (Kapunda and Akinkugbe 2005: 153). In order to achieve the goal of developing an efficient and competitive export-oriented industrial sector, the policy thrusts include the following:

- Vigorous pursuance of trade and negotiations with both bilateral and multilateral bodies to ensure that such negotiations lead to maximum market access for Botswana exports and lowest possible prices for the inputs required by Botswana industry;
- Development of the capacity to use international data-banks to locate competitive inputs;
- Identification of export opportunities and making such information available to the private sector;
- Encouragement of investors and entrepreneurs to use incentive schemes to improve labour productivity and to achieve competitive unit labour costs;
- Establishment of appropriate mechanisms to develop utility rate policies for public monopolies, whether operated by public or private interest;

- Freedom of investors in the trade competitive sectors to make decisions regarding industrial location and technology, guided by areas with a high potential for industrial location;
- Development and support of programmes by the ministries dealing with commerce and industry, in partnership with private organizations, to assist new and expanding exporters;
- Promotion of small, medium and micro enterprises (SMMEs) trade (Republic of Botswana 1998: 12).

As part of the process of implementation, the government established a high-level national committee for the implementation of the industrial policy, and provided measures of special support to such implementing organisations as the Botswana Development Corporation (BDC), Botswana Export Development and Investment Agency (BEDIA) and the Financial Assistance Policy (FAP)/Citizen Entrepreneurial Development Agency (CEDA).

Despite the seemingly good industrial development policy, the contribution of manufacturing to GDP has been fluctuating at around 4 per cent, for the past 10 years. This figure is less than the 6 per cent at independence. The trend is even worse for the agricultural sector. In both sectors the growth rates are relatively low. For illustration see Table 3.1.

Furthermore, the contribution of manufacturing to international trade in terms of export has declined since 1998, contrary to expectation from the export-oriented strategy introduced in that year. These trends may be viewed as an indication of a relative low degree of industrialization based mainly, on the one hand, on consumer goods like food processing, drinks and textiles and, on the other hand, the dominance of the mining (diamond) sector. It is also a sign of diversification to other sectors including services. The negative impact of globalization has also its share in this case as earlier noted.

The Case of Tanzania

In 1961, Tanzania[3] inherited a private-investor-oriented industrial strategy based on reports by A.D. Little, Inc. and World Bank. During that time, the manufacturing sector contributed only 4 per cent to GDP compared to agriculture's 60 per cent;[4] moreover, 80 per cent of manufactures consumed in the country were imported (Rweyemamu 1973: 49). Export also depended largely on the agricultural sector, mainly cash crops like cotton, sisal and coffee. Three years later, a comprehensive 5-year planning system was introduced.[5] It incorporated the import-substitution strategy

Table 3.1: Real Growth Rates, Contribution to GDP and Total Export of Manufacturing and the Dominant Mining Sector in Botswana (1993/94 prices) (percentage)

Year	Manufacturing			Mining			Agriculture*		
	Growth Rate	Contribution to GDP	Contribution to Export	Growth Rate	Contribution to GDP	Contribution Export	Growth Rate	Contribution to GDP	Contribution Export*
1966	7.0	6.0	15.0	-	-	-	8.5	42.7	70.0
1985	0.5	3.2	14.8	30.0	50.0	74	6.0	5.6	8.0
1998	5.3	4.6	20.0	28.6	32.1	76	5.9	3.3	4.0
2000	3.5	4.1	9.0	13.0	36.5	89	-8.7	2.4	2.0
2001	-3.5	4.0	9.0	16.8	34.7	9.0	9.9	2.4	1.0
2002	0.2	3.9	9.0	-3.5	35.9	90	-2.6	2.2	1.0
2003	3.1	3.7	9.0	10.9	34.7	90	1.8	1.5	1.0
2008**	2.0	4.0	8.9	3.9	35.0	89	2.0	1.5	1.0

Notes: * Mainly beef
   ** Estimates

Sources: Computed by the author using Data from Central Statistical Office (2009), Kapunda & Botlhole (2009), Republic of Botswana (2006); Narayana et al (2005).

to guide industrialization. The private sector dominated the economy until 1967 when the Arusha Declaration formalized the beginning of socialism (Ujamaa). All major means of production were then nationalized and central planning was enforced. During the first 15 years after independence (1961-1976) the economy's growth and provision of basic goods as implied in the import-substitution strategy was fairly satisfactory. Average real GDP growth was about 5.4 per cent during the period while the manufacturing sector grew at a higher average of 7.8 per cent.[6]

The Third Five-Year Plan (1976-1981) set the rates of growth for manufacturing sector and GDP at 9.3 per cent and 6.0 per cent, respectively. The plan was actually the first phase of the Long-Term Industrial Plan based on the Basic Industry Strategy (BIS) – 1975-1995. This strategy was basically a reaction against the import-substitution strategy which was criticized on the ground (among others) that its implementation could not be met essentially because of increasingly high costs of imported inputs. Consequently, the expected foreign exchange saving and related advantages were not realized. The long-term priorities of the BIS were:

i.   Establishing engineering and metal working industries, workshops for manufacturing spare parts, tools and machine parts in order to enhance self-reliance and expand the local market for iron and steel;

ii. Establishing basic industries particularly iron/steel, coal, chemicals and construction materials industries;

iii. Establishing medium and small-scale industries in the regions, districts and in villages with a view to producing basic necessities where most consumers reside and spread industries in the regions and zones;

iv. Expanding agricultural processing industries and producing exportable products so as to increase the country's foreign exchange earnings;

v.   Increasing scientific, technical and technological knowledge by expanding the training of workers in industries and by establishing centres for industrial services and technology;

vi. Increasing technical and industrial co-operation with friendly neighbouring countries and various international institutions so as to strengthen the industrial economy;

vii. Making efforts to utilize local raw materials available in the country in order to implement the above-mentioned targets and objectives.

Like many other African economies, Tanzania faced economic crisis in the late 1970s and early 1980s due to both external and internal factors. The external factors, among others, were: sharp increases in petroleum prices first experienced in 1973-74 and further price doubling in 1979-80; the break-up of the East African Community; the severe drought experience in 1981/82 and 1983/84; the 1978/79 war with Amin's Uganda; and, the country's worsening terms of trade.

Most of the internal factors revolved around the choice of inappropriate development policies and strategies and misappropriation of resources (Bagachwa 1992: 24). Between 1980 and 1985, the real GDP growth was 1.2 per cent while manufacturing was declining at a rate of -4.3 per cent, indicating de-industrialization. By 1986, like many other African economies (except Botswana as noted earlier), Tanzania had to embark on the World Bank/IMF-supported structural adjustment programme. In 1986-89 the economy grew at 3.7 per cent and manufacturing at 2.7 per cent (Bagachwa 1992: 23). Although the improvement of the growth rate may be partially attributed to the SAPs/reforms, the external factor impact of the crises had slowed down and there were also internal adjustments to allow improvement in economic growth. The SAPs did not accommodate long 5-year plans. Three years were initially recommended and, later on, annual/rolling plans were promoted in favour of free market mechanism. The 20-year Basic Industrial Strategy to end in 1995 became obsolete despite its importance for gaining economic independence.

Although the manufacturing growth rates and contribution to real GDP have increased in the 2000s, the contribution to export is still relatively low (see Table 3.2). This is partially attributed to high international competition. As was the case of Botswana, the impact of globalization on competition elaborated in the subsequent section has its share in the trend.

Global and Regional Challenges and Opportunities

As noted earlier, Botswana and Tanzania and the rest of Africa face the challenge of the growing intensity of competition at both global and regional levels. At global level, the free trade and comparative advantage tend to be over-emphasized especially by already industrialized countries so that Africa indefinitely continues specializing in production and importation of primary goods at the expense of industrialization. Furthermore, the role of the state is expected to focus on maintenance of the enabling environment for private investment and free trade. Industrial policies and export-oriented strategies have been crafted in some countries like Botswana and Tanzania to create the enabling environment.

Table 3.2: Real Growth Rate and Contribution of Manufacturing, Mining and Agriculture to GDP and Total Export in Tanzania (1992 prices) (per cent)

Year	Manufacturing			Mining			Agriculture*		
	Growth Rate	Contribution to GDP	Contribution to Export	Growth Rate	Contribution to GDP	Contribution Export	Growth Rate	Contribution to GDP	Contribution Export*
1961	8.0	4.0	5.0	8.5	1.0	8.0	6.0	60.0	85.0
1985	5.0	9.1	10.5	18.0	1.0	7.6	3.0	50.0	90.0
1998	8.0	8.3	6.1	27.4	2.0	12.9	1.9	49.1	50.2
2000	4.8	8.3	6.5	13.9	2.3	6.5	3.4	48.1	44.1
2001	5.0	8.4	7.2	13.5	2.5	6.6	5.5	48.0	27.1
2002	8.0	3.9	7.3	15.0	2.7	6.7	5.0	47.5	21.0
2003	8.6	8.6	6.8	18.0	3.0	7.2	4.0	46.7	19.3
2008**	8.5	9.1	7.1	16.3	3.6	11.0	4.0	44.7	15.5

Note: * Estimates
Sources: Rweyemanu (1973); Bagachwa (1992); United Republic of Tanzania; Kapunda (2008) Economic Survey.

Although experience has shown some positive impacts in some countries like Tanzania, such as relatively impressive growth rates of GDP, manufacturing and mining; improvement of degree of quality and market competitiveness of some consumer products like beer, bottled water, cigarettes and textiles; privatization and joint venture; and improvement of availability of inputs/raw material for industries including SMEs, the negative impacts remain a challenge. For example, the flood of cheap and mostly low-quality products from China and elsewhere, including used textiles, has contributed to the closure of some local plants. The situation was even worse in some countries like Botswana where textile industries import all the basic inputs. These are normally imported at high prices. Thus, producing and selling such products at low competitive prices becomes uneconomic (Kapunda 2003a, 2003b). Second, the (expected) reduction or removal of subsidies on important industries for rural poverty alleviation (micro, small and medium industries) and other strategic industries, affects their performance negatively (Kapunda 2006). Third, since private investors are interested in projects with the least pay- back period, industries remain unbalanced in favour of small and light consumer industries. Private investors shy away from the intermediate and capital goods sector, whose pay-back period may take five or more years. However, intermediate and capital goods industries are strategic in ensuring industrial linkages, intensive use of domestic inputs, and economic independence in the long run. Fourth, foreign investment tends to be over- emphasized at the expense of local investment. As argued elsewhere, practically all African countries use imported technology. It is the responsibility of African countries to learn and adopt such technology and create their own technology in the long run (Kapunda, 2007:119). Last, but not least, there is also the problem of unfair competition and other anti-competitive practices against local fir ms and consumers. Tanzania and Botswana have tried to address the problems by launching competition/trade policies. Tanzania crafted a trade policy for a competitive economy and export-led growth in 2003, and in 2005 Botswana adopted a competition policy to address the problem (see Appendices A and B). However, effective implementation of these policies is yet to be seen and evaluated. Furthermore, during implementation, care should be taken on the interpretations of some of the objectives. One of the specific objectives of Tanzania's trade policy, for instance, is 'encouragement of higher value-added on primary exports'. This objective should not be interpreted in favour of the Ricardian theory of comparative advantage, for Tanzania or Africa in general to focus on primary (agriculture and mining) exports and take it easy on the secondary (manufacturing) exports, especially in the long run.

Regarding challenges and opportunities at regional level the following comments are in order. First, the expected competition and free trade even within regional blocs like SADC, SACU and EAC require the industrial sector to produce products of high quality at low, competitive prices. As noted in the case of Tanzania, effort towards that direction has been made in some consumer industries like food and drinks. However, more has to be done to include all products. In general, Africa should take the positive aspects of regional and international competition as an opportunity to encourage the manufacture of quality products; thereby improving revenue and profitability (see also Oosthuizen 2006; Kapunda 2000). Second, as noted earlier, countries within regions such as SACU and EAC have to design and implement appropriate harmonization of industrial policies while accommodating global trade agreements such as those related to WTO and Economic Partnership Agreement (EPA). This is important in the case where some countries are less industrialized in the region. Botswana, for instance, faces more stiff competition for industrial goods from the more industrialized South Africa so are the other less industrialized SACU members – Lesotho, Namibia and Swaziland. This renders development of the manufacturing sector a difficult task. The situation is also applicable in Tanzania where its industrial products have to face competition with those from South Africa or Kenya, given that the country is a member of both SADC and EAC. SACU, however, is in a more advanced stage in harmonization of industrial and related policies. The new SACU Agreement adopted in 2002 includes, among other aspects, the following harmonization objectives:

i.   Permitting national protection of infant industries in Botswana, Namibia, Lesotho and Swaziland (BNLS) for eight years;

ii. Harmonization of policies in industry, trade and agriculture;

iii. Harmonization of product standards and technical regulation within common customs area;

iv. Promotion of fair competition, significant increase in investment and economic development;

v.   Facilitation of the cross-border movement of goods between members;

vi. Establishment of effective transparent and democratic institutions which will ensure equitable trade benefits to members; and

vii. Facilitation of equitable sharing of revenue from customs excise and additional duties. (Sentsho and Tsheko 2005: 259).

However, these measures are not adequate. Further, harmonization of the industrial sector should be encouraged, especially those related to longer period of protecting infant and strategic industries; investment and tax incentives; and individual country policy interests. Also, the implementation of the objectives needs to be accelerated. Countries like Botswana should take advantage of the opportunities implied in the objectives. As argued elsewhere (Kapunda and Akinkugbe 2006), the continuation of the protection of infant industries for a specific period should be treated as an opportunity to promote industrialization. However, the future challenge in the industrial sector should be able to produce high quality products at low costs in order to compete regionally and internationally. Botswana should also take advantage of the new revenue distribution formula based on country's share of intra-SACU imports and GDP since it is in favour of Botswana's high GDP. This revenue should be used judiciously and substantially in favour of industrial development in Botswana. The government expenditure should include bailing out important industries during the current recession.

Third, apart from harmonization opportunities, less industrialized countries may consider integration of manufacturing industries from the more industrialized countries within the region. Botswana, for instance, can turn its relative disadvantage of small market and lower technological level into an opportunity by integrating its industrial activities into those of South Africa. Through government integration, for example, manufacturing agreements could be negotiated with selected major manufacturers under which Botswana would produce and supply component parts to South African producers instead of establishing production units of competing brands. Such agreements seem viable in such industries like motor vehicle manufacture, electronic and household appliances and agricultural equipment.[7] Fourth, through integration and adaptation and eventually creation of technology from abroad, Botswana and other African governments should take the opportunities of making the foundation and long-term plans for intermediate and capital goods industries which are not given priorities by the private sector due to their long pay-back period. As argued elsewhere (Kapunda 2007: 125), the governments should encourage foreign investors to invest in such industries by providing effective investment incentives such as long payment holidays, or even embarking on joint ventures with them.

Lastly, the industrial sector should take advantage, not only of regional harmonization and integration but also benefits from international trade opportunities such as the African Growth Opportunity Act (AGOA) and the European Union (EU). Botswana, for instance should take advantage of the EU markets to promote more beef exports. However, they should take extra caution of possible negative impact of such agreement and counter-react accordingly.

It should also be underscored that there is a need to rethink the industrial development strategies and policies in Africa towards harmonization. This could appropriately be done first at regional levels. The recent agenda on SACU industrial policy harmonization is commendable (Vickers 2008).

Conclusion

This chapter has examined globalization and regional challenges and opportunities in industrial policy, development and trade in Africa, focusing on Botswana and Tanzania. Both of them are members of SADC and also belong to other regional blocs: SACU and EAC respectively. Botswana was not subjected to structural adjustment programmes (SAPs) like many other African countries including Tanzania. The current globalization, however, has positively and negatively affected both countries like other African countries. Botswana and other African countries should take advantage of the opportunities arising from the positive impact of globalization. However, they should counter-react to the negative impact of globalization and the implied unregulated free trade and unfair competition. The visible hand of the government together with the private sector, small businesses and civil society in each country should regulate the negative impacts which tend to exacerbate industrial development and consumer welfare through various ways, such as effectively implementing competition policy, implementing appropriate industrial policy, protecting infant and strategic industries, and planning and establishing long-run intermediate and capital good industries, which ensure economic independence. This requires prudent use of resources like minerals as the case of Botswana and domestic savings in addition to foreign investment. This is directly in line with Guy Mhone's view.

Countries in regional blocs like Botswana and Tanzania have to face the challenge of designing and implementing appropriate harmonization industrial policies while maintaining national industrial policies and interest and accommodating other global trade agreements. These countries should also take advantage of the opportunities arising from regional industrial policy harmonization. Furthermore, they should take advantage of the international opportunities like those implied in AGOA, EPA and others, but not compromise their national interest.

Botswana's economy has been a relative success largely due to prudent and accountable government which managed to shift resources obtained from the high price of diamonds and non-processed minerals into education and wealth generation for the citizens. Consequently, the country is one of the few African countries which upgraded from least developed countries to middle-income countries. This essentially explains why Botswana was not subjected to structural adjustment programmes unlike many other African countries.

Notes

1. See, for instance Mhone's summary paper, 'Labour Market Discrimination and Its Aftermath', in , P. Bond, 2007, *Southern Africa'*..
2. Details are in CODESTRIA's Announcement and Call for Proposals on the 'Guy Mhone Memorial Conference on Development: Rethinking Trade and Industrial Policy for African Development', 2008, and Dede Amanor-Wilks' 'Africa Commodities', in *Botswana Mmegi* Newspaper of 20 May 2008, p. 10.
3. Tanganyika by then. The name changed to Tanzania after Tanganyika and Zanzibar United in 1964.
4. This percentage also includes a small part of the mining activities.
5. Prior to the 5-year planning system, there was a 3-year plan (1961-1963) based essentially on the 1960 Report of the World Bank Mission.
6. Calculated using data from National Accounts of Tanzania (various issues) & Bagachwa (1992: 23).
7. For details see Kapunda and Akinkugbe (2006) and Sentsho and Tsheko (2005).

References

Adongo, J., 2008, 'Development Integration and Industrial Policy in SACU: The Case of Namibia', in Vickers, B., *Industrial Policy in the Southern African Customs*, Midrand, South Africa: Institute for Global Dialogue.

Bagachwa, M. S. D., 1992, 'Background, Evolution, Essence and Prospects of Current Economic Reforms in Tanzania', in Bagachwa, M. S. D., Mbelle, A. V. Y. and Van Arkadie, B., eds, *Market Reforms and Parastatal Restructuring in Tanzania*, Dar-es-Salaam: Economics Department & Economic Research Bureau, University of Dar es Salaam.

Bond, P. ed., 2007, *Beyond Enclavity in African Economies: The Enduring Work of Guy Mhone*, Durban: Centre for Civil Society, University of KwaZulu-Natal.

Central Statistics Office (CSO), 2009, *National Accounts Statistics: Statistics Brief*, Gaborone: CSO. Chachage, S. L. C., 2003, 'Intellectuals and Africa's Renewal', Paper presented at the CODESRIA Anniversary Conference, Addis Ababa.

Collier, P., 1999, 'Globalisation: How Should Africa Respond', *AERC Research Newsletter*, Nairobi: AERC.

Edigheji, O., 2004, 'Globalisation and the Paradox of Participatory Governance in Southern Africa: The Case of the New South Africa', *African Journal of International Affairs*, Vol. 1, Numbers 1 and 2. Harvey, C., Siphambe, H. and Segosebe, E., 2000, *Globalisation and Sustainable Human Development: Progress and Challenges for Botswana*, UNCTAD/UNDP Occasional Paper. Kapunda, S. M., 2000, 'Globalisation and Its Impact on Industrial Performance and Employment in Africa: The Case of Tanzania'. Paper presented at OSSREA Congress, Dar-es-Salaam.

Kapunda, S.M., 2003a, 'Post Liberation Industrial Development and Policy In Botswana: A Regional Perspective', Paper presented at 30th CODESTRIA Anniversary Conference, Gaborone, 18 – 19 October, 2003.

Kapunda, S. M., 2003b, 'Reform and Industrial Development and Trade in East Africa: The Case of Tanzania', Paper presented at 30th CODESTRIA Anniversary Conference, Addis Ababa, 30 - 31 October.

Kapunda, S. M. and Akinkugbe, O., 2005, 'Industrial Development in Botswana' in Siphambe, H. K., Narayana, N., Akinkugbe, O. and Sentsho, J., eds, *Economic Development of Botswana*, Gaborone: Bay Publishing Co.

Kapunda, S. M. and Akinkugbe, O., 2006, 'Botswana's Industrial Development Policy and Policy Harmonisation within SACU', Research Report presented to the Institute for Global.

Dialogue (IGD), Johannesburg.

Kapunda, S.M., 2006, 'The Economic Threat of Globalisation and Small and Medium Enterprises in Africa', in Narayana, N., ed., *Issues of Globalisation and Economic Reforms*, New Delhi: Serial Publication, pp.555 – 564.

Kapunda, S.M., 2007, 'Beyond the Impasse of African Industrial Development: The Case of Botswana, Tanzania and Zambia', *Africa Development*, Vol. XXXII, No. 4, pp. 117-126.

Kapunda, S. M., 2008, 'Growth, Employment and Poverty Alleviation Strategies: The Case of Tanzania', in Wohlmuth, K., *New Growth and Poverty Alleviation Strategies for Africa*, Bremen: University of Bremen, Germany.

Kapunda, S. M., and Botlhole, T. D., 2009, 'Growth, Employment and Poverty Alleviation Strategies: The Case of Botswana', in Wohlmuth, K., *New Growth and Poverty Alleviation Strategies for Africa*, Bremen: University of Bremen, Germany.

Lall, S., 1994, 'Industrial Policy: The Role of Government in Promoting industrial and technological development', *UNCTAD Review*, pp. 65 – 90.

Lall, S., 2004, 'Reinventing Industrial Strategy', UNCTAD G24 Discussion Paper No. 28, April.

Kulindwa, K. and Mbelle, A. V. Y., 2001, 'Environmental Consequences of Globalisation on Natural Resources Exploitation and Export Performance', in Mbelle, A. V. Y., Mjema.

G.D. and Kilindo, A. A. L., *The Nyerere Legacy and Economic Policy Making in Tanzania*, Dar-es-Salaam: Dar-es- Salaam University Press.

Mhone, G., 2007, 'Labour Market Discrimination and Its Aftermath', in Bond, P., ed., *Beyond Enclavity in African Economies: The Enduring Work of Guy Mhone*, Durban: Centre for Civic Society, University of KwaZulu-Natal.

Narayana, N., Siphambe, H.K., Akinkugbe, O. and Sentsho, J., 2005, 'Botswana Economy – An Overview' in Siphambe, H. K., Narayana, N., Akinkugbe, O. and Sentsho, J., eds, *Economic Development of Botswana*, Gaborone: Bay Publishing Co., pp. 19–28.

Narayana, O. Akinkugbe and Sentsho, J., *Economic Development*, Gaborone: Bay Publishing Company, pp. 149-169.

Oosthuizen, G.H., 2006, *The Southern African Development Community*, Midrand: Institute for Global Dialogue.

Republic of Botswana (RB), 1999, *Industrial Development Policy*, Gaborone: RB. Republic of Botswana (RB), 2005, *Competition Policy*, Gaborone: RB.

Republic of Botswana (RB), 2006, *Annual Economic Report*, Gaborone: RB.

Rweyemamu, J. 1973, *Underdevelopment and Industrialisation in Tanzania*, London: Oxford University Press.

Satyanarayan, A., 2006, 'Globalisation: Impact of Sickness In Small Scale Industries', in N. Narayana, ed., *Issues of Globalisation and Economic Reforms*, New Delhi: Serial Publications. Siebert, H. and Koop, J., 1990, *Institutional Competition: A Concept for Europe?* Aussenwirtschaft 45, pp. 439 – 62.

Sentsho & Tsheko, 2005, 'Botswana in the Context of Regional Economy', in Siphambe, H. K., Narayana, N., Akinkugbe, O. and Sentsho, J., eds, *Economic Development of Botswana*, Gaborone: Bay Publishing Co., ,pp. 25–269.

Shivji, I.G., 2003, 'The Rise, Fall and the Insurrection of Nationalism in Africa', A Keynote paper presented at CODESRIA Anniversary Conference, Addis Ababa.

United Republic of Tanzania (URT), 2003, *Trade Policy for a Competitive Economy and Export-led Growth*, Dar-es-Salaam: URT.

United Republic of Tanzania, (URT), 2006, and other various issues, *Economic Survey*, Dar-es-Salaam: URT.

Vickers, B., ed., 2008, *Industrial Policy in the Southern African Customs Unions, Proceedings of a workshop on harmonising industrial policy in SACU*, Midrand, South Africa: Institute for Global Dialogue.

Appendix A

Competition Policy and Law in Tanzania

The main objective of the competition policy is to address the problem of concentration of economic power arising from market imperfections, monopolistic behaviour in economic activities and consequent restrictive business practices. (Restrictive business practices affect the consumer either by higher prices and unacceptable quality standard or limitations on the availability of goods and services).

Trade Policy in Tanzania

The main objective of trade policy is in line with Vision 2025; that is, to promote a diversified and competitive export sector, enhance efficient domestic production so as to achieve a long term current account balance and consequently stimulate higher rates of growth and development.

Specific objectives include:

- Building a diversified competitive economy to enhance the generation of foreign exchange;
- Encouraging higher value-added on primary exports;
- Stimulating investment in export-oriented areas in which Tanzania has comparative advantage;
- Promoting domestic production and technological change consistence with the required productivity increase;
- Encouraging improvement of efficiency of imports utilization;
- Maximizing utilization of complementarities in regional and international trade;
- Achieving and maintaining long-term balance in the current account.

The ultimate objective of trade policy is to enhance earning power so as to address Tanzania's key priority of poverty eradication in fulfilment of the fundamental human rights for all citizens as enshrined in the constitution of the United Republic of Tanzania.

(United Republic of Tanzania 2003: 81, 103).

Appendix B

Competition Policy in Botswana

The objectives of the Competition Policy are:

- Preventing and redress unfair business practices adopted by firms against consumers and small businesses in Botswana;
- Preventing and redress anti-competitive practices in the Botswana economy and remove unnecessary constraints on the free play of competition in the market;
- Enhancing economic efficiency, promote consumer welfare and support economic growth and diversification; Complementing other government policies and laws;
- Enhancing the attractiveness of the Botswana economy for foreign direct investment by providing transparent, predictable and internationally acceptable regulatory mechanisms for firms to engage in economic activities;
- Supporting other policy initiatives such as citizen economic empowerment and access to essential services without prejudice to the pursuit of the overall efficiency and competitiveness of the economy; and
- Achieving deregulation where regulation is no longer needed. (Republic of Botswana, 2005)

4

Economic Reforms in Zambia and India: Comparative Trade and Industrial Policy during 1991-1992

Euston Chiputa

Introduction

Both Zambia and India embarked on full-throttle liberalized economic trajectories during the 1991-1992 period. This involved relaxing the long-standing economic policies centred on restrictive trade and industrial policy frameworks. Up to 1991-92, both countries had emphasized import-substitution industrialization (ISI). Both countries had put in place restrictive import and export policy measures through heavy taxation of exports and imports of goods and services. By 1991, both Zambia and India faced imminent economic collapse. In Zambia, both the macro and the micro-economic fundamentals were upside down; interest and exchange rates had skyrocketed while supplies of essential goods and services had all but dried up. The change of government in that year, with the Movement for Multi-party Democracy (MMD) assuming power on a populist front of liberalizing both the political and economic landscapes, gave impetus to the resolve for reforms in the political and the economic sectors of Zambia. In India also, by 1991, inflation had soared to levels beyond the generally tolerated one-digit threshold.[1] Like in Zambia, India's macro and microeconomic fundamentals had regressed, resulting in a near bankruptcy status for the country in 1991. Therefore, both Zambia and India had to embark on full liberalization at that time. Before then, India had tried to liberalize its economy from since the late 1970s and early 1980s; but these were half-spirited measures compared to the reforms of 1991.

In Zambia, on the other hand, the Mulungushi and Matero reforms of 1967/68 and 1969/70, respectively, had seen a national economic trade and industrial policy shift from a generally liberalized and private sector-driven trade and industrial policy framework to a nationalized, state-driven policy trajectory. In the 1980s, attempts were made to liberalize the economic landscape, especially through relaxation of price controls, which in 1986 had led to food riots on the Zambian Copperbelt. Therefore, while both Zambia and India had undertaken partial trade and industrial policy reforms in the 1980s, it was not until 1991-92 that both countries embarked on full-scale economic reforms.

It has been argued in some circles that *capital flight* and lack of positive responses by foreign investors forced the Zambian government to embark on *de-privatization*.[2] Generally, both Zambia and India had become socialist states, given the high levels of state ownership and control of some of the major means of production. The trade and industrial policy reforms embarked upon in 1991-92 entailed a full-circle retreat from the socialist economic policy agenda to a capitalist one in Zambia; but it meant a calibrated policy retreat from the socialist system in India, to an economic brand-mix of the two economic systems – capitalism and socialism. In both Zambia and India, this involved relaxing the long-standing economic policies centred on restrictive trade and industrial policy frameworks. Up to 1991-92 both countries had emphasized import-substitution industrialization (ISI). Both countries had put in place restrictive import and export measures, through heavy taxation of export and import of goods and services . State officials repeatedly stated that their objective was to protect the infant local industries. Through development planning, Zambia and India had ended up with lopsided economic trajectories in their continued attempts to steady the supply of consumer goods and services,. In both countries, the rigid economic policies evolving around import-substitution industrialization were not yielding the desired socio-economic progress. Thus, both countries resorted to economic reform with emphasis on trade and industrial policy reform.

Zambia did away with the use of development planning blueprints upon the change of the political system from one-party state to multi-party democracy in November 1991. In India, on the other hand, while development planning blueprints were being churned out as developmental guides (indicative planning), a rigid following of the blueprints to the letter was significantly watered down. Emphasis was transferred to market liberalization. However, after implementation of liberalization in both countries, the immediate results showed positive trends in India and negative ones in Zambia.[3] In this reform process, the particular need for trade and industrial policy rethinking was imperative.

Trade and Industrial Policy Reform could Contribute to Reinvigorating the Economies

Several factors were responsible for Zambia and India's change of development paradigms in 1991-92. The inward looking economic policy frameworks of both countries were now seen as hindrances to economic growth and overall national development. Zambia's regressive economic trajectory was cited as being in need of immediate economic surgery. Zambia's dependent *trade and industrial systems* also militated against the adoption of aggressive ways of addressing the nation's imbalances that had led to economic dependence. Although there was no such high-level dependence in India as in Zambia up to 1991, there was need to free the energies of the private sector *in trade and industry* from restrictive investment and *trade* policies in order to attract more investment and engender economic growth and national development on a higher scale. In addition, there was need to promote and energize the small scale private sector to play a significant productive role. There was also need to free the voice of the civil society whose advocacy was a cardinal factor in speaking for the voiceless small-scale agricultural producers and business entities.

Zambia's unbearable debt burden, under-performing public and private sector ventures, and overall negative economic growth indicators all pointed to the need for a different approach towards the nation's economic malaise in order to get the economy on the track to recovery, growth and development. Zambia's trade and industrial policy framework needed to be remodelled from import-substitution industrialization that had been followed up to 1991-92, towards an export-focused industrialization policy in order to earn foreign exchange and to create jobs, both of which were in short supply.

Although piecemeal reforms in India had begun way back in the late 1970s and early 1980s, the 1991-92 reforms were most comprehensive. In Zambia, the political tumult of the 1990/91 campaign for multi-party democracy carried with it the tag of economic liberalization and privatization. The 1990-91 period particularly witnessed some of Zambia's worst economic indicator deteriorations (with GDP indicators between 0.2 and 1.0 per cent, well below even those in some African countries, engulfed by civil conflicts). Essential goods like groceries were in perpetual short supply, foreign exchange was a nightmare to find, thus, exacerbating the country's socio-economic meltdown. The combination of planned economic management and a one-party state had made matters worse in Zambia compared to India where a multi-party democratic order was in place. While the year 1991 ushered in an economic and political breakthrough from the 'dirigiste' past in India, it ushered in a worse economic situation in Zambia, at least in the first few years after 1991.

Because Zambia's industrial policy framework had been state-dominated and, thus state-dependent, the role of the private small-scale, medium and large-scale enterprises had been crowded out of the national economic space. When the state enterprises faltered and failed to engender economic growth, the whole national economy suffered. On the other hand, India's quick post-1991 economic recovery could be attributed to that country's recognition of the crucial role of the private sector, small- scale, medium and large-scale enterprises. When the Indian political and economic landscape suffered the severe economic plunge of 1991-92, the private sector enterprises remained resolute. Many of them were able to take advantage of their own private initiatives to generate local solutions which enabled them to avoid being inundated by the economic malaise that devastated the public or state enterprise landscape.

Policy Shift Imperatives in Zambia

A look at the socio-economic trajectory in Zambia up to 1991 is very revealing. When the Movement for Multi-party Democracy (MMD) under Frederick Chiluba defeated the 27-year-old United National Independence Party (UNIP) government of President Kenneth Kaunda in the October 1991 Presidential and Parliamentary Elections, it was on a platform to structurally transform Zambia both economically and politically. The MMD government assumed power on a popular platform on which Zambians endorsed whatever measures would reverse the many and embarrassing years of economic collapse and ruin. The people of Zambia had accepted, during the MMD pre-election campaign trails across the length and breadth of Zambia that they were willing to 'bite the bullet' if that would restore the nation's economic sanity and prosperity. The Chiluba administration, therefore, embarked on a liberalization and privatization programme with such speed as had never been seen before anywhere in Africa. Zambia's trade and industrial policy framework had to undergo a reform trajectory if the liberalization and privatization programme was to be achieved. The hope of both the MMD leadership and the nation at large was that the benefits of the new measures would yield quick, tangible results. The immediate results and those that followed a few years later belied the expectations. To appreciate how this came to be, there is a need to consider the historical factors that had led to the meltdown in the Zambian socio economic landscape.

The Zambian trade and industrial policy framework could not be restructured without a structural transformation of the entire economic setup because the many years of economic deterioration had left the economy structurally paralyzed. Between the mid-1970s and 1991, the Zambian economy underwent 'a virtually uninterrupted spiral towards extreme poverty and other very high levels of human deprivation, aid-dependence and debt distress'.[4] The main problem was the failure by the governing party to redress economic imbalances whenever and wherever they appeared. In addition, the crowding out of the private sector from the national economy left the Zambian economy too vulnerable to withstand the economic vagaries. This contrasted sharply with the Indian situation which allowed the private sector adequate space to participate and contribute to driving the economy in the right direction.

Zambia's Economic Downswing: Some Historical Factors

Zambia's economic problems began just a decade after independence. While the political leadership was in the process of implementing the economic and political changes contained in the Mulungushi (1967/68) and Matero (1969/70) reform packages, and the 'One Party Participatory Democracy' (1972) respectively, the economic situation in the country soon began to betray their efforts. Despite the fact that the economic crisis brought about by the Unilateral Declaration of Independence (UDI) in 1965 had decisively been dealt with, there soon appeared other difficulties. Firstly, there was a sudden increase in the price of crude oil by the Organization of Petroleum Exporting Countries (OPEC) in 1973.[5] This negatively affected the supply of foreign exchange for non-oil producing African countries like Zambia. Although it is often argued that the plunge in the prices of copper on the London Metal Exchange was seen in Zambian political circles as a factor in the decline of Zambia's economic fortunes in 1973, this did not take place until after 1975 when the price began to fall steadily.[6] The reduced receipts from copper exports were also a result of reduced copper production, not just a function of collapsed prices. Between 1980 and 1990, Zambia's copper production slumped from a high of 682,000 tonnes to 440,000 tonnes.[7] Apart from lower prices being a cause for lower production of copper, there was also a continuing shortage of spares and machinery for the mines, owing to the continued lack of recapitalization of the mining industry. On this score, both trade and industrial policy reforms had become inevitable for Zambia.

While the Zambian government was trying to come to terms with the impact of the oil crisis, the nation continued to face increasing problems of rapid population growth (about 3 per cent per annum), unemployment, rural-urban migration, and greater poor-rich and rural-urban differentiation. By 1975, the formal sector employment stood at about 300,000 to 400,000, while almost 40 per cent of the population resided in urban areas. Issues of food security also became critical as the nation continually failed to meet its food requirements. One important sore point in this regard was Zambia's weak trade and industrial policy framework in the agricultural sector. While the government had embarked on import-substitution industrialization – for example, through the construction of the Nitrogen Chemicals of Zambia (NCZ) fertilizer plant in Kafue, 45 kilometres south of the capital Lusaka – no industrial policy trajectory was targeted at agricultural machinery or even the simplest agricultural spares and components. These continued to be imported, from the smallest bolts and nuts to the most sophisticated components needed to keep the fertilizer plant running. Moreover, even the raw materials for fertilizer manufacturing had to be imported. This defect was not only applicable to agriculture, but to all other sectors of the Zambian economy. The Zambian economy also continued to be heavily dependent on the external world economy for the consumption of its raw material (especially copper and other mineral) products, for grants and loans, and for various raw materials and other industry input supplies. This kept the Zambian economy in a perpetually precarious state, as it remained vulnerable to any shock arising from the global economy. As a result, in December 1971, the Zambian government had to devalue the currency at the time of the worldwide exchange rate realignment, and in January 1972 introduced a tight budget. For the first time since independence, the country felt the financial drought. The Mulungushi Reforms of April 1968 had marked the first step in the radicalization of Zambia's economic policy, while, on the political front, the end of multi-party politics in 1972 also ended consensus politics in Zambia.[8]

The government's common reference to the *Leadership Code* further worsened the situation. *Leadership Code* was a term used to refer to the government's policy that prohibited all leaders in government, civil servants, parastatal company chiefs and their workers, and all workers in quasi-government employment, from engaging in any other gainful employment or form of business that would earn them extra income besides their official emoluments. While Zambians in private business had their businesses limited to specific capital limits by the Mulungushi Reforms, their counterparts in employment were constrained by the

Leadership Code. Not much tax revenue could accrue to the state treasury from indigenous businessmen and women and employees due to these state-imposed constraints. The two prohibitions fatally crippled the Zambian entrepreneur. The prohibitions also created conditions which increased the syndrome of citizens' dependency on the state. To ameliorate the citizens' suffering, the state had to resort to subsidies to enable citizens access the necessities of life. The introduction of meal coupons for the low-income citizens in urban areas contributed significantly to Zambia's deteriorating economic status in the late 1980s. Mealie-meal coupons were introduced in 1988 by Kenneth Kaunda's one-party (UNIP) government, intended to cushion the urban poor from the debilitating price rises and the resultant socio- economic deprivation.

Zambia's involvement in the liberation struggle in Southern Africa was another of the factors that imperilled the economy both directly and indirectly. During the liberation wars Zambia lost enormously in economic and human terms. Often, the Portuguese, South African and Rhodesian white regime troops crossed into Zambia to cause mayhem among the local and refugee populations. They blew up such infrastructure as bridges, railways, buildings and refugee camps. The cost of reconstruction and rehabilitation, the loss of lives, plus the inflow, transportation, and feeding of refugees and displaced Zambian populations put a severe toll on the Zambian economy.

Zambia's Debt Regime

Given the dire economic straits and the depleted foreign reserves base, the Zambian government resorted to borrowing from both bilateral and multilateral lenders from 1976. This marked the beginning of Zambia's debt burden that later turned into a crisis.[9] While the national debt was mounting, the performance of the economy was declining. The parastatal companies were major culprits in this downturn of the economy. Many of them were unable to live up to the expectations of the nation in terms of effective delivery of economic and social goods and services. This was more so in the implementation of the trade and industrial policy framework emanating from the Mulungushi and Matero reforms of 1968 and 1970, respectively. They continually relied on fresh injections of state capital (subsidies) to remain afloat. Their dilemma was partly a result of over-employment, due to nepotism , coupled with such other factors as sheer incompetence of some of the parastatal managers, , corruption and other related vices. Valdes sums up the crisis in the parastatals when he said government burdens itself with economic functions it cannot perform efficiently and yet neglect other functions which cannot be provided by the private sector, such as primary education in rural areas, road construction and agricultural research.[10]

In 1974, Zambia's total debt portfolio was less than US $500 million, but in 1983 the government obtained the first major loan from the International Monetary Fund (IMF), in the sum of Kwacha 253.54 million (US $322 million). By 1984, it had borrowed some more funds from the World Bank.[11] Zambia also borrowed heavily and received grants from individual countries such as Canada, the United States, Britain, Denmark, Iraq and Japan, among others. Zambia borrowed from foreign private banks such as Standard Chartered Bank, European Investment Bank and the International Development Bank of Denmark, the Arab Bank for Economic Development, so that at the end of 1983 the total national indebtedness shot up to K3.16 billion (US $ 2.5 billion). By 1984 the debt had risen to more than US $ 4 billion, making Zambia one of the world's largest debtors in per capita terms at the time. This formed about 84 per cent of the country's Gross National Product (GNP). By 1991, Zambia's debt had risen to over US$ 7 billion![12] By this time, it had joined the ranks of the heavily indebted developing countries and its debt portfolio was rising rapidly.

Zambia's debt increased rapidly partly because of what may be termed as the naivety of the country's political leadership. They believed that the loans so contracted would be repaid once the slumped copper prices improved. President Kaunda even stated that 'in due course prices of copper will move upward once more'.[13] This was in spite of the stark reality of copper's falling prices and production levels and the declining revenue therefrom. The naivety of the political class, together with their propensity to spend in order to keep the restless urban populations calm, through subsidized living, further pushed the economy into a devastating plunge.[14] Zambia's spiralling indebtedness could also be attributed to external factors such as the declining world primary commodity prices and increasing world prices of manufactured goods. This was in addition to the oil price hikes of 1973 and 1978, already discussed above. DeLancey recognizes that, these external factors, in combination with domestic policy shortcomings, resulted in a slowing of economic growth. A similar oil crisis in 1978 and declining world prices for primary commodity exports of Africa, along with continued domestic policy deficiencies, led to a period of actual economic decline in the 1980s and the first half of the 1990s.[15]

The role of foreign experts who came from Western countries formed part of this external nexus. Their advice often failed to resolve the crises; instead, it usually accentuated them. The main weakness was that foreign experts often based their conclusions on Western models, which were different from the African situation. There was a marked difference in the Indian scenario where the use of foreign experts was negligible, if any. India had long recognized the dire need for indigenous expertise in all fields, by expanding and improving tertiary education. In fact, some of Zambia's foreign experts, especially in education, health, agriculture and commerce, came from India.

Zambia's declining economic fortunes translated into reduced per capita incomes and lower overall human development. Zambia's real per capita income was estimated at US$500 in 1980, but by 1989 it had slumped to US$290.[16] Gamani Corea states that African countries were plagued by poverty, very high rates of population growth, low growth rates of GDP, etc.[17] Although Corea's statement refers to the African continent generally, Zambia's economic situation could not be described to be any better, though the levels of poverty were not very high during the first decade of independence. It was after the mid-1970s that the major signs of decline in the Zambian economy began to show. Real GDP stagnated between 1980 and 1987, averaging only 0.2 per cent growth per annum, resulting in a markedly lower standard of living.[18]

Socio-economic Meltdown

The strain of the combined economic difficulties made the Zambian government embark on drastic budgetary cuts in social services provision. A lot of the revenue had to be used to service the debts accrued from previous loans. At the same time, the political class did not wish to give up their propensity for luxury. Instead, hospitals, schools, roads and public transport were the first to bear the brunt of reduced funding. It was not unusual to find patients lying on beds without mattresses and linen, and without appropriate treatment, due to lack of equipment, medicine and even medical staff. In the schools, it was very common for pupils to be taught by untrained teachers employed by the state, or to find a school of up to 300 to 400 pupils with only two teachers - a man and his wife as headmaster and deputy headmaster, who also acted as senior teacher and class teacher. It became common for travellers to spend many days at bus stations awaiting public transport to ferry them from one part of the country to another.

While the population was growing at a rate of 2.5 to 3.3 per cent per annum, there was no provision for new jobs. Many parastatal industries began to run at either half capacity or less. The neglect of rural areas and government's concentration on pampering the volatile urban populations with subsidies made matters worse for the rural dwellers. Many resorted to migrating to urban centres in search of non-existent jobs. DeLancey sees the rural-urban drift as assumptive of structural problems in the agricultural sector.[19] The increasing poverty levels, lack of jobs and the government's neglect of rural areas translated into deep-rooted economic differentiation between urban and rural Zambians. In 1969, President Kaunda recognized the problem when he asserted:

> I should … remind you that we, the workers, we the urbanites, have had it very good indeed since independence at the expense of our own brothers and sisters, the peasants, in our rural areas. We should remember that apart from the fact that the wage earners' sector had increased its earnings by 32 per cent (1964–68) to the tune of K780 million, that for our 80 per cent peasant population in rural areas rose from about K112 million in 1964 to about K116.

Moreover, such sectors as mining, construction and transport registered zero or very low growth rates, with marked decline in formal sector employment.

Enter the IMF and the World Bank

Faced with difficulties in acquiring foreign exchange, debt servicing, poor economic performance of the parastatal companies, dwindling food supplies, and growing import bills, the government was forced to 'surrender' to the dictates of the International Monetary Fund (IMF) and the World Bank. Like elsewhere, the IMF and World Bank's prescribed panacea was to introduce economic austerity measures. These involved currency devaluation and freeing the price regime by cutting food subsidies. Both measures led to price hikes on all goods and services, and higher inflation. To salvage the foreign exchange situation, the government was advised by the Fund and Bank experts to commence a programme of foreign exchange auctioning. Foreign exchange auctioning involved a weekly offer (auction) of foreign currency (mostly US dollars and British Sterling) by the Bank of Zambia (Central Bank) so that banks and companies could bid for its purchase. This was implemented in 1985, but it was soon impaired by chronic shortages of the foreign exchange to be auctioned, mostly a result of shortfalls in copper revenues and inflationary acceleration in money supply. The accompanying sharp currency depreciation eroded the people's confidence in the auction programme. At the start of the auction in October 1985, the exchange rate was ZK5.00 to US$1.00, but by the time the programme was halted in March 1987, the rate had reached ZK15.00 to US $1.00. This meant a currency depreciation of 200 per cent, within 18 months.[20]

The 1976–88 period was one of acute shortages of literally all basic essential commodities, except political rhetoric. Queues for commodities as sugar, maize (corn) meal (Zambia's staple food), cooking oil, detergents and soaps became very familiar sights in Zambia. Smuggling of essential goods, especially into Congo-Kinshasa, coupled with corruption in acquiring essential commodities, made life nightmarish for the majority of ordinary Zambians. As stated earlier, it was not uncommon either for long distance travellers to spend several days at bus stations before finding a bus to take them to their respective destinations. The price of maize meal had been rising steadily, and then it suddenly shot up by up to 50 per cent at the end of 1985.[21] To worsen matters, the government made its first attempt at implementing the Structural Adjustment Programme (SAP) by liberalizing agricultural marketing.[22] With no respite for the majority of the workers and other citizens, food riots broke out in 1986 on the Copperbelt, the nation's economic nerve centre. Several lives were lost as the police attempted to quell the riots.

Acts of Desperation?

In an attempt to remedy the situation and prevent future riots, President Kaunda introduced the mealie-meal *coupon* system, intended to subsidize the staple food, maize meal, for the vulnerable low-income urban consumers. Coupons were issued to designated urban families and individuals on a monthly basis. The coupons would then be exchanged for bags of maize meal at the shops.[23] However, the coupon system, besides being open to abuse, was yet another way of offering subsidies to consumers, not producers who had the capacity to boost production. The government removed subsidies from production by removing the fertilizer price differential subsidy, but reintroduced the subsidy on consumption in order to pamper the urban consumers. This was more for political expediency than economic rationale. The government was more wary of the urban poor's reaction to increased food prices and the consequences, in the wake of the tragic Copperbelt food riots of 1986. Moreover, the coupon system also benefited the targeted vulnerable urban workers less. It was greatly abused and instead it enriched some businessmen and those entrusted with its administration. Shawa admits that administration of the coupon system was very difficult as households not meant to benefit did so, although it was initially intended for only those in low-income wage employment.[24] From 1991, the standard of living had shrunk to about half of what it had been shortly after independence, with the per capita GDP falling from about US$650 to about US$290,[25] a decline of more than 50 per cent.

Policy Shift Trajectory in Zambia

Upon assuming power in November 1991, the new MMD government embarked on a New Economic Recovery Programme (NERP), aimed at restoring economic resilience, productivity and overall economic growth.

To this end, a structural programme was started in 1991, with a focus on privatization, liberalization of trade and exchange markets, introduction of a cash budget, reforms in health, education and the public sector, increasing the productivity of the agricultural sector and improving the infrastructure.[26] The reforms were intended to both liberalize the economy and privatize state (public) enterprises 'through market-based stabilization policies and promotion of the private sector as a prime mover of the economy'.[27] Fiscal and monetary policies were implemented to redress the various imbalances that had held the entire economy to ransom. The measures included lowering the rate of inflation and interest rates, establishing a market-based competitive exchange regime, as well as a diversified and market-led export base and ensuring food security. The Zambian leadership's understanding of privatization was that it had to be done in the quickest time possible. The Government created the Zambia Privatization Agency (ZPA) through the Privatization Act No. 21 of 1992,[28] to drive the privatization process. However, since the MMD government assumed power towards the end of the year (November 1991) their reform policies could only begin in earnest the following year. Before the privatization exercise was launched, the government took to resolving the long-standing problems of fiscal and monetary reforms.

Government decided to free interest rates so that market forces could determine the appropriate rates according to demand and supply. It also liberalized interest rates in 1992. However, as Simatele states:

> Within six months, the lending rate had risen by over 260 percentage points from 47 per cent in December 1992 to 171% in June 1993. The deposit and Treasury bill rates increased over the same period from 46.8 per cent to 97.9 per cent and 47 per cent to 164.9 per cent respectively.[29]

Borrowing investible capital became extremely difficult at such bank interest rates, which made doing business in Zambia practically impossible. The resulting economic plunge could not inspire confidence in the ordinary people as their socio-economic conditions continued to worsen rather than recover and improve.

In agriculture, the new government abolished subsidies, and declared that market forces should rule the marketing of agricultural inputs and produce. Suddenly, the rural producers found themselves at the mercy of private maize buyers and input dealers, the so-called 'briefcase businessmen'. The role of the cooperative movement that had replaced the National Agricultural Marketing Board (NAMBoard) was negated. For the immediate period, the rural farmers found themselves with produce, especially maize, that they could not sell at a guaranteed price, but a negotiated and often much lower one, as they had to haggle with all sorts of buyers from the urban areas. Many a time rural farmers were swindled. As far as the rural dwellers were concerned, this became the biggest failure of the MMD government of President Frederick Chiluba. Yet, again, even the new Zambian government failed to realign the trade and industrial policy to garner the required resources for agriculture and rural development. Merely liberalizing the agro-market without a correct policy to ensure cost-effective production and distribution of both produce and inputs in the agricultural industry could not ameliorate the deterioration of agriculture and the utter neglect of the rural dwellers.

In education and health, reforms were embarked upon to realign the two service sectors. This saw the introduction of 'user fees' in institutions of learning and medical facilities. The irony of the user fees was that they came at a time when poverty levels and the Human Immuno-deficiency Virus & Acquired Immuno-Deficiency Syndrome (HIV&AIDS) were debilitating the population. Although HIV&AIDS patients were exempted from paying medical fees, very few Zambians, if any, could declare openly their HIV status at that time. Further still, extremely few Zambians could accept to undergo an HIV test, unless it was for studies abroad or for employment. Instead of enhancing education and health provision, the fees became a hindrance, as most families could just not afford even the lowest of the fees. Many children began to leave school and to take to the streets as a way of life. Many patients could not seek treatment due to inability to pay medical bills.

When the privatization programme began in 1992, the target was to privatize a total of 280 state enterprises, including the nation's economic lifeline, the mines, which proved quite intractable at first. A disagreement arose among the national leaders as to whether the mines should be sold as one entity or privatized in an unbundled fashion. Eventually the supporters of the unbundled formula carried the day. Another disagreement was over the pricing for what Francis Kaunda, the former Chief Executive of the Zambia Consolidated Copper Mines (ZCCM), called 'Selling the

Family Silver'.[30] The privatization of the mining industry took an entire decade to conclude.

No Results Yet

These measures were expected to usher in 'miracle' cures especially among the population, whose expectations and enthusiasm for change had clearly been demonstrated at the October 1991 elections. The expectations were fuelled by the increases in aid releases to Zambia from the donor and lender community after the elections. However, the immediate results of the economic restructuring process did not support the highly anticipated 'miracle' cures. For example, Nokkala notes that the status of the poor actually deteriorated, instead of improving.[31] Lise Rakner points out that several years after the launch of the liberalization and privatization policies in Zambia, the country's economic growth indicators, like job creation and poverty reduction, remained weak, and the economy actually declined to levels worse than the 1991 levels.[32] Therefore, in the immediate period following the implementation of the liberalization and privatization measures in Zambia, the results were disappointing. Kayizzi-Mugerwa argues that:

> In spite of the government's market 'radicalism', the growth response in Zambia has for much of the 1990s been poor both in absolute terms and in comparison to its neighbours... It is clear in retrospect that while the government's wide-ranging policies needed to be buttressed by equally ambitious political reforms, there were, reminiscent of the Kaunda era, too few human and financial resources to ensure success. Thus, although the government quickly embarked on the Zambian equivalent of the 'big bang', projecting a policy profile as different from that of UNIP as possible, the fundamentals had changed little.[33]

The miracle turn-around of the economy promised during the 1990-91 campaigns for multi-party politics and the eventual elections in 1991 proved a nightmare for the population as the economy shrunk further and further.

The situation was very different in India where the results were almost instantaneous after the liberalization measures were put to work during the 1991-92 period. In Zambia the emphasis was placed on changing from state ownership to private and mostly foreign ownership of the means of production. Zambians did not have the levels of investable capital that the foreigners had, because many years of state regulation against private Zambian ownership of means of production had prevented Zambians from amassing adequate financial resources to take up such challenges. The growth of an indigenous capitalist class in Zambia had been drastically curtailed by the many years of state regulation and intolerance to indigenous private capital. In a way, trade policy did benefit, through the liberalization and denationalization measures that the Chiluba government put in place, so that now anyone could export to Zambia. However, liberalization and denationalization alone were not enough to engender an adequate policy paradigm shift towards production of much-needed industrial equipment, goods, machine spares and tools that are critical to any industrialization process. Opening up the Zambian import and export market was all that was done. The industrial policy put most emphasis on resuscitating the mining industry. In many instances, the MMD government's industrial policy even negated the few industries that had been built up under the Kenneth Kaunda regime up to 1991. The liberalized trade and industrial policy framework stifled the infant industries, as they found themselves suddenly in competition with subsidized foreign producers on the Zambian market.

Trade and Industrial Policy Shift in India

When the Indian government embarked upon the sweeping economic structural reforms in 1991, the action was premised on the weaknesses that threatened to cripple the economy, especially in the 1990-91 period. The economic reforms of 1991 and after were an acceleration of the earlier reforms that had begun in the mid-1980s.[34] While the immediate cause of the 1991-92 economic restructuring in Zambia was the change of government the previous October, which had been occasioned by the many years of socio-economic regression, in India the immediate factor was the economic crunch of 1990-91. Bimal Jalan states that:

> In August 1990 India's fragile economy was plunged into a deep crisis by the adverse impact of the crisis in the gulf. For the next ten months, the economy was teetering on the brink of collapse as the country passed through two changes of government, a general election and several other events. Then in July 1991 the picture changed dramatically. A series of new policy measures was announced with a view to restoring confidence. The budget of the new government marked the beginning of liberalization and fiscal correction...[35]

The 1990 economic crisis in India was a sudden crunch whose most immediate precipitation was the Gulf crisis of 1990-91, caused by the United States and the Allies' invasion of Iraq in February 1991. On the surface, neither the long-term nor the immediate pre-1990 economic scenario suggested any immediate economic slump in India. At least up to late 1989 the economic atmosphere in India was perceived to be normal; in fact, India was even being praised universally for its economic management. With the country's national income growth at 5.5 per cent per annum through the 1980s, and industrial growth posting an 8 per cent annual growth rate, coupled with the achievement of food self-sufficiency, there was no cause to fear a sudden economic plunge of the magnitude of the 1991 crisis.[36]

India's Economy: Some Historical Factors

Up to 1990, the Indian economy had resiliently withstood the various economic vagaries that had arisen over the years. The economy had withstood the mid-1960s droughts through concessional food imports. The United States government's loan concession for wheat, termed Public Law (PL 480), was the main item of the concessional imports of that time, but was curtailed in 1965 by the American government as a sign of disapproval of India's war with Pakistan. In the 1973 drought, the Indian government successfully mounted a food imports strategy, this time through direct purchase on the open market. In 1979, the severe food shortage arising also from drought was managed, this time purely on local food resources. India had built up national buffer food stocks over the few years, out of the experience of previous disasters, to fall upon in times of similar distress. The Indian economy also successfully weathered the economic storm emanating from both the 1973 and 1978/79 oil crises.[37] Premised on these successes, the Sixth Five-Year Plan (1980-85) states that: 'The most significant achievement of the planning period has been the fact that the Indian economy has achieved a greater degree of resilience to cope with disturbances in the international economy.'[38]

Thus, capacity was built up so that future economic distresses could be handled without recourse to foreign aid. This fell in line with the 1949 Parliamentary decision against the importation of food grains from abroad after 1951 except when necessitated by 'widespread failure of crops or for the purpose of building up a central reserve'.[39] Therefore, even when drought conditions occurred in the Chhatisgarh region of Madhya Pradesh, the upper reaches of Sirmur District of Himachal Pradesh, as well as in Garhwal in Uttah Pradesh, in 1991, the Government was able to use food stocks in reserve to bail out the drought-affected areas.[40]

Low Economic Growth

Although India's economic growth was impressive, it was not fast enough to meet the challenge of poverty. Elsewhere in this study, it has been argued that the poverty levels that India inherited at independence were so deeply entrenched that poverty could not be eradicated or reduced significantly given India's economic growth rates of up to 4 per cent. According to Datta, even after concerted efforts at poverty reduction in the post-colonial period, by the end of the sixties, poverty in India was in the range of 40 per cent, while 'the Planning Commission in 1979-80 estimated that the percentage was 51 in the rural areas, 38 per cent in urban areas and 48 per cent in the aggregate'.[41] Significant reduction in poverty levels was held back particularly by the slowdown in economic growth at different periods from independence to 1991. In fact, by 1991, the Indian economy reached a point of nearly defaulting on her financial obligations. This made the need for structural adjustment and economic reform imperative. However, the 1990-91 economic crisis in India, sudden as it appeared to be, was actually a culmination of long-standing latent weaknesses and limitations in the Indian economy stretching back to the period of independence. Mukherjee argues that the 1991 fiscal and balance of payments crisis resulted from both long-term and short-term constraints that had built up in the Indian economy over the years.[42]

One of the problems that led to the crunch in the Indian economy in 1991 was that structural weaknesses had bred inefficiency in the economy. While India's high level of protection of indigenous industries had successfully deepened and widened the country's industrial base, and thereby shielded the country from foreign dependence, along the way the protectionist mechanisms had began to breed inefficiency and technological backwardness in Indian industry. The plethora of restrictive rules and regulations (commonly referred to as the 'license quota' Raj) stifled internal and external competition and the spirit of entrepreneurship and innovation. The application of the Monopoly and Restrictive Trade Practices (MRTP) Act (1969), coupled with the reservation of some industrial sectors for small-scale industry, disjointed the business environment of large-scale firms. Further, the reservation of certain areas for the small-scale entrepreneurs actually worked against small-scale industry because it excluded them from benefiting from economies of scale and research and development (R & D) activities. Moreover, India's growing public sector, which controlled the 'commanding heights' of the Indian economy that had been critical to India's industrial development, began to emerge as a burden to the country, as inefficiency crept into operations. The public sector had diversified the country's industrial structure, especially in the areas of capital goods and heavy industry. Thus, the public sector took a leading role in reducing India's dependence on foreign capital, foreign equipment and technology.[43]

Unfortunately, a combination of political and bureaucratic pressure led to overstaffing, while appointment of politicians as managers opened the industries to manipulation by trade union activists and rendered them incapable of exercising effective and efficient control over the firms under their charge. Public sector enterprises became loss-making entities and havens of rampant corruption. Their failure to run economically caused manifold losses and low investment efficiency, resulting in very high capital output ratios. Mukherjee indicates that 'estimates for the (Indian) economy as a whole show that the capital used per unit of additional output or the incremental capital output ratio (ICOR) kept rising, it being a little over 2.0 during the First Plan and reaching 3.6 during the Third Plan ... (and) ... between 1971 and 1976 the ICOR had touched a high of 5.76 ... Even during the eighties ... the (simple) average rate of financial return on employed capital in public sector enterprises was as low as 2.5 per cent'.[44]

Another internal factor that led to India's economic downswing was the manner in which the state structure and democratic landscape functioned. Strong and articulate demands on state resources from various sections of the nation led to a gradual negation of fiscal prudence from the mid-seventies. Government expenditure began and continued to rise unabated, fuelled by a 'proliferation of subsidies and grants, salary increases with no relationship to efficiency or output, overstaffing and other "populist" measures such as massive loan waivers'.[45] Budgetary allocations became a means of political bargaining among the various sections of the Indian political spectrum. The resulting fiscal profligacy caused very sharp rises in the country's fiscal deficits. Mukherjee argues that India's consolidated government (centre and states) fiscal deficits rose sharply from 4.1 per cent of GDP in 1974-75 to 6.5 per cent in 1979-80, 9.7 per cent in 1984-85, peaking at 10.4 per cent in 1991.[46] These weaknesses arose in the Indian economy mainly because the overall positive growth rates (averaging over 5.5 per cent GDP growth) came from over-borrowing and over-spending, not increased savings and investment.

External Factors

It has been argued that a major shortcoming in India's economic growth path was her failure to take advantage of the new enabling economic environment on the international scene, which had emerged by the mid-1960s. This argument revolves around the view that the inward-looking character of the industrialization process has been one of the more persistent traits of the planning strategy that India originally adopted during the mid-fifties. From the mid-sixties onwards it became evident that the process of industrialization could not continue in the same trend.[47]

Being inward-looking, India's industrialization policy favoured satisfaction of domestic demand (which any sound economy does anyway), with a slant towards import substitution. This in turn had other side effects that impacted negatively on the economy's growth frontier, especially as regards India's failure at international competitiveness due to technological backwardness. Chakravarty argues that one widely diagnosed cause of India's growing lack of competitiveness in the international market is the so-called 'technological lag'. The Indian economy is often described as a 'high cost economy', and a very prominent factor for the high level of costs is the 'obsolete' nature of much technology utilized in Indian industry.[48] The resultant effect of not participating effectively in the international economic arena, especially for trade purposes, was the shortage of foreign exchange. The foreign exchange crunch led to the June 1966 devaluation of the rupee by 36 per cent, in the hope that transitional assistance would come India's way from abroad once the economy began to show signs of opening up. However, the anticipated exports growth did not materialize, until 'between 1970-71 and 1981-82 (when Indian) exports increased nearly 5-fold at current prices, implying an annual rate of growth of 15.9 per cent'.[49] These benefited from the newly opened Gulf market for Indian exports.

In the wake of the first worldwide oil crisis of 1973, the net terms of trade turned against the Indian export drive; but by 1978 the situation had been put under control. This was unlike the Zambian situation where there was no turn-around in the economic plunge, resulting from the 1973 oil crisis and went on into the 1978-79 crisis. However, the 1978-79 oil crisis threw India's economic gains to the wind. Although India handled the crisis was well, compared to other developing countries, the crunch left an indelible imprint on India's export performance. This was unlike the Zambian situation where there was no change in the economic downturn resulting from the 1973 oil price hike, which lasted up to the next oil crisis of 1978-79. Like all other developing countries (Zambia inclusive), India faced a hostile international environment premised on declining import demand in developed countries, which were also in deep recession from 1980. The protectionist tendencies in the developed countries added to the economic strain that was already growing so that India's textiles, garments, shoes, iron and steel, iron ore and leather, faced very stiff barriers, while the fall in unit values of some of these products made them less prospective as exportable commodities. These factors were crowned by India's own infrastructure constraints, especially in power and transport. The Indian export environment was made unfavourable domestically by 'lack of coherent domestic policies as India's share in world traditional export growth declined'.[50] The result was that in the 1960s India's balance of payments position began to get precarious. The Sixth Plan acknowledges that: 'With very few exceptions, India has been having a negative balance of trade throughout the last thirty years. The balance of payments problems facing the country during the Sixth Plan are likely to be acute and will require innovative approaches to cope with the situation. The trade deficit in the basic year of the Plan, 1979-80, estimated at Rs.2, 370 crores is higher than ever before.[51]

Although the economy remained resolute and poised for growth, there were serious disruptive undercurrents taking place during the 1980s. According to Mohan, India's exports, as a function of GDP, declined from 7.8 per cent back in 1929 to 4.3 per cent in 1986. He concluded that: 'The Indian tragedy is not that we adopted an anti-export bias in the 1950s, when everyone else did, but that we did not change in the 1960s when world trade grew by leaps and bounds.'[52] Shortly before the 1990-91 crisis, the West was praising India as a showcase of success, at least in economic circles. Both the World Bank and the International Monetary Fund (IMF) acceded to India's 'healthy' economic growth parameters up to 1988, yet India's 'balance of payments had already turned quite uncomfortable by the end of 1988 and foreign debt was rising sharply'.[53]

When the Gulf Crisis of 1990-91 came, it found the Indian economy in a very vulnerable state. Coupled with the political fluidity at the centre during that period, the Indian economy reached a near dead-end. The political and economic difficulties of the 1990-91 period even delayed the launch of the Eighth Five-Year Plan, which, instead of commencing in 1990/91 only started in 1992. The only available escape route was liberalization. When the minority National Congress government of Prime Minister Narasima Rao embraced sweeping economic reforms in July 1991, it quickly restored a respectable amount of confidence in the economy.

India's Policy Shifts

From July 1991 the newly elected government introduced several reforms in order to restore confidence in the Indian economy. The events that led to the crisis were both economic and political. Politically, the worsening conditions from 1988 to 1991 had telling effects on the economy. Political uncertainty developed and affected the government's ability to control 'burgeoning fiscal and current account deficits'.[54] The failure by any one political party to win an outright majority to form a stable government in the November 1989 elections left a void. A new coalition formed a shaky government. When the Deputy Prime Minister was fired in July 1990, it was followed by other political problems. The announcement that the Mandal Commission Report would be implemented, coupled with the Ayodhya conflict over the Ram Janambhoomi-Babri Masjid, led to a breakdown of law and order in several states of India. The government lost its majority in Parliament in November 1990, just after one year in power. The takeover of power by another minority government did not portend any political stability at the centre. The new government failed to present the national budget in Parliament in February 1991. The following month, that government also resigned. This triggered fresh elections in May and June of that year. The new (also minority) government borne out of those elections became the fourth government in two years.[55] The new minority National Congress government of Prime Minister Narasima Rao and Finance Minister Manmohan Singh presented its budget in July 1991. Measures were instituted, targeting an immediate reduction of India's fiscal deficit. Liberalization of the economy, that is, significantly (though in a calibrated manner) opening the doors of the Indian economy to market forces became a reality. This was because, as Mukherjee puts it, 'reform of the dirigisme, control-ridden and inward-looking economy was long overdue'.[56] The calibrated manner in which the Indian economic landscape was liberalized differed sharply from the Zambian situation, where liberalization was rapid and wholesale.

To reduce the fiscal deficit, the government opted to devalue the exchange rate of the Indian rupee to the tune of about 20 per cent in order to bring it at par with the market margin. The liberalization of trade involved policy reforms, which gave Indian companies more freedom to import goods and services at reasonable rates of taxation. Industrial controls were also relaxed to create an enabling and conducive environment for industries to be able to access their input and service requirements more easily.

Another reform measure involved the breakup of the long-standing industrial licensing system, which had held back industrial growth. The Monopoly and Restrictive Trade Practices (MRTP) Act of 1969 which had severely handicapped large business firms was also abolished. The restrictions that had been placed on foreign direct investment (FDI) were eased, just as the encumbrances that had stifled the capital and financial market sectors were lowered. In addition, a bold step was taken to gradually disinvest from public enterprises. This was echoed in the Eighth Five-Year Plan (1992-97) in which the necessity to diminish the role of the public sector in India's economic life was emphasized. Therefore, India's 1991 liberalization strategy was a concerted effort to break away from the past in order 'to free the economy from stifling internal controls as well as equip it to participate in the worldwide globalization process to its advantage'.[57] Here, again, lay a major dichotomy between the Zambian and the Indian trade and industrial policy reform trajectories. In Zambia, the reform in 1991-92 came like a whirlwind, whereas in India it was undertaken with a lot of caution. In the end, the results proved more lasting and effective in India, unlike in Zambia where the results appeared shaky and prone to erosion. From then on, the Indian economy began to score on the economic recovery chart. By 1992, most of India's negative economic trends had been reversed and set on a growth path. India's gross domestic product (GDP) recovered from a low of 0.8 per cent during 1991-92 and had increased to 5.3 per cent by 1992-93 and on to 6.2 per cent in 1993-94, such that over the next three years India's economic growth touched the 7.5 per cent mark. At that rate, India was almost catching up with the East Asian economic high fliers. Further, industry recovered and posited a growth rate of 2.3 per cent in 1992-93, and shot up to 6 per cent from a meagre less than 1 per cent prior to the reforms. By 1995-96 industrial production in India had reached an all- time high of 12.8 per cent. Other sectors that recorded dramatic recoveries included the Indian Stock Market whose total capitalization as a proportion of GDP catapulted from 13 per cent in 1990 to 60 per cent in 1993. By 1995, the Indian stock market had the largest number of listed companies in the world.[58] Liberalization injected a breath of life into the Indian economy so that thereafter the negative economic trends remained confined to the days of the pre-liberalization era. In Zambia, on the other hand, given a weaker trade and industrial policy base, and a very small and weak indigenous capitalist base, the 1991-92 economic reforms could not engender instantaneous benefits as happened in India.

Conclusion

While recovery in India was swift and dramatic following the 1991 sweeping economic reforms, the situation was very different in Zambia. The major cutting line between the two liberalization experiences was that India put emphasis on fiscal and monetary reforms, coupled with a gradual disinvestment programme. India also allowed the private sector to thrive, in a political landscape where democracy was a major ingredient. The existence of a vibrant civil society, trade unions and opposition political parties which were allowed adequate space to operate enabled them to play a pivotal role in the governance system of the country. This gave India more leverage in undertaking well debated and, thus, often consensual industrial policy directions. In Zambia, on the other hand, the 1991-92 period marked the re-emergence of political parties, the emergence of civil society organizations, and the reinvigoration of the trade union movement. Thus, the fact that these were just re-emerging in Zambia in the post-1991 elections, left Zambia's economic policy framework without much debate, criticism and analysis. Zambia's industrial policies, and other national policies for that matter, were being implemented without public scrutiny; it was as if they were fool proof.

In Zambia, the fiscal and monetary measures were coupled with a sudden and traumatic privatization programme. The end result was massive poverty arising from job losses in the hastily privatized public enterprises, and the privately owned companies that opted out of the country, due to the radical liberalization programme. Pensioners lost their life pensions and other people lost investments in banks that went under. Given Zambia's high tax regime, locally manufactured goods could not compete with the highly-subsidized, cheap, imported products that began to flood the Zambian market. Manufacturing industries like Dunlop Zambia Limited, Chloride Zambia, Colgate Palmolive, and several others uprooted their machinery and relocated to other countries like Zimbabwe.

Therefore, instead of injecting a life-saving change into the Zambian economy, liberalization and privatization in general, and the reform of the trade and industrial policy regime from 1992 in particular, left a sense of betrayal, despondency and devastation. While the 1991 Indian trade and industrial policy reform trajectory ushered in an optimistic era of accelerated economic prosperity, with the economic indicators showing an upturn, the hope of the Zambian reform bearing fruit, especially immediately after 1992, looked quite bleak. All the interim economic indicators pointed towards economic deterioration rather than improvement. The implication was that tangible socio-economic results would only begin to show after at least a decade of a spirited economic reform process including the reform of trade and industry. Indeed, after 2002, Zambia's economic prospects began to brighten up, as the privatized mining industry and other economic sectors began to respond positively to the improving world economic system. This could form very fertile ground for a future study. It can also be noted that the major industrial policy shift bottlenecks in the 1991-92 period were partly due to the Zambian economy's reliance on majority state control and drive of the whole economy. There was not much space left to the private sector, nor was there any such space for divergent political views. This vacuum led the state to formulate and undertake unabashed industrial policy routes without adequate checks and balances. There were also no buffer economic sectors in the form of private small, medium and large-scale enterprises which could fill the void when state enterprises faltered (as they frequently did).

Recommendations

One of the main recommendations is that state-oriented policy frameworks should be coupled with private sector-anchored and driven policy directions. Private sector-driven policy directions could fill the void left whenever the state is unable to successfully carry out necessary industrial policy changes. In India, unlike in Zambia, the private sector's small-scale industries were able to take advantage of state weaknesses in responding to economic advantages arising from the Indian state's failure in economic management. Indian private sector small-scale industries were able to produce small industrial machines and tools which came in handy among rural Indians in resolving economic operational challenges. These were machines that could, for example, shell peanuts; extract juice from sugar cane, and other such small-scale machines for performing various functions that made life easier and operations more economical. In Zambia, such small-scale machines were imported. Zambia could have taken advantage of the diverse Zambian people's age-old traditional technologies and industrial knowhow, such as blacksmithing, to make hoes, axes and other tools. This could then be scaled up by providing more modern methods of fashioning such tools. Over the years, industrial production of such tools could then be embarked upon, thereby cutting off importation of such tools. This, in turn, would also provide the much needed employment with the multiplier effects that go with such innovations. Buttressed by state policy this industrial capacity could continually be scaled up and eventually blossom into a significant tools manufacturing industry.

The 1991-92 economic down-swing and industrial policy difficulties faced in Zambia could have been avoided by ensuring that the local skills base of the Zambian people was anchored in local technological advancement. This should have involved industrial policy shift directed at improvement of local indigenous technologies. The societies which used their traditional industries and local technologies, improved on them and scaled up their productive capacities, have moved up the industrialization ladder of the world economies. So, the medium and small-scale entrepreneurs should augment themselves to boost their production potential through resilience and by seizing business opportunities as they arise.

The role of the civil society organizations in Zambia could also be increased in order to give the small producers a mouthpiece with which to articulate various concerns and challenges affecting them. This could help the state realize how best to re-orient industrial policy from exclusive focus on large-scale industrial concerns to an all-embracing policy framework.

Drawing from the Indians' quick resolution of their industrial policy bottlenecks using home-grown solutions after the 1991-92 economic malaise, and Zambia's failure with the use of foreign solutions during the same period, it would be safe to state that solutions to Africa's economic difficulties in general, do not lie in asking for donor aid or foreign expert advice, but in local, home-brewed solutions.

Only when Africa and its leaders realize that development cannot be anchored on foreign solutions can Africa's industrial policy drive begin to yield the kind of development that the people of Africa desire. With different home-grown industrial policies and strategies, Zambia began to record sustainable economic gains. The Indian situation, with all its weaknesses, clearly shows that allowing the local indigenous entrepreneurs adequate space in the economy enabled the Indian economy to survive a very severe economic whirlwind as the resilience of the private sector, comprising the small, medium and large-scale enterprises, compensated for the weaknesses of the state enterprises.

Notes

1. A. Sen, 'Radical Needs and Moderate Reforms', in J. Dreze and A. Sen, eds., *Indian Development: Selected Regional Perspectives*, New Delhi, Oxford University Press, 1996, p.1; E. K. Chiputa, 'Development Planning in Zambia and India: A Comparative study from Independence to 1991', PhD. Thesis, Jawaharlal Nehru University, New Delhi, 2006, p.2; J. Bhagwati, *India in Transition: Freeing the Economy*, Delhi, Oxford University Press, 1994, p.35.

2. Jonathan, H. Chileshe, *Third World Countries and Development Options: Zambia*, New Delhi, Vikas Publishing House, 1986, p. 109; J. Shawa, 'Zambia', in A. Valdes and K. Muire- Lereche, eds., *Agricultural Policy Reforms and Regional Market Integration in Malawi, Zambia and Zimbabwe,* Washington DC: International Food Policy Research Institute, 1993, p. 140; D. Rodrik and A. Subramanian, 'Why India can grow at 7 per cent a Year or More: Projections and Reflections', *Economic and Political Weekly,* April 17, 2004, pp. 1591-96.

3. These sentiments were expressed by Professor Thandika Mkandawire during my presentation of this paper at the Guy Mhone Conference organized by CODESRIA in Lusaka, Zambia, on 27 July 2008.

4. India's economic growth indicators picked up within a short time of the implementation of the 1991 reforms, whereas in Zambia economic growth continued to slide downwards even after the reforms of 1991-92.

5. H. Van Der Heijden, 'Zambian Policy-making and the Donor Community in the 1990s',World Institute for Development Economics Research (WIDER) Discussion paper 2001/87, September 2001, p. 1.

6. V. DeLancey, 'The Economies of Africa', in A. Gordon and D. Gordon, eds., *Understanding Contemporary Africa,* London, Lynne Rienner Publishers, 1996, p. 103.

7. S. Chipungu, 'The State, Technology and Peasant Differentiation in Zambia: A Case Study of the Southern Province, 1930-1986', Lusaka, Historical Association of Zambia, 1988, pp. 193-194. Chipungu refutes the copper price slump thesis as a major factor in Zambia's economic plight at the time of the first major oil price hikes in 1973.

8. Van Der Heijden, 'Zambian Policy-making and the Donor Community in the 1990s', p. 3.

9. A., Martin, *Minding Their Own Business: Zambia's Struggle Against Western Control,* London, Hutchinson and Co. Ltd., 1972, p. 77; C. Gertzel, C. Baylies and M. Szeftel, 'Introduction: The Making of the One-Party State', in Cherry Gertzel, ed., Carolyn Baylies and Moris Szeftel, *The Dynamics of the One-party State in Zambia,* Manchester, Manchester University Press, 1984, pp. ix and 17.

10. DeLancey, 'The Economies of Africa', in Gordon and Gordon, eds., *Understanding Contemporary Africa,* pp. 17-18.

11. A. Valdes, 'The Macroeconomic and Overall Policy Environment Necessary to Complement Agricultural Trade and Price Policy Reforms', in A. Valdes and K. Muir-Leresche, eds., *Agricultural Policy Reforms and Regional Market Integration in Malawi, Zambia and Zimbabwe,* Washington DC., International Food Policy Research Institute, 1993, p. 19.

12. Chipungu, 'The State, Technology and Peasant Differentiation in Zambia: A Case Study of the Southern Province,' *1930 – 1986,* p. 199.

13. Chipungu, 'The State, Technology and Peasant Differentiation in Zambia: A Case Study of the Southern Province, 1930 – 1986', p. 199. Chipungu discusses Zambia's indebtedness in the 1980s at length; see also F.R. Fernholz, 'Debt Management and Debt Relief during the 1990s in Zambia', in Bill and McPherson, eds., *Promoting and Sustaining Economic Reform in Zambia,* London: Harvard University Press, 2004, p. 263.

14. Chipungu, 'The State, Technology and Peasant Differentiation in Zambia: A Case Study of the Southern Province, 1930 – 1986', p. 205.

15. R. Douglas, ed., *Rural Transformation in Tropical Africa,* Belhaven Press, London, 1988, p.3. His words in the Introduction hold true for Zambia's situation at the time.

16. DeLancey, 'The Economies of Africa' in Gordon and Gordon, eds., *Understanding Contemporary Africa,* p. 103.

17. Shawa, 'Zambia', in Valdes and Muir-Leresche, eds, *Agricultural Policy Reforms and Regional Market Integration in Malawi, Zambia and Zimbabwe*, p. 139.

18. G. Corea, 'Introduction', in K. P. Ghosh, ed., *Developing Africa: A Modernization Perspective*, London, Greenwood Press, 1984, p. 3, and Ghosh in the same book p.47, discusses the impact of the oil price hikes and the slowdown in the growth of world trade in primary commodities.

19. Shawa, 'Zambia', in Valdes and Muir-Leresche, eds., *Agricultural Policy Reforms and Regional Market Integration in Malawi, Zambia and Zimbabwe*, p. 139.

20. DeLancey, 'The Economies of Africa', in Gordon and Gordon, eds., *Understanding Contemporary Africa*, p. 108; see also United Nations Economic Commission for Africa, *Economic Survey of Africa Vol. III: East African Sub-region*, New York, United Nations, 1971, p. 6, where it is noted that Zambia and Rhodesia (Zimbabwe) had the largest proportion in the East and Central African sub-region (15–20 per cent) of their populations living in towns and cities.

21. Chipungu, 'The State, Technology and Peasant Differentiation in Zambia: A Case Study of the Southern Province, 1930 – 1986', p. 141.

22. Shawa, 'Zambia', in Valdes and Muir-Leresche (eds.) *Agricultural Policy Reforms and Regional Market Integration in Malawi, Zambia and Zimbabwe*, p., 139.

23. Shawa, 'Zambia', in Valdes and Muir-Leresche, eds., *Agricultural Policy Reforms and Regional Market Integration in Malawi, Zambia and Zimbabwe*, p. 141.

24. Chipungu, 'The State, Technology and Peasant Differentiation in Zambia', p. 197.

25. http//www.fao.org/docrep/003/v4595e/v4595e06.html, P. Ojermark and C. Chabala, *The Development of Independent Cooperatives in Zambia: A Case* Study, Rome, Food and Agriculture Organization, 1994, p. 8.

26. Shawa, 'Zambia', in Valdes and Muir-Leresche, eds., *Agricultural Policy Reforms and Regional Market Integration in Malawi, Zambia and Zimbabwe*, p. 146.

27. Shawa, 'Zambia', in Valdes and Muir-Leresche, eds., *Agricultural Policy Reforms and Regional Market Integration in Malawi, Zambia and Zimbabwe*, p. 148.

28. Der Heijden, 'Zambian Policy-making and the Donor Community in the 1990s', p. 2.

29. M. Nokkala, 'Simulating the Effects of Debt Relief in Zambia', World Institute for Development Economics Research (WIDER) Discussion paper, WDP 2001/118, October 2001, p. 2.

30. C. Fundanga, Governor of the Bank of Zambia, 'Zambia's Economic Outlook – What We Learnt in the Last 40 Years and Where Do We go from Here?' Paper presented at the Chartered Institute of Marketing Accountants (CIMA), Zambia, Annual Business Discussion on the theme 'Zambia's Economic Outlook- What Have We Learnt in the Last 40 Years and Where Do We go from Here?' Lusaka, 7 January 2005 (Unpublished) p. 3.

31. http://www.zpa.org.zm/zpaintro.htm, 'About the ZPA'.

32. http://www.handels.gu.se/epc/archive/00003481/01/Simatele%5Favhandl.pdf, M. Simatele, 'Financial Sector Reforms And Monetary Policy In Zambia', PhD. Thesis, Göteborg University, 2004, p. 34.

33. F. Kaunda, *Selling the Family Silver*, Kwazulu-Natal, Interpak Books, 2002, the book discusses the sale of the Zambian mines during the post-1991 liberalization period.

34. Nokkala, 'Simulating the Effects of Debt Relief in Zambia', p. 3.

35. L. Rakner, *Political and Economic Liberalization in Zambia, 1991–2001*, Uppsala, Nordiska Africainstitutet, 2003, pp. 78–79.

36. S. Kayizzi-Mugerwa, 'Explaining Zambia's Elusive Growth: Credibility Gap, External Shocks and Reluctant Donors', in M. Lundahl, ed., *From Crisis to Growth in Africa*, London/New York, Routledge, 2001, pp. 132-133.

37. P. Bardhan, *The Political Economy of Development in India*, Expanded Edition, New Delhi, Oxford University Press, 2003, p. 119.

38. B. Jalan, 'Introduction', in B. Jalan, ed., *The Indian Economy: Problems and Prospects*, New Delhi, Penguin Books India (P) Ltd., 1992, p. vii.

39. Jalan, 'Introduction', in Jalan, ed., *The Indian Economy: Problems and Prospects*, p. ix.

40. A. Sen, 'How is India Doing?' in R. A., Choudhury et al, eds., *The Indian Economy and its Performance since Independence*, New Delhi, Oxford University Press, 1990, pp. 10-11.

41. Government of India, Planning Commission, *Sixth Five-Year Plan, 1980-85*, chapter I, p. 26.

42. Government of India, *Constituent Assembly of India (Legislative) Debates*, Vol. III, March 19, 1949.

43. GOI, *Lok Sabha Debates, First Session, Tenth Lok Sabha*, Vol. 2, No. 11, July 24, 1991.

44. B. Datta, *Indian Planning at the Crossroads*, Delhi, Oxford University Press, 1992, p. 18.

45. A. Mukherjee, 'Indian Economy, 1965-91', in B. Chandra, A. Mukherjee and M. Mukherjee, *India after Independence, 1947-2000*, New Delhi, Penguin Books, 1999, p. 357.

46. Mukherjee, 'Indian Economy, 1965-91', in Chandra, Mukherjee and Mukherjee, *India after Independence, 1947-2000*, p. 358.

47. Mukherjee, 'Indian Economy, 1965-91', in Chandra, Mukherjee and Mukherjee, *India after Independence, 1947-2000*, pp. 358-359.

48. Mukherjee, 'Indian Economy, 1965-91', in Chandra, Mukherjee and Mukherjee, *India after Independence, 1947-2000*, pp. 361-362.

49. Mukherjee, 'Indian Economy, 1965-91', in Chandra, Mukherjee and Mukherjee, *India after Independence, 1947-2000*, pp. 362-363.

50. S. Chakravarty, *Development Planning: The Indian Experience*, Oxford, Clarendon Press, 1987, p. 69.

51. Chakravarty, *Development Planning: The Indian Experience*, p. 64.

52. Chakravarty, *Development Planning: The Indian Experience*, p. 70.

53. GOI, Planning Commission, *Sixth Five-Year Plan, 1980-85*, Chapter 1, p. 25.

54. GOI, Planning Commission, *Sixth Five-Year Plan, 1980-85*, Chapter 6, p. 205.

55. R. Mohan, 'Industrial Policy and Controls', in Bimal Jalan, ed., *The Indian Economy: Problems and Prospects*, New Delhi, Penguin Books India (P.) Ltd., 1992, pp. 88-89.

56. Jalan, 'Introduction', in Jalan, ed., *The Indian Economy: Problems and Prospects*, pp. ix-x.

57. Jalan, 'Introduction', in Jalan, ed., *The Indian Economy: Problems and Prospects*, p. x.

58. Jalan, 'Introduction', in Jalan, ed., *The Indian Economy: Problems and Prospects*, p. xi.

References

Austeen, Ralph, 1987, *African Economic History: Internal Development and External Dependency*, London: James Currey.

Bardhan, P., 2003, *The Political Economy of Development in India*, Expanded Edition, New Delhi: Oxford University Press.

Bhagwati, Jagdish, 1994, *India in Transition: Freeing the Economy*, New Delhi: Oxford University Press.

Chakravarty, S., 1987, *Development Planning: The Indian Experience,* Oxford: Clarendon Press. Chileshe, Jonathan, H., 1986, Third *World Countries and Development Options: Zambia,* New Delhi: Vikas Publishing House.

Chipungu, Samuel, 1988, 'The State, Technology and Peasant Differentiation in Zambia: A Case Study of the Southern Province, 1930-1986', Lusaka, Historical Association of Zambia.

Chiputa, Euston, K., 2006, 'Development Planning in Zambia and India: A Comparative Study from Independence to 1991', PhD. Thesis, Jawaharlal Nehru University, New Delhi. Corea, G., 'Introduction', in K. P. Ghosh, ed., 1984, *Developing Africa: A Modernization Perspective,* London: Greenwood Press.

Datta, B., 1992, *Indian Planning at the Crossroads,* New Delhi: Oxford University Press.

DeLancey, V., 1996, 'The Economies of Africa', in Gordon, A. and Gordon, D., eds, *Understanding Contemporary Africa,* London: Lynne Rienner Publishers.

Douglas, R., ed., 1988, *Rural Transformation in Tropical Africa,* London: Belhaven Press. Economic Intelligence Unit, 1982, 'Zambia', *Quarterly Economic Review,* Annual Supplement. Fernholz, F.R., 2004, 'Debt Management and Debt Relief during the 1990s in Zambia', in Bill and McPherson, eds, *Promoting and Sustaining Economic Reform in Zambia,* London: Harvard University Press.

Fundanga, C., Governor of the Bank of Zambia, 2005, 'Zambia's Economic Outlook – What We Learnt in the Last 40 Years and Where Do We go from Here?' 7 January Unpublished paper presented at the Chartered Institute of Marketing Accountants (CIMA), Zambia, Annual Business Discussion on the theme 'Zambia's Economic Outlook- What Have We Learnt in the Last 40 Years and Where Do We go from Here?' Lusaka.

Gertzel, C., Baylies, C. and Szeftel, M., 1984, 'Introduction: The Making of the One-Party State', in Cherry, Gertzel, ed., *The Dynamics of the One-party State in Zambia,* Manchester: Manchester University Press.

Government of India (GOI), 1949, Constituent Assembly of India (Legislative) Debates, Vol. III, March 19.

GOI, 1991, Lok Sabha Debates, First Session, Tenth Lok Sabha, Vol. 2, No. 11, July 24. GOI, Planning Commission of India, 1980, *Sixth Five-Year Plan, 1980-85,* New Delhi: Planning Commission of India. http://www.zpa.org.zm/zpaintro.htm, 'About the ZPA'.

Jalan, Bimal, 'Introduction', in Jalan, Bimal, ed., 1992, *The Indian Economy: Problems and Prospects,* New Delhi: Penguin Books India (P.) Ltd., pp. ix-xxiii. Kaunda, F., 2002, *Selling the Family Silver,* Kwazulu-Natal: Interpak Books.

Kayizzi-Mugerwa, S., 2001, 'Explaining Zambia's Elusive Growth: Credibility Gap, External Shocks and Reluctant Donors', in M. Lundahl, ed., *From Crisis to Growth in Africa,* London/New York: Routledge, pp. 132-146.

Leys, Colin, 1996, *The Rise and Fall of Development Theory,* Oxford: James Currey.

Markakis, John, Curry, Junior and Robert, L., 1976, 'The Global Economy's Impact on Budgetary Policies in Zambia', *Journal of African Studies, 3,* 4, pp.403-427.

Martin, Anthony, 1972, *Minding Their Own Business: Zambia's Struggle Against Western Control,* London, Hutchinson and Co. Ltd.

Mukherjee, A., 1999, 'Indian Economy, 1965-91', in B. Chandra, A. Mukherjee, and M. Mukherjee, *India after Independence, 1947-2000,* New Delhi: Penguin Books, pp. 351-364.

Mukherjee, Aditya, 1999, 'Economic Reforms since 1991', in Chandra, B., Mukherjee, M. and Mukherjee, A., *India after Independence, 1947–2000,* New Delhi: Penguin Books India (P.) Ltd., pp. 365-373.

Nokkala, M., 2001, 'Simulating the Effects of Debt Relief in Zambia', World Institute for Development Economics Research (WIDER) Discussion paper, WDP 2001/118.

Ojermark, P., and Chabala, C., 1994, *The Development of Independent Cooperatives in Zambia: A Case Study,* Rome: Food and Agriculture Organization. (http//www.fao.org/docrep/003/v4595e/v4595e06.html).

Prebisch, Raul, 1980, Cited in Vijay Kelkar, 'India and the World Economy: A Search for Self-Reliance', Paper presented at the seminar on 'Jawaharlal Nehru and Planned Development', held on 11-14 January.

Rakesh, Mohan, 1992, 'Industrial Policy and Controls', in B. Jalan, ed., *The Indian Economy: Problems and Prospects,* New Delhi: Penguin Books India (P.) Ltd., pp. 85-115.

Rakner, Lise, 2003, 'Political and Economic Problems in Zambia: 1964-1991', Abstract, in Lise Rakner, *Political and Economic Liberalization in Zambia,* Uppsala: The Nordic Africa Institute.

Republic of Zambia, CSO, 2000, *Census of Population and Housing: Zambia Analytical Report,*Vol. 10, November 2003.

Republic of Zambia, 1978, National Assembly, Daily Parliamentary Debates, Budget Address by Finance Minister, Friday, 27 January.

Republic of Zambia, 1979, *Third National Development Plan, 1979-83,* Lusaka: National Commission for Development Planning.

Rist, Gilbert, 2002, *The History of Development: From Western Origins to Global Faith,* London: Zed Books.

Rodrik, Dani, and Subramanian, Arvind, 2004, 'Why India can grow at 7 per cent a Year or More: Projections and Reflections', *Economic and Political Weekly,* April 17, pp. 1591-96. Sen, Amartya, 1990, 'How is India Doing?' in R.A. Choudhury, et al, eds, *The Indian Economy and Its Performance Since Independence,* New Delhi: Oxford University Press, pp. 7-22.

Sen, Amartya, 1996, 'Radical Needs and Moderate Reforms', in Jean Dreze, and Amartya Sen, eds, *Indian Development: Selected Regional Perspectives*, New Delhi: Oxford University Press. Seshamani, Venkatesh, 1977, 'Zambia's Industrial Strategies: Problems and Prospects', *African Social Research*, Nos. 37/38, December 1996-January 1977, pp. 75-86.

Shawa, Julius, J., 1993, 'Zambia', in Alberto Valdes and Kay Muire-Lereche, eds, *Agricultural Policy Reforms and Regional Market Integration in Malawi, Zambia and Zimbabwe*, Washington DC., International Food Policy Research Institute.

Simatele, M., 2004, 'Financial Sector Reforms and Monetary Policy in Zambia', PhD. Thesis, Göteborg University. Accessed at: http://www.handels.gu.se/epc/archive/00003481/01/Simatele%5Favhandl.pdf,

Turok, Ben, 1979, 'The Penalties of Zambia's Mixed Economy', in Ben Turok, ed., *Development in Zambia*, London: Zed Press.

United Nations Economic Commission for Africa, 1971, *Economic Survey of Africa Vol. III: East African Sub-region*, New York: United Nations.

Valdes, A., 1993, 'The Macroeconomic and Overall Policy Environment Necessary to Complement Agricultural Trade and Price Policy Reforms', in A. Valdes and K. Muir-Leresche, eds, *Agricultural Policy Reforms and Regional Market Integration in Malawi, Zambia and Zimbabwe*, Washington DC: International Food Policy Research Institute.

Van Der Heijden, Hendrik, 2001, 'Zambian Policy-making and the Donor Community in the 1990s', World Institute for Development Economics Research (WIDER) Discussion Paper 2001/87.

5

The Emergence of China in Cameroon: Trade Impact and Evolution of Trade Configuration

Sunday A. Khan

Introduction

Cameroon established diplomatic relations with the People's Republic of China in March 1971. Over the next 36 years of diplomatic ties, Cameroonian presidents have paid six official visits to China, but the first ever visit to Cameroon (part of an eight-nation African tour) by a Chinese President (Hu Jintao) was in January 2007. This among others things, is a clear indication of China's increasing interest in Cameroon and Africa in general. China now accounts for about 20 per cent of the world's population and has recorded an annual average growth rate of close to 10 per cent in the last two decades (Kaplinsky 2007). According to Broadman (2007), during the 1990-1994 and 1999-2004 periods, the annual average growth rate of African exports to China was 20 per cent and 48 per cent, respectively. China has become an important player in the global economy and politics, actively participating in global institutions. No country can ignore China anymore. China's intensification of relations with developing countries has been attributed to the need to secure raw materials for its hungry booming economy and markets for its manufactures. Whether we like it or not, China is presenting a new and significant challenge to the global economy and particularly developing economies. However, many of these countries are not yet making efforts to assess the extent and the potential impact of the emergence of China on their economies. They seem to be overwhelmed by the aid pledges and infrastructural projects from China and are overlooking the overall impact on their economies.

To gain an insight into the economic relations between China and Cameroon, we examine one of the traditional channels of interaction – trade (other economic channels are investment and aid flows, but data paucity prevents us from considering them in this study). Cameroon's traditional trading partners have been European countries, and top among them has been France, its former colonial master. Trade with Asia, and especially China, has been very low, but is increasing rapidly. On the eve of Hu Jintao's arrival in Cameroon,[1] the Chinese ambassador declared that from January to November 2006, the volume of trade between the two countries went up by 101 per cent compared to 2005 (*Cameroon Tribune* 30 January 2007). Increased trade between Cameroon and China offers a lot of opportunities, and equally some challenges to the Cameroonian economy. China's demand for Cameroon's primary commodities offers a huge opportunity for the government. Similarly, relatively cheap manufactured imports from China impact positively on the living conditions of poor Cameroonians. However, increased trade with China constitute a challenge to the Cameroonian economy and society. The huge influx of cheap Chinese manufactured goods poses a serious threat to fragile local producers; some of whom have been exporting in the sub-region and even beyond. The existence of such potential advantages and risks requires regular and systematic assessment so as to know how to minimise the risk while maximizing the benefits arising from the emergence of China in the global economy. The rhetoric from the Chinese leadership about a new strategic relationship with Cameroon based on 'sincere friendship', 'equality', 'reciprocal benefit', and 'win-win cooperation'[2] as emphasized in a speech by the Chinese president during his visit to Cameroon should not be taken for granted.

The objective of this study, therefore, is to examine the nature of trade (exports and imports) relations between China and Cameroon and how these have modified Cameroon's trade configuration and their potential impact on various stakeholders in the country. This will entail assessing the size and composition of trade with China and also the effect on trade with Cameroon's traditional Western partners like France, Germany, The Netherlands, Spain, etc. It also implies identifying and evaluating the potential implications for the relevant stakeholders in Cameroon like consumers, producers, government, wage earners, etc.

Theoretical Framework

A large part of the literature holds that trade is important for growth. Such a conclusion derives from studies concluding that outward-oriented economies consistently have higher growth rates than inward-oriented economies. This neoclassical view has been supported by the phenomenal growth and industrialization records of Asian countries like Hong Kong,

Singapore, Korea and Taiwan, and later Malaysia and Thailand. These countries are often compared with those in Latin America and Africa that opted for the import-substitution strategy. Over the last 30 years, these Asian countries approximately doubled their standards of living every ten years (Giles and Williams 2000). China and India are the latest to join this group and thus lend more support to the argument that openness to trade leads to more rapid growth. Some authors like Krueger (1995) identify trade policy as the crucial element of economic policy. The World Bank (1993) considers the experiences of these Asian countries as a model for development.

The literature outlines a number of channels through which more trade openness can impact positively on the economy. First, an expansion in trade (especially exports) may promote specialization in the production of export products, which in turn may boost the productivity level and may cause the general level of skills to rise. This may then lead to a reallocation of resources from the (relatively) inefficient non-trade sector to the higher productive export sector. The productivity change may lead to output growth. An outward-oriented trade policy may also give access to advanced technologies, learning by doing, and better management practices that may result in further efficiency gains in the overall traded-goods sector. The larger international market permits economies of scale to be realized in the export sector. Lastly, a larger export sector would make available more of the resources necessary to import in a more timely fashion both physical and human capital, including advanced technologies in production and management, and for training higher quality labour (Giles and Williams 2000; Ben-David and Loewy 1998; Fosu 1990).

Some authors have, however, been expressing worries about the exaggerated enthusiasm for trade liberalization. Rodrik (1999: 25), observes that 'just as the advantages of import-substitution policies were overstated in an earlier era, today the benefits of openness are oversold ...' The interventionist policies of East Asian governments (through human capital development, technology and industrial policies) are often cited as being instrumental in forging the comparative advantage enjoyed by these countries (Wade 1990; Amsden 1989). Their rapid growth cannot therefore be attributed solely to their openness to trade. Governments in many developing countries do advocate for some level of protection (even temporary) for local firms, so as to allow them time to raise their productivity to levels compatible with international competition. According to Yanikkaya (2003), despite the wide consensus about the positive association between trade flows and growth, the literature on the effects of trade restrictions on growth has reported mixed results. Another strand of the literature stresses the possibility of reverse causation between trade and growth, i.e., instead of trade policy leading to growth, growth can also cause trade. A study by Jung and Marshall (1985) finds inconclusive evidence on the direction of causality, while Harrison (1996) finds that openness and growth Granger-cause each other in both directions.

A consensus on trade and growth linkages should allow developing countries to formulate trade policies that could raise growth and foster development. If more trade is seen to promote growth, then the barriers which restrict imports and reduce the externality effects of exporting should be reduced. If, on the contrary, growth is sourced largely internally, then trade liberalization should be checked and programmes for human and physical capital investment and increased research and development promoted (Wälde and Wood 2004). It is within the context of a choice between inward-orientation and outward-orientation that we examine the nature of trade between Cameroon and China and the potential impact on the local economy. To examine the impact on various stakeholders in the economy, we use an analytical approach derived from Kaplinsky (2007). This approach innvolves in distinguishing between complementary and competitive impacts; as well as direct and indirect impacts. The direct impact results from trade between China and Cameroon, while the indirect impact is due to China's role in the world as a major player, capable of influencing global prices, and consequently affecting even countries not trading directly with them. A synthetic view of the proposed framework (limited to trade interactions) is summarized in Table 5.1.

Table: 5.1: A Synthetic View of the Complementary/Competitive and Direct/Indirect Impacts of Trade with China

	Direct	Indirect
Complementary	Increased export income, and employment	Higher global prices for Cameroon's exports
	Cheap inputs for industries Cheap consumption goods	Lower global prices for imports of especially capital goods from other countries
Competitive	Displacement of existing and potential local producers by cheap Chinese products – De-industrialization Wages and jobs are threatened by cheap Chinese products	Competition in external markets – falling prices and markets – falling prices and falling market shares for export of manufactures

Source: Adapted from Kaplinsky (2007) and Khan and Baye (2007)

This framework can potentially enable us to sort out opportunities from threats, and identify winners and losers from increased trade between Cameroon and China. Different stakeholders in the same country may be affected differently, and it is possible for a stakeholder to be both a gainer and a loser. Gainer or loser groups can either be consumers, local firms and/or the government. Information for the study is obtained largely from the statistical annals of the National Institute of Statistics and the Department of External Trade and Industry (Ministry of Trade and Industry) in Cameroon.

Size, Significance and Composition of Trade with China

Cameroon had been trading with China even before the establishment of diplomatic relations in 1971. The volume of trade leaped to more than CFAF 112 billion in 2000, up from only about CFAF 50 billion in 1999. In this section, we describe the nature and extent of trade links between Cameroon and China. We examine separately exports, imports and the bilateral trade balance with China, and comparatively with other major trading partners.

Exports to China and other Major (Export) Destinations

Cameroon's exports to China were relatively low prior to 1999, but they shot up by more than 200 per cent within a year to stand at more than CFAF 80 billion in 2000, representing almost 7 per cent of Cameroon's total exports, from barely 2.7 per cent in 1999. China was then ranked sixth among Cameroon's main export destinations in 2000. This, however, was the peak of Cameroon's exports to China, as they took a downward trend from then onward. By 2005, exports to China declined to barely CFAF 36 billion, representing only 2.5 per cent of Cameroon's total exports. China fell to the eighth position among Cameroon's export partners. Therefore, while Cameroon's exports to the world increased from CFAF 1,179 billion in 2000 to CFAF 1,476 billion in 2005, exports to China were on a steady decline as shown in Table 5.2. Compared with other major trading partners (Figure 5.1 and Table 5.A1 in the Appendix), exports to China are very low. For period of 2002-05, Cameroon's main export partners where Spain (20.7 %), Italy (14 %), France (12.8 %), Holland (10 %) and USA (7.1 %). Over the same period, exports to China averaged only 3.5 per cent annually. This is reflected in trade with some of the regions in the world. More than two-thirds of Cameroon's exports go to the EU, while less than 10 per cent goes to East Asia; and this share is on a downward trend.

Table 5.2: Exports to China, Share and Rank among Major Export Destinations (million CFAF)

Year	China	World	China's Share (%)	China's Rank
1999	26,682	985,492	2.7	6
2000	80,819	1,178,597	6.9	5
2001	75,619	1,281,902	5.9	6
2002	54,197	1,252,866	4.3	6
2003	56,923	1,301,893	4.4	6
2004	33,134	1,256,789	2.6	8
2005	36,221	1,475,969	2.5	8

Source: INS – Institut National de Statistique (2004, 2006)

Figure 5.1: Share of Exports to Main Destinations

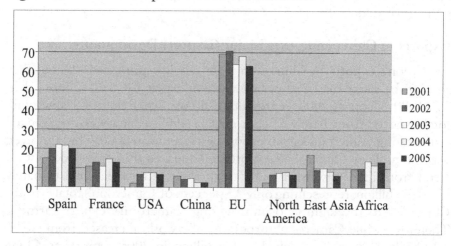

The composition of Cameroon's exports to China is limited to a few primary commodities: crude oil, wood and cotton (Table 5.A2 in the Appendix). The export of crude oil to China, which represented more than 50 per cent of all export to China, ended in 2003, perhaps due to declining oil production in Cameroon, and because China secured better oil deals elsewhere. Beginning in 2004, raw cotton replaced crude oil as the principal export commodity to China, representing almost 75 per cent of all exports to this country. Therefore, by 2005, Cameroon exported only cotton and wood-related products to China. The cotton exports and wood exports to

China, however, represented only 40 per cent and 4 per cent respectively of the total export of these commodities by Cameroon. Cameroon's other main exports commodities like crude oil, cocoa, coffee and banana are exported essentially to Spain, Italy, France, Holland, etc. Such export performance is rather disappointing, as it indicates is that Cameroon is not yet reaping much from the huge demand for raw materials by China. However, it also represents opportunities for increasing exports to China. First, by increasing wood and cotton exports, and then exploring the possibility of diversifying exports to other commodities produced abundantly in Cameroon like cocoa, coffee, banana, etc.

Imports from China and other Major (Import) Sources

Unlike exports, imports from China have been on a steady rise. In 2005, Cameroon imported goods from China worth almost CFAF80 billion, up from barely CFAF23 billion in 1999. China's share of total exports to Cameroon consequently moved from 2.8 per cent to 5 per cent, and China became Cameroon's third source of imports after France and Nigeria,[3] up from the ninth position in 1999 (see Table 5.3). While Cameroon's total imports increased by 88 per cent between 1999 and 2005, imports from China increased by 231 per cent.

Apart from Nigeria, none of Cameroon's traditional trading partners witnessed an increase in exports to Cameroon like China. Between 2002 and 2005, they all lost import shares in Cameroon: France (27 %), USA (45 %), Germany (23.5 %), Italy (18 %), Holland (14 %), Japan (13 %) etc. China's share of Cameroon's imports increased by almost 40 per cent within same period.[4]

The rapidly rising share of imports from China has therefore meant a reduction of imports from some of Cameroon's traditional partners. If we look at some major trading regions (Figure 5.2), it is clear that imports from the EU are high, but declining, while those from East Asia are relatively low and are increasing steadily. Imports from North America are also declining while those from Africa are rising, but largely dominated by hydrocarbon imports from Nigeria.

Table 5.3: Imports from China, Share and Rank among Major Import Sources (million CFAF)

Year	China	World	China's Share (%)	China's Rank
1999	22,912	811,226	2.8	9
2000	31,474	1,052,203	3.0	8
2001	36,629	1,356,767	2.7	8
2002	46,331	1,294,971,	3.6	7
2003	50,331	1,251,561	4.0	5
2004	58,442	1,365,047	4.3	7
2005	75,796	1,524,180	5.0	3

Sources: INS – Institut National de Statistique (2004, 2006)

Figure 5.2: Share of Imports from main Sources

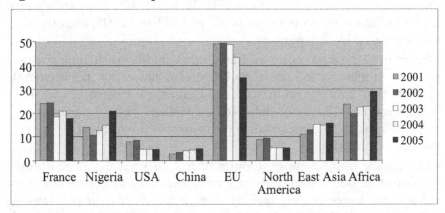

While exports to China are on essentially two commodities, imports from China cover a wide range of products. Before 2003, cereals (especially rice) were the main import commodities, taking almost 50 per cent of all imports; but by 2005 this dropped to less than 2 per cent. Cereals are imported essentially from Thailand, France and India. Other import categories have seen substantial increases in imports from China. The share of total imports of machinery, transport and other equipment from China has increased from only 1.3 per cent in 2001 to 8 per cent in 2005. Similarly, the share of other manufactured goods imported from China increased from 8 per cent to 33 per cent within the same period. Most of these commodities were hitherto imported from Western countries, and especially Europe. Table 5.A4 in the Appendix, which provides more details on imports from China, indicates that most of the commodities witnessed an increase of more than 75 per cent between 2000 and 2005.

Trade Balance with China and other Major Trading Partners

Higher imports and lower exports have led to a negative trade balance with China since 2004. From a trade surplus of almost CFAF 50 billion in 2000, Cameroon had a trade deficit of almost CFAF 40 billion in 2005. The trade surplus with China started a downward trend in 2001, and turned into a trade deficit by 2004 (Table 5.4). Concerned with the worsening trade balance with China, the president of Cameroon raised the issue in a speech to the visiting Chinese president in February 2007: 'We wish to benefit from export quotas for some of our products like coffee, cotton, cocoa, banana, just to name a few; so as to re-equilibrate as much as possible, the trade balance between our two countries' (*Cameroon Tribune*, 2 February 2007: 3). However, there is no known official policy or strategy to deal with this huge trade deficit with China or even to assess the potential impact on the economy. The *de facto* picture could be worse if we factor in the observation that some goods imported from some other countries are actually made in China. An example is imports from Dubai (United Arab Emirates) which rose from about CFAF 1 billion in 2000 to more than CFAF 6.5 billion in 2005. These goods are all made in China. It should be noted that Cameroon exports virtually nothing to the United Arab Emirates. Goods labelled as made in China are also imported from other countries like Nigeria.

Table 5.4: Cameroon's Trade Balance with China and the World (million CFAF)

| | China | | | World | | |
	Exports	Imports	Balance	Exports	Imports	Balance
1999	26,682	22,912	3,770	985,492	811,226	174,266
2000	80,819	31,474	49,345	1178,597	1052,203	126,394
2001	75,619	36,629	38,990	1281,902	1356,767	-74,865
2002	54,197	46,331	7,866	1252,866	1294,971	-42,105
2003	56,923	50,331	6,601	1,301,893	1,251,561	50,332
2004	33,134	58,442	-25,308	1,256,789	1,365,047	-108,258
2005	36,221	75,796	-39,575	1,475,969	1,524,180	-48,211

Source: INS – Institut National de Statistique (2004, 2006)

Cameroon's overall negative trade balance cannot be attributed solely to China, as the balance with France, Germany, and Japan has also always been negative (Table 5.A5 in the Appendix), though Cameroon has a consistent trade surplus with others countries like Spain, Italy and Holland. However, while the deficit with France has been declining, that with China is on the rise, a reflection of the widening trade deficit with East Asian countries (Figure 5.3). The trade balance with the EU has been and continues to be largely positive. The improving trade balance with North America largely reflects Cameroon's trade with the USA. The evolution of trade with China might likely be a determinant of the trend of Cameroon's future trade balance.

Figure 5.3: Cameroon's Trade Balance with some Partners and Regions

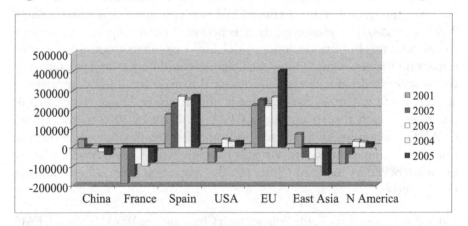

Potential Impact of Trade with China

The potential impact evaluation largely expresses likelihoods/probabilities, i.e. expressing the conditionality of an occurrence. This is attributed to the fact that our analysis relies on secondary data, while a detailed impact analysis requires primary data.

Complementary Impact

Exports to China directly impact on a number of stakeholders in Cameroon. The first among which is the government who gets additional revenue in the form of royalties and various forms of taxes from the export of wood products and cotton provide to China. Though declining, export income from China amounted to more than CFAF80 billion in 2000. According to Global Forest Watch (2000), in 1998, the logging sector accounted for 28 per cent of non-petroleum export revenues. The government also benefits from cotton exports, especially as the production and export of cotton are overseen by a government parastatal – SODECOTON.[5] Exports to China, therefore contribute positively to Cameroon's fiscal balance, as well as the current account balance. Exports to China also provide direct benefits of jobs and more income to areas or localities where these commodities are harvested. The villages from which timber is exploited receive a fixed percentage of the royalties received from timber cutters. This is used to finance community projects in education, health, rural roads, water, etc. As the government tries to limit the export of timber, more jobs are created in the logging industry. Global Forest Watch (2000), reports that in 1998, roughly 55,000 people were directly or indirectly employed in the logging industry in Cameroon.

The import of cheap consumer goods from China is benefiting many Cameroonians, especially the middle and lower income groups. The gain is not only in the lower prices, but also the large variety of goods now accessible to a large portion of the population. There are certainly more welfare gains in importing a TV set from China than from France. Yet, there are persistent complaints about the lower quality of these goods compared to goods imported from the West or even those produced locally. But this is not enough to deter buyers, as the price-quality ratio favours Chinese imported goods. The manufacturing sector, especially small- and medium-sized enterprises are also benefiting directly from cheap capital and intermediary inputs from China. The machinery, transport and other equipment commodity group is one of the fast-growing import categories from China. From only about CFAF5 billion in 2001, imports in this category rose to almost CFAF25 billion in 2005. The cost of production is substantially reduced, thus making such firms more competitive.

The government is expected to gain and also lose from increased imports from China. The gain is in terms of increased revenues from import tariffs. The loss is due to foregone income tax from those losing their jobs, and also tax from firms closing down because of competition from Chinese imports. The extent of the net effect can only be got from a detailed survey of SMEs producing similar items. China's insatiable demand for primary commodities has raised their international prices, thus indirectly increasing Cameroon's export income, even for commodities not exported to China like crude oil. A barrel of crude oil is now selling for more than US$100, partly as a result of China's demand. The rising prices of Cameroon's primary commodity exports and the falling prices of manufactured imports, poses a serious problem to the Cameroonian economy, as it risks being locked in the primary sector if this pattern of trade continues to grow. The cheap imports help to destroy the industrial sector while the primary sector is expanding thanks to the rising demand. If this is not checked, the prospects of industrialization will be compromised and the economy will be locked in the production of primary products.

Competitive Impact

Given that China and Cameroon mainly export manufactured and primary commodities, respectively, one would normally not expect any competition between these countries. However, it should be noted that Cameroon has the most developed manufacturing sector within the Central African sub-region, and exports a reasonable quantity of manufactured goods to countries like Gabon, Chad, Congo, Côte d'Ivoire and Togo. The share of industrial products in total exports stood at 26.5 per cent in 2002, down from 30.7 per cent in 2001 (INS 2004). It is in this sector that China is likely to pose a serious competitive challenge to Cameroon (and a threat to the budding industrial sector); especially concerning those commodities equally produced and consumed locally or exported by Cameroon. While cheap capital goods imports should have a positive direct complementary impact on local firms, the direct competitive impact might be deleterious. Firms in Cameroon, especially those producing similar goods to Chinese imports, are likely to face a lot of difficulties competing on the domestic market as the consumer goods from China are cheaper. So the firms might be winning and losing at the same time. On the balance, their survival depends on their ability to innovate and remain cost-competitive. However, if increased (low-priced) imports from China replace only high-priced imports from other sources, in the absence of local production, welfare should be increased.

Another likely group of losers from increased competition from Chinese imports is local labour and their trade unions. A number of firms are reducing wages and/or laying-off workers so as to remain competitive. Others are winding-up because they cannot compete with cheap Chinese imports, especially small businesses in clothing and footwear. This implies that many people are likely to lose their jobs because of competition from China. To better appreciate the indirect competitive impact of China, we examine the evolution of Cameroon's exports to the Central African sub-region (a traditional market for Cameroon's manufactured exports), and the impact on some specific commodities also exported by China to the sub-region.

As shown in Table 5.5, Cameroon's exports to the Central African sub-region declined sharply from CFAF105 billion to CFAF55 billion between 2003 and 2005; a reduction of more than 47 per cent within two years, following a steady increase up to 2003. Exports to the different countries in the sub-region followed the same trend. For all the countries under consideration, Cameroon's exports for 2003 were greater than for 2005. It is likely that competition from cheap Chinese exports may be responsible for dwindling exports within the sub-region. An examination of some specific products can better reveal the competitive impact of imports from China. We have selected two sets of products that are exported by both Cameroon and China within the Central African sub-region. These are perfumes/toiletries and batteries. Table 4.6 clearly indicates that Cameroon's export of these products declined sharply in the period under consideration. In 2005, total exports of perfumes/toiletries were not even a tenth of what they were in 2001 – declining by more than 90 per cent. The trend for battery exports is not much different – falling from CFAF2.3 billion to CFAF0.71 billion between 2003 and 2005.

Table 5.5: Cameroon's Exports to the Central African Sub-Region (Million CFAF)

	2001	2002	2003	2004	2005
Congo Republic	13,817	14,775	11,813	11,877	11,049
Gabon	11,477	12,994	24,866	19,904	15,009
Equatorial Guinea	7,328	6,881	17,646	15,702	9,544
Central African Republic	3,812	9,905	7,580	5,993	5,989
Chad	8,502	27,001	26,509	14,586	13,865
DR Congo	19,869	7,963	16,556	11,043	0
Sub-Regional Total	**64,805**	**79,515**	**104,971**	**79,104**	**55,455**

Source: INS – Institut National de Statistique (2004, 2006)

Table 5.6: Some Manufactured Exports of Cameroon (Million CFAF)

	2001	2002	2003	2004	2005
Total perfumes and toiletries	3,501	3,316	1,795	1,224	315
Total battery exports	47	1,884	2,275	781	706
Batteries to Gabon	- - - - -	- - - - -	1,324	617	472

Source: INS – Institut National de Statistique (2004, 2006)

A close examination of battery exports to Gabon (the hitherto main export market for made-in-Cameroon batteries), indicates a decline from 908 tonnes in 2003 to only 278 tonnes in 2005 – a drop reduction of more than 69 per cent (INS, 2004, 2006). A pack of four Size-AA batteries made in Cameroon (Hellesens) cost CFAF300, while a similar pack imported from China (Royal)[6] sells at just CFAF100; i.e. almost 67 per cent less despite incurring additional costs like custom duty, insurance, transport costs, etc. The price differential should be much larger in other markets in which batteries from the two countries are competing, as batteries from Cameroon would incur additional costs to enter those markets. Therefore, the manufacturing sector is losing as a result of Chinese competition, not only directly in the domestic market, but also indirectly in the sub-regional market – their backyard.

Conclusion

By and large, the European Union countries remain Cameroon's major trading partners, supplying on average about 45 per cent of imports and buying about 67 per cent of its exports. However, China's share of the Cameroonian market has been increasing rapidly in the last few years at the expense of European countries, especially France and Germany. China's share of imports increased from 2.7 to 5 per cent between 2001 and 2005, while that of France declined from 24.1 per cent to 17.7 per cent during the same period. China then moved from the seventh to become Cameroon's third import source. Exports to China have, however, been evolving in the opposite direction, consequently aggravating the trade deficit between the two countries. In 2005, China alone accounted for 82 per cent of Cameroon's total trade deficit. The emergence of China and its trade with Cameroon is gradually changing the latter's trade configuration. If the present trend should persist, China (and East Asia in general) might replace

France (and the EU) as Cameroon's main import source in the near future. We suspect that the trend in other sub-Saharan Africa countries might not be very different. This is an issue because goods imported from China pose a more competitive threat to locally manufactured goods than those from Europe, which are generally more expensive and allow some market space for local industry. It is common to find imports from China cheaper than locally-produced goods.

However, trade with China is providing Cameroonians with cheap and diverse consumption and capital goods, though issues of quality abound. These imports pose a competitive trade not only in the domestic market, but also in Cameroon's export market in the Central African sub-region. Wages and employment are also likely to be affected. Specialization in the export of primary commodities (due to rising global prices) and import of cheap manufactures from China risk undermining the industrial sector and locking Cameroon in primary activities. Trade with China presents both opportunities and challenges, and it is advisable for Cameroon (and other African countries) to systematically and regularly assess the nature and impact on their economies in view of maximizing the benefits and reducing the risks. Else, Chinese aid and infrastructural projects will overshadow other potentially damaging economic interactions with China, especially the effect of cheap imports on the industrialization process. Unfortunately, Cameroon did not offer alternative exchanges and productive capacity relations with China but simply switched from European countries to China. So it is not surprising to see the repetition of the same mistakes. It is even worse as Cameroon did not protect itself and its Small and Medium Enterprises (incentives and market) from the cheap imports, often poor-quality processed goods from China. As a result, Cameroon serves more as a spring – board for China to improve Chinese industries.

Notes

1. While in Cameroon, Hu Jintao demonstrated the largesse of the Chinese towards Cameroon with the signing of eight agreements, amounting to almost CFAF65 billion, made up of grants and soft loans.
2. Extracted from Hu Jintaos' speech in Cameroon (*Cameroon Tribune* 31 January 2007) — translated by the author from French.
3. Imports from Nigeria are essentially hydrocarbons – 99.7% of imports in 2005.
4. The large increase in imports from China is entirely consistent with China's increase in world exports, and especially to Africa. This is attributed to the increased competitiveness and variety of Chinese manufactured exports *vis-à-vis* the rest of the world. According to Sandrey (2007), exports to Africa increased from US$7 billion in 2003 to US$18.7 billion in 2005 – a nearly threefold increase.

5. French acronym for Cotton Development Company
6. Hellesens batteries are produced in Cameroon by PILCAM, while Royal batteries are produced by the China Royal Battery Company Ltd. There are about five different brands of batteries in Cameroon imported from China.

References

Amsden, A.H., 1989, *Asia's Next Giant: South Korea and Late Industrialization*, New York: OxfordUniversity Press.

Ben-David, D. and Loewy, M. B., 1998, 'Free-trade, growth, and convergence', *Journal of Economic Growth,* Vol. 3, pp. 143–70.

Broadman, H., 2007, 'Africa's Silk Road: China and India's New Economic Frontier', Washington, DC: The World Bank

Cameroon Tribune No 8778/4977 of Tuesday, 30 January 2007

Cameroon Tribune No 8780/4979 of Thursday, 1 February 2007

Cameroon Tribune No 8781/4980 of Friday, February 2, 2007

Fosu, A., 1990, 'Exports and Economic Growth: The African Case', *World Development,* Vol. 186, pp. 831-835.

Giles, J.A. and Williams, C. L., 2000, 'Export-led Growth: A Survey of the Empirical Literature and some Non-Causality Results. Part 1', *The Journal of International Trade and Economic Development,* Vol. 93, pp. 261–337.

Global Forest Watch, 2000 *An Overview of Logging in Cameroon: A Global Forest Watch Cameroon Report,* Washington, DC: World Resources Institute.

Harrison, A., 1996, 'Openness and growth: A time-series, cross-country analysis for developing countries', *Journal of Development Economics,* Vol. 48, pp. 419–447.

INS (Institut National de la Statistique), 2004, '*Annuaire Statistique du Cameroun 2004*', Yaoundé : INS.

INS (Institut National de la Statistique), 2006, '*Annuaire Statistique du Cameroun 2006*', Yaoundé : INS.

Jung, S.W., and Marshall, P. J., 1985, 'Exports, growth and causality in developing countries', *Journal of Development Economics,* Vol. 18, pp. 1–12.

Kaplinsky, R., 2007, 'The Impact of China and India on the Sub-Saharan Africa: A Methodological Framework', A Framework Paper for AERC Project on 'The Impact of Asian Drivers on Sub-Saharan Africa'.

Khan, S.A. and Baye, F. M., 2007, 'China-Africa Economic Relations: The case of Cameroon'. Case Study Report for the AERC project on 'The Impact of Asian Drivers on Sub-Saharan Africa'.

Krueger, A.O., 1995, *Trade Policies and Developing Nations,* Washington, DC: Brookings Institution.

Rodrik, D., 1999, The New Global Economy and Developing Countries: Making Openness Work, Washington, DC: Overseas Development Council.

Sandrey, R., 2007, 'The African Merchandise Trading Relationship with China', *Inside AISA*, Number 3 and 4, October/December.

Wade, R., 1990, *Governing the Market: Economic Theory and the Role of Government in East Asian Industrialization*, Princeton, New Jersey: Princeton University Press.

Wälde, K. and Wood, C., 2004, 'The Empirics of Trade and Growth: Where are the Policy Recommendations?' *International Economics and Economic Policy*, Vol. 1, pp. 275–292.

World Bank, 1993, *The East Asian Miracle: Public Policy and Economic Growth*, New York: Oxford University Press.

Yanikkaya, H., 2003, 'Trade Openness and Economic Growth: A Cross-Country Empirical Investigation', *Journal of Development Economics*, Vol. 72, pp. 57– 89.

Appendices

Table 5.A1: China and other Destinations of Cameroon's Exports (values – million CFAF; Shares – %)

	2002		2003		2004		2005	
	Value	Share	Value	Share	Value	Share	Value	Share
Spain	249,628	19.9	284,633	21.9	269,039	21.4	290,491	19.7
Italy	238,053	19.0	175,116	13.5	149,945	11.9	173,305	11.7
France	161,068	12.9	139,820	10.7	184,365	14.7	186,836	12.7
Holland	160,460	12.8	138,133	10.6	111,575	8.9	112,549	7.6
USA	84,987	6.8	98,044	7.5	94,669	7.5	98,871	6.7
China	54,197	4.3	56,932	4.4	33,134	2.6	36,221	2.5
Belgium	26,625	2.1	32,677	2.5	50,760	4.0	60,671	4.1
Taiwan			34,256	2.6	15,901	1.3	14,592	1.0

Source: INS – Institut National de Statistique (2004 and 2006)

Table 5.A2: Composition of Exports to China (Million CFAF)

Description	2000	2001	2002	2003	2004	2005
Crude oil	69,603	68,565	39,954	33,879	0	0
Raw cotton	0	0	65	12,244	21,457	26,917
Rough wood	9,351	3,994	7673	3,598	3,437	5,463
Simply worked wood	1,818	2,861	6,041	6,814	7,514	2,498
Wood chips and waste	47	169	438	357	275	688
Other exports	0	30	26	40	451	655
Total	**80,819**	**75,619**	**54,197**	**56,932**	**33,134**	**36,221**

Source: INS – Institut National de Statistique (2004 and 2006)

Table 5.A3: China and other Sources of Cameroon's Imports (values - million CFAF; Shares - %)

	2002		2003		2004		2005	
	Value	Share	Value	Share	Value	Share	Value	Share
France	314,780	24.3	227,749	18.2	285,746	20.9	269,611	17.7
Nigeria	139,084	10.7	158,372	12.7	204,399	15.0	320,521	21.0
USA	108,433	8.4	59,316	4.7	67,050	4.9	70,581	4.6
Japan	58,691	4.5	70,882	5.7	58,746	4.3	59,316	3.9
China	46,331	3.6	50,331	4.0	58,332	4.3	75,796	5.0
Belgium	51,866	4.0	49,166	3.9	62,284	4.6	56,134	3.7
Germany	60,511	4.7	44,863	3.6	58,615	4.3	55,121	3.6
Italy	43,277	3.3	39,485	3.2	36,467	2.7	41,247	2.7
Holland	36,233	2.8	37,315	3.0	28,971	2.1	36,324	2.4

Source: INS – Institut National de Statistique (2004 and 2006)

Table 5.A4: Composition of Imports from China (Million CFAF)

Description	2000	2001	2002	2003	2004	2005
Cereals	14,748	17,734	23,648	14,757	10,229	5
Footwear and accessories	1,381	1,519	1,587	5,650	9,840	8,513
Machines, electrical and mechanical components	2,907	3,219	5,053	6,772	9,015	13,389
Road vehicles; tractors	424	492	898	2,000	3,596	6,913
Ceramic products	795	1,624	1,739	2,360	3,651	5,487
Manufactures of metals	1,066	1,000	1,341	1,641	2,096	3,550
Plastic materials	530	929	1,034	1,233	1,501	3,526
Fish and shell fish	0	18	162	360	162	2,574
Rubber	589	670	735	1,180	1,863	3,260
Travel goods, leather articles etc	1,072	1,207	982	1,590	1,794	3,183
Synthetic or artificial fibres	596	929	388	661	1,327	2,320
Medical equipments etc.	426	516	914	842	991	1,881
Pharmaceutical products	468	464	671	586	602	1,633
Clothing accessories	201	946	320	599	974	1,592
Photographic apparatus and optical goods, etc	864	598	0	1,147	1,059	1,280
Diverse chemical products	106	192	357	684	706	1,267
Other textiles and confectionaries	368	303	557	813	842	1,088
Other Imports	4,933	4,269	5,945	7,456	8,194	14,335
Total	31,474	36,629	46,331	50,331	58,442	75,796

Source: INS – Institut National de Statistique (2004 and 2006)

Table 5.A5: Trade Balance with Trading Partners and Regions (million CFAF)

	2001	2002	2003	2004	2005
Spain	172,273	230,419	268,971	250,443	271,118
Italy	305,544	194,776	135,631	113,478	132,058
France	-190,159	-153,712	-87,929	-101,381	-82,775
Holland	90,464	124,227	100,818	82,604	76,225
USA	-80,561	-23,446	38,728	27,619	28,290
China	38,990	7,866	6,601	-25,198	-39,575
Belgium	-33,241	-25,241	-16,489	-11,524	4,537
Taiwan	101,958	10,905	32,387	14,289	13,012
India	3,830	1,319	-13,720	-4,918	-12,803
Germany	-83,097	-42,523	-30,021	-47,072	-41,301
Nigeria	-179,713	-128,580	-148,703	-191,346	-312,165
Japan	-60,536	-57,880	-58,278	-57,312	-47,102
UK	-11,191	-23,738	1,594	25,161	47,623
EU	219,583	250,822	220,280	264,438	402,772
North America	-89,534	-37,613	29,819	23,799	18,519
East Asia	68,277	-56,615	-61,109	-100,229	-148,914
Africa	-202,140	-128,075	-104,800	-165,495	-248,740
Latin America	-10,021	-23,284	-7,436	-35,439	-56,995

Source: INS – Institut National de Statistique (2004 and 2006)

PART TWO

**Trade and Industrial Policy:
Regional and International Context**

PART TWO

Trade and Industrial Policy:
Regional and International Context

6

EU-Africa Economic Partnership Agreements: Risks, Rewards and Requisites for Agricultural Trade and African Development

Aderibigbe S. Olomola

Introduction

The European Union (EU) and the African, Caribbean and Pacific (ACP) countries have been involved in the negotiation of Economic Partnership Agreements (EPAs) as established in the Cotonou agreement. The EPAs were to be negotiated during a 5-year preparatory period which was to end on 31 December 2007 such that the agreement would come into force on 1 January 2008. The negotiations which began in September 2002 entered the substantive phase in 2006 in various areas including agriculture. Events have shown that conclusions could not be reached by the end of 2007 (Olomola 2008). In the negotiations, ACP countries are split into six regional groups out of which four, which fall within Africa (West Africa, Eastern and Southern Africa, Central Africa and Southern Africa Development Community), will be the focus of attention in this paper. For Africa, negotiations involving agriculture are very crucial since agriculture remains the foundation of most African economies and African peoples' livelihoods. Indeed, sustainable development of trade in agriculture is expected to lead to sustainable development of the economies of African countries.

Though there are variations, the level of dependence on agriculture appears to be high in all the regions of Africa. As shown in Table 7.1, the share of agriculture in total GDP averaged 33.5 per cent between 2000 and 2004 in West Africa. The number of people employed in agriculture stood at an average of 65 per cent during the period, while the average number of undernourished people was 24.7 per cent of the total population. In Eastern/Southern Africa, agriculture's share in total GDP averaged 27.7 per cent between 2000 and 2004. The proportion of people employed in agriculture stood at an average of 72.6 per cent and was the highest during the period. The proportion of undernourished people was also the highest, being an average of 37.7 per cent of the total population. In Central Africa, the share of agriculture in total GDP averaged 30.1 per cent between 2000 and 2004. The number of people employed in agriculture stood at an average of 60.4 per cent during the period while the average number of undernourished people was 32.3 per cent of the total population. In Southern Africa, the share of agriculture in total GDP is the least with an average of 17.4 per cent between 2000 and 2004. The number of people employed in agriculture stood at an average of 50.3 per cent during the period while the average number of undernourished people was 30.1 per cent of the total population (Table 6.1). Despite the high level of dependence on agriculture, the performance of the sector is still very low judging by the high level of under-nourishment among the population. Food is still not generally available at affordable prices.

The significance of agricultural export earnings and the contribution of individual commodities also vary considerably in the various sub-regions. Between 1995 and 2000, coffee accounted for 83 per cent of export earnings in Uganda, 76 per cent in Burundi and 62 per cent in Ethiopia. In Malawi, tobacco made up 59 per cent of export earnings, while sugar accounted for 87 per cent of the earnings in the Gambia. During the same period, Guinea Bissau derived 83 per cent of its export earnings from cashew nut and in Somalia livestock accounted for 55 per cent of the export earnings. In Seychelles, fish made up 59 per cent of the export earnings (Table 6.2). The significance of agricultural trade has continued to grow over the last few years and many African economies are becoming increasingly agricultural commodity-dependent.

In West Africa, the share of agricultural export in total export earnings between 2001 and 2003 stood at 79.7 per cent in Guinea Bissau, followed by Burkina Faso (69 %), Chad (60.2 %), and Cote d'Ivoire (55 %). The ratio of agricultural export to agricultural GDP is exceptionally high in the case of Cote d'Ivoire (89.5 %), which is the largest producer of cocoa in the world. In Central Africa, Sao Tome and Principe – a country dependent on more than one commodity export earnings – appears to be the only country where agricultural export is significant in relation to agricultural GDP and in terms of its contribution to total GDP.

Table 6.1: Indicators Related to Agriculture and Development in Africa

EPA Region	Share of Labour Force in Agriculture (%) (2000-2004)	Degree of Under-nourishment (%) (2001-2003)	Share of Agriculture in Total GDP (%) (2000-2004)
West Africa	65.0	24.7	33.5
Eastern/ Southern Africa	72.6	37.7	27.7
Central Africa	60.4	32.3	30.1
Southern Africa	50.3	30.1	17.4

Adapted from Kasteng, 2006.

In East Africa, the share of agricultural export in total export earnings is well over 50 per cent, especially in Burundi, Tanzania, Somalia, Ethiopia and Djibouti. It is only in Kenya that the ratio of agricultural exports to agricultural GDP is more than 50 per cent. In Southern Africa, Malawi is the most agriculture-dependent country, with its agricultural export having a massive share of about 95 per cent of total exports in the same period. Relative to agricultural GDP, agricultural export is significant in Botswana, Mauritius, Malawi, Namibia, South Africa and Swaziland (Olomola 2007). The EU is a major export destination for many commodities from the various EPA regions in Africa. The West Africa EPA region is the largest exporter of agricultural products to the EU (32.3 %), followed by Eastern and Southern Africa (24.9 %), and Southern Africa (22.6 %). Lower levels of export are recorded in the Caribbean (11.0 %), Central Africa (6.2 %) and the Pacific (4.0 %). Between 2000 and 2004 exports to the EU followed an increasing trend from the various EPA regions although the increase has been at different rates ranging from 14.6 per cent in the Caribbean to 61.1 per cent in West Africa. Of all the EPA regions, West Africa is by far the largest destination for EU agro-food exports (47.5 %) while exports to the Pacific are by far the smallest (0.1 %). The existing trade regime as entrenched in the Cotonou agreement has tended to support positive trade balance in favour of all the EPA regions (with the exception of Central Africa) during the period (Table 6.3).

Nonetheless, concern is growing about the ability of African countries to compete effectively in the international market and maintain a positive trade balance in the context of the on-going negotiations for EU-Africa EPAs and the paradigm shift in the trade relationship between the EU and

Table 6.2: Countries Dependent on Agricultural Commodities for Export Earnings Annual Average Export Data US$, 1995-2000

S/N		>50 (%) of export earnings		20-49 (%) of export earnings		10-19 (%) of export earnings	
1	Cocoa			Sao Tome & Principe[a]	48		
				Cote d'Ivoire	28		
				Ghana[a]	27		
2	Coffee	Burundi[a]	76	Rwanda[a]	48	Madagascar[a]	15
		Ethiopia	62			Kenya[a]	13
		Uganda	83			Tanzania[a]	16
						Congo, Dem. Rep[a]	11
						Central African Republic[a]	11
3	Cotton			Burkina Faso	41	Togo 17	
				Chad[a]	37	Central African	
				Benin	34	Republic[a]	12
				Mali[a]	34	Tanzania[a]	11
4	Tobacco	Malawi	59	Zimbabwe	29		
5	Tea			Kenya[a]	24	Burundi[a]	12
				Rwanda[a]	21		
6	Vanilla			Comoros	35		
7	Sugar	Gambia[a]	87	Mauritius	23	Swaziland[a] 18	
		Djibouti[x]	45				
8	Cashew Nut	Guinea Bissau	83				
9	Livestock	Somalia	55			Chad[a]	18
						Mali[a]	18
						Sudan	14
						Niger[a]	14
						Namibia[a]	12
						Djibouti[a]	17
10	Fish	Seychelles	59	Mozambique	32	Namibia[a]	19
				Sao Tome and Principe[a]	30	Cape Verde	19
				Madagascar[a]	30	Gambia[a]	15
				Senegal	30	Mauritania[a]	14
				Sierra Leone[a]	25	Morocco	11

Source: Adapted from: DFID 2004, 'Rethinking Tropical Agricultural Commodities', August.

its former colonies. EPAs require reciprocity – that the ACP countries open their markets to EU exports – whereas they previously enjoyed non-reciprocal preferential access to EU markets. For many of these ACP countries, which are least developed, this poses very significant challenges. Greater challenges are even to be expected by non-LDC countries that seem to have no genuine alternatives at the moment. In general, the EPAs negotiations present both an opportunity and a threat for the ACP countries.

Table 6.3: EU Average Trade with the EPA Regions (2000-2004) in US$1,000

EPA Region	Exports to the EU	(%)	Change (2000-2004) (%)	Imports from the EU	(%)	Change (2000-2004) (%)	Trade Balance
West Africa	3,003,184	32.3	+61.1	1,937,373	47.5	+41.4	+1,065,811
Eastern & Southern Afr.	2,315,184	24.9	+14.7	396,825	9.7	-14.9	+1,918,359
Central Afr.	484,048	5.2	+14.9	530,818	13.0	+43.9	-46,770
Southern Afr.	2,104,796	22.6	+73.9	766,743	18.8	+72.1	+1,338,053
Caribbean	1,025,656	11.0	+14.6	439,341	10.8	+2.6	+583,315
Pacific	375,796	4.0	+20.1	5,961	0.1	+75.7	+369,835
ACP Total	**9,308,664**	**100**	**+39.7**	**4,077,061**	**100**	**+35**	**+5,231603**

Source: Kasteng, 2006. Based on UN Comtrade Statistics.

The opportunity is to expand their exports to the EU, increase earnings and stimulate development; while the threat lies in a possible destruction of domestic industries from an influx of cheap imports from the EU. The need, therefore, arises to identify the key areas of adjustment and the types of adjustment which will possibly yield desired outcomes given the level of development and available resources. Specifically, the objectives of this paper are (i) to determine the potential impacts of the EU-Africa EPAs, through a critical review of contemporary literature on this subject, (ii) examine the risks and challenges of agricultural FTAs, (iii) undertake a comparative analysis of the approaches to agricultural liberalization in EU FTAs in selected countries with a view to drawing lessons for successful EU-Africa EPAs, and (iv) proffer a configuration of agricultural liberalization for EU-Africa EPAs that will ensure a 'win-win' paradigm of agricultural trade and genuine partnership for African development.

Review of the Potential Impact of the EU-Africa EPA

The theory of economic integration stipulates that an EPA should have a number of economic effects. Most importantly, an EPA involves preferential trade arrangement with two basic trade effects, one in which trade between partner countries expands in accordance with international comparative advantage, and the other in which trade between countries expands as a result of the preferential treatment given to imports from within the region as compared to those from the rest of the world. The former effect has been identified as 'trade creation', where domestic products are substituted by imports of lower-cost goods produced by a country's partner, and the latter as 'trade diversion', which stands for the shift in imports from the least-cost exporter to the more expensive product from the partner nation (Viner 1950).Trade creation is associated with a welfare gain as it means a shift from an inefficient to an efficient source of supply.

Trade diversion, on the other hand, is associated with a welfare loss, as it means a shift in imports from an efficient to an inefficient source of supply. In the case of ACP imports, this would translate into a substitution of non-preferred products from, for instance, the United States or Japan, by preferred EU imports. While this categorization is a helpful description of the effects of the formation of a Free Trade Agreement (FTA), it depicts only part of the economic effects of such an arrangement. Further likely effects are, for example, losses in tariff revenues due to the preferential tariff elimination; economies of scale due to an enhanced economic market; terms of trade effects due to changes in relative export and import prices; as well as dynamic effects, such as gains from increased competition, capital inflows and the transfer of external technology. A country that enters an EPA may experience a welfare gain or loss, depending on the country's unique situation. As a consequence, the impact of the EPAs on individual ACP countries has to be analysed empirically (Borrmann et al 2005). So far, only a few empirical studies have examined the likely impact the EPAs could have on trade flows or government revenue and various economic and financial indicators in Africa.

Bussolo (1999) analysed the welfare impact for and policy options of the South African Development Community (SADC) within a general equilibrium framework. His results indicate that – in comparison to the base run – a unilateral trade liberalization by SADC would be better by far in terms of real GDP growth rates than a regional EPA with the European Union. For Eastern Africa, McKay et al (2000), using a partial equilibrium model, estimated the (static) welfare impact of a regional EPA with the EU. In the case of a complete trade liberalization vis-à-vis the EU, Tanzania and Uganda are both likely to encounter a decline in welfare levels, though falling consumer prices, due to lower import prices and increased competition, are benefiting consumers in East Africa. By and large, their results are driven by the lost tariff revenue on EU imports. Like Bussolo, they point out that their findings have to be interpreted with caution, as severe data restrictions limit the choice of the model used and the reliability of the estimated effects.

Busse and Großmann (2004) estimated the trade effects and fiscal impact of the EPAs on West African countries using a partial equilibrium model. The model assumed that under the likely terms of any EPA agreement, tariffs facing EU exporters in West Africa are to be phased out over a period of twelve years from 2008 to 2020 and focused on the final stage, in which all tariff barriers have been eliminated. In the case of a complete tariff liberalization vis-à-vis EU imports in all West African countries, total imports from the EU are expected to increase in the mid-scenario in the range of 5.2 per cent (Guinea-Bissau) to 20.8 per cent (Nigeria). Apart from Nigeria, relatively high trade effects can be expected in Benin (increase in total imports by 1.6 %), Cape Verde (11.7 %), Senegal (11.5 %) and Togo (10.9 %). The reasons for this outcome are mainly above-average tariff rates for EU imports and/or relatively high import-duty collection-efficiency ratios. In absolute terms, the increase in total imports in Nigeria is by far the largest in West Africa, due to the magnitude of both overall and EU imports. Trade creation exceeds trade diversion (in absolute levels) in all scenarios and all West African countries. For trade creation, the increase in EU imports in the mid scenario ranges from 3.6 per cent in Mali to 12.5 per cent in Nigeria. Again, relatively high trade barriers vis-à-vis EU imports are the main reason for the larger trade effects in Nigeria. The trade diversion effects are somewhat smaller. From the perspective of non-preferred imports, the largest decline can also be expected in Nigeria with a decrease of US$229 million or 7.6 per cent.

Apart from the impact on trade flows, the tariff elimination will lead to a decline in import duties and, hence, total government revenue. In absolute terms, the decline in import duties in the mid scenario ranges from US$2.2 million in Guinea-Bissau to US$487.8 million in Nigeria. As a share of total import duties, the decrease will be largest in Cape Verde with a decline of 79.9 per cent. More importantly, import duties can be a significant source of total government revenue. A considerable decline would affect the revenues of West African governments and their ability to provide public goods. From this perspective, Cape Verde and Gambia will be particularly affected with an estimated decline in total government revenue, in the mid-scenario, of 19.8 and 21.9 per cent, respectively. As a share of

GDP, the percentage figures for both countries amount to 4.1 and 3.5, which are very large numbers. Based on these calculations, both countries would face a severe impact on their economies. The reasons for the far above average (relative) decline in import duties and government revenues are Cape Verde's and Gambia's relatively large share of EU imports to their GDP, their dependence on import duties to finance public expenditures and their relatively high collection efficiency ratios. In contrast to Cape Verde and Gambia, the overall impact on government revenue would be somewhat smaller in other West African countries. Still considerable effects can be expected in Ghana and Senegal with a decline in government revenue in the magnitude of 10 to 11 per cent. Given that these countries already have relatively large budget deficits, the importance of the impact of the EPA on government revenue becomes clearly visible.

The results clearly indicate that a few product categories are sensitive in almost all West African countries with respect to changes in trade flows. More specifically, apparel and clothing, other made up textile articles, and footwear, gaiters and the like will be highly affected by an EPA. To a lesser degree, but still considerably affected are: sugars and sugar confectionery, preparations of cereal, flour, starch/milk, essential oils and resinoids, soap and organic surface-active agents, manufactures of straw, esparto and other, cotton, carpets and textile floor coverage, knitted or crocheted fabrics, cars, trucks, motorbikes, furniture, bedding, mattress, and toys, games and sports requisites. For these products, the changes in total imports, measured in absolute and relative terms, are far above average. According to Busse and Großmann (2004), the estimated trade effects occur only if European exporters lower their export prices in line with the tariff elimination. If EU exporters engage in anti-competitive behaviour as they gain market power in the aftermath of trade liberalization either individually or collectively, they may leave market prices unchanged and increase their profits instead. In this circumstance, ECOWAS countries will lose import duties without gaining the advantage of lower import prices. Thus, economic welfare would definitely decline. In general, this outcome is more likely to occur in less competitive markets. Other studies, for example, Bussolo (1999) and McKay et al (2000), which analyse the welfare impact of the EPAs on the South African Development Community (SADC) and Tanzania/Uganda respectively, support these results. The authors indicate that regional EPAs with the EU may lead to a decline in welfare levels, as the losses in tariff revenues exceed any gains from trade through lower import prices, and that a unilateral trade liberalization by African ACP countries would be far better for real GDP growth rates.

Recently, the impact searchlight has been beamed on Ghana to examine the development implications of the EU Economic Partnership Agreement (Patel 2007). The study shows that the potential benefit is limited in view of the liberalization policies already put in place by the Ghanaian government and conclude that (i) Ghanaian firms will be unable to withstand competition from EU imports (ii) EPA will constrain industrial policy and jeopardise future development and (iii) EPA will worsen the performance of the agricultural sector (see Box 6.1). These results indicate that both LDCs and non-LDC African ACP countries need to face considerable challenges if they comply with the so-called WTO compatible reciprocal liberalization policies inherent in the EPAs.

Box 6.1: Potential Impact of EPA on Non-LDCs: The Case of Ghana

Potential Benefits

In theory, liberalization could benefit Ghanaian domestic sectors that are heavily dependent on imported capital goods for their production, if the price of these inputs were to decrease due to the lowering of tariffs. However, the potential benefit of this are likely to be low for Ghana because the government has already liberalized unilaterally and applies a tariff of between 0-5 per cent for raw materials and capital goods. Ghanaian firms also have access to tariff concessions, which are applied on imported inputs into nominated end-uses, such as agricultural implements and machinery, fishing nets and pharmaceuticals. Eliminating tariffs against imported EU goods might also mean cheaper (imported) goods for Ghanaians. However, this depends on traders passing on lower prices to consumers. This potential benefit must also be seen in the context of the impact on production and broader long-term national development.

Adverse Effects

Inability to Withstand Industrial Competition from EU imports. The elimination of tariffs on EU imports will force many Ghanaian domestic producers to compete directly with EU firms. Although greater exposure to competition from imports can theoretically lead to greater innovation and efficiency gains if local firms are able to adapt, the ability of Ghanaian producers to compete with EU imports is highly constrained by the severe supply-side constraints they face. If tariff protection was removed, many Ghanaian producers would no longer remain profitable due to their much lower levels of industrial productivity and competitiveness, compared to the EU. While industrial development is a key part of Ghana's policies, domestic firms are still hindered by the lack of infrastructure and weak institutions, low levels of value-addition and the small-scale nature of production. *EPA Will Constrain Industrial Policy and Jeopardise Future Development.* Beyond the one-off effect of lowering tariffs, an EPA will also affect an ACP country's development by binding tariff liberalization. An EPA is likely to freeze the tariff reduction commitments made by African countries, meaning that countries will not easily be able to increase their tariffs once they have made commitments to lower them. Hence, it is crucial to remember that EPAs will have an impact both on a country's present and future prospects. Binding tariff levels impacts on a government's ability to use tariff policy as a means of encouraging production, sheltering industries and nurturing them to move up the 'value-chain' into areas where there is more value-added in the goods that are produced. Although tariff policy is not the only mechanism available to governments to help industrial development, it can be an important part of a government's policy strategy along with other instruments, including policies to improve infrastructure and human capital accumulation.

EPA will Worsen the Performance of the Agricultural Sector. If Ghana is forced to liberalize under the EPA, agricultural producers would be adversely affected by cheaper and (often heavily subsidized) EU agricultural exports. For example, in 2002 the EU spent over US$1 billion subsidizing dairy exports; over US$39.4 million in export subsidies for 132,2000 metric tonnes of milled rice; and roughly US$11.1 million on subsidies for wheat exports (Miencha 2005; USDA 2003). In the context of an FTA, these subsidized agricultural exports would lower the price of these products in Ghana, pushing domestic producers out of the market. Although liberalization has the potential to result in cheaper imports, the costs of losing Ghana's productive sectors to EU competition must be considered in terms of the country's dynamic, long-term development interests. Indeed, even the EU's own commissioned Sustainability Impact Assessment (SIA) Report states that if West African countries were forced to fully liberalize this would result in import surges in the agro-industry. The estimates are that imports would increase by 16 per cent for onions, 15 per cent for potatoes, 16 per cent for beef, and 18 per cent for poultry.

Source: Adapted from Patel, 2007

Risks and Challenges of Agricultural FTAs

Free trade agreements in agriculture often emphasize the promise that all farmers will find prosperity by increasing their export market shares. By and large, the free trade model in agriculture is flawed and has been regarded as one of the major causes of hunger and poverty around the world. Indeed, farmers do not export, multinational corporations do. Instead of leading to prosperity for farmers, free trade has driven an export-led corporate model of agriculture that has substantially increased the dumping of agricultural commodities onto world markets at below the cost of production. Moreover, small-scale farmers, who make up about 70 per cent of the population in some of the poorest countries in the world, cannot compete with these below-cost imports. In many cases, these farmers can no longer support themselves on their land, and are forced to migrate to other areas in search of a better life. Agribusiness groups have flourished under the free trade system while farmers in developing countries have been losing out. The world has increasingly witnessed the consolidation of the food and agriculture system of developed countries at the expense of small farmers, healthy food and rural communities in Africa (see Olson and Spieldoch 2007). The lessons from the Indian experience on free trade are not in any way encouraging to any African ACP country. Agricultural liberalization in particular has resulted in deleterious consequences for Indian agriculture and farmers (see Box 6.2).

Box 6.2: Free Trade and Indian Agriculture

Agriculture constitutes a vital part of India's economy and of its workforce. India started trade liberalization reforms in agriculture in the 1990s and is a founding member of WTO, signing its various agreements including the 'Agreement on Agriculture'. This latter agreement especially was about reducing domestic support/subsidies by developed countries while reducing tariff and non-tariff barriers by developing countries to enhance market access and more open trade in agriculture across countries .Consequently, along with many other developing countries, India reduced tariffs and import duties, and also removed quantitative restrictions on agricultural import while, on other hand, total domestic farm support provided by developed countries has not shown any significant decline. In United States, subsidy to 90,000 farmers has increased 700 times since 1996. Meanwhile, India's domestic support to her 600 million farmers is actually negative to what she is allowed to provide under AoA. With such scenario, international prices of many agricultural commodities went to their lowest limit in international markets and the Indian market started getting flooded with cheap imports which increased by 300 per cent in value terms between 1996-97 and 2003-04. On the other hand, India's export actually declined from 1995 to 2001 with marginal recovery in recent years. A poor Indian farmer, with minimal domestic support cannot compete with heavily subsidized products from developed countries. Hence, more than 25,000 farmers committed suicide from indebtedness and many farmers started moving to urban areas as unskilled labour, leading to steady decline in agricultural workforce and the sector's share in GDP. Consequently, there is deceleration in output of all agricultural produce touching its lowest limit in recent years, threatening food security and self-sufficiency of the country.

Sources: *(http://www.wto.org/English/docs_e/legal_e/ursum_e.htm)(http://www.twnside.org.sg/title/2099.htm) (http://www.icrier.org/pdf/WPper cent20177.pdf) (http://www.oxfam.org.au/campaigns/mtf/povertyhistory/docs/sharmapaper.pdf) (http://www.navdanya.org/dwd/dwd/news/04july15.htm)*

Given the fact that many people in Africa heavily depend on agriculture for their livelihood, it is important to identify the risks and challenges inherent in the EU-Africa EPA with a view to making necessary remedial measures that will be advanced in the continuing EPA negotiations for ultimate entrenchment in the agreements. If the negotiations are to proceed in such a way as not to worsen the economic and social conditions of African countries, the following risks and challenges must be considered.

EPAs Will Expose African Countries to Devastating EU Competition

Least developed countries (LDCs) are normally exempt from reciprocity in the WTO. However, if they accept to join a Free Trade Area as currently defined by Article XXIV of GATT, they must also commit to maximizing the elimination of their trade barriers. Although the EU made a widely published gesture to offer all LDCs duty and quota-free access to the European market through the so-called 'Everything but Arms' initiative of 2001, under EPAs, as currently foreseen, LDCs will be denied the preferences and be required to open their markets. If forced to liberalize, agricultural producers would be adversely affected by cheaper and (often heavily subsidised) EU agricultural exports.

Although liberalization has the potential to result in cheaper imports, the costs of losing Africa's productive sectors to EU competition must be considered in terms of the region's dynamic, long-term development interests. In the case of West Africa, for instance, even the EU's own commissioned Sustainability Impact Assessment (SIA) Report (2004) states that if the countries were forced to fully liberalize, this would result in import surges in the agro-industry. The estimates are that imports would increase by 16 per cent for onions, 15 per cent for potatoes, 16 per cent for beef, and 18 per cent for poultry. These sectors identified by the report must not be viewed as the only ones that are likely to be adversely affected by liberalization – the SIA report excluded several fruits and vegetable products from their analysis due to the lack of available price data. With such an undue competition, there will be little incentive for African producers to diversify into more 'value-added' products, or for entrepreneurs to invest in developing new capacity, given the uncertain domestic and regional markets for products competing with EU imports. This could exacerbate the primary commodity export dependency syndrome, and thus limit the prospects for industrialization and job creation.

African Countries Will Face Substantial Adjustment Costs

Many African countries have not fully recovered from the debilitating impact of commodity crises, structural adjustment, debt, the HIV pandemic and war. They are, therefore, not in a position to provide the fabulous financial resources that will be required to address the supply constraints and to provide the social and other compensatory measures which will be necessary in the event of exposure to competition with EU imports. Meanwhile, the EU has not agreed to make sufficient commitments for the additional resources that will be needed during the preparation, establishment and the operation of the EU-Africa Free Trade Areas. In other words, African countries are expected to make immense commitments without any assurance of being able to pay for them. Indeed, a recent study of Ghana concludes that under the funding programme of the European Development Fund (EDF) for the period 2008-2013 (which will be a crucial period for adjustment if an EPA is signed), African countries will receive no extra resources for EPA support. This coupled with slow disbursement rates and operational weaknesses of the EDF funding mechanism, has raised considerable doubts about whether the EU's promise of aid for trade will be meaningfully delivered in the context of EPAs (see Patel 2007).

Reduction in Government Revenue is a Major Obstacle to Development

The elimination of tariffs will have important implications for government revenue as many African countries rely heavily on import taxes for their fiscal income. Removing this source of income will dramatically reduce African countries' spending abilities and institutional capacity and will require investments in alternative tax systems. Even then it is not certain that alternative tax systems in some countries can provide an equal amount of government revenue. In any case, additional financial resources will be needed for the sustained support of fiscal restructuring processes in Africa.

A study conducted by the Common Market for East and Southern Africa, a regional trade bloc, in 2002 found that if all EU imports entered that region duty-free, governments would lose about 25 per cent of their trade taxes and about 6 per cent of total tax revenue. Another study, by Germany's Hamburg Institute of International Economics, estimated that declines in import duties in countries of the ECOWAS would range from the equivalent of $2.2 million in Guinea-Bissau to $487.8 million in Nigeria. The decline would be sharpest in Cape Verde, where 80 per cent of import revenues are likely to be lost. If no adjustments on spending were made, Cape Verde and the Gambia would incur budget deficits of 4.1 and 3.5 per cent, respectively. On average, ECOWAS countries are highly dependent on import duties, which account for 14.7 per cent of government revenue and 2.5 per cent of GDP (see ECDPM 2006). In Ghana, specifically, import duties account for 15.5 per cent of total government revenue. It has been estimated that EPA liberalization would result in a potential loss of about US$90 million in government revenue in Ghana. This is equivalent to 1.8 per cent of GDP and 10.3 per cent of government expenditure (Busse et al 2004). The removal of tariffs will slash African ACP governments' budgets and very likely hit spending on health and education. For example, Burundi's potential loss of US$ 7.6 million in tax revenue is equivalent to losing a dollar per person in social spending. Zambia is predicted to lose US$15.8 million – equal to the government's annual spending on HIV/AIDS (Powel 2007).

Reciprocity is Unjustified on Account of Preference Erosion

Trade preferences for African countries are further being eroded through WTO-led liberalization and other bilateral schemes between the EU and third countries, which has resulted in improved market access for non-ACP developing countries. The value of the existing ACP preferences has diminished as a result of the reform of the European Common Agriculture Policy (CAP). Access to EU markets has proved to become more difficult due to tight rules of origin and a variety of non-trade barriers, including strengthened Sanitary and Phyto-Sanitary (SPS) measures. In other words, the value of the existing market access that the ACP countries are expected to pay for at a high cost, is continuously declining.

Threat to African Industrial Development

The deals will allow African markets to be flooded with subsidised European products. This will damage the development of value-added goods, including sectors such as agro-processing, clothing and textiles (often seen as the basis of industrialization), while hitting small and medium producers and poor workers. ACP negotiators are concerned that in the short term, their industries will be unable to compete with European companies, and that in the long term this could undermine the economic sectors upon which their future economic development could rest. Bilateral trade rules set at the WTO state that countries should eliminate 90 per cent of trade barriers over a period of around ten years. There is a fierce debate about how flexible these rules are in terms of the percentage of trade African countries would have to open, and the timescale over which it would occur. But the bottom line is that through EPAs, African countries have to open up, and at a pace dictated by WTO rules rather than their development needs.

EPA Will Undermine Regional Integration

EPAs are being negotiated between the EU and six regional groupings – the Caribbean, the Pacific, East Africa, West Africa, Southern Africa and Central Africa. Strengthening regional trade is important, particularly in Africa, to help small economies grow. However, the EPA groupings threaten to fracture home-grown attempts to pursue regional integration. The first potential problem is that least-developed countries already have market access into the EU through the 'Everything but Arms' agreement. They therefore have little incentive to join an EPA, because it asks them to open their markets but gives them little in return. Given that less-developed countries make up three quarters of African nations, this is a major obstacle threatening to split poor countries from their richer, regional neighbours. The second potential problem is that the EPA negotiating groups do not match existing African regional groups, and in fact overlap. The aim of regional integration is to have a common external tariff, which requires a regional coherence of African trade policies (in the same way that the EU has its own 'common market'). But having overlapping loyalties – one to an EPA regional group, the other to another African regional group – undermines this.

Following further trade liberalization, existing processes of regional co-operation and integration between ACP countries will be hijacked, as the EU (i) enforces the tendency of narrowing down regional co-operation and integration processes to trade liberalization, (ii) forces the scope and pace of that liberalization, (iii) causes the break up of regional configurations, and (iv) wants to be part of any region through free trade agreements. Building up trade within Africa is more important than exporting to the EU. This is supposed to be a key aim of EPAs, but they are set to undermine it. Imports from the EU to Burkina Faso, for example, would increase by about 8 per cent or US$40 million, while also displacing Burkina Faso's exports to other West African countries, which would drop by more than 6 per cent (or US$2 million) as a result.

EPA Will Undermine Achievement of MDGs

The Millennium Development Goals (MDGs) were signed by 189 heads of states and governments in 2000. Midway through the 15-year time frame set for the achievement of the MDGs (as at 2007) the emerging picture is that though there is tremendous progress made by some African countries on some specific goals, most of the goals and targets are unlikely to be met by 2015 by many African countries unless there is renewed political will and citizen activism. With the notable exception of North Africa, most African countries are off the mark in the countdown to 2015. Achievement of the MDGs will be further severely constrained on account of the tax revenues that will be lost through trade liberalization. Many governments rely on the revenue they collect from trade tariffs. For example, in Uganda, trade taxes represent 48 per cent of total government revenue. The removal of tariffs on EU imports could reduce poor-country governments' revenues drastically, and thus adversely affect their spending on health, education and other essential services. The EU has failed to give a guarantee to African countries that it will make up for any revenue losses that EPAs bring about, thus creating further unease amongst the concerned governments.

Approaches to Agricultural Liberalization in EU FTAs

This section presents a comparative analysis of EU free trade agreements with selected countries – the Euro-Mediterranean Agreements involving seven trade partners (Tunisia, Morocco, Israel, Jordan, the Palestinian Authority, Algeria and Lebanon) as well as agreements with South Africa, Mexico and Chile as far as agriculture is concerned. The analysis is to be conducted to show the relevance and provide examples and options as to how best to structure the liberalization of agriculture within the on-going

EPA negotiations and to draw useful lessons. Since the first Euro-Mediterranean Conference in November 1995, the EU and twelve Mediterranean countries have been engaged in negotiating Association Agreements. The overall objective is to form, by 2010, one Euro-Mediterranean free trade area from the separate agreements in place. To date, bilateral Association Agreements have been concluded with seven trade partners: Tunisia (1995), Israel (1995), Morocco (1996), Jordan (1997), the Palestinian Authority (1997), Algeria (2001) and Lebanon (2002). The seven MED partners are heterogeneous with regard to agriculture. For instance, the agricultural sector generates a large proportion of GDP and employment in Morocco and Tunisia (14 % and 12 %, and 45 % and 29 %, respectively) compared to much lower figures in Israel (3 % and 4 %). The Products are mainly Mediterranean fruits and vegetables, potatoes, olives and olive oil and wine. The MED agreements aim at establishing a WTO-compatible free trade area for all products, with a transitional period of up to twelve years. Yet no specific liberalization roadmap has been defined for the agricultural sector as a whole. Specific concessions for liberalization have been determined for certain products only.

In South Africa the agricultural sector plays a minor role compared to the industrial sector in terms of GDP and employment (contributing 3 per cent and 4 per cent, respectively). South Africa's main agricultural product is maize, followed by sugarcane and wheat. Major export commodities are citrus fruits, cane sugar and wine. The EU and South Africa concluded their Trade, Development and Cooperation Agreement (TDCA) in 1999, and the TDCA has been provisionally in force since January 2000. Mexico's agricultural sector is characterized by a low share in GDP (4 per cent) but a high share in overall employment (45 %). The main Mexican products exported to the EU are coffee, vegetables and spirits. The major imports from the EU are oilseeds, dairy products and wine. Mexico initiated a major agricultural policy reform in the early 1990s affecting its most important crops, i.e. copra, cotton seed, barley, rice, soy, sorghum, sunflower, and wheat. Import controls and government direct price supports to producers were abolished, and subsidies to agricultural inputs, credit and insurance were drastically reduced. The EU and Mexico signed their Economic Partnership, Political Coordination and Cooperation Agreement, also known as the 'Global Agreement', in December 1997. The agreement came into force in October 2000.

Chile's agricultural sector contributes a relatively minor proportion of the country's GDP and employment (11 % and 14 %, respectively). Main agricultural products are cereals, fodder, sugar-beets, potatoes and vegetables. Due to the inverted growing season, fruits have become a particularly important product exported to northern countries. Wine has also gained increased status as a key export product. The EU-Chile Association Agreement which was signed in November 2002 has very detailed provisions on trade and also covers services, investment, government procurement, intellectual property rights, competition, customs procedures and, in annexed agreements, wine and spirits and SPS standards.

As shown in Table 6.4, six basic instruments are applied separately or in combination to achieve trade preferences for the countries involved in the various FTAs, beyond the provisions of WTO most-favoured-nations (MFN) status. They are:

   i.   Tariff concessions

   ii.   Tariff rate quota (TRQ) concessions

   iii. Safeguard clauses

   iv. Specific rules of origin for agricultural products

   v.   Options for flexible adjustment to a partner's market access

   vi. Other specifics which are topics not common to all agreements

It is also clear from Table 6.4 that domestic support is not part of the FTAs; thus, there are no domestic support-related provisions in the agreements. In all the agreements, the pattern of product coverage of liberalized imports into the EU reflects the degree of EU domestic protection and the risk or existence, of internal surpluses for the respective products. In this connection, three general rules apply: (i) high domestic production leads to a low willingness for tariff reduction, as this could undermine high domestic prices, (ii) high domestic production supplemented by risks of internal surpluses leads to additional restrictions on imports by not extending TRQs, and (iii) existing remarkable surpluses increase EU interest in improving its access to the markets of the contracting partner. Details of how these instruments apply to the various EU FTAs under review are presented in Table 6.4.

Table 6.4: Comparison of Instruments of EU Free Trade Agreements

Instruments for Trade Preferences	Euro-Mediterranean for Agreements	EU-South Africa (TDCA)	EU-Mexico Global Agreement	EU-Chile Association Agreement
1) Tariff Concessions	- Tariff concessions are not a central instrument. - Only the agreement with Lebanon defines concrete steps for tariff reductions by the EU trade partner, starting five years after the agreement enters into force	• The transition period for the completion of the tariff reduction schedule is twelve years on the side of South Africa and ten years on the EU side. • The reduction of duties takes place in six different reduction schemes in the case of the EU and four reduction schemes in the case of South Africa. Products whose de-nomination is protected within the EU are excluded from trade liberalization. This pertains especially to cheese and wine (Art. 13 and 9).	- The Global Agreement sets out a transition period of ten years for the implementation of all liberalization commitments. - As many as eight different liberalization schemes are defined for both the EU and Mexico. - In schedules which foresee complete liberalization, the longest transitional periods for the EU and Mexico are nine and ten years, respectively. - Products whose denomination is protected within the EU are excluded from trade liberalization. This pertains especially to cheese and wine (Art. 8, 10).	- The Association Agreement defines a transition period of maximum ten years for trade liberalisation of agricultural commodities and processed agricultural products. - There are four tariff elimination schedules in which the EU completely eliminates duties with transitional periods of zero, four, seven and ten years. In addition, duties are partially liberalized in four other product schemes (Art. 71). On the Chilean side, liberalization takes place in three schedules of zero, five and ten years, in which tariffs for the respective products are phased out completely.
2) Tariff Rate Quotas	- The most important quotas refer to some of the strategic products such as citrus fruits, tomatoes, apples, olive oil, cut flowers and wine - TRQs granted in favour of the EU mainly relate to cereals and sugar and corresponding products. - All agreements except that with Algeria define an increase of quota volume by 3 per cent per year, but just for some products.	- Tariff rate quota concessions are implemented for some of the products that are excluded from the overall liberalisation process. - Some quotas are established for those products that do not benefit from immediate liberalization. Annual growth rates are defined.	- Tariff rate quotas are conceded by the EU for imports originating in Mexico. - No annual growth rate is defined, but the contracting parties can make further concessions according to a review clause.	- An annual growth rate is specified per product. Quotas for meat increase by 10 per cent of the original quantity. The rest of the quotas increase by 5 per cent of the original quantity, except those for sugar confectionery, cocoa pre-parations and sweet biscuits, waffles and wafers, which do not increase.

Table 6.4: Comparison of Instruments of EU Free Trade Agreements (Continued)

Instruments for Trade Preferences	Euro-Mediterranean for Agreements	EU-South Africa (TDCA)	EU-Mexico Global Agreement	EU-Chile Association Agreement
3) Safeguard Clauses	-All agreements contain common safe-guard clauses, though there are no spe-cific agricultural safeguard provisions. -As for the EU's entry price system (EPS), which constitutes a special EU safeguard for fruits and vegetables, the agreement with Morocco is the only MED agreement that foresees a seasonal reduction of the EPS with respect to some favoured products. -The concessions are limited to certain periods of the year and defined quantities. -The agreed entry price is below the MFN entry price.	-Agriculture is integrated into a common safeguard clause which lays down requirements for applying the safeguards, applicable safeguard measures and procedures. -Compared with the other agreements, South Africa has achieved more flexibility to initiate so called 'Transitional Safeguard Measures' (Art. 25) during a transition period of twelve years. The TDCA contains no shortage clause.	Only a common safeguard clause exists (Art. 15). It describes the requirements for implementing safeguard measures, timeframes for consultation and the need for compensation. A shortage clause (Decision, Art. 16) defines conditions for justifying export restric-tions similar to GATT Article XI.	In addition to a common safe-guard and shortage clause (Art. 92 and 93), a special safeguard clause for agricultural products is defined and extended to processed agricultural products (Art. 73, called the emergency clause). The clause contains provisions for measures that may be applied in case of emergency (e.g. raising tariffs to the pre-liberalization level), as well as the timeframe for consultations before such measures enter into force (30 days) and regulations for imme-diate actions under exceptional circumstances (provisional measures for a maximum of 120 days).

Table 6.4: Comparison of Instruments of EU Free Trade Agreements (Continued)

Instruments for Trade Preferences	Euro-Mediterranean for Agreements	EU-South Africa (TDCA)	EU-Mexico Global Agreement	EU-Chile Association Agreement
4) Rules of Origin	-For agriculture-specific rules of origin, the general provisions apply. -Bilateral cumulation is valid for all MED agreements. No specific GIs are named.	-Some provisions concern the extension of 'origin' to countries which are not joining the FTA. Products containing components from other ACP countries are defined as originating in South Africa (and thus receive TDCA preferences) if the value added in South Africa exceeds the imported ACP value. Beyond the value requirement, products need not undergo additional working or processing in South Africa. -Any 'working or processing carried out within SACU shall be considered as having been carried out in South Africa, when further worked or processed there'. -Geographical indications are covered in the separate Agreement on Trade in Wine and the Agreement on Trade in Spirits.	-General provisions for qualification as originating product apply and bilateral cumulation is valid. -Geographical indications are tackled by the separate Agreement on the Mutual Recognition and Protection of Designation of Spirit Drinks. Mexico protects all European designations and the EU protects Tequila and Mezcal in accordance with existing domestic law.	-The general provisions for conferring goods to origin status apply and bilateral cumulation is applicable (Art. 1-6).

Table 6.4: Comparison of Instruments of EU Free Trade Agreements (Continued)

Instruments for Trade Preferences	Euro-Mediterranean for Agreements	EU-South Africa (TDCA)	EU-Mexico Global Agreement	EU-Chile Association Agreement
5) Options for flexible Adjust-ments	-Options for flexible adjustments are foreseen in the form of both the review and flexibility clauses applying to all agreements. -The review process terminates five years after the agreement enters into force. -In case of applying the flexibility clause, resulting disadvantages for one party shall be balanced by further concessions from the other.	-Options for flexible adjustments are included in the TDCA by means of both a review clause and a flexibility clause (Art. 18 and 20). The review clause states that within five years of the TDCA entering into force, further liberalisation steps shall be considered especially for those products that are excluded from total tariff reduction. The flexibility clause allows the parties, after agreement has been reached in the Cooperation Council, to amend the agricultural arran-gements in the TDCA as a result of changes in domestic agricultural policies. Yet it also requires that the party amending the arrangements make liberalisation concessions at an equivalent level on imports from the other party	Options for flexible adjustments are offered through a review clause (Art. 10). This review clause is much more precise than those in other agreements. The clause provides for further liberalisation of agricultural trade after an evaluation by the JointCouncil within the first three years of the agreement's enfor-cement. The Global Agreement also explicitly mentions a review of the TRQs (also within three years), as well as of the EU's protection of denomination (in accordance with developments in intellectual property rights). It further specifies that where appropriate' the relevant rules of origin shall be reviewed as well. No flexibility clause is included.	Options for flexible adjustments are integrated by means of a review clause (called the evolution clause), thus providing opportunities to further enhance liberalisation three years after the implementation of the agreement (Art. 74). No flexibility clause is included.

Table 6.4: Comparison of Instruments of EU Free Trade Agreements (Continued)

Instruments for Trade Preferences	Euro-Mediterranean for Agreements	Eu-South Africa (TDCA)	Eu-Mexico Global Agreement	Eu-Chile Association Agreement
6) Other Specifics	-For agriculture-specific rules of origin, the general provisions apply. -Bilateral cumulation is valid for all MED agreements. No specific GIs are named.	-Some provisions concern the extension of 'origin' to countries which are not joining the FTA. Products containing components from other ACP countries are defined as originating in South Africa (and thus receive TDCA preferences) if the value added in South Africa exceeds the imported ACP value. Beyond the value requirement, products need not undergo additional working or processing in South Africa. -Any 'working or processing carried out within SACU shall be considered as having been carried out in South Africa, when further worked or processed there'. -Geographical indications are covered in the separate Agreement on Trade in Wine and the Agreement on Trade in Spirits.	-General provisions for qualification as originating product apply and bilateral cumulation is valid. -Geographical indications are tackled by the separate Agreement on the Mutual Recognition and Protection of Designation of Spirit Drinks. Mexico protects all European designations and the EU pro-tects Tequila and Mezcal in accor-dance with existing domestic law.	-The general provisions for conferring goods to origin status apply and bilateral cumulation is applicable (Art. 1-6).

Source: European Centre for Development Policy Management (ECDPM) 2004

Emerging Lessons from the Comparative Analysis of Bilateral EU FTAs

A number of key messages are derived from the above analysis which can provide guidance as to the measures to be taken by African countries in negotiating the EPA with the European Union. They are summarized as follows.

Trade in agricultural products is far from being completely liberalized

The EU and its trading partners retain many tariff barriers concerning market access. So the agricultural parts of EU FTAs contend with the conflict of trade liberalization on the one hand and national interests to limit market access on the other hand. The analysis of the different EU FTAs shows that the EU excludes important products from the targeted free trade. The EU's domestic protection and support pattern for certain agricultural products can be identified as a key factor determining these exceptions. For those products that are excluded from liberalization, the EU grants important concessions by admitting market access within the limits of TRQs. Concerning the liberalization process, two different approaches for agriculture can be discerned.

Clear definition of the products that benefit from preferential market access (the MED agreements)

This approach limits the overall coverage of products. It defines the first steps of the liberalization process, though an overall roadmap is missing. Flexibility with respect to further steps to an advanced liberalization is granted by a review clause.

Definition of timetables for the overall liberalization process

The FTAs in respect of South Africa, Mexico, Chile and Lebanon for imports into the EU define timetables with differing start dates and lengths of the liberalization process. Again, important products are excluded and they are favoured by concessions within the limits of TRQs. Allocating agricultural products to different timetables or exemptions from free trade and restricting market access to TRQs increases the controllability of the liberalization process. Additional flexibility is achieved by review clauses concerning products that are exempted from free trade. Thus, though the agreements aim at liberalization, important agricultural products remain excluded from free trade. The main products excluded from liberalized import into South Africa are beef, swine, goats, sheep, sugar, some dairy (butter and other fats and oils derived from milk, dairy spreads, cheese and curd, ice cream, sweet corn, maize and maize products, barley and barley products, wheat and wheat products and chocolate. In the case of Mexico the main products include bovine animal, beef, swine, poultry, dairy, eggs, potatoes, bananas, cereals except buckwheat, roasted coffee, some oil and fats, (palm oil, cobra oil, animal fats or oil) sugar, cocoa, grape juice and grape most and rum; while the main products excluded from liberalized import into Chile are dairy, leguminous vegetables, sweet corn, wheat and meslin flour, wheat groats, and pellets of cereals, vegetable oil and margarine and sugar. With respect to agriculture the agreements with South Africa, Mexico and Chile cover a wider range of issues and products, especially those connected to trade of wine and spirits. The Chile agreement includes additional provisions concerning cooperation to enhance sustainable agriculture and capacity building, possibly providing ways to intensify bilateral relations beyond trade liberalization.

Flexible Rules of Origin

Especially in the case of South Africa, flexible cumulation of origin across a large number of third countries is a unique feature distinguishing the TDCA from other agreements. These lessons are taken into consideration in articulating the configuration of agricultural trade in respect of the EU-Africa economic partnership agreements in the following section. Essentially, the position of rigidity in the key elements of the negotiation should be vacated. There is need for flexibility in the pursuit of liberalization, definition of rules of origin and in the commodities that will benefit from preferred access.

Configuration of Agricultural Trade in the EU-Africa EPA

This section, examines the structure of agricultural liberalization in the context of the EU-Africa EPAs. It begins with a highlight of the key issues in the basic trade in food and agricultural products under an EPA and makes recommendations to address the issues and ensure that the EPAs lead to sustainable development of agriculture, promote economic growth and reduce poverty in Africa.

Key Challenges and Structural Issues to be Addressed

The critical issues to be addressed in this section of the chapter from Africa's standpoint in terms of the structure of the basic trade in food-and-agricultural products under an EPA are:

i.   The multidimensional process of erosion of the value of traditional ACP agricultural trade preferences;

ii.   The challenge posed by the cost-increasing effects of EU food-safety;

iii.   Standards and associated compliance and verification challenges;

iv.   The growing product differentiation in the EU market which is of increasing price significance and the need to shift patterns of production in response to this changing situation;

v.   The growing competitive challenge faced on the EU market from highly competitive developing-country agricultural exporters as wider EU agricultural trade policy evolves;

vi.   New competitive challenges which will be thrown up in serving national and regional markets for food-and-agricultural products as a result of the enhanced price competitiveness of EU food-and-agricultural exports;

vii.   The extent of tariff-elimination commitments to be entered into by ACP regions on food-and-agricultural products;

viii. The time-frame for the elimination of tariffs by ACP regions on food-and-agricultural products;

ix.   The nature of the safeguard measures to be allowed in sensitive food-and- agricultural product sectors.

Recommendations for Improved Agriculture under the EU-African EPAs

Meeting the Challenge of Reciprocity

TThe process of CAP reform is explicitly intended to enhance the price competitiveness of EU agricultural production for internal and international markets. This is achieved by shifting the basis of EU agricultural support from support for agricultural prices to support to agricultural producers. The provision of direct aid payments to farmers allows prices of basic agricultural commodities to fall without undermining EU farm incomes. This enhances the price competitiveness of EU agricultural products and simple value-added food products on both domestic and export markets. This has already witnessed an expansion of EU exports of simple value-added food products to African countries in those sectors where the process of CAP reform is most advanced (e.g., cereals) and those in which agricultural raw materials are used as a basic input (e.g., the livestock sectors). The process of CAP reform which affects all EU agricultural sectors is impacting on the markets of an increasing number of agricultural and simple value-added food products. The dismantling of tariff protection around African markets for agricultural and simple value- added food products, in the face of enhanced EU export price competitiveness, could potentially undermine efforts to move up the value chain in serving national and regional markets throughout the whole of Africa. The EPAs should therefore, emphasize the following:

- Trade agreements with the EU should have provisions for adequate market protection instruments against the influx of cheap EU agricultural and food products into Africa.

- Maintaining tariff protection until such time as the EU has dismantled all forms of export support impacting on EU-ACP food-and-agricultural trade.

- Establish pre-emptive safeguard measures involving the monitoring and surveillance of trade in food-and-agricultural products benEfiting directly and indirectly from the deployment of EU agricultural support programmes, so as to prevent market disruption in sensitive African food-and-agricultural product sectors.

Preference Erosion

Complete removal of all residual tariffs charged on ACP food-and-agricultural product exports (e.g., removing the £0.15/kg special duty on ACP beef exports and the removal of all special duties on sugar-based products). Remove all remaining quantitative restrictions on duty-free access for ACP food-and-agricultural products exports – from grapes to sugar.

Costs associated with EU Food Safety Standards

Across a range of products the profitability of traditional ACP agricultural exports is being squeezed by declining EU prices and rising food-safety costs.

Recommendation

Establishment of a wider range of targeted 'aid for trade' programmes to defray private-sector costs associated with meeting EU food-safety standards (in line with support extended internally within the EU) and to support the establishment and operation of public food-safety control systems in Africa.

Increased Competitiveness

With increased agricultural liberalization, many traditional African suppliers cannot compete on price with the highly competitive developing-country agricultural producers that are increasingly gaining market share in the EU. If traditional ACP suppliers are to profitably serve the EU market then they will need to be assisted in moving up the value chain to reduce their dependence on the prices of basic agricultural commodities.

Production of Higher Value-added Products

In many markets for traditional temperate agricultural products, the process of CAP reform is substantially reducing market prices in the EU. This is being compounded by the associated process of dismantling bilaterally and multilaterally EU systems of tariff protection, which is further increasing competition on the EU market. The emergence of a range of non-traditional low-cost agricultural suppliers into international trade is also intensifying competition on basic agricultural markets in the EU. All of this requires ACP suppliers to move up the value chain, to the production of higher-value food products if ACP countries are to profitably develop their trade in food-and-agricultural products with the EU. A shift to value-added agriculture involving expanded production, increased productivity and processing of major export commodities should be an appropriate mechanism to address the unfavourable international price of export crops and to achieve the desired growth in export revenue. Nonetheless, a big challenge in Africa is how to ensure that the value-added activities leading to the production of tradable commodities actually take place within the local communities in order to minimize transaction costs and contribute to the growth of the non-farm sector. In this connection, it is important to stress that emphasis should not only be on changing the market value of what local producers have to sell, but also on ensuring increased investment in the communities where the commodities are produced. The local communities must be empowered to have control over the activities in the value chain and to gain direct access to markets and remain competitive in the markets. By and large, given the other constraints faced in ACP countries, targeted programmes of 'aid for trade' support will be required if ACP producers are to transit from the export of raw materials to that of value-added commodities.

Coping with Increasingly Differentiated EU Markets

The EU market is increasingly fragmenting into two distinct parts: the 'necessity purchase' and 'luxury purchase' components. Internally, the EU is seeking to shift European agricultural production towards serving the 'luxury purchase' component of the EU market. In the 'necessity- purchase' component of the market consumers make purchase decisions based exclusively on price. In the 'luxury purchase' component of the market in contrast, 'quality' standards, ethical factors or methods of production, play a more important role in the purchase decisions of consumers than price considerations. As the floor price for basic commodities has been allowed to fall, so the gap between prices of bulk commodities and differentiated products has widened. Indeed, 'luxury purchase' products and 'necessity purchase' products are now subject to divergent price trends: rising prices for 'luxury purchases' and stagnant or declining prices for 'necessity purchases'. This carries important implications for ACP producers who will have to make the transition from simply 'trading' into general EU markets, to 'marketing' specific differentiated products into particular components of the EU market. This will require targeted 'aid for trade' support in identifying 'luxury purchase' components of the EU market and supporting investment in developing production to serve these components of the EU market.

Rules of Origin

The Cotonou agreement provides for 'full cumulation' whereby ACP exports will only qualify for preferences for any processing that has been carried out in the EU, other ACP countries and South Africa. To enhance value-added agriculture, there is the need for 'global cumulation' where African exports can contain inputs that have been processed across all ACP regions and other developing countries.

Safeguard Measures

There is need to define a special safeguard and shortage clause for various categories of agricultural products with provisions for measures that may be applied in case of emergency (e.g., raising tariffs), as well as the timeframe for consultations before such measures enter into force.

Food Security Clause

On account of food security, the agricultural sector should be regarded as a sensitive sector and a number of commodities produced by small-scale farmers should be considered for placement on the list of exclusion from reciprocity.

MDGs Clause

The EPA should include an MDG clause in which full attainment of MDGs will be a condition for re-opening discussions on possible reciprocity, as concerns agricultural liberalization. The clause should also have provisions for increased flow of ODA to address supply-side and other structural constraints, boost production capacity, strengthen competitiveness and diversify the economies in African ACP countries.

Improved Regional Trade and Agricultural Development

African leaders and policy makers are moving towards a realignment of priorities in the promotion of agricultural growth as evidenced by concrete initiatives that have been taken early in the 21st century (see Box 7.3). Nonetheless, the persistent crisis in African agriculture and its inability to perform its role meaningfully is sufficient evidence that action plans alone will not modernize and transform the sector into an engine of growth. In this connection, the following recommendations should be considered.

- Priority should be given in the EU-Africa EPA for improved access to food; progress towards the Maputo commitments, including 10 per cent of African national budgets devoted to the agricultural sector and rural development; and to enhanced intra-Africa trade in agriculture, including staple foods.

- This also deserves an increased investment into Africa's small producers, rural entrepreneurship and private sector development, allowing them to improve supply capacity, and hence take advantage of any trading opportunities, especially those within Africa.

- The Maputo commitment therefore needs to be matched by 10 per cent EU development resources.

- Additional resources should be set aside to mitigate the expected negative effects of climate change especially on small-scale producers.

- Implementation of the Comprehensive Africa Agricultural Development Programme (CAADP) at regional and national levels needs to be accelerated, with particular attention to the involvement of non-state actors such as small farmers' associations.

Box 6.3: Initiatives for Improved Agricultural Growth and Food Security in Africa

The Maputo Declaration

Prompted by the urgent need to revitalize the agricultural sector in African countries the Maputo Declaration called on Member States to: adopt sound policies on agricultural and rural development; prepare collaborative bankable projects under CAADP for the mobilization of resources: and allocate at least 10 per cent of their national budgetary resources to the agricultural sector within five years. The Declaration also called for: the active participation of all the key stakeholders at the national and regional levels in all aspects of Africa's food and agricultural production; the establishment of food reserve systems that are based on regional and sub-regional food self-sufficiency to fight hunger and poverty; increased cooperation with Africa's development partners aimed at addressing the effects of their subsidies on the development of African agriculture and providing better access for Africa's exports; and the acceleration of the process of establishing the African Investment bank as provided for in the Constitutive Act of the AU.

The AU/NEPAD Comprehensive Africa Agriculture Development Programme (CAADP)

The Comprehensive Africa Agriculture Development Programme (CAADP) was designed to serve as an integrated framework of development priorities aimed at halting and reversing the decline of the agricultural sector in Africa. CAADP focuses investments into four mutually reinforcing pillars. Pillar 1 emphasizes the need for expansion of the area under sustainable land management and reliable water control systems. Pillar 2 underlines the need for improvement of rural infrastructure and trade-related capacities and market access; Pillar 3 focuses on increasing food supply and reducing hunger, by accessing improved technology, so as to enable small farmers to play a major role in increasing food availability close to where it is most needed. Pillar 4 is a long-term pillar which focuses on agricultural research, technological dissemination and adoption to sustain long-term productivity growth. A Companion Document on livestock, fisheries and forestry sub-sectors has also been prepared and been endorsed.

Creation of the Department of Rural Economy and Agriculture within the AU Framework

The Maputo Summit institutionalized the Commission's mechanism for initiating and promoting policies and strategies for developing Africa's rural economy and improving livelihoods by approving the creation of the Department of Rural Economy and Agriculture (DREA) within the new structure of the African Union Commission. The department was thus charged withthe responsibility of promoting measures to reverse the continent's low agricultural productivity, achieve overall agricultural growth in its broadest sense (i.e., including crop and livestock sub-systems, forestry and fisheries), and enhance environmental sustainability and sustainable use of natural resources. In preparing its Strategic Plan, DREA has worked in close collaboration with the NEPAD Secretariat, the Regional Economic Communities (RECs), Member States, regional and international institutions, Civil Society Organizations and a number of the continent's development partners.

The Sirte Declaration on Agriculture and Water

The Sirte Declaration focused on the challenges of implementing integrated and sustainable development in agriculture and water in Africa. Cognizant of the urgent need to respond adequately to Africa's critical problems of hunger, poverty and disease by employing innovative, complementary and comprehensive approaches, the Second Extraordinary Summit of African Heads of State and Government which was held in Sirte, Libya in February 2004, called on Member States to commit themselves to: the development of African agriculture in all its dimensions, including the promotion of the production of strategic agricultural commodities; livestock and fisheries development; the development of agricultural implements; and water and natural resources especially the development of the continent's river basins. The Declaration also called for: the strengthening and/or establishment of Centres of Excellence for the development of African agriculture in all its ramifications; the strengthening and/or establishment of banks for genetic resources for agriculture and livestock; the provision of registration mechanisms for intellectual property rights; the enhancement and/or establishment of early warning systems at the regional level and their coordination at the continental level to avert the negative impact of drought, desertification, floods, natural disasters, and pests; and the establishment of information networks for agricultural production and food security and input and output marketing.

Source: Africa Union, 2005

There should be provision of conditional agricultural subsidies in Africa to support small farmers and producers throughout the value chain to ensure sustainable supply of their products especially in local markets.

Energy crops for bio-fuels could offer market opportunities for African smallholders, benefiting employment creation, income generation and local energy security. However, large-scale mono-cultures have proven detrimental to small producers, the local environment, land rights and food security. Development of such plantations needs to be discouraged and production promoted only under strict sustainability criteria. There are several reasons in support of greater intra-regional trade in Africa. First, it is likely to increase incentives for large private traders to invest in the fixed costs of setting up large trading operations to profit from annual fluctuations of local marketable surpluses within wider areas. This is one way of addressing the problem of limited economies of scale in individual countries where marketing activities are in the hands of small-scale operators. Second, is the potential to reduce fluctuations in prices both within and across seasons, if harvests are imperfectly correlated (or, better still, negatively correlated) across the regional trading bloc. Third, intra-regional trade is apt to provide a valuable outlet for surpluses as national production of a given commodity approaches 'self-sufficiency', thus reducing the extent of the price fall during years of bumper harvest. Fourth, it can stimulate additional production growth through local specialization based on comparative advantage, in which case regional produce may replace imports from international markets (Poulton et al 2006).

The emphasis on regional integration as a precursor to integration of Africa into the global economy should be given a pride of place especially in view of the emerging global food crisis and the adverse consequences of the astronomic price increases in the oil market. The price of crude oil on the international market is now about US$100 per barrel and is predicted to increase (2011 prices). The world is yet to find a solution to the oil 'bomb' which is likely to spark off stagflation in many poor import-dependent economies. The integration in the various EPA regions in Africa should not be seen only in terms of trade in goods and services; it should promote complementarity in production and investment opportunities so that, overall, Africa would be in a position to effectively resist the importation of inflation which is now building up in the developed countries and which is likely to wipe out the gains being made in some countries in terms of poverty reduction and economic growth.

Creation of African Commodity Exchange

While efforts are being made to re-direct the EPA towards improved development of agriculture in Africa, it will be necessary to look inwards to design innovative approaches to create improved market access to encourage individual African countries to trade within the continent. Thus, for the purpose of income generation, stabilization and poverty reduction the bottlenecks in the marketing system have to be removed to improve intra-Africa trade. For Africa, overall, there is a need to increase the geographical coverage of commodity markets and improve farmers' access to markets in general. Improved market access has the potential to bring individual producers the information they need to negotiate more effectively. With a better knowledge of market prices, producers can engage in contracts with more favourable terms than hitherto has been the case, in order to hedge against price drops. In view of the foregoing, the establishment of an African Commodity Exchange is recommended. This is an issue that can be taken up at the level of the African Union. Fortunately, Agricultural Commodity Exchange (ACE) is now operational at the level of individual countries in Africa, thus there are lessons to be learnt. Many of them have been designed to ensure a fair, orderly, and efficient marketing system to encourage smallholder farmers to produce more for the market; to benefit domestic agro-industry through a more efficient and reliable supply chain; and to enhance export competitiveness by getting the domestic market in order. It should be possible to begin by conducting studies on the performance of the existing ACEs and the feasibility of establishing one at the continental level

Conclusion

Free trade agreements in agriculture often emphasize the promise that all farmers will find prosperity by increasing their export market shares. By and large, the free trade model in agriculture is flawed and has been regarded as one of the major causes of hunger and poverty around the world. The potential benefit appears to be limited in view of the liberalization policies already put in place in many countries. Evidence suggests that both LDCs and non-LDC African ACP countries will face considerable challenges if they comply with the so-called WTO compatible reciprocal liberalization policies inherent in the EPAs. A review of the potential impact of African regional EPAs with the EU shows that there may be a decline in welfare levels, as the losses in tariff revenues exceed any gains from trade through lower import prices, and that a unilateral trade liberalization by African ACP countries would be better by far for sustained economic growth and development. Thus, it is expected that changes in the EPAs in the current form will be required in several areas, especially in terms of (i) doing away with arbitrary time frames and setting realistic time that reflects the pace of development in Africa, (ii) reviewing the rules of origin and the demand for reciprocity, (iii) providing concrete assurance to address resulting revenue losses by African countries, (iv) supporting regional initiatives aimed at developing African agriculture, and (v) ensuring that African countries are not constrained in attaining the MDGs. The agricultural sector should be regarded as a sensitive sector and should be exempted from any rule of reciprocity. On the domestic scene, African governments must ensure that appropriate policies are put in place to transform the agricultural sector from being exporter of raw materials to exporter of value-added commodities that enhance their revenue generation potential and guarantee sustainable livelihood for the masses of the people that depend largely on agriculture.

References

Africa Union, 2005, 'Status of Food Security and Prospects for Agricultural Development in Africa', report of the AU Ministerial Conference of Ministers of Agriculture, held in Bamako, Mali, from 31 January - 1February 2006. (https://www.google.com.ng/url?sa=t&rct=j&q=&esrc=s&source=web&cd=1&cad= rja&ved=0CDcQFjAA&url=http%3A%2F%2Fwww.africa-union.org%2FRural%2520 Agriculture%2FMIN%2520CONF%2520BKO%25202006%2FFAO%2FEn%2FEnglish_ Food_Security_Bamako.doc&ei=4R_oUbO_HtG3hAebhIDoBw&usg=AFQjCNEE-xxvmJwLwH-r8jWJIGBRoE8Hhg&sig2=AdPwXZTLDFzd_aKMyanFAQ&bvm= bv.49478099,d.ZG4).

Borrmann, A., Busse, M. and S. Neuhaus, 2005, 'EU/ACP Economic Partnership Agreements: Impact, Options and Pre-requisites', *Intereconomics*, Vol. 40, No. 3: May/ June, pp.169- 176.

Busse, M. and H. Großmann, 2004, 'The Impact of ACP/EU Economic Partnership Agreements on ECOWAS Countries: An Empirical Analysis of the Trade and Budget Effects', Hamburg Institute of International Economics (HWWA) *Discussion Paper* No. 294.

Bussolo, Maurizio, 1999, Regional or Multilateral Agreements? An Evaluation of Southern-Africa Trade Policy Scenarios, Overseas Development Institute, London, mimeo.

ECDPM, 2004, 'Comparing EU Free Trade Agreements: Agriculture', *In Brief*, No. 6A, July, European Centre for Development Policy Management.

ECDPM, 2006, 'Overview of the Regional EPA Negotiations: West Africa-EU Economic Partnership Agreement', *In Brief*, No. 14B, November , European Centre for Development Policy Management.

Kasteng, Jonas, 2006, 'Agriculture and Development in the EPA Negotiations', Swedish Board of Agriculture, International Affairs Division, December.

McKay, Andrew, Chris Milner and Oliver Morrissey, 2000, 'The Trade and Welfare Effects of a Regional Economic Partnership Agreement', CREDIT Research Paper 00/08, University of Nottingham.

Miencha, F., 2005, 'Background Studies on Kenya's Trade and Industrial Policy Plans and Implications of EPAs for Kenya's Key Sectors', Report for EcoNews Africa and Traidcraft Exchange, August 2005.

Olomola, Ade S., 2007, 'Strategies for Managing the Opportunities and Challenges of the Current Agricultural Commodity Booms in SSA', An Invited Paper Presented at the IX Senior Policy Seminar of the African Economic Research Consortium (AERC), Held at Hilton Yaounde, Cameroon, 27 February - 1 March.

Olomola, Ade S., 2008, 'EU-AFRICA Economic Partnership Agreements: Pre-Requisites and Policy Options', Paper Presented at the Research and Policy Dialogue on Economic and Political Integration and Alternatives to EPAs, Organized by CODESRIA, Hilton Addis-Ababa Hotel, Ethiopia, 9-11 June.

Olson, R. Dennis and Spieldoch, Alexander, 2007, 'Behind the Secret Trade Deal: What about Agriculture, Commentary, 21 May, The Institute for Agriculture and Trade Policy, Minneapolis, Minnesota, USA.

Patel, Mayur, 2007, 'Economic Partnership Agreements between the EU and African Countries: Potential Development Implications for Ghana'. (*www.realizingrights.org*).

Poulton, Collin, Kydd, Jonathan and Dorward, Andrew (2006) 'Overcoming Market Poulton, Collin, Kydd, Jonathan and Dorward, Andrew (2006) 'Overcoming Market Constraints on Pro-Poor Agricultural Growth in Sub-Saharan Africa', *Development Policy Review* 24(3): 243-277.

Sustainability Impact Assessments of the EU-ACP Economic Partnership Agreements, 2004, 'Phase I Regional SIA: West African ACP Countries', January .

USDA, 2003, EU Trade Policy Monitoring on Export Subsidies. GAIN Report No. E. 23156.

Viner, Jacob, 1950, '*The Customs Union Issue*', New York: Carnegie Endowment for International Peace.

7

Trade Facilitation: Implications for Intra-African Trade in a Globalized Economy

Ntangsi Max Memfih

Introduction

Generally, there is a tendency for policy makers and researchers to focus more on policy than natural barriers to trade. However, recent evidence generally and certainly in some African countries suggests that natural barriers may be a more important source of trade cost than trade policy, and may well be a significant factor contributing to the sluggish response to trade liberalization in Africa. Indeed, a study reported by the World Trade Organization (2004), indicates that for the majority of sub-Saharan African countries, transport cost incidence for exports (the share of international shipping costs in the value of trade) is five times higher than tariff cost incidence (the trade weighted *ad valorem* duty actually paid). It is increasingly being realized that tariffs, quotas and other trade policies are only one element of the overall cost of trade and that efforts to improve customs procedures, minimize the trade distorting impact of standards and reduce transport costs may have higher payoff than reciprocal reductions in overt trade policy barriers. This is because logistical, institutional and regulatory barriers are often more costly and generate no offsetting revenue (World Bank 2005). For instance, Milner, Morrissey and Rudaheranwa (2001) calculated and compared the effective protection of imports, and implicit tax on exports due to transport costs, to the protection due to trade policy barriers for Uganda. The results of their investigation revealed that natural protection on domestic sales arising from transport costs was high, being equivalent to an effective rate of protection of 48 per cent on average in 1994 (about a quarter higher than protection due to trade policy).

They also found that the implicit tax associated with transport costs was as high as 100 per cent for manufactured goods, almost 40 per cent for food products, almost 25 per cent for coffee, cotton and tea, and about 25 per cent for fish.

However, transport costs are only one of the transaction costs associated with trade. If other constraints, such as market information and reliable utilities (electricity and telecommunications) could be quantified, the implicit taxation of exporters associated with transaction costs would be even higher. Therefore, while trade policy reforms are important to improve incentives and encourage efficiency, they would be more effective if transaction costs resulting from natural barriers are also lowered. Indeed, the African Export-Import Bank (AFREXIMBANK) (2003), attributes recent growth in the value of intra-African trade (an increase in the rate of growth in value from 4.7 per cent in 2002 to about 13.5 per cent in 2003, and in the share of intra-African trade in total African trade to 9.6 per cent in 2003 from 9.1 per cent in 2002 and 9.5 per cent in 2001 to improvement in shipping and air-links between Southern and West Africa; pursuit of external trade and payment reforms; and reduction in tariff and non-tariff barriers to intra-African trade aided by more intense pursuit of regional integration.

Evolving Definition and Scope of Trade Facilitation

In a narrow sense, trade facilitation efforts simply address the logistics of moving goods through ports or more efficiently moving documentation associated with cross-border trade. More recent definitions have been broadened to include the environment in which trade transactions take place, that is, the transparency and professionalism of customs and regulatory environments, as well as harmonization of standards and conformity to international or regional regulations. The International Chamber of Commerce (ICC) (www.iccbookshop.com) defines trade facilitation as 'the adoption of a comprehensive and integrated approach to simplifying and reducing the cost of international trade transaction, and ensuring that the relevant activities take place in an efficient, transparent and predictable manner based on internationally accepted norms and standards and best practices'. However, trade facilitation should not only be perceived as a 'transportation or customs problem', but rather a broader issue which straddles many aspects of weak capacities that exist in many developing countries, and inhibit their effective participation in international trade. This notwithstanding, trade facilitation is not the concern of developing countries only.

Indeed, developed countries are leading the clamour for trade facilitation measures in the WTO. It has become prominent among WTO issues because the international business community is increasingly demanding for greater transparency, efficiency, and procedural uniformity of cross-border transportation of goods; as well as the need for an efficient legal redress mechanism, proper co-ordination between customs and other inspection agencies, use of modern customs techniques and improvement of transit regimes.

Constraints to Intra-African Trade: Key Issues of Trade Facilitation

The Physical Movement of Consignment (Transport and Transit): High Transport Costs

According to ECA (2004) in ARIA, transport costs are high in Africa in general and in landlocked African countries in particular – averaging 14 per cent of the value of exports compared to 8.6 per cent for all developing countries – and higher still for many countries, such as Malawi (56 %), Chad (52 %) and Rwanda (48 per cent) (Table 7.1). Other studies also indicate that transport costs in Africa are the highest in the world. A report by the United Nations Conference on Trade and Development (UNCTAD) shows that the freight cost as a percentage of total import value was 13 per cent for Africa in 2000 compared to 8.8 per cent for developing countries and 5.2 per cent for industrial countries. At the sub-regional level, the freight costs of West Africa as a percentage of total import value was 14 per cent while those of East and Southern Africa, including the Indian Ocean region was 15.2 per cent. The ratio of North Africa stood at 11 per cent (UNCTAD 2002). In practice, data on the costs of inland transport are extremely difficult to obtain, except for some specific case studies. This difficulty is associated with political considerations in some cases which distort information and the non-existence of information since a lot of informality is involved

Table 7.1: Transit Costs in Selected African Countries and World Groups, 2006

Country or Group of Countries	Transport and Insurance (US$ Millions)	Exports of Goods and Services (US$ Millions)	Transit Costs as a Share of Value of Exports (%)
Botswana	230	3,030	8
Burkina Faso	70	272	26
Burundi	23	96	24
Central African Republic	59	179	33
Chad	99	190	52
Ethiopia	240	979	25
Lesotho	43	263	15
Malawi	214	385	56
Mali	229	644	36
Rwanda	70	144	48
Swaziland	30	1,085	3
Uganda	269	757	36
Zambia	216	1,255	17
Zimbabwe	379	2,344	16
Landlocked Countries	3,706	26,314	14
Least Developed Countries	4,277	24,640	17
Developing Countries	109,055	1,268,581	9

Source: ECA, 2004 and UNCTAD Data, 2008

Table 7.2 provides some examples of land transport costs for selected routes in Africa. It shows that there exist large differentials in road transport costs across routes. An additional kilometre on the route from Douala to N'djamena, for example, is three times more expensive than on the route from Maputo to Johannesburg (World Trade Organization 2004). Other studies also find large cost differentials across routes. For example, the cost of shipping from Durban to Lusaka, 1,600km away, is 2,500 dollars, whereas the cost of shipping from Durban to Maseru (Lesotho), only 347 kilometres, is 7,500 dollars (Limoa and Venables 2001).

Table 7.2: Estimated Unit Transport Costs for Container and Selected Routes in 2005

	Route	Costs ($ per km)
Dar-es-Salaam-Kigali	1,650	3.0
Dar-es-Salaam-Bujumbura	1,750	3.0
Douala-N'djamena	1,900	4.2
Lome-Ouagadougou	1,000	2.6
Lome-Niamey	1,234	2.6
Mombasa-Kampala	1,440	2.3
Maputo-Johanesburg	561	1.4

Source: Extracted from World Trade Report 2007

Inadequate Transport Infrastructure

African countries recognized the importance of transport infrastructure in general and regional transport infrastructure networks in particular to their development prospects as far back as the 1960s, just after most of them attained independence. As a result, several transport infrastructure development initiatives have emerged over the years. One of the most ambitious of these initiatives is the Trans African Highways (TAH) network, conceived in the early 1970s. However, several years after its conception, missing links still exist in the TAH network, especially at border areas. An analysis of 103 cross-border TAH links (TAH sections leading to border posts) shows that 33 per cent are unpaved roads in various conditions - good, fair and poor; 16 per cent are paved roads in poor condition; and 38 per cent are paved roads in good or fair condition. This clearly illustrates the poor state of physical integration between African countries. Using the missing TAH links as a measure of road integration, ECA (2004) shows that there is disparity in the level of physical integration across the continent (Table 7.3). Overall, the road sub-sector in Africa is in a deplorable state. The total length of roads in the region is 2,064,613 kilometres out of which only 29.7 per cent is paved, the remaining portion being either earth or gravel roads. In addition to its low density, distribution, and the fact that a large proportion is unpaved, a sizeable chunk of Africa's road network is in a state of disrepair. For instance, 34 per cent of paved roads and 55 per cent of unpaved roads in CEMAC were in poor condition in 2005. Similarly, 34 per cent of paved roads and 68 per cent of unpaved roads in COMESA were in poor condition in the same period.

Table 7.3: Physical Integration of RECs in 2006

Regional Economic Community	Total TAH Links	Missing Links	Missing Links as a Share of Total (%)
COMESA	15,723	2,695	17
EAC	3,841	523	14
ECCAS	10,650	4,953	47
ECOWAS	10,578	2,970	28
IGAD	8,716	2,423	28
SADC	11,454	2,136	19
UMA	5,923	1,110	21

Source: ECA, 2004 and UNCTAD Data, 2008

Poor Interconnection of African Railway Networks

The African rail network is currently estimated to be about 89,380 km long, with a density of 2.96 km per 1,000 sq. km. Three railway gauges predominate in Africa, i.e. 1.067m, 1.000m, and 1.435m, thus causing limitations in the physical integration of the railway networks in various sub-regions. The interconnections of the network is relatively poor, especially in Central and Western Africa, and the available rolling stock is still very low compared to other regions of the world. Disjointed railway networks result in frequent loading and off-loading of goods, which increases delays and transport costs. To compound things, the maintenance of existing railway networks is very poor.

Inefficient Transport Operations

Inefficiency of transport services is manifested in several ways including: high vehicle prices, poor market information, existence of transport cartels, poor knowledge of operating costs, poor operating practices, and poor routine maintenance, all of which lead to high vehicle operating costs and low vehicle utilization. Transport operators usually transfer the burden of high vehicle operating costs to consumers by raising fares. Similarly, operators increase fares to offset low revenues due to low vehicle utilization.

Numerous Roadblocks

The phenomenon of roadblocks poses a serious challenge to trade in Africa. It results in excessive delays and substantial increase in transport costs. *The Economist* (December 2002) reported 47 roadblocks between Douala and Bertoua in Cameroon, a distance of about 500kms. Nearly all ECOWAS member states also maintain numerous checkpoints, where drivers are sometimes subjected to administrative harassment and extortion (Table 7.4).

Table 7.4: Checkpoints along Major ECOWAS Highways in 2004

Highways	Distance (km)	Number of Checkpoints	Checkpoints per 100km
Lagos-Abidjan	992	69	7
Cotonu-Niamey	1,036	34	3
Lome-Ouagadougou	989	34	4
Accra-Ouagadougou	972	15	2
Abidjan-Ouagadougou	1,122	37	3
Niamey-Ouagadougou	529	20	4

Source: ECOWAS Official Site, 2003 and ECA, 2004

According to the report of a review of the status of implementation of the Trans African Highways network, jointly commissioned by the Economic Commission for Africa (ECA) and the African Development Bank (ADB) in mid-2003, the payment at checkpoints between Abidjan and Ouagadougou varies between 1,000 FCFA and 5,000 FCFA. On the Trans-Sahelien Highway between Ouagadougou and Niamey, a distance of 529 km, the payment by a loaded truck is estimated at about 100,000 FCFA, and on the Douala-Bangui road, a distance of 1450km, the total cost of passage is estimated to be between 250,000 FCFA and 300,000 FCFA. These examples illustrate a common reality that transporters face in Africa. The resultant loss of time and increase in vehicle operating costs from these stops are considerable. The trip from Bangui in the Central African Republic to Douala in Cameroon, which can be done in three days given the poor state of the road, usually takes between 7 to 10 days. A study on transit transport in ECOWAS in 1999 revealed that enormous amounts of time and money are wasted each year at checkpoints in the region. Overall, lost revenue was estimated at 2 billion FCFA yearly (www.ecowas.int).

Police Escorts, Limited Use of Containers and Multimodal Transport Operations

Added to the numerous checkpoints is the risk of goods being diverted from their intended destination. To solve this problem, some countries such as Cameroon, Kenya and Nigeria have introduced a transit monitoring system in the form of police escorts. However, transport operators in Kenya complain bitterly about these escorts because they contribute to delays and result in additional costs – the police usually escorts convoys of trucks and the journey only begins when several trucks are ready to depart. Operators also have to pay for the security provided by these police escorts. A more efficient way of preventing the diversion of goods into the domestic market of transit countries could be the use of containers. Indeed, elsewhere in the world, the growth of containerization has given a new impetus to the door-to-door movement of goods under the responsibility of Multimodal Transport Operators (MTOs).

Variations in Technical Standards of Vehicles

The proliferation of rules and regulations hampers international transportation of goods in Africa, as it leads to uncertainty and a multiplicity of forms and procedures. For instance, variations in approved technical standards for vehicles in different sub-regions of Africa block free competition between transport operators. Table 7.5 shows that if standards were applied, a 22-metre long truck operating in Nigeria, a member State of ECOWAS, would not be allowed to operate in neighbouring Cameroon, a member State of CEMAC, whose maximum allowable vehicle length is 18 metres. Similarly, transport operators would not be able to load their trucks to the maximum payload if they decide to do business across ECOWAS, CEMAC, COMESA since each of these sub-regions apply different axle load and weight limits.

Variation in Transit Charges

Transit charges constitute an additional burden for transport operators in Africa. At present, there are divergences in transit costs among member states in different African sub-regions, resulting in lack of transparency and high road user charges. This needs harmonization.

Table 7.5: Technical Standards for Vehicles in Different RECs, 2004

RECs	Axle Load Limit (Tonne)			Max. Load	Max. Length	Max. Height	Max. Width
	Single Axle	Tandem Axle	Triple Axle	(Tonnes)	(Metres)	(Metres)	(Metres)
CEMAC	13	21	27	50	18	4	2,5
COMESA	10	16	24	n.a	22	n.a	n.a
ECOWAS	12	21	25	51	22	4	2.5

n.a is not available

Source: ECA 2004 and ECOWAS 2005

Problems Related to Crew Members

Agreements regulating transport operations at sub-regional level do not always take into account questions relating to crew members, i.e. the driver and apprentices. These employees are confronted with administrative problems concerning their documents (driving licences, residence permits, work permits, etc.). For COMESA and SADC countries, visas are not required for Commonwealth citizens, but for countries not belonging to this institution such as Rwanda, Burundi, and the Democratic Republic of Congo, crew members on vehicles in transit must pay each time for entry visas into those other countries. This constitutes a barrier to the free movement within the sub-region and increases transport costs.

Import and Export Procedures

The key problems here include excessive documentary requirements; outdated official procedures; insufficient use of automated systems; lack of transparency, predictability and consistency in customs activities; and lack of modernization and cooperation of customs and other governmental agencies.

Excessive Documentary Requirements and Outdated Official Procedures

According to estimates by UNCTAD, on average, customs transaction involves 20-30 different parties, 40 documents, 200 data elements 30 of which are repeated at least 30 times and the re-keying of 60-70 per cent of all data at least once. Frequently, documentation requirements are ill-defined and traders are not adequately informed on how to comply with them, thus increasing the potential for errors. This problem is even worse at borders, especially as border posts and customs offices are, in most cases, physically separated.

Insufficient Use of Automated Systems

The lack or insufficient use of automated processes and information technology is a major cause of delays, costs and inefficiencies, as paper documents are usually presented at the time of border crossing, and verification of the information submitted takes place at that time.

Lack of Transparency, Predictability and Consistency in Customs Activities

Lack of transparency and predictability is a major source of uncertainty as regards costs and time involved for international trade transactions. When the necessary information on applicable regulations is not readily available, trade operators have to spend resources in order to obtain information. Enterprises operating in an environment that is not transparent need to spend more resources to obtain regulatory information. Furthermore, they will frequently have to add expenses for bribes, penalties and administrative or judicial appeals. As these additional expenses do not usually vary according to the value of the goods or the volume of sales, they serve to increase the operational costs per unit and put firms in developing countries in a weaker position than larger firms.

Lack of Modernization of, and Cooperation among, Customs and other Governmental Agencies

Customs departments and other government agencies involved in trade are often inefficiently structured internally. Common problems include inadequacies in physical infrastructure, training and education, inefficient emoluments of staff, and lack of co-ordination and co-operation between customs administrations as well as between customs and tax administration.

Safety and Security

The need for more stringent security procedures in the face of the recent wave of international terrorism is becoming more and more important and poses a new and very serious challenge to customs administration as well as to operators, especially in the maritime and air transport sub-sectors. There is a growing need to balance between safety and security and the smooth flow of goods and services.

Information and Communication Technology (ICT)

The African region as a whole lags behind others regions in the use of modern information technology in domestic as well as international trade activities. Telecommunications services are inadequate, inefficient and very expensive, availability of mobile cellular phones is still limited, expensive, and non-existent in some rural areas. Africa has the lowest internet diffusion in the world. However, there is a wide variation in the use of ICT across Africa, as shown in Table 7.6. Communications in Africa depends largely on outside operators. In ECOWAS, only 2.8 per cent of transit traffic relies on routing facilities within the sub-region, while the rest uses

Canadian, European and US operators. Transit traffic represents 29 per cent of total traffic and 41 per cent of direct traffic. There are some encouraging signs in the ICT sector. For example, fixed line telephone connectivity has increased in most regional economic communities as policies on foreign investment have been liberalized (ECA 2004). The use of mobile telephone services has also increased with the greater openness of markets and cross-border investment in service provision. Egyptian and South African telephone companies have been active in establishing mobile telephone companies in other African countries. Internet connectivity is also increasing rapidly in Africa.

Table 7.6: Mobile Telephone and Internet connectivity by Regional Economic Community, 2004

Regional Economic Community	Estimated Population (000)	Cellular Sub-scribers per 100 people	Internet Users per 10,000 people
CEMAC	31,705	5.2	21.8
CEN-SAD	339,092	2.5	57.5
CEPGL	67,331	0.5	0.9
COMESA	436,824	5.8	35.0
EAC	88,722	1.5	23.7
ECCAS	99,186	3.6	7.6
ECOWAS	226,888	2.0	27.2
IGAD	166,835	0.8	12.5
IOC	18,603	15.6	115.5
MRU	15,620	0.5	14.1
SACU	51,249	11.3	490.5
SADC	284,115	10.1	147.1
UEMOA	71,635	1.9	57.2
UMA	77,900	5.2	129.3
Total	**1,810,959**		**63.6**

Source: Compiled from ITU Data, 2006

International Payments Mechanisms, Insurance Requirements and Customs Guarantees

ECA studies reveal that the documentary credit payment system is the most popular international payment system in Africa. However, this practice is characterized by cumbersome and complex procedures. The basis of the system is a series of checks in which the progress of goods towards the buyer is pinned to the progress of payment to the seller. The process is time-consuming, requires physical movement of documents between different banking establishments in two different countries and is not well understood and badly managed by many users. Indeed, it has been reported that half of all requests for payment are rejected on grounds of documentary inconsistencies. In addition, the system is open to fraud.

Insurance

Concerning road transport, African regional economic communities have introduced common insurance schemes. COMESA, for example, has the third party motor insurance scheme (Yellow Card) that provides for third party insurance cover, valid in all the transit and destination states including medical bills for crew. CEMAC and ECOWAS have also introduced similar schemes.

Customs Guarantee

Customs security is one of the major difficulties in freight transit. This has to be ensured by the establishment of a financial guarantee and mechanism that makes sure that goods in transit do not enter the transit country market without the necessary taxes and customs duties being paid. Guarantee payments represent a high cost for transport operators. In Africa, however, no sub-regional organization has managed to establish a satisfactory system. In the case of ECOWAS countries, texts are applied differently. Customs services in Cote d'Ivoire and Senegal, for example, require bank guarantees. Burkina Faso, Benin and Niger have all instituted guarantee funds, with the guarantee being cumulative (paid in each of the countries transited) and non-reimbursable.

Multiplicity of Currencies and Exchange Rate Arrangements

Monetary unions can generate potential large benefits for African countries through increased trade flows, and economic growth. Monetary integration implies a medium-to-long term move towards forms of fixed exchange rates, with countries eventually adopting a common currency. However, exchange rate arrangements in Africa are currently fragmented. Multiplicity of currencies increases international trade costs as businessmen are confronted with the cost of changing from one currency to another. This has been identified as one of the contributing factors to the high cost of international transport operations in Africa.

International Trade Standards

As a barrier to trade, the issue of international trade standards is more relevant to Africa's trade with the rest of the world than to intra-African trade. In recent years, an increasing mass of standards and technical regulations governing the admissibility of imported goods into an economy has emerged for various reasons. In principle, the purpose of such standards is to ensure that the products available in markets meet minimum requirements, irrespective of their origin. Yet, it is often argued that some countries (mostly industrial countries) tend to use standards and regulations as a substitute for tariffs and quantitative restrictions. That is, while the process of trade liberalization has imposed the removal of most of classical trade barriers, these countries continue protecting some sectors by using standards to constraint imports from lower-cost developing countries.

Existing Efforts to Facilitate Intra-African Trade

Over the years, considerable efforts have been made at national, bilateral, sub-regional, regional and international levels to facilitate intra-African trade. Such efforts have included, inter alia, the signing of conventions, protocols and agreements, and the development of institutions and trade facilitation initiatives.

National Efforts to speed up Customs Operations - The Tunisian Experience

The Tunisia TradeNet (TTN) is an automated system that provides a one-stop trade documentation-processing platform connecting the principal actors of international trade. It serves as a tool for exchanging international trade documents, maritime community documents and other administrative documents; payment of documentary credits and settlement of duty taxes. It is also a tool for business transactions such as processing purchase orders, shipment and delivery bills, invoices and transfer orders. In terms of international financial transaction, the TTN facilitates the exchange of bills of lading between Tunisian banks and European banks. In addition, the TTN serves as a marketplace where offers and requests are made and transactions processed. Prior to the creation of TTN in February 2000, the complexity of trade documentation processing in Tunisia resulted in delays in clearance of goods for imports.

Bilateral Cooperation

Numerous bilateral agreements on international road transport have been entered between African countries. For instance, it has been estimated that in UEMOA, only 30 per cent of the rules governing road transport are sub-regional, the remaining 70 per cent being either bilateral or national. It has also been indicated that there are more than 100 agreements between UEMOA member states in the area of transport. Good examples of bilateral cooperation between transit and landlocked countries are those between Cameroon and its landlocked neighbours of Chad and the Central African Republic. Among other things, these conventions identify transit corridors to be jointly managed by the national land freight authorities of Cameroon and its neighbours, specify the percentage of freight to be transported by Cameroonian transporters and their counterparts from the landlocked countries, and clearly stipulate that all vehicles in possession of specified documents plying the identified corridors should only be subjected to limited controls at jointly selected checkpoints.

Efforts to Facilitate Trade at Sub-Regional Levels

In central Africa, several conventions governing international transport have been signed including the inter-state convention for the transportation of miscellaneous goods by road (CIETRMD); the inter-state convention for multimodal freight transport; the regulation on transportation of dangerous goods, and the Inter State Transit agreement for Central African countries (TIPAC). CEMAC countries have also adopted a community highway code and a civil aviation code; created an international commission for the Congo, Oubangui and Sangha Basin; and signed a protocol on maritime cooperation as well as an agreement on air transport between member states. With regard to ECCAS, a community road network was adopted in 1988. In 2003, a transport master plan was also adopted in the sub-region.

In West Africa, ECOWAS and UEMOA have adopted two conventions on transport: the Inter-State Transport Convention (TIE) and the Inter-State Road Freight Transit Convention (TRIE). These conventions, both of which were signed in 1982 and have entered into force, define the conditions of road transport between member states and provide the transit, without interruption, of freight.

ECOWAS has introduced a common vehicle insurance scheme known as the Brown Card. This is a scheme that covers third-party liability and medical expenses. In addition, ECOWAS adopted the Automated System for Customs Data (ASYCUDA) in 1990, and in 1998 it launched the Trade Opportunity Management System to foster trade and investment by disseminating information on trade and business opportunities and promoting business contacts among economic operators in the community. Presently, ECOWAS, and UEMOA are working on the establishment of joint border posts, which, among other things, would address the issue of variation in working hours at adjacent border posts, which leads to delays.

In Eastern and Southern Africa, COMESA and SADC have protocols covering the area of transport. COMESA and SADC have also adopted measures aiming to facilitate transport and transit between member states (Table 7.7). In addition, some East African countries, form part of transport corridor initiatives such as the Northern and Central Corridor initiatives. The Northern Corridor links the landlocked Great Lakes countries of Burundi, Rwanda, Uganda and Eastern Democratic Republic of Congo, to the Kenyan seaport of Mombasa, while the Central Corridor connects the port of Dar es Salaam to the same landlocked Great Lakes countries.

Continental Initiatives

Several continental initiatives are enhancing the effectiveness of communications at the national level and promoting intra-African trade and regional integration. These include the African Telecommunication Union, the Regional African Satellite Communications Organisation, the African Information Society and the New Partnership for Africa's Development.

African Telecommunications Union

The African Telecommunications Union, established in 1999, seeks to foster the rapid development of information and communication technology in Africa to improve service, access, and interconnections between African countries. It has a wide range of objectives covering such issues as joint capacity building, regional policy convergence, financing of joint projects, exchange of information and standardization of tariffs and technology.

Regional African Satellite Communications Organizations

The Regional African Satellite Communications Organization (RASCOM), created in the early 1990s by African telecommunications ministers, has as its main objective to extend affordable telecommunications services to the entire population of Africa, by setting up telecommunications infrastructure based on satellite technology. It also aims to establish direct links between African countries.

Table 7.7: COMESA and SADC Transport and Trade Facilitation Measures

Measures Adopted by COMESA	Measures Adopted by SADC
Harmonized Axle load limits	Single customs declaration of goods
COMESA carrier licence and transit plates	Harmonization of weight limits and vehicle dimensions
Harmonized road transit charges	Harmonization of road transit charges
Customs Regional Bond Guarantee	Legal framework for overload control
The COMESA Customs Declaration	Adoption of community insurance scheme
Third Party Motor Insurance (Yellow Card)	SADC road design standards
ACIS – The Advance Cargo Information System	SADC road design signalsDefining a regional trunk road network
ASYCUDA – The Automated System for Customs Data	SADC Drivers Licensing – harmonizing the training of drivers and delivering of driving licences
Inter-Railway working agreement between railways companies	SADC region has adopted the concept of Development Corridors and Spatial Development Initiatives (SDI)

Source: ECA 2004

African Information Society Initiative

The African Information Society Initiative, launched by ECA in 1995, was designed to bridge the digital divide between Africa and the rest of the world. It intended to provide a guiding framework for African countries in modernizing and interconnecting their information and communication infrastructure and services.

The Pan-African Telecommunications Network (PANAFTEL)

PANAFTEL was aimed at setting up a continent-wide telecommunications network directly linking neighbouring countries. The project proved unsuccessful, however, due to political diversity, concentration on international links instead of national networks, cultural differences, and financial constraints.

The New Partnership for Africa's Development (NEPAD)

NEPAD which was formed in 2001 is a holistic, and integrated sustainable development initiative for the economic and social revival of Africa. The primary objective of the initiative is to eradicate poverty in Africa and to place African countries, both individually and collectively, on a path of sustainable growth and development in order to halt the marginalization of Africa in the global economy. One of its key concerns is enhancing trade between African countries.

Efforts by International Organizations for Trade Facilitation

The Sub-Saharan African Transport Policy Programme (SSATP) has been particularly active in the facilitation of intra-African Trade. The SSATP was instrumental in setting up and operationalizing the RECs Transport Coordination Committee in February 2005. It worked with this committee to develop an implementation plan for RECs activities to be funded by SSATP. These activities include the establishment of observatories of abnormal practices, port security audits, establishment of corridor committees, harmonization of legal/regulatory arrangements at border posts, and technical assistance. NEPAD has recognized transport and trade facilitation as a priority area in its infrastructure action plan, and within this framework, the African Development Bank (AfDB), European Union, USAID and Japan are providing support to RECs such as ECOWAS and UEMOA. The RECs are being provided with funds to set up observatories of abnormal practices, pay for the services of transport and trade facilitation experts at their Secretariat, and to evaluate the status of transit corridors as well as to reconstruct some of these corridors.

The Way Forward

Providing Adequate and Efficient Transport Infrastructure and Services

Specific actions required to improve transport infrastructure include: maintaining and rehabilitating existing roads, expanding the road network to isolated areas, widening roads with narrow lane and shoulder widths, and where necessary, adjusting horizontal and vertical alignments taking into consideration the increased use of heavy vehicles; increasing the connectivity of railway sections with different track gauges; replacing obsolete and inappropriate equipment at ports with modern container handling facilities, developing container terminals at ports to facilitate efficient handling and storage of containers; developing more dry ports to serve both landlocked countries as well as interior areas of coastal countries; and training of local staff to run containerized systems that are highly mechanized and computerized, and quite useful for multimodal transport operations.

Removing Illegal Roadblocks and preventing Diversion of Goods on Africa's Roads

Without any doubt, the challenge of removing roadblocks and preventing the diversion of goods on Africa's roads is enormous. These problems are extensive, deep-rooted and inherently difficult to come to grips with. Overall, improvements have to be based on political agreements and interventions from the highest government levels. This is, in fact, a prerequisite to sustainable solutions. The New Partnership for Africa's Development (NEPAD), through its Peer Review mechanism, could play a leading role in this regard.

Speeding up Customs and Border Crossing Procedures

The problem of slow and cumbersome border procedures could be addressed by reducing the number of trade documents and copies required and harmonizing the nature of the information to be contained in these documents. Such trade documents should also be designed and standardized in accordance with international accepted standards, practices and guidelines and should be adaptable for use in computer systems.

Promoting the Use of New Technology

Several African countries are using automated customs systems such as the Automated System for Customs Data (ASYCUDA) or other systems like the Tunisia TradeNet, to simplify and speed up customs procedures However, there is a need to enhance capacity through training.

Improving on Governance

Good governance is perhaps the single most important factor in promoting trade, eradicating poverty and promoting development. Around the world, more people are recognizing that governance matters for development; that institutions, rules and political processes play a big role in whether trade flourishes between countries, whether economies grow, whether children go to school, whether development moves forward or backward. So, facilitating trade and thus development is not just a social, economic and technological challenge; it is also an institutional and political challenge. Studies have shown what poor governance means for ordinary citizens schools without teachers, courts without justice, local bureaucrats demanding bribes at every turn, etc. Much of the recent debate has focused on what makes institutions and rules effective, including transparency, participation, responsiveness, accountability and the rule of law (Ntangsi 2007). The NEPAD Initiative could act as a springboard on which good governance practices in Africa could be instituted provided its African Peer Review Mechanism (APRM) is functional and respected

Conclusion

Despite the seriousness of the issues addressed above, resource and capacity constraints faced by African countries in general and sub-Saharan African countries in particular, may make it extremely difficult to address all the problems simultaneously. Although a comprehensive approach is necessary in the long term, actions need to be prioritized in a rational way in the medium and short terms. Furthermore, the need for regional approaches and strategic partnerships to complement national measures must be stressed, since international trade involves the use of infrastructure and services of at least two countries. This is especially true for landlocked countries with key transit facilities lying outside their territorial boundaries. A regional approach can be an efficient means of coordinating actions, setting priorities, reviewing progress, mobilizing resources, allocating funds, and monitoring contribution levels, with regard to solving common problems.

References

African Development Bank, 2003, *Globalization and Africa's Development*, Tunis: African Development Report.

African Export-Import Bank, 2003, 'African Trade Report 2003 - Leveraging Emerging Opportunities in a Changing World' (http://www.uneca.org/eca_resources/Major_ECA_Websites/crci/trade_facilitation.html)

Buyonge, Creck and Kireeva, Irina, 2008, 'Trade Facilitation in Africa: Challenges and Possible Solutions', *World Customs Journal*, Vol. 2, No. 1, pp. 41-54. Available at: www.worldcustomsjournal.org.

Collier, P. 2002, *Primary Commodity Dependence and Africa's Future*, Washington, DC: World Bank.

Economic Commission for Africa (ECA), 2004, 'Assessing Regional Integration in Africa (ARIA I)', Addis Ababa: ECA.

ECA, 2004, 'Economic Report on Africa - Unlocking Africa's Trade Potential', Addis Ababa: ECA.

ECOWAS, 2010, 'ECOWAS Aid for Trade Review meeting-Introduction', 26-27 January, Abuja: ECOWAS.

ECOWAS, 2005, 'New Project Launched for Increased Intra-Regional Trade on Agriculture Products', Press Release, Abuja.

Ellis, S., 1997, 'Rapid Appraisal Techniques for Identifying Maintenance Priorities on Low Volume Roads', Transport Research Laboratory, PR/OSC/122/97. (www.uneca.org/crci/trade_facilitation.html).

ITU, 2006, ITU Information Society Statistics Database. (http://www.itu.int/ osg/spu/publications/digitalife/statisticalhighlights.html)

Limao, N. and Venables, A., 2001, 'Infrastructure, Geographical Disadvantage and Transport Costs', Mimeo, Washington DC/New York: World Bank and Columbia University. Longo, Roberto and Sekkat, Khalid, 2001, 'Obstacles to Expanding Intra-African Trade', *OECD Working Paper* No. 169.

Milner, C, Morrissey, O, and Rudaheranwa, N., 2001, 'Policy and Non-Policy Barriers to Trade and Implicit Taxation of Exports in Uganda., *The Journal of Development Studies*, Vol. 37, No. 2, December ,Tennessee State University College of Business.

National Board of Trade, 2003, Trade Facilitation from a Developing Country Perspective, Report, Stockholm Report.

Ntangsi Max Memfih, 2007, 'Managing the Brain Drain Crises in African through Pan Africanism: The Case of the NEPAD Initiative', *The International Journal Series on Tropical Issues,* Vol. 8 No. 3, September, Pacificam, Douala.

Ntangsi Max Memfih, 2004, 'The NEPAD Initiative and the Challenges of Agricultural Development and Food Security in Africa', Paper presented at the CODESRIA/DPMF International Collaborative Conference, 26 - 28 January, Addis Ababa.

Ntangsi Max Memfih, 2003, 'The NEPAD Initiative: A Basis for Fostering Economic Development in the CEMAC Zone', in *Central Africa: Crises, Reforms and Reconstruction*, E.S.D. Fomin and John W. Forje, eds, Dakar: CODESRIA Book Series.

The Economist, 2002, 'The road to hell is unpaved', 21 December , pp. 65-67.

UNCTAD, 2001, 'Transit System of Land Locked and Transit Developing Countries', TD/ BILDC/AC.1/17.

UNCTAD, 2008, *Handbook of Statistics*, New York and Geneva: United Nations. UNCTAD, 2004, *World Investment Report, 2004: The Shift Towards Services*, New York and Geneva: United Nations.

UNCTAD, 2002, *Review of Maritime Transport 2002*, Geneva: United Nations.

World Bank, 2005, 'Global Economic Prospects - Trade, Regionalism and Development', Washington DC: World Bank.

World Trade Organisation, 2004, *World Trade Report*, Geneva: WTO.

8

Facilitating the Production and Export of Manufactured Goods in Africa and Asia/Pacific: A Comparative Analysis Using Panel Data

Oluyele Akinkugbe

Introduction

The role of international trade in industrialization, economic growth and development has long been a topic of interest to economists and policy makers worldwide. A large number of studies have examined this relationship empirically (Myrdal 1957; Harberler 1959; Maizels 1968; Michaely 1962; Reidel 1984; Singer and Grey 1988; Ng and Yeats 1997), and the results confirmed Kravis's (1970) conclusions that international trade provides an important stimulus to industrialization and economic growth. Economic theory, therefore, seems to suggest a relatively direct and simple chain of causality: human development is enhanced through income growth; income growth becomes greater with more cross-border trade; trade is increased through conscious efforts directed at industrial expansion and trade facilitation. Consequently, interest has been high in identifying factors constraining a country's capacity to accelerate its industrial output and fully engage in trade, and in examining policy options towards increasing such capacities. It is widely recognized that high foreign tariffs and non-tariff restrictions reduce a country's trade below potential levels. Equally important, perhaps, is that self-imposed restrictions and high production and transaction costs can have similar adverse effects of reducing trade volume and industrial output, as well as the ability to compete efficiently in global commerce. The increasing move in recent times towards globalization, adherence to the World Trade Organization

(WTO) rules, as well as membership of many regional trade blocs have led to a gradual dismantling of tariff and non-tariff barriers to trade, the removal of other forms of constraints and technical barriers (TBT) in the way of a free flow of goods and services – thus fostering trade through trade facilitation. Despite the efforts already made in that regard, these remain major hurdles to be scaled to attain expanded trade and competitiveness in Africa.

Countries in Africa often export a narrow range of products (Collier 1998; Wohlmuth 2005). A study by Morrissey and Filatotchev (2000) noted that in the late 1990s, 39 of 47 African countries depended on two primary commodities for over half of their export earnings. As a result, these countries were highly vulnerable to commodity terms-of-trade shocks. Diversifying exports away from primary commodities into manufacturing, which currently accounts for only a relatively modest share of GDP and even more modest share of exports, could reduce this vulnerability. In addition to reducing vulnerability to shocks, increasing exports might boost income by increasing economic growth (Soderbom and Teal 2003). The conjecture, therefore, is that if export results in industrial productivity and income improvements, policies that promote industrialization and trade – or at least remove biases that discourage these – might ultimately result in greater competitiveness in the global market. Higher income, accelerated growth rate, and sustained economic diversification can then follow.

This chapter examines why government policies still continue to discourage industrial production and export, even in the light of reductions in tariff and non-tariff barriers in many African countries in recent times. The barriers include restrictive trade and poor customs regulations and administration, which are all related issues of trade facilitation.

Trade and Industrial Growth Facilitation – A General Theoretic Consideration

In the broadest sense, trade and industrial growth facilitation encompasses the domestic policies and technical regulations, institutions, standards and infrastructure associated with the movement of goods across borders. In this regard, facilitation can be conceptualized as improving efficiency in administration and procedures, along with improving logistics at ports and customs, streamlining the regulatory environment, deepening harmonization of standards and conforming to international regulations in the drive to attain free movement of goods and global trade competitiveness. Defined in this way, trade facilitation can be measured using four broad indicators (Wilson et al 2003a, 2003b, 2004): *Port*

Environment – designed to measure the quality of infrastructure of maritime, road, air and rail transportation – (transport corridors and airports); *Customs Environment* – designed to measure direct customs costs as well as administrative transparency of customs and border crossings; *Regulatory Environment* – designed to measure an economy's approach to regulations and; *E-business Usage* – designed to measure the extent to which an economy has the necessary domestic infrastructure (such as telecommunication, financial intermediaries, and logistic firms) and using networked information to improve efficiency.

A number of previous studies shared this view of the conceptualization of trade facilitation and used same to empirically examine the impact, positive or otherwise, of the indicators on trade expansion and output growth in Africa. For instance, Clarke (2005) finds that African manufacturing enterprises are less likely to export to countries with restrictive trade and customs regulation and poor customs administration. Longo and Sekkat (2004) examine the possibility of expanding intra-African trade with a gravity model, but also pay attention to obstacles to intraregional trade. They show that insufficient infrastructure, mismanagement of economic policies and internal political tensions are the main obstacles to trade in African countries. Limao and Venables (2001) also show that poor infrastructure accounts for 40 per cent of predicted transport costs for coastal countries and up to 60 per cent for landlocked countries. De Groot et al (2003) also show that a better quality of formal institutions tend to increase trade. Rodrik et al (2002) conclude that the quality of institutions has a significant and positive effect on country's total trade flows. Otsuki et al (2001) find that African export of cereals, nuts and dried fruits will decline by 4.3 (cereals) and 11 per cent (nuts and dried fruits) with a 10 per cent tighter European Union standard on aflatoxin contamination levels of these products. Francois and Manchin (2007) also find that exports performance depend on institutional quality. In the case of sub-Saharan Africa (SSA), Limao and Venables conclude that intra-SSA trade costs are substantially higher and trade volumes substantially lower than those for non-SSA countries. Also, in Africa, relatively high trading costs at the border, low resources complementary between member countries, small market size, and poor transport infrastructure limit both intra- and inter-regional trade (Yang and Gupta 2007; Foroutan and Pritchett 1993; Njinkeu and Foss 2006).

In this era of dynamic and changing global trade patterns, the costs of moving goods across international borders is just as important as tariffs – if not more important – in deter mining the cost of landed goods and the competitiveness of nations in global trade. Therefore, the ability of countries to deliver goods and services on time and at the lowest possible costs is a key determinant of integration into the world economy. Some recent studies have shown, for instance, that it costs more to transport goods from Durban in South Africa to neighbouring countries in the Southern African region than it costs to ship the same tonnage of goods from Singapore to Durban. This may explain why the issues of trade facilitation or part of the so-called Singapore issues are critical aspects of recent WTO negotiations and the broader DOHA Development Agenda.

Export and Trade Facilitation of Africa's Manufactured Goods: A Situation Analysis

Manufacturing accounts for only a relatively modest share of value added in most African countries (except for South Africa). Table 8.1 reveals that Africa's participation in the global trading system has been quite marginal, and has not recorded any marked improvement since 1980. In actual fact, Africa's percentage share in world export declined from 5.8 per cent in 1980 to an all-time low of 2.08 per cent in 1995. It has since increased – albeit marginally – to 3.3 per cent in 2008. The case of SSA follows exactly the same pattern; declined from 2.46 per cent in 1980 to 1.01 per cent in 1995.

Table 8.1: Africa's Percentage Share of World Exports, 1980 – 2008

	1980	1990	1995	2000	2001	2002	2003	2004	2005	2006	2008
Europe	42.85	47.04	44.52	40.08	41.99	42.74	43.77	42.83	40.79	40.10	38.82
America	14.44	14.99	15.04	16.43	15.99	14.61	13.25	12.56	12.13	12.04	11.14
Africa	5.86	3.08	2.08	2.28	2.23	2.26	2.37	2.52	2.85	2.78	3.30
SSA excl. RSA	2.46	1.23	0.86	1.01	0.98	1.03	1.07	1.15	1.33	1.33	1.66
Asia	18.0	16.94	20.99	23.7	23.08	24.04	24.54	26.0	27.85	28.29	29.76

Source: UNCTAD, Handbook of Statistics, 2006/07, 2009

The current reported figure for 2008 is 1.66 per cent. Table 8.2 also shows that Africa as a whole (sub-Saharan Africa and North Africa as represented by MENA) lags significantly behind the rest of the regions of the world on account of manufacturing value added as percentage of GDP. In 2006, manufacturing value added was only equal to about 14.3 per cent of GDP as opposed to about 32 per cent in East Asia and the Pacific and 18.3 per cent in Latin America and the Caribbean. The difference between the successful Asian economies and sub-Saharan Africa is even more pronounced when looking at manufactured exports (Table 8.2). Manufactured exports as a percentage of total merchandise exports were above 80 per cent in East Asia and the Pacific in 2006 and about 53 per cent in Europe and Central Asia for the same period – compared to just 33 per cent in sub-Saharan Africa. As a percentage of GDP, Clarke (2005) indicated that manufactured exports from sub-Saharan Africa were just about 3 per cent.

In terms of the factors that may directly or indirectly impact on Africa's manufactured exports performance, Table 8.3 reveals quite clearly that even though tariffs have been falling over the years in most of Africa, customs and trade regulations might have imposed some noticeable constraints. In many African countries, it takes a relatively long time for exports and imports to clear customs procedures and, in some cases, additional informal payments to customs officers are needed to ensure timely processing. In addition to long processing times, the paper work associated with importing and exporting can be burdensome (Milner et al 2000; World Bank 2004). Furthermore, and as reported in the investment climate surveys, some enterprises need to complete additional procedures, such as obtaining import or export licenses, to import intermediate inputs, raw materials or capital goods and to export their final products. Table 8.3 shows that whereas the average number of days to clear exports in Africa is over 6 days, it is 3.8 days in Asia. For imports, the same exercise takes about 10 days in Africa and just over 5 days in Asia.

Table 8.2: Regional Manufacturing Value Added and Manufactured Exports, 1995 – 2004

	Exports of goods and services (% of GDP)		Manufactures exports (% of merchandise exports)		Manufacturing, value added (% of GDP)		
	1995–2006	2000	1995–2006	2006	1995	2000	2006
East Asia & Pacific	29.84	36.10	59.93	80.19	29.84	30.02	2.03
	47.30.	—	80.37	—	--	18.87	2007
Europe & Central Asia	--	40.88	--	56.44	22.31	18.17	18.34
	40.10.	—	45.99	—	14.37	—	—
Latin America & Caribbean	--	20.63	32.25	57.73	13.34	—	12.56
	25.70	—	52.71	—	23.64	—	—
Middle East & North Africa	--	—	—	—	18.23	—	18.95
	14.37	28.40	—	19.26	16.57	—	—
South Africa	57.80	—	14.70	54.31	14.29	—	—
Sub-Saharan Africa	23.64	27.87	--	31.15	—	—	—
	29.85	—	52.99	—	—	—	—
	16.57	32.35	--	—	—	—	—
	35.48	—	33.30	—	—	—	—

Source: World Development Indicators, 2008 (online)

Table 8.3: Customs and Trade Regulations and Days for Exports and Imports to Clear Customs

	% of Enterprises Reporting Trade and Customs Regulations as a major or very severe problems		Days for exports and Imports to clear customs (average)	
	Exporters	Non-Exporters	Exports	Imports
Africa	**40.1**	**32.6**	**6.1**	**9.9**
Kenya	47.0	39.1	4.5	9.6
Tanzania	41.2	26.6	11.7	18.5
Senegal	37.9	35.4	6.4	7.3
Asia	**27.9**	**11.7**	**3.8**	**5.4**
China	32.3	9.6	5.4	7.5
India	16.9	11.5	–	–
Philippines	34.6	13.9	2.3	3.3

Source: World Bank, Investment Climate Assessment, 2004

Literature Review and Methodology

The greatest challenge faced by researchers over the years has to do with obtaining conceptually acceptable measures of trade facilitation which can meet policy makers' needs. That is, how do research results assist policy makers to reallocate scarce resources in order to encourage the flow of trade? Should policy makers start with such measures of trade facilitation as port modernization, customs reforms, regulatory harmonization or e-commerce infrastructure? All these reforms are clearly important and needed in any country for improved export performance, but limited resources – that confront most Africa countries – imply that not all of them can be addressed at the same time, and therefore some prioritization may be necessary. The empirical literature on trade facilitation is limited, since attention only began to shift in this direction after the emergence of the WTO and the negotiation rounds in 1994, as well as the DOHA Development Agenda (of which one of the contentious issues was, and still is, the Singapore issues). Maskus, Wilson, and Otsuki (2001a) addressed some of the more important empirical methods and challenges in quantifying the gains of trade facilitation in the area of harmonized regulations. The Asia Pacific Foundation of Canada (1999) outlines the relative importance of the three kinds of trade facilitation measures (customs, standards and regulatory conformity, and business mobility) for APEC business but did not assess the impact on APEC of trade facilitation improvements. Other empirical analysis, such as APEC (1999), UNCTAD (2001), and Hertel et al (2001) used CGE models to quantify the benefits of improved trade facilitation on trade flows. Similarly, studies such as those by Freund and Weinhold (2001), Fink et al (2002), Moenius (2000) and Wilson et al (2003, 2004) used the gravity models and found that bilaterally shared standards, decrease in communications costs, enhanced port efficiency, improvements in customs and financial resources to trade significantly promote the expansion of trade, whereas regulatory barriers tend to deter trade. Furthermore, Otsuki, Wilson and Sewadeh (2001a, 2001b) applied the gravity model to the case of food safety standards, and found that African exports of cereals, nuts and dried fruits will decline with a tighter EU standard on aflatoxin contamination levels of these products.

The analysis undertaken for this chapter departs in a way from the methodology applied in earlier studies; we had explored the use of panel regression technique of one-way error component random effects model. The fixed effect model was tried but rejected based on the results of the Hausman specification test. The use of Panel Data technique in this regard enabled us to exploit the inherent advantages of large number of data points – increased degree of freedom and reduced colinearity among the explanatory variables – that are associated with such large data points and, of course, increased efficiency of econometric estimates. The basic structure of the equation estimated is:

$$ln(V_i^t) = b_1 ln PE_i + b_2 ln CE_i + b_3 ln RE_i + b_4 ln EB_i + b_5 ln(GNPPC_i) + b_6 ln(TTP_i) + b_7 ln(ICT_i) + b_8 ln(TPC_i) + ''»_i + å_i^t$$

(1)

Where i stands for the countries in the sample and t denotes trading years (t = 1995... 2006). The dependent variable denoted as V_i^t stands for Manufactures exports as percentage of total merchandise exports. This is a preferred choice since the use of aggregate exports, which will then include fuels; ores and metals may distort the results of the analysis. The terms PE_i, CE_i, RE_i and EB_i denote country i's indicators of port efficiency, customs environment, regulatory environment and e-business usage. GNPPC denoted per capita GNP, TTP indicates Tax and trade policy variables; ICT indicates indicators of Information and Technology, while TPC represents indicators of Transport, Power and Communications. The parameters b'_s are the coefficients to be estimated, whereas the time invariant term $"»_i$ is the exporter-specific intercept that is expected to capture variation in trade flows due to the unobserved difference in quality of goods, domestic policies and border costs in exporting countries. The term $å^i_i$ is the error term that is assumed to be normally distributed with mean zero. Equation (1) was estimated twice (once each for the African data series and the APEC data series), using the panel regression estimation technique.

Data and Data Sources

Pooled, cross-country, annual time series data for the period 1995 – 2006 for 20 African countries and 10 selected member countries of APEC were used for the empirical analyses. The major source of data is the World Development Indicators (WDI) 2007 (online). One major problem with the dataset is the issue of missing data points. Given this problem, we resorted to the use of the variables for which consistent data were available for the period 1995 to 2004. This same problem also necessitated the use of only 20 African countries in the sample[1], since for many of the African countries, WDI 2007 (online) reported missing points for most the variables considered. By taking this route, we might have been able to reduce the problem of random fluctuations in the data and, at the same time, exploit the time-series properties of the data set.

Variables

The dependent variables used for the analysis is Manufactured exports (percentage of merchandise exports) (MANEX). The explanatory variables on the other hand derive from the conceptualization of trade facilitation as previously explained. Moreover, due to lack of sufficient series on variables that could have constituted better proxies for the indicators for selected countries, we were constrained to the use of the following explanatory variables: real per capita GDP (RGDPPC) (+) – to measure market size of the economy (used essentially as a control variable); taxes on exports (% of tax revenue) (OPEN) (-) (an indication of restrictive trade policy regime); number of start-up procedures to register a business (NSTART) (-) – to measure the stringency of, transparency and stability of local regulations; aircraft departures (AIR) (+) – a measure of international linkage; Fixed and mobile phone subscribers per 1,000 people (PHONESUB) (+) – a measure of infrastructure development; corruption perception index (PERCEPTN) (+); domestic credit to the private sector (% of GDP) (CREDIT) (+) – a measure of the development of the domestic financial system; international telecoms, outgoing traffic (INTT), (proxy for ICT) (+) and a measure of e-commerce; Procedures to enforce a Contract (NFORCEP) (-) – a measure of the transparency and ease of enforcement of environmental regulation. Summary statistics for the data sets, which consist of twelve annual observations for each country and each variable, are provided in Tables 8.4a and 8.4b. The tables provide a general view of the data. As can be observed, there are no excessive inter-country variations in the data for most of the variables.

Table 8.4a: Summary Statistics – African Data Set

Variables	Mean	Std. Error	Minimum	Maximum
MANEX	34.725	26.714	0.207	90.602
AIR	21129.936	28101.595	700.000	146800.001
RGDPPC	1182.239	1162.874	156.302	4289.377
PERCEPTN	3.479	1.382	0.690	6.400
NFORCEP	31.625	12.208	16.000	58.001
INTT	216.341	142.489	31.833	649.689
OPEN	69.220	23.308	0.0001	132.304
NSTART	11.125	2.239	5.000	14.000
CREDIT	39.222	43.891	-77.377	159.542
PHONE	86.985	120.916	1.873	559.462

Source: Author's computations

Table 8.4b: Summary Statistics – APEC Data Set

Variables	Mean	Std. Error	Minimum	Maximum
Variables	Mean	Std. Error	Minimum	Maximum
MANEX	66.905	27.671	11.127	95.425
AIR	78315.084	36248.656	1814.449	1.74785.225
RGDPPC	7030.633	8879.504	657.995	32249.690
PERCEPTN	4.831	2.335	1.700	9.400
NFORCEP	5.443	6.734	2.757	18.995
INTT	1814.449	1590.015	439	7625.869
OPEN	126.423	109.505	0.000	473.509
NSTART	7.380	4.270	0.001	13.000
CREDIT	85.214	53.906	15.656	210.417
PHONE	47.855	45.870	1.816	192.590

Source: Author's computations

Following the standard practice in empirical analysis that involves time-series data, the data were tested for stationarity using the panel unit root tests procedure developed by Pedroni (1999). This test rejected the null of unit root at the 5 per cent significance level.[2] The data were also tested for heteroscedasticity using the white's test, and checked for multi-collinearity. Similarly, the null of heteroscedasticity was rejected at the 5 per cent significance level.

The correlation matrix and the variance inflation factor (VIF), respectively reported in Tables 8.5a and 8.5b (African Data set) and 8.6a and 8.6b (APEC data set), do not indicate the presence of severe multicollinearity among the explanatory variables.[3] The correlation matrix clearly shows that the pair-wise correlation is almost non-existent for most of the variables. The only two variables for which there appears presence of some positive correlation are Real GDP per capita and Corruption Perception Index in the African data set and OPEN, Real GDP per capita in the APEC data set. But even for these variables, the correlation coefficients do not significantly exceed 0.8 as to pose a serious multicolinearity problem. For multicollinearity to cause a serious problem, the rule of thumb is that the correlation coefficient between two regressors must exceed 0.8 (Brooks 2008: 51).

Table 8.5a: Correlation Matrix – African Data Set

	Air	Rgdppc	Perceptn	Nforcep	Intt	Open	Nstart	Credit	Phone
Air	1.000	0.406	0.259	0.048	-	-0.448	-0.245	0.079	0.328
Rgdppc	0.406	1.000	0.737	0.024	0.474	0.358	0.101	0.328	0.073
Perceptn	0.259	0.737	1.000	-0.216	-	0.339	-0.251	0.126	0.550
Nforcep	0.048	0.024	-0.216	1.000	0.156	0.450	0.547	0.143	-0.069
Intt	-0.474	-0.028	0.39	3.156	1.000	0.321	-0.139	-0.536	-0.111
Open	-0.448	0.358	0.339	-0.450	0.321	1.000	-0.139	-0.536	0.111
Nstart	-0.245	-0.101	-0.251	0.547	-0.139	-0.091	1.000	-0.190	-0.104
Credit	0.079	0.328	0.126	0.143	-0.536	-0.291	-0.190	1.000	0.372
Phone	0.328	0.073	0.550	-0.069	-0.111	0.390	-0.104	0.372	1.000
				0.139					
				-0.536					
				-0.111					

Source: Author's computations

Table 8.5b: Correlation Matrix – APEC Data Set

	Air	Rgdppc	Perceptn	Nforcep	Intt	Open	Nstart	Credit	Phone
Air	1.000	0.754	0.787	0.354	0.585	0.736	-0.139	0.495	0.645
Rgdppc	0.754	1.000	0.827	0.403	0.767	0.885	-0.210	0.663	0.877
Perceptn	0.787	0.827	1.000	0.536	0.724	0.708	-0.206	0.632	0.763
Nforcep	0.354	0.403	0.536	1.000	0.621	0.402	0.243	0.205	0.498
Intt	0.585	6767	0.724	0.621	1.000	0.798	0.187	0.514	0.906
Open	0.736	0.885	0.708	0.402	0.798	1.000	-0.115	0.669	0.848
Nstart	-0.139	-0.210	-0.206	0.243	0.187	-0.115	1.000	-0.338	0.122
Credit	0.495	0.663	0.632	0.205	0.514	0.669	-0.388	1.000	0.611
Phone	0.645	0.877	0.763	0.498	0.906	0.848	0.122	0.611	1.000

Source: Author's computations

Results

The Panel regression results of the estimated equation for the two data sets (Tables 8.6a and 8.6b) indicate that to a reasonable extent, the approach adopted for the analysis in this chapter – generating a set of distinct trade facilitation indicators and using them in a regression model––is generally successful. Table 6a shows that coefficients of the nine trade facilitation measures are generally significant at conventional levels (but for Aircraft Departures that is only marginally significant); and all are of the expected signs. Table 6b on the other hand shows the results for the selected APEC member countries. The estimated coefficients are all significant at conventional levels; all also turning out with expected signs.

Worthy of further elaboration is the use of the Corruption Perception Index (CPI). As reported by Transparency International (TI), CPI relates to perception of the degree of corruption as seen by business people and country analysts in the reporting countries. It ranges between 10 (highly clean) and 0 (highly corrupt). We resorted to the use of this variable since we could not find any reliable series on port efficiency (customs efficiency). In this regard, our conceptualization is that CPI could serve, both as an indication of the level of corruption in a country (which of course deters investment and trade flows) as well as customs environment. Our choice in this regard is further reinforced by the well-known fact that in many African countries, irregular additional payments connected with import and export permits, business licences, exchange controls, tax assessment, police protection or loan application may in a very significant way constitute serious constraint to trade flows. The positive relationship between CPI and manufactured exports that derive from the regression results indicate that cleaner countries are likely to be highly productive and export more manufactured goods.

Finally, by way of caveat, it must be mentioned that the estimated coefficients may be biased due to the sample selection bias that results from omitting observations with zero trade (Wall 2000). Downward bias is likely for the coefficients on the trade facilitation measures because observation with zero trade caused by poor conditions of trade facilitation, other things being equal, are ignored. The implications of this selection bias could not be examined because the data source (WDI 2007) does not distinguish zero trade from missing records.

Table 8.6a: Panel Regression Results (Random Effects Model) – African Countries

Variables	Estimated Coefficients	p-values	Variance Inflation Factor (VIF)
Constant	10.6186	0.00	1.7430.
Rgdppc	7806	0.020	1.989
Credit	0.6756	0.002	2.189
Nstart	-0.8531	0.045	1.336
Nforcep	-0.0161	0.035	2.321
Intt	-0.0941	0.000	1.996
Air	0.4461	0.118	2.698
Open	0.5821	0.001	1.897
Perception	0.3324	0.013	2.436
PHONE	1.8247		0.000
	2.085		
No. of Observations	200		
No. of Countries	20		
R^2	0.678934		

Notes: A p-value that exceeds 0.10 indicates that the parameter estimate is not significant at 1%, 5% and 10% levels.

Source: Author's computations

Table 8.6b: Panel Regression Results (Random Effects Model) – APEC Countries

Variables	Estimated Coefficients	p-values	Variance Inflation Factor (VIF)
Constant	5.2715		0.032
Rgdppc	2.384		
Credit	0.8225		0.0126
Nstart	1.439		
Nforcep	- 0.6641		0.004
Intt	2.358		
Air	-0.9931	0.001	1.748
Open	0.5821	0.001	1.897
Perception	0.3324	0.013	2.436
PHONE	1.8247		0.000
	2.085		
No. of Obervations	120		
No. of Countries	10		
R^2	0.879316		

Notes:	A p-value that exceeds 0.10 indicates that the parameter estimate is not significant at 1%, 5% and 10% levels.

Source: Author's computations

Summary and Conclusion

Despite significant reductions in tariff and non-tariff barriers in many African countries in recent times, government policies, including restrictive trade and poor customs regulations and administration – all related issues of trade facilitation – still continue to discourage export. In this chapter, we have examined the relationship between the indicators of trade facilitation and trade flows (manufactured goods export) through the use of pooled, time series data that were obtained from the World Bank, World Development Indicators (WDI 2007) for 20 selected African countries, and 10 APEC member countries for the sake of comparison.

The results show that significant improvements in infrastructure, well-functioning institutions, and e-business usage may expand trade; whereas regulatory barriers and the perception of corruption in a country will deter trade in the two regions; though on almost all counts, APEC seemed to have performed a lot better than Africa, an indication of better functioning policy and institutional space.

The distinguishing feature of this chapter rests in the use of different indicators of trade and industrial growth facilitation and examining their relative efficacy on manufactured goods exports in a multi-country framework. In the context of quantifying the benefits of trade and industrial growth facilitation efforts in Africa and APEC, or anywhere in the developing world for that matter, this multiple-indicator approach as suggested in the literature, as well as the panel estimation method employed in this chapter, may enhance the efficacy of targeted policy design and implementation.

Our recommendations are that governments in the different African countries will need to emulate the drive towards best practices in creating a favourable investment climate and well-functioning institutions, which seem to be driving the success of APEC regional member countries in trade and industrial expansion in the global value chain. Reform policies and programmes have to be targeted at the different indicators for Africa to be globally competitive in manufactured goods export, and to enable it to escape the commodity export dilemma that has plagued Africa's development far too long.

Notes

1. The 20 African countries in the sample are: Algeria, Botswana, Cameroon, Egypt, Ghana, Kenya, Madagascar, Malawi, Mali, Mauritius, Morocco, Mozambique, Namibia, Nigeria, Senegal, South Africa, Tanzania, Tunisia, Uganda, and Zambia; while the 10 Asian Pacific Economic Cooperation Countries (APEC) countries are: Indonesia, Philippines, Peru, China, Malaysia, Thailand, Mexico, Chile, Singapore and Hong Kong.

2. The test was carried out by expressing the explanatory variables in the same form as they appear in the regression equations. The Augmented Dickey-Fuller statistics for panel and group under null of unit root or no cointegration with 9 regressors are -4.01 and -4.87, respectively. Thus, the null of unit root is rejected. A computer printout of the results is available on request from the author (yeleakinkugbe@gmail.com).

3. The VIF was calculated from auxiliary regressions as VIF $= 1/1\text{-}R2j$, where R2j is obtained by regressing each explanatory variable included in the original regression on the remaining explanatory variables. A value of VIF higher than 10 usually indicates the presence of multicollinearity.

References

Akinkugbe, O., 2007, 'A Panel data Analysis of Trade Facilitation Issues and manufactured Goods Export in sub-Saharan Africa', *The Botswana Journal of Economics*, Vol. 4, Issue 7, pp. 28-37.

Asia Pacific Economic Co-operation (APEC), 1999, 'Assessing APEC Trade Liberalization and Facilitation', Update by Economic Committee of APEC, September, Singapore: APEC.

Asia Pacific Foundation of Canada, 1999, *Survey on Customs, Standards and Business Mobility in the APEC Region*, Vancouver: APF Canada.

Brooks, C., 2008, *Introductory Econometrics for Finance*, Cambridge: Cambridge University Press.

Clarke, G. R. G., 2001, 'Does Internet Connectivity Affect Export Performance? Evidence

Clarke, G.R.G., 2005, 'Beyond Tariffs and Quotas: Why Don't African Manufacturers Export More?' *World Bank Working Paper* No. 3617, Washington DC.

Collier, P., 1998, 'Globalization: Implications for Africa', in Zubair, Iqbal & Khan, Moshin S. ,eds, *Trade Reform and Regional Integration in Africa*, Washington DC: International Monetary Fund.

De Groot, H.L.F., Linders, G.J., Rietveld, P., and Subramanian, U., 2003, 'The Institutional Determinants of Bilateral Trade Patterns', Tinbergen Institute Discussion Paper, TI 2003-044/3.

Fink, C., Matoo, A. & Neagu, C. I., 2002, 'Trade in International Maritime Services: How Much Does Policy Matter?', *World Bank Economic Review*, Vol.16, No.2, pp. 81-108.

Foroutan, F. and Pritchett, L., 1993, 'Intra-sub-Saharan African Trade: Is It Too Little?' *Journal of African Economies*, 2(1), 74-105.

François, J. and M. Manchin, M., 2007, 'Institutional Quality, Infrastructure and the Propensity to Export', Policy Research Working Paper, No. 4152, World Bank: Washington, D.C.

Frankel, J. A., 1997, *Regional Trading Blocs in the World Economic System*, Institute for International Economics, Washington, D.C., Processed.

Freund, C. & Weinhold, D., 2000, 'On the Effect of the Internet on International Trade', *International Finance Discussion Papers*, No. 693, 2000, Board of Governors of the Federal Reserve System, New York.

Harberler, G., 1959, 'International Trade and Economic Development', in J.D. Theberge, ed., *Economics of Trade and Development*, New York.

Hertel, T. W., Walmsley, T, & Itakura, K., 2001, 'Dynamic Effect of the "New Age" Free Trade Agreement between Japan and Singapore', *Journal of Economic Integration*, Vol. 16, No. 4, pp. 446-84.

Kravis, I., 1970, 'Trade as a Handmaiden of Growth: Similarities between the Nineteenth and Twentieth Centuries', *The Economic Journal*, December.

Limao, N. and A.J. Venables, A.J., 2001, 'Infrastructure, Geographical Disadvantage, Transport Costs, and Trade', *World Bank Economic Review*, 15(3), 451-479.

Longo, R. and Sekkat, K., 2004, 'Economic Obstacles to Expanding Intra-African Trade', *World Development*, 32(8), 1309-1321.

Maizels, A., 1968, *Exports and Economic Growth in Developing Countries*, Cambridge, Massachusets.

Maskus, K. E. & Wilson, J. S., 2001, *Quantifying the Impact of Technical Barriers to Trade: Can it be done? Studies in International Economics*, Ann Arbor: University of Michigan Press.

Maskus, K. E., Wilson, J. S. & Otsuki, T., 2001, 'An Empirical Framework for Analyzing Technical Regulations and Trade', in Keith Maskus, & J. S.Wilson, eds, *Quantifying the impact of technical barriers to trade: Can it be done? 2001,* Ann Arbor: University of Michigan Press.

Michaely, M., 1962, *Concentration in International Trade,* Amsterdam: North Holland.

Milner, C., Morrissey, O. & Rudaheranwa, N., 2000, 'Policy and Non-Policy Barriers to Trade and Implicit Taxation of Exports in Uganda', *Journal of Development Studies*, Vol. 37, No. 2, pp. 67–90.

Moenius, J., 2000, 'Three Essays on Trade Barriers and Trade Volumes', Unpublished Ph.D. Dissertation, University of California, San Diego.

Morrissey, O., & Filatotchev, I., 2000, 'Globalization and Trade: The Implications for Exports from Marginalized Economies', *Journal of Development Studies*, Vol. 37, No. 2, pp. 1–12.

Myrdal, G., 1957, *Rich Lands and Poor*, New York.

Ng, F. & Yeats, A., 1997, 'Open Economies Work better! Did Africa's Protectionist Policies cause its marginalization in World Trade?' *World Development*, July, pp. 351-89.

Ng, F. & Yeats, A., 2000, 'On the recent trade performance of sub-Saharan African Countries: Cause for hope or more of the Same?', *Africa Region Working Paper Series*, No. 7, Washington DC: World Bank.

Njinkeu, D. and Fosso, P.B., 2006, 'Intra-African Trade and Regional Integration', Prepared for the ADB/AERC International Conference on Accelerating Africa's Development Five Years into the Twenty-first Century, Tunis, 22-24 November.

Njinkeu, D. Wilson, J. and Fosso, P.B., 2009, *Expanding Trade within Africa: The impact of Trade Facilitation*, ILEAP Background Brief No. 14, ILEAP, Toronto.

Otsuki, T., Wilson, J. S. & Sewadeh, M., 2001a, 'What Price Precaution? European Harmonisation of Aflatoxin regulations and African groundnut Exports', *European Review of Agricultural Economics*, Vol. 28, No. 3, pp. 263-284.

Otsuki, T., Wilson, J. S. & Sewadeh, M., 2001b, 'Saving Two in a Billion: Quantifying the Trade Effect of European Food Safety Standards on African Exports', *Food Policy*, No. 26, Washington DC: World Bank,.

Pedroni, P., 1999, 'Critical Values for Cointegration Tests in Heterogeneous Panels with Multiple Regressors', *Oxford Bulletin of Economics and Statistics*, Vol. 61, pp. 653-70.

Riedel, J., 1984, 'Trade as an Engine of Growth Revisited', *Economic Journal*, 1984, March, pp. 231-46.

Rodrik, D., Subramanian, A., and Trebbi, F., 2002, *Institutions Rule: The Primacy of Institutions on Integration and Geography in Development Economics*, Washington DC: IMF, WP/02/189.

Soderbom, M. & Teal, F., 2003, 'Are Manufacturing Exports the Key to Economic Success in Africa?' *Journal of African Economics*, Vol. 12, No. 1, pp. 1–29.

Singer, H.W. & Gray, P., 1988, 'Trade Policy and Growth of Developing Countries', *World Development 1988*, No. 3.

Tinbergen, J., 1962, Sharing the World Economy: Suggestions for an International Economic Policy, New York: Twentieth Century Fund.

United Nations Conference on Trade and Development, 2001, *E-Commerce and Development Report*, Geneva: UNCTAD.

United Nations Conference on Trade and Development (UNCTAD), 2007, *Handbook of Statistics 2006/07*, Geneva: UNCTAD.

United Nations Conference on Trade and Development (UNCTAD), 2009, *Handbook of Statistics 2009*, Geneva: UNCTAD.

Wall, H. J., 2000, 'Gravity Model Specification and the Effects of the Canada-US Border', *Federal Reserve Bank of St. Louis Working Paper Series*, 20000-024A, St. Louis.

Wilson, J. S., Mann, C., Woo, Y. P. Assanie, N., & Inbom Choi, I., 2002, *'Trade Facilitation: A Development Perspective in the Asia-Pacific Region'*, Asia Pacific Economic Cooperation, Singapore.

Wilson, J.S., Mann, C. L., & Otsuki, T., 2003a, *Trade Facilitation and Economic Development: Measuring the Impact*, World Bank Working Paper, No. 2988, Washington DC: World Bank.

Wilson, J.S., Mann, C. L., & Otsuki, T., 2003b, 'Trade Facilitation and Economic Development: A New Approach to Quantifying the Impact', *The World Bank Economic Review,*2003, Vol. 17, No. 3, pp. 367-389.

Wilson, J.S., C.L. Mann and T. Otsuki, T., 2004, *Assessing the Potential Benefit of Trade Facilitation: A Global Perspective*, World Bank Working Paper 3224, Washington, DC: World Bank.

Wohlmuth, K., 2005, *African Development Perspective Yearbook: Escaping the Primary Commodities Dilemma*, Vol. 11, 2005, Hamburg/London: VERLAG Munster.

World Economic Forum, 2005, *'Global Competitiveness Report'*, Geneva: World Economic Forum.

World Bank, 2004, *Investment Climate Assessment: Enterprise Performance and Growth*, Washington DC World Bank.

World Bank, 2007, *World Development Indicators*, Retrieved from https:// publications.worldbank.org/register/WDI2007.

World Bank, 2008, *World Development Indicators*, Retrieved from https:// publications.worldbank.org/register/WDI2008; 18 July 2008.

Yang, Y. and Gupta, S., 2007, 'Regional Trade Arrangements in Africa: Past Performance and the Way Forward', *African Development Review*, 19(3), 399-431.

9

Africa's Development, Climate Change and Carbon Trade: Whose Agenda is it, Anyway?

Godwell Nhamo

Introduction

As the Kyoto Protocol came into force in February 2005, a carbon rush began to gain steam in the financial industry. Investors predicted that carbon trade could become one of the largest markets in the world with trading volume worth between US$60 and US$259 billion by 2008 and some unlikely actors were already gearing up to profit from this new, invisible market. Foremost among them was the World Bank (Foreign Policy in Focus 2005: 1).

The ratification of the Kyoto Protocol (KP) in February 2005 moved the world towards a global consensus on the need to address the negative developmental and environmental impacts associated with global warming and climate change. Since then, both state and non-state actors have moved even closer to this consensus that was being spearheaded by the United Kingdom, a country that scored a first in 2008 by passing a Climate Act (UK Government 2008). Climate change is now as much a global environmental issue as it is developmental and economic, requiring urgent attention. The Fourth Assessment Report (AR4) of the Intergovernmental Panel on Climate Change (IPCC) predicts that by 2020 there could be hundreds of millions of environmental refugees and conflicts over land due to severe climate change impacts resulting in reduced economic growth (McCarthy et al. 2007).

The AR4 also reports that income inequalities between poor and rich countries will increase. Although this must be viewed with caution, the African continent is predicted to be the most affected, with increased droughts, crop failure, spread of human disease and rising sea levels. To mitigate climate change, the developed countries (listed under KP's Annex 1) have engaged the developing (non-Annex 1 or host Party) countries, some from Africa under the KP's CDM. Among the leading host countries for the CDM project implementation is the CIBS block – A block made up of China, India, Brazil and South Africa. These countries are today commonly known as newly industrialized or emerging economies.

Ayre and Callway (2005) see the economic pillar in sustainable development overshadowing environmental and societal issues. To them, the processes surrounding the birth of the KP were highly controlled by the rich countries. Such countries decided how much poor countries should pay, and how much the rich countries should do to control climate change and clean the air. The aspect of Africa being controlled has a long history: from slave trade that provided free, forced and cheap labour, through the partitioning and scramble of Africa, to the introduction of the Structural Adjustment Programmes and conditional development aid, denied and eventually controlled trade in ivory and now the KP and post-KP that restricts our development potential through restricted emissions.

Understanding Climate Change: The Bigger Picture

Climate change has been identified as a critical environmental and developmental concern of the twenty-first century, not only in Africa, but the world over (SADC-REEP 2007). Key developmental and trade issues are increasingly being linked to climate change, an aspect that challenges us to understand and closely monitor this complex web of inter-and intra-relationships of phenomena. The changing climate generally impacts on the economic, socio-political and environmental pillars of development. More specifically, climate change negatively impacts the provision of land resources, food security, freshwater, marine environments, forests and woodlands, biodiversity, poverty, disease, and governance, to name but a few of the phenomena. Of late, different regional and national governments' understanding on climate change have even caused further fragmentation in the continent. This serves us no good and plays well into the hands of our trade 'enemies'. Understanding this web of relationships and addressing critical points associated with it becomes the departure point for effectively addressing key developmental concerns within the context of the KP.

Climate change as recognized by the Intergovernmental Panel on Climate Change (IPCC) refers to any change in climate over time, whether due to natural variability or as a result of human activity. This usage differs from that in the United Nations Framework Convention on Climate Change (UNFCCC), where climate change refers to a change of climate that is attributed directly or indirectly to human activity that alters the composition of the global atmosphere and that is in addition to natural climate variability observed over comparable time periods. Due to the fact that the IPCC is currently shaping policy around climate change globally, its definition for climate change is adapted for this publication. The UNFCCC aims at monitoring anthropogenic GHG emissions. Carbon dioxide (CO_2), methane (CH_4) and nitrous oxide (N_2O) are among the chief GHGs listed in the literature (Rehan and Nehdi 2005).

KP's Clean Development Mechanism

The KP framework established the CDM as a global mechanism to achieve cost-efficient GHG reductions in developing countries. The CDM allows governments and companies in developed countries to invest in CDM projects in order to earn Certified Emission Reduction Units (CERs), which can be used towards meeting their 2012 emissions reduction targets. Developed countries under the KP are expected to reduce GHG emissions on average by 5.2 per cent between the period 2008 and 2012 based on their 1990 base year levels (Ellis et al 2007). The schematic representation of how the CDM and the CERs work is given in Figure 9.1.

Figure 9.1: The Clean Development Mechanism and CERs

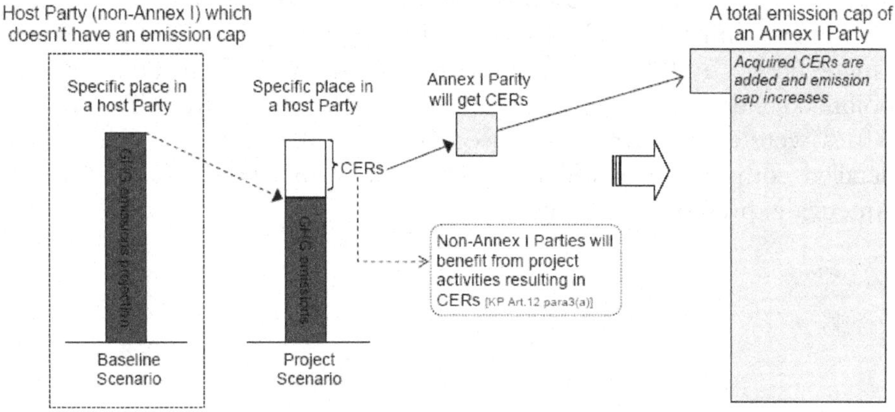

The purpose of CDM is to provide support to developing countries in achieving sustainable development (Lopes 2002) through the implementation of CDM projects in a range of sectors that include energy, waste management, industrial processes, transport, construction, oils and natural gas as well as fuel combustion. The developed countries that have ceilings for GHG emissions (known as emission caps), help developing countries which do not have emission caps, to implement projects that reduce GHG emissions (Muzino 2007). Based on the IPCC Second Assessment Report (Lopes 2002), one unit of CER (Figure 1) is equal to one metric tonne of carbon dioxide equivalent (CO_2e). This CO_2e is calculated according to the Global Warning Potential (GWP), based on an index allowing expression of the quantities of different GHGs in terms of CO_2e. Hence the CO_2e makes it possible to add up the reductions of different gases.

CDM Investment Climate

The CDM investment climate index (ICI) is critical when dealing with CDM project investment. The CDM ICI is computed using parameters such as: the Institutional Investor Country Rating (based on the macroeconomic environment index, the public institutions index and the technology index), The Transparency International Corruption Perceptions Index, the ratification of the KP, the appointment of a Designated National Authority (DNA), acceptance of a methodology or registration of a project by the Executive Board, and the purchase of climate certificates by selected international funds (Satoguina 2006). The CDM ICI measures the investment climate for CDM projects in given host countries. This index ranges between 100 points, considered to be the highest, and zero (0) points considered to be the lowest. As at 2006, the top five CDM ICI in Africa were South Africa, Morocco, Tunisia, Mauritius and Uganda. A detailed comparison of top five CDM ICI from Africa, Asia and Latin America is presented in Table 9.1.

Table 9.1: CDM ICI from Africa, Asia and Latin America

Region	Country	Rank (top five)	CDM ICI (maximum 100 points)	Regional Classification
Africa	South Africa	1	76.4	Good climate
	Morocco	2	70.9	Satisfactory climate
	Tunisia	3	52.6	Adequate climate
	Mauritius	4	52.2	Adequate climate
	Uganda	5	49.7	Adequate climate
Asia	Korea (Republic)	1	89.9	Good climate
	India	2	84.5	Good climate
	Philippines	3	74.7	Satisfactory climate
	China	4	74.3	Satisfactory climate
	Indonesia	5	73.8	Satisfactory climate
Latin America	Chile	1	94	Very good climate
	Mexico	2	86	Good climate
	Brazil	3	83	Good climate
	Costa Rica	4	75	Satisfactory climate
	Panama	5	74	Satisfactory climate

Source: Compiled after (DNA of China 2007; DNA of South Africa 2006; DNA/National CDM Authority of India 2006;Hirschle & Paulo 2006)

CDM projects Status

As at 26 April 2010, a total of 2,165 CDM projects had been registered by the Executive Board of the UNFCCC. Out of these total, 1,647 CDM projects were from the Asia and the Pacific region while 464 were from Latin America and the Caribbean (UNFCCC Secretariat 2007a). Africa had a mere 41 CDM projects registered and the category 'Other' constituted the remaining 13 CDM projects. The distribution of these projects in terms of percentages is shown in Figure 9.2.

Figure 9.2: Global Distribution of CDM Projects

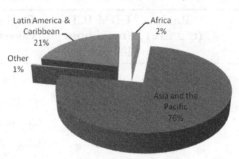

Source: Computed from http://cdm.unfccc.int (accessed 26 April 2010)

Jung (2006) drew policy implications concerning the geographical distribution of CDM projects. The improvement of the CDM institutional mechanism and capacity building was deemed the most appropriate transmission mechanism for the promotion of a more equitable distribution of CDM projects. The author also noted that host nations with very small climate change mitigation potential may still remain unattractive to CDM investment even if they were to improve their institutions and capacity. This is the main case with most African countries.

How Clean is the KP's CDM?

This is the question that has been asked since the conceptualization of the KP and one which should continue to be asked into the future. The realization to qualify development as 'clean' means there was other development that was not clean – resulting in high levels of pollution, particularly from the developed world. One would probably metaphorically use the term 'clean' as an opposite of 'dirty' development that characterized the histories of developed countries from the days of slave trade, through industrial revolution and colonial rule to the current debates on globalization that have led to continued environmental decay (Nhamo 2006). The KP assumes that carbon trade will clean the atmosphere of excess GHGs, alleviate poverty and work towards the attainment of the Millennium Development Goals (MDGs). Originally proposed by Brazil as the Clean Development Fund (CDF), based on the polluter-pays principle, the proposal did not get joy from especially the USA and Australia that strongly disputed historical accumulation of GHGs in the computations. According to Nhamo (2006), the CDF would be financed by contributions from developed countries, which exceeded their GHG emission quotas (estimated at US$3.33 per unit). The realized revenue would have been used to finance the present-day CDM projects. In this regard, climate equity and justice was declined paving the way for market-oriented capitalist approach to environmental management.

The KP evolved in part from the fact that reducing GHG emissions in developing countries at an estimated cost of US$1-US$4/tonne of CO2e is considerably cheaper than in developed countries with costs up to US$15/tonne of CO2e. To avoid abuse, the KP advocates for strict monitoring regime led by the Designated National Authority (DNA) that is tasked with regulating and approving CDM projects.

Facilitation of the Carbon Trade

Under the KP, all GHGs (chief among them, carbon dioxide, methane and nitrous oxide) are converted to their carbon dioxide equivalent (CO_{2e}). One carbon credit unit is equivalent to one tonne of CO2e. The CO2e then allows a Rand (Dollar) value to be attached, thereby allowing trading on the international market. There is a series of steps that are involved in CDM project cycle. The key ones include (a) the preparation of the Project Design Document (PDD); (b) Validation and Approval; (c) Registration; (d) Monitoring; (e) Verification and Certification; and (f) Certification and Issuance of the Certified Emission Reductions – CERs). Details concerning these and other stages are presented in Table 9.2.

It is from the above generic CDM project cycle that host countries are given the jurisdiction to develop their own and similar CDM approval and evaluation criteria. The KP requires that each host country should designate a national authority for the CDM (Lee, Plourde & Bogner 2004). The Designated National Authority (DNA), as it is known, is the legal entity or institution designated by the host country to manage the CDM project implementation processes. Given that one of the KP's two key goals is to assist developing countries that host CDM projects to achieve sustainable development, a key and early function of the DNA is to develop 'sustainability criteria' that will be used by the DNA to judge whether a proposed CDM project will contribute to the sustainable development of the country. If such a finding is made, then the project should receive the approval of the host country. This approval is a prerequisite for a CDM project and a factor that investors consider, often waiting for the DNA to indicate its support for a project before deciding whether to invest in it or not.

Climate Change and Development

Until the twenty-first century, climate change was viewed largely as an exclusive environmental concern that had very limited relevance to development policy-makers and practitioners. Similarly, development approaches have been given less attention within the climate change

Table 9.2: Generic Stages in CDM Project Cycle

Stage	Description	Responsibility
Host country approval	Approval at the national level by the Designated National Authority (DNA), consistent with domestic laws and political priorities.	Project developer
Project Design Document	Identification of a concept and development of the project design documents such as baseline estimate, additionality, sustainable development contributions, monitoring and verification plan and stakeholders' opinion.	Project developer or participants
	Third party validation of baselines and other details to confirm that CERs as claimed by the project are considered realistic.	Designated Operation Entity (DOE)
Validation and Approval	Approval is when the DNA of each party involved confirm their voluntary participation and the DNA of the host country attest that such CDM project contributes to the sustainable development of the country	National Authority Authority
Registration	Registration of the project activity with the CDM Executive Board, once the project has received host country approval.	CDM Executive DOE Board on demand of
Financing	Investor providing capital in the form of debt or equity; investors may/may not be carbon buyers.	Project developer
Implementation Monitoring	Building, commissioning and initiating operations. During commissioning and further operations, the progress and GHG offsets are to be monitored.	Project developer Project developer
Verification	Independent assessment of project performance against the validated design.	DOE
Certification and issuance of CERs	Based on the verification report, the CDM Executive Board certifies and issues CERs.	Executive Board

Source: Lee, Plourde and Bohner (2004)

community, who instead favour natural science approaches focusing on reducing GHG emissions (Huq, Reid & Murray 2006). For the first time in the history of the United Nations (UN) Security Council, the subject of climate change was discussed during the 62nd Session of the United Nations' General Assembly in New York September 2007. The nexus between climate change (science and policy making) and development is presented in Figure 9.3. Some of the landmarks highlighted in Figure 9.3 will be briefly deliberated upon.

The term 'sustainable development' was popularized by the World Commission on Environment and Development (WCED) in its 1987 report entitled *Our Common Future*. The aim of the WCED was to find practical ways of addressing environmental and developmental problems of the world. *Our Common Future* reported on many of the global realities and recommended urgent action on eight key issues to ensure that development was sustainable, among them: population and human resources; food security; the urban challenge; energy; industry; species and ecosystems; managing the commons; and, conflict and environmental degradation. In a way, these eight key issues were identified as some form of early indicators to sustainable development. Since then and due to the contested nature of the concept 'sustainable development and sustainability', a myriad of definitions have emerged (see, Lowe 1990; Singh and Titi 1995; Barboza 2000).

Figure 9.3: Nexus of Climate Change and Development

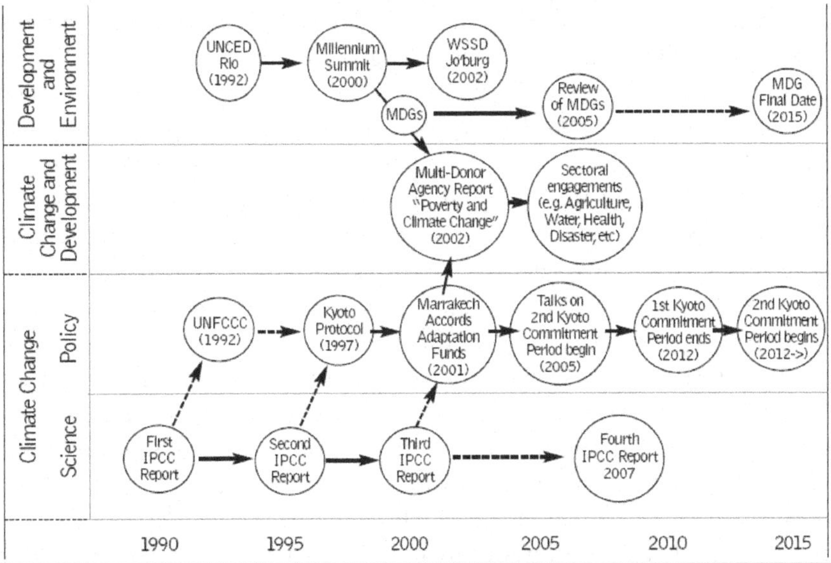

Source: Huq, Reid and Murray, 2006: 8.

Our Common Future's definition of sustainable development was also adopted during the UN Earth Summit of 1992 (UNCED 1992) that came up with Agenda 21. However, in as much as *Our Common Future's* definition takes cognisance of people, many environmental policies and legislation, both at the global and national, scales hardly recognize them as the primary focus of development (Jacobs, cited in Cahill 2002:2). In this respect, Jacobs identifies equity (commitment to meet basic needs of the poor), quality of life (i.e., economic growth should not be taken as equal to human well-being), and participation (involving as many stakeholders as possible in environmental policy processes) as additional key themes in attaining sustainability. Cahill (2002) also warns of the need to distinguish between the concepts sustainability and sustainable development. He maintains that the former refers to the end-state, whereas the latter refers to the means by which that end is achieved. However, the two terms are often used interchangeably.

As is the case with democracy and globalization, the concept of sustainable development 'has become one of the most ubiquitous, contested, and indispensable concepts of our time' (Castro 2004: 1). Although first introduced in response to environmental issues and crises, sustainable development has been defined primarily by the mainstream tradition of economic analysis, which tends to marginalize the issue of ecological sustainability itself. Several other authors have criticised different implications of *Our Common Future's* definition for being 'too vague, for not defining what needs are, or for not saying what are the mechanisms to achieve an environmentally sustainable society' (ibid). The definition, in any case, reflects a political compromise between growth and environmental sustainability that the pro-growth delegations at the United Nations could accept.

The main shortcoming of the mainstream approach to sustainable development, of which climate change mitigation under the KP falls, has been that it is driven by the capitalist economy. This implies that it is about sustaining development rather than developing sustainability in the ecological sense (Castro 2004). To this effect, priorities are placed on ensuring that environmental conditions are managed so as to ensure maximum long-term capital accumulation. In this respect, neoclassical environmental economics gravitates toward a weak sustainability hypothesis at best. Here it is assumed that in most cases, human-made capital can substitute for natural capital, so that in all but a few cases, there are no real limitations to industrial growth imposed by the environment. Market mechanisms can be adjusted to ensure that environmental factors are taken account of, with no real alteration in the fundamental character of the capitalist economy. This is true even when one traces discourses around climate change. Given this scenario, more critical perspectives are needed if any kind of meaningful sustainable development, which has to be about sustaining the environment even more than sustaining economic develop-ment is to be achieved. For this purpose the Marxist critique, and especially environmental Marxism, is essential. Environmental Marxism combines a devastating political-economic critique of the main tendencies of capital accumulation with a commitment to radical social transformation and thus, is able to challenge mainstream sustainable development theory on its own ground in the form of a deep and wide-ranging alternative (Castro 2004).

The Millennium Development Goal (MDG) 7 (UNDP 2003) to which the overarching aim is to eliminate poverty, stipulates the need to ensure that environmental sustainability is achieved at the lowest possible scale, that is, the household. Three targets are set: to integrate the principle of sustainable development into national policies and programmes by 2015; have the proportion of people without access to safe drinking water, and by 2020, achieve significant improvement in the standards of living of at least 100 million squatter residents. The risk of urban squatters still stands. Fragile (and even stable ecosystems) easily succumb to heavy population densities resulting in the depletion of naturally occurring life support systems and quality of life issues like waste management and sanitation. To address the ills of unsustainable development in Africa, the New Economic Partnership for Africa's Development (NEPAD) that also places the need to eradicate poverty at the core of its agenda has put in place an Action Plan for the Environment Initiative (NEPAD 2002). The initiative notes that Africa is rich in natural resources including land, minerals, biological diversity, wildlife, fresh water, fisheries and forests. However, rapid population growth, rising poverty levels (including the widening gap between the rich and the poor) and inappropriate development practices are mentioned as major factors leading to degraded environments (UNEP 2003). The NEPAD initiative sets 11 action plans grouped according to areas of concern or programmes. Some of the programmes include: integrated waste and pollution control; the management of cities and the management of coastal and marine resources (NEPAD 2002). Although this is a significant achievement, issues pertaining to climate change are not given adequate space and clarity by the NEPAD, particularly the KP and how Africa should engage with it.

Africa and the Copenhagen Climate Summit

There is now a general consensus on mitigation, adaptation, technology and financing as the fundamental pillars for addressing climate change. However, major disagreements remain between countries on the distribution of responsibilities and commitments and the relative significance and sequencing of these measures for different regions of the world. This is mainly due to the large differences in relative shares in contributions to GHG emissions (the cause of global warming), distribution and nature of predicted future impacts of climate change, relative costs of and capacities to invest in effecting the two response measures among countries, regions and sectors. The 2007 Bali Conference is cited as one of the key landmarks to Copenhagen 2009. The Bali Conference managed to effectively launch negotiations to craft a new international climate change agreement by the end of 2009. It spelt out a clear roadmap for these talks (Africa Union 2007). Some of the notable immediate results were particularly important for developing countries, not least in the areas of adaptation funding, technology transfer and reducing emissions from deforestation. The Bali Conference also established a roadmap for negotiations on the new emission targets for industrialized countries under the Kyoto Protocol, along with defining the scope and content of the upcoming review of the Protocol. Some of the landmarks from the Bali Road Map are outlined in Box 9.1.

Box 9.1: Landmarks from the Bali Road Map

Road Map seeks to finalise a post 2012 regime by December 2009 in Copenhagen, Denmark.Discussion on mitigation by developed and developing countries was particularly contentious. Parties agreed to a proposal by India and other developing countries, to a text referring to nationally appropriate mitigation actions by developing country parties in the context of sustainable development, supported by technology and enabled finance and capacity building in a measurable, reportable and verifiable manner. The decision on long-term action under the Convention was thus adopted.Bali decided that the process shall address enhanced national/ international action on mitigation, as well as enhanced action on adaptation, technology development and transfer, and provision of financial resources and investment. On adaptation, the conference decided to address a range of issues, including international cooperation to support urgent implementation of various adaptation actions, taking into account the immediate needs of developing countries that are particularly vulnerable to the adverse effects of climate change, especially least developed countries, small island states and African countries.The Bali Action Plan calls for the road to Copenhagen 2009 to be an open process − open to the private sector, international organizations and civil society. This offers opportunities for the business community, along with international financial institutions, to contribute. With private investments constituting 86 per cent of investment and financial flows related to climate change, businesses are key to the solution.

Source: Africa Union (2007: 12)

The climate negotiation environment is dynamic, volatile and at times explosive. This has been true of the pre and Copenhagen talks that witnessed the developing countries walking out twice (once in Barcelona and once in Copenhagen). The developing countries, particularly those from Africa, have now realized that they have been for a long time left on the margins of negotiations and at times excluded in some informal rounds of talks where 'things' happen. The discords and tensions during climate negotiations were evident during:

2000: In The Hague the Kyoto Protocol Rule Book was left half done as parties broke up angrily without agreement (Ingham 2009)

2009: In November the Africa Group walked out during the preparatory Barcelona round of talks (Drexhage 2009)

2009: On Monday, 14 December, the Africa Group, supported by the G77 walked out again and boycotted Copenhagen for five hours (Cartiller 2009). The delegates returned only after there was guarantee that they would not be sidelined during talks about the future of the Kyoto Protocol.

The main reason for the walkouts was that developing and poorer nations wanted to see decisions that would lead to a 40 per cent drop in greenhouse gas (GHG) emissions by 2020 based on 1990 levels (Otton 2009). Against the backdrop of walkouts in Copenhagen, the China versus USA platform has been growing strong. The Vice Foreign Minister of China, He Yafei, was cited as acknowledging that 'China would not be the fall guy if there were a fiasco' (Ingham 2009). In confirmation of the frustration that emerged during Copenhagen, the coordinator of the G77 Group, Bernadiat de Castro Muller was cited indicating that the group was faced with a process in which it had no control which was 'totally undemocratic, totally untransparent' (Otton 2009). Watts (2009) also reveals the drama that took place during Copenhagen 2009. Watts records that:

Negotiators played the conference like a football team intending a 0-0 draw. Their strategy was defensive; their tactics were tough; and their tackling of opponents occasionally brutal. At the opening of the high-level segment, China's chief negotiator Su Wei interrupted the Danish chair, the most public of a series of moves aimed at undermining the authority of the host. With the support of other emerging economies India, Brazil and South Africa they shot down all attempts to make emissions cuts legally binding or to set long-term goals for reducing greenhouse gases.

Within the formal and informal negotiating, groupings are key players. These are men and women that have experience in the climate negotiations from both an individual and institutional orientation. Harris (2009) identified 15 such key individuals for Copenhagen 2009 (COP 15) round of negotiations (Figure 9.4).

Figure 9.4: COP 15 Key Players

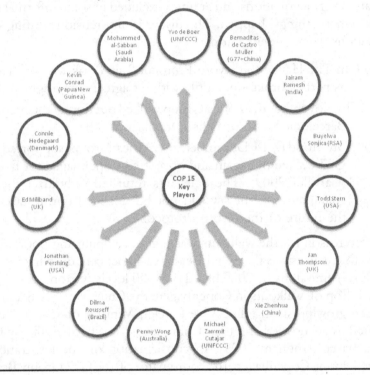

Source: Author

In its submission to the AWG-LTCA, the African Union (2009b) indicated its wish to have a shared vision on long term cooperative action. Such a vision would see parties to the UNFCCC working based on common but differentiated responsibilities and respective capabilities. The African Union also expected action to be taken in an equitable manner taking historical responsibility into account. This proposal meant that Africa would not do as much as Annex 1 countries. Africa would do its bit in terms of voluntary nationally appropriate mitigation actions (NAMAs). The NAMAs would include appropriate measures to reduce GHG emissions through a number of measures that include: increased forestry cover; stabilizing forest carbon stocks; and, enhanced carbon sinks. Further details regarding other Copenhagen 2009 positions from within Africa and its associated formal negotiating groups are shown in Table 9.3.

Table 9.3: African and Related Blocs' Views on Copenhagen Outcomes

Country	Block represented	Views
Algeria	Africa Group	Expressed serious concerns with the lack of progress at previous meetings and reminded parties that Africans are already impacted by climate change through increased droughts, health hazards, food scarcity and migration. Africa called for transparent and equitable negotiations during the high-level segment.
Sudan	G77+China	Called upon parties to observe the principles of good faith, transparency, inclusiveness and openness. He emphasized the need for the Copenhagen agreed outcome to ensure full implementation of developed country party commitments under the Convention.
Lesotho	Least Developed Countries	Urged countries not to betray 'the expectations of the anxious global population' and highlighted the importance of adaptation, financing, technology and capacity-building support, and underlined the need for contributions to the LDC Fund to finance countries' most immediate adaptation needs.
Grenada	Alliance of States Small Island	Urged an ambitious outcome responding with the urgency needed and guaranteeing the long-term survival of small island developing states (SIDS), LDCs, and other vulnerable groups. A political outcome was inadequate and that SIDS would 'have to consider our options' if a legally-binding outcome is not achieved. She said a final agreement must address emission reductions by all major emitting countries and limit temperature increase to below 1.5°C and atmospheric greenhouse gas concentrations to 350 ppm. She indicated that any agreement should also provide for stable, predictable and adequate financing for adaptation, capacity building, technology and mitigation.

Source: Compiled after IISD (2009: 3)

During further deliberations, South Africa was supported by Grenada from the AOSIS as she suggested that 'issues related to mitigation by developed countries, market approaches and finance' (IISD 2009: 6) be forwarded to the political level. There were also contestations in terms of procedures as Egypt supported India's view that the Protocol process should take precedence and that the reports from informal gatherings and groups like the 'friends of the chair' go through the COP/MOP or COP before being forwarded to Heads of State (IISD 2009: 6).

Although not a country from the African Group, Nicaragua raised fundamental points. She requested that the Copenhagen Accord be treated as a submission from only the UNFCCC parties who crafted and negotiated it. The key parties were those led by the USA and Basic. This meant that the proposed Copenhagen Accord had to be issued as a miscellaneous document. Nicaragua further proposed that the COP and COP/MOP be suspended and allow the AWG for both the UNFCCC and the Kyoto Protocol as prescribed in the two-track negotiating systems to continue. To reveal the contestations behind the closed Copenhagen doors, Nicaragua further proposed that a decision be taken to 'mandate inclusive and transparent consultations, as appropriate' during Mexico in 2010 where COP16 would take place. Following extensive consultation, the COP President Rasmussen accepted reissuing the proposed Copenhagen Accord as a miscellaneous document and also indicated in the document which countries had crafted the draft document. Following this ritual, Nicaragua was asked to compromise and withdraw its proposal to suspend the COP and COP/MOP (IISD 2009). Such is the drama that comes with climate negotiations and decisions that follow thereafter.

In the end, Basic + USA drew up the Copenhagen Accord excluding the EU. The Basic Group is made up of Brazil, China, India and South Africa. The Copenhagen Accord was further discussed by 25 heads of state. The Accord was presented to other countries present 'giving them one hour to read and sign on' (Oxfam 2009: 6). The EU reluctantly accepted the Copenhagen Accord although many developing countries including those from Africa refused to endorse it. As such COP15 'noted' as opposed to 'adopting' the Copenhagen Accord (Black 2009). Reacting to the Copenhagen Accord, Sudan condemned it, stressing that:

> it threatens the lives and livelihoods of millions of people in developing countries, including the African continent. He referred to the financial commitment of US$100 billion in the document as 'a bribe', saying that a commitment to 2°C would ask Africa to 'sign an incineration pact' and was based on values that 'tunnelled six million people in Europe into furnaces.

Sudan's comments referring to the Holocaust (IISD 2009) were not well received by certain countries, among them the UK, Mexico, Canada, Grenada, Norway and the EU. This group of countries called upon Sudan to withdraw its statement. However, no record could be obtained that the statement was withdrawn. Such tense relationships during climate negotiations can have serious future consequences for a developing nation like Sudan as it might find itself sidelined in terms of climate assistance from the developed countries. In an earlier statement by the African Group, a position was presented that the continent was not in Copenhagen as a victim of the past climate injustice but as a future stakeholder in the climate space (African Union 2009a).

More responses to the Copenhagen Accord came from Lesotho (representing the LDCs), Ethiopia (for the African Union) and Algeria (for the African Group), the EU, Russian Federation, the Philippines, Singapore and Japan. The response sort of 'supported' the Copenhagen Accord. Many parties to the UNFCCC noted that it was a compromise document (ISSD 2009). However, Papua New Guinea was reported complaining of the inadequate negotiating capacity and support from Africa. Papua New Guinea indicated that some G-77+China parties were being represented by weak public servants. To her dismay, such public servants were to blame for removing a lot of substance from the Copenhagen Accord although the USA insisted that there had been participation of about 30 countries in the development of the Copenhagen Accord (IISD 2009). South Africa also highlighted a procedural error and pointed out that technically, the COP decision had been adopted during the COP/MOP plenary and requested that the record be corrected so that the decision is under the COP, rather than the COP/MOP. South Africa also made a request to note that the Accord took place outside of the UNFCCC process and proposed that parties submit their intended support of the Accord in the record of the session (IISD 2009: 9).

Policy Pointers and Way Forward for Africa

In the light of the foregoing, it is apt to submit that the current KP set-up has not been Africa's home-grown agenda; hence it has been somebody's agenda. To this end, African and other governments from the (least) developing nations must unite their voices and demand that the post-2012 arrangements reflect and present a fair and level trading platform in carbon. The single biggest challenge for CDM is the failure to have developing countries earn carbon credits (Nhamo 2006). To this end, a number of Latin American countries are considering taking voluntary targets, which earn them carbon credits. Costa Rica, for example, produced their own Certified Tradable Offsets which they have put up for sale. African countries are in a position to manage their own domestic permit trading system by applying regional standards and their own national legal systems and financial institutions. The technological aspect under the current CDM could be maintained as part of international cooperation to improve system design and to share best practices. The CDM protocol in China is spelt out in its *Interim Measures for Operation and Management of CDM in China of 2004* (Xuedu 2005). From the protocol, CDM projects have to be submitted for approval to the Chinese DNA by the owners of the underlying projects, an issue alleged to limit consultants from the direct communication with the Chinese authorities, and limits the eligibility of project owners to *Chinese funded or Chinese-holding enterprise*. The regulation excludes many foreign owned enterprises from implementing CDM projects. In terms of benefit sharing, revenue from the transfer of carbon credits are owned jointly by the Government and the project owner, with allocation ratio of the revenue to be decided by the Government. The Government also reserves the right to review and approve the price as well as the commercial terms of the carbon credit transaction. This has been done to protect Chinese interests in a market which is characterized by imbalances in negotiation power and knowledge of the market, risks, commercial terms, and contracts (Nygard, Murray & Streck 2005).

Given that a number of African countries have stable investment climates, a number of CDM projects are mushrooming. However, due to various threats (risks, uncertainty, ignorance in some sections of community and indeterminacy) associated with the CDM that have resulted in a non-legally binding Copenhagen Accord, there is need to apply the Earth Summit's precautionary principle in all dealings. The following suggestions are therefore made as a way forward.

Keeping negotiations within the UNFCCC framework: An alternative leaked Danish presidency negotiation text (Oxfam 2009) caused havoc in Copenhagen and a blanket of mistrust emerged. The leaked document seemingly favoured Annex 1 countries and the wrath from Non-Annex 1 countries almost stalled the talks (Vidal & Watts 2009). The proposal contained thereof sought to replace the two-track approach with a single new agreement. This resulted in Brazil, China, India and South Africa presenting an alternative proposal based on the two-track approach. Although the proceedings finally got back to focus on official texts, negotiating time had been lost and never to be recovered. In the 2010 round of further talks, Africa must be on the lookout for such side-tracking in order to maximize negotiation time in Mexico. The Africa Group must continue lobbying for the reformation of the United Nations system of governance. Although this has been on the agenda for a long time now, the need to reform the United Nations system was highlighted by Ed Miliband of the UK (Miliband 2009) following the shame in Copenhagen 2009. In his article entitled 'The Road from Copenhagen' featured in *The Guardian*, Miliband wrote:

> There is a wider question, too, about the structures and nature of the negotiations. The last two weeks at times have presented a farcical picture to the public. We cannot again allow negotiations on real points of substance to be hijacked in this way. We will need to have major reform of the UN body overseeing the negotiations and of the way the negotiations are conducted.

With such support emerging from one of the dominating forces in the United Nations system of governance, the time could be ready for Africa to push further the agenda of reform. In addition, the Africa Group should stick to polishing the existing twin official texts done under the UNFCCC system. These texts are said to contain much more promise than the Copenhagen Accord (Oxfam 2009).

Use of CDM project quota system: to safeguard biased investment in sectors considered 'low hanging fruit' of easy carbon credit picking such as landfill gas and hydropower (Nhamo 2006).

Need for capacity building and sustained awareness raising programmes: At all governance levels including sub-regional groupings, national governments, provinces and/ or states and municipalities.

Mobilization of more local financial resources: This could be done as part of Socially Responsible Investment (Corporate Social Responsibility) from the corporate world and earn government and other local players 'carbon credits' for the benefit of the environment and future generations even outside the CDM like the Costa Rica experience.

Role of national GHG mitigation and adaptation policies and legislation: African governments can put in place shared or individual policies and legislation leading to GHG capture, especially from landfills and other agreed sources for energy generation and other uses. Currently, South Africa and other Southern African Development Community countries like Zimbabwe have in critical shortages of electricity, an aspect that has a huge potential to slow development and economic growth.

Adaptation and not mitigation the key for addressing climate change in Africa: The CDM mechanism is predominantly based on mitigation and has resulted in select few countries, among them Egypt, Morocco and South Africa benefiting from the proceedings. This is an aspect that can easily lead to the re-partitioning of the continent in the name of CDM implementation. CDM is therefore likely to be some kind of privilege for the selected few economies as in most cases investors are not interested due to limited returns. This is an aspect that is supported by the small percentage of CDM potential in Africa compared to the overall global picture that is dominated by the Asian and Latin American continents. Hence, measures that channel more energy towards adaptation (how Africans can live with the changing climate) are more suitable for the continent.

A call for climate justice and Right to economic growth: Given that the African continent emits near insignificant levels of GHG, the original call by Brazil for the Clean Development Fund still makes much sense. This means those that pollute more must in fact pay more. To date, the USA has refused to ratify the KP yet it calls upon the emerging economies such as South Africa to have caps. Africa has full rights to economic growth and the argument is cemented by our low per capita GHG emissions. If one was to use average per capita GHG emissions compared to those from the developed world, Africa might only need to start cutting on emissions in three to four decades ahead. In 2003, for example, USA individuals were far bigger emitters, at 20 tonnes per capita against China's 3.2 tonnes and a world average of 3.7 tonnes.

Capability a key issue: Although there is a common goal globally, countries must meet this according to their respective capabilities. Developed countries must significantly cut their emissions and stop thinking of profiteering from ailing economies from Africa and the south.

Forest resources a huge plus for Africa: Although there has not been a clear-cut way of assessing how much climate change mitigation the African forests are playing and will continue to play, this resource remains pivotal to our post-KP positioning. Collectively, a position must be taken to assess how much sink the forest cover is providing. Stronger legislation curbing logging and other destructive activities could then be put in place to permit continued industrial growth (Nhamo 2009a).

Promoting co-leadership in climate matters: The need to have developing countries like those from Africa taking responsibility in climate change matters must be promoted (Nhamo 2009b). A co-leadership model recognises the existence and interface of leaders and co-leaders. In CC Co-leadership places this narrative at the centre, driving various kinds of leaders and co-leaders as well as leadership and co-leadership tied to numerous CC leadership zones. Among some of the leadership zones are: the mitigation, adaptation, financing, technology, social dynamics, and policy framework.

Call for a fair, ambitious and legally binding deal: The road to Mexico 2010 and deliberations during the COP16 thereof should witness the African continent taking over from where they left in Copenhagen with regards to a call for a fair, ambitious and legally binding post-KP deal.

Conclusion

Africa's development, climate change and carbon trade: Whose agenda is it anyway? This is the question this chapter attempted to address. From the deliberations thereof, it was evident that the carbon trade mechanism under the Kyoto Protocol is certainly not beneficial to many African countries. As modern day commentators have noticed, the clean development mechanism (CDM) under the Kyoto Protocol might as well be known as the China Development Mechanism or the Asian Development Mechanism since most of the projects have been implemented in China, India and other Asian countries. If Latin America's Brazil and Mexico are brought into the picture, then there is certainly very little to say about the CDM with regard to Africa's growth and development.

Following COP15 in Copenhagen, Denmark 2009; COP16 in Cancun, Mexico 2010; and COP17 in Durban, South Africa 2011, Africa's climate change agenda has taken a new twist and emphasis. African governments have made it clear that theirs is to prioritize climate change adaptation as the overarching building block in terms of addressing climate change. Africa needs to learn more on coping strategies rather than preventing climate change happening. African governments have realized that their dependence on agriculture and associated resources like water, forestry, tourism, wildlife and fisheries presents a compelling case to prioritize adaptation. African governments are also worried about climate mitigation as one of the key aspects of the emerging green global economy following the global financial crisis of 2008. Africa is worried about jobs creation and wishes to see programmes that address climate change intertwined with the agenda to create sustainable employment opportunities and reduce extreme poverty. Given that climate change adaptation has been prioritized into the future, African governments are now interested in having programmes that address finance, technology and international property rights, capacity building and awareness, negotiations and mitigation as aligned to the adaptation agenda. To this end, the Green Climate Fund operationalized during COP17 in Durban is seen as one of the conduits upon which the adaptation agenda can be realized fully in Africa. Needless to say, the so-called Green Climate Fund is supposed to be generated from the developing countries that have neglected their earlier commitments in terms of aid funding as history judges them. Hence African governments still need to do more to generate revenue to push this adaptation agenda from an African perspective and at national levels. From Cancun and Durban COPs, African and other developing regions lobbied and managed to have adaptation as one of the key climate negotiation decisions emerging from the two COPs. In Durban, agriculture and climate change was also deliberated and this is now going to be one of the negotiation aspects under adaptation and related thematic focus areas in the global negotiation space into the future.

The latest developments in global climate change negotiations bear testimony to a call in this chapter for a vigilant African continent that sees itself with an increasing and irreversible, pro-active, pro-participatory role regarding the post-Kyoto Protocol trade mechanisms. African countries should be encouraged to continue calling with one voice for a fair trade mechanism within both the second Kyoto Protocol commitment period ending in 2015 as well as the transitional period to 2020, when all countries will be required to take action to reduce carbon emissions. A number of key observations have been made in the chapter, among them: a call for the use of CDM project quota system; need for capacity building and sustained awareness raising programme; mobilization of more local financial resources; role of national GHG mitigation and adaptation policies and legislation; call to prioritize climate change adaptation and not mitigation; call for climate justice; right to economic growth and co-leadership in climate change. Hopefully, this work will add to the body of knowledge enhancing Africa's climate negotiating power.

References

Africa Union, 2007, 'Climate change: African perspectives for a post-2012 agreement', Addis Ababa: AU Secretariat.

African Union, 2009a, 'Statement by H.E. Meles Zenaoui, Prime Minister of Federal Democratic Republic of Ethiopia, on behalf of the African Group, Copenhagen, Denmark, 16, December 2009', Addis Ababa: Africa Union Secretariat.

African Union, 2009b, 'The Copenhagen decisions: Submission on the outcome of the Ad Hoc Working Group on Long Term Cooperative Action under the Convention under item 3', Addis Ababa: Africa Union Secretariat.

Ayre, G. and Callway, R., 2005, *Governance for Sustainable Development,* London: Earthscan.

Black, R., 2009, *Copenhagen climate deal meets qualified UN welcome.* (http://news.bbc.co.uk/2/hi/science/nature/8422133.stm). 23 December 2009.

Cahill, M., 2002, *The environment and social policy,* London: Routledge.

Cartiller, J., 2009, *Climate code red' at UN talks, warns Nigeria.* (http://www.mg.co.za/article/2009-12-14-climate-code-red-at-un-talks-warns-nigeria). 15 December 2009.

Castro, C. J., 2004, 'Sustainable development: Mainstream and critical perspectives', *Organisation & Environment,* Vol. 17, pp. 195-225.

DNA of China, 2007, *CDM-Market Brief: China,* Cologne: German Office of Foreign Trade/Deutsche Investitions.

DNA of South Africa, 2006, *CDM-Market Brief: South Africa,* Cologne: German Office of Foreign Trade/Deutsche Investitions.

DNA/National CDM Authority of India, 2006, *CDM-Market Brief: India,* Cologne: German Office of Foreign Trade/Deutsche Investitions.

Drexhage, J., 2009, *The Barcelona Negotiations on Climate Change: Where the Spirit Is Willing?,* London: International Institute for Sustainable Development.

Ellis, J., Winkler, H., Corfee-Morlot, J. and Gagnon-Lebrun, F., 2007, 'CDM: Taking stock and looking forward', *Energy Policy,* Vol. 35, pp. 15-28.

Foreign Policy In Focus, 2005, *A carbon rush at The World Bank,* Washington DC: Foreign Policy In Focus.

Harris, J., 2009, *Copenhagen climate conference: The key players,* (Available: http://www.guardian.co.uk/environment/2009/nov/30/copenhagen-key-players), 17 December.

Hirschle, A. and Paulo, S., 2006, *CDM-Market Brief: Brazil,* Cologne: German Office of Foreign Trade/Deutsche Investitions.

Huq, S., Reid, H. and Murray, L. A., 2006, *Climate change and development links,* London: International Institute for Environment and Development.

IISD, 2009, *Summary of the Copenhagen climate change conference: 7-19 December 2009,* Toronto: International Institute for Sustainable Development.

Ingham, R., 2009, *Walkout heightens failure fears over climate summit.* (http://www.mg.co.za/article/2009-12-14-walkout-heightens-failure-fears-over-climate-summit), 15 December.

Jung, M., 2006, 'Host country attractiveness for CDM non-sink projects', *Energy Policy,* Vol. 34, pp. 2173-2184.

Lee, C. A., Plourde, D. M. and Bogner, J. E., 2004, 'Landfill gas recovery: South Africa's low handling fruit for carbon credits trading', in Institute of Waste Management of Southern Africa, eds, *WasteCon2004,* pp. 52-60.

Lopes, I. V., 2002, *The Clean Development Mechanism (CDM): A Brazilian Implementation Guide,* Rio de Janeiro: Fundação Getulio Vargas.

McCarthy, M., Castle, S. and Naidu, E., 2007, 'Climate change wars loom over scarce resources'. *The Sunday Independent,* 8 April.

Miliband, E, 2009, 'The road from Copenhagen'. (http://www.guardian.co.uk/commentisfree/2009/dec/20/copenhagen-climate-change-accord). 26 December 2009.

Muzino, Y., 2007, *CDM in Charts Version 1.0 March 2007: China,* Ministry of Environment/Institute for Global Environmental Strategies: Beijing.

NEPAD, 2002, *A summary of NEPAD Action Plans,* Johannesburg: NEPAD.

Nhamo, G., 2006, 'Why can't we clean up our own act?', *South African Labour Bulletin,* Vol. 30, pp. 10-13.

Nhamo, G., 2009a, 'Climate Change: Double Edged Sword for African Trade and Development', *International Journal of African Renaissance,* Vol. 4, pp. 117-139.

Nhamo, G., 2009b, 'Co-leadership in climate change: An agenda for 2013 and beyond', *Politikon: South African Journal of Political Studies,* Vol. 36, pp. 463-480.

Nygard, J., Murray, A. and Streck, C., 2005, 'Clean Development Mechanism in China: Taking a proactive and sustainable approach', *The Sino Sphere Journal,* Vol. 8, pp. 5-11.

Otton, C., 2009, 'World leaders try to save floundering climate summit', (http://www.mg.co.za/article/2009-12-15-world-leaders-try-to-save-floundering-climate-summit), 16 December 2009.

Oxfam, 2009, 'Climate shame: get back to the table: Initial analysis of the Copenhagen climate talks', London: Oxfam.

Rehan, R. and Nehdi, M., 2005, 'Carbon dioxide emissions and climate change: Policy implications for the cement industry', *Environmental Science and Policy,* Vol. 8, pp. 105-114.

SADC-REEP, 2007, *Environmental issues and crises,* Howick: Southern African Development Community - Regional Environmental Education Programme.

Satoguina, H., 2006, 'Analysis of CDM experience in Morocco and lessons learnt for West African Economic and Monetary Union: Case study: Benin, Burkina Faso, Niger and Togo', Hamburg: Hamburgisches Welt-Wirtschafts-Archiv (HWWA) and Hamburg Institute of International Economics.

UK Government, 2008, *Climate Change Act,* London: UK Government.

UNCED, 1992, *Agenda 21,* New York: UN Secretariat.

UNDP, 2003, *Human Development Report 2003: Millennium development goals - A compact among nations to end human poverty,* New York: Oxford University Press.

UNEP, 2003, *Global environment outlook 3: Past, present and future perspectives,* London: Earthscan.

UNFCCC, 2009, *Copenhagen Accord,* Copenhagen: United Nations Framework Convention on Climate Change.

NFCCC Secretariat, 2010a, *Registered projects by host parties.* (http://cdm.unfccc.int), 26 April 2010.

UNFCCC Secretariat, 2010b, *Registered projects by region.* (http://cdm.unfccc.int), 26 April 2010.

UNFCCC Secretariat, 2010c, *Distribution of registered activities by scope.* (http://cdm.unfccc.int), 26 April.

Vidal, J. and Watts, J., 2009, *Copenhagen: The last-ditch drama that saved the deal from collapse,* (http://www.guardian.co.uk/environment/2009/dec/20/copenhagen-climate-global-warming), 21 December.

Watts, J., 2009, *Copenhagen summit: China's quiet satisfaction at tough tactics and goalless draw,* (http://www.guardian.co.uk/environment/2009/dec/20/copenhagen-climate-summit-china-reaction), 21 December.

Xuedu, L., 2005, 'Chinese CDM policy: Clarifications to some misunderstood issues', *The Sino Sphere Journal,* Vol. 8, pp. 19-20.

PART THREE

Intellectual Property Rights, Technology Transfer and Culture Policy

10

Intellectual Property and Technology Transfer Towards African Countries: Is International Law a Beneficial Policy?

Patrick Juvet Lowe

Introduction

The adoption of the treaty instituting the World Trade Organization (WTO) in 1994 ended the Uruguay Round's negotiations. It was followed by a development, without precedent, of the debate on intellectual property. This debate has extended into the discussions of experts and non-experts – leading to contradictory arguments between proponents and opponents of the system – and into national and regional legislations to include the changes brought by the new treaty. In fact, to the WTO treaty was annexed the Trade-Related Aspects of Intellectual Property Rights (TRIPS) Agreement that extended the obligation to respect intellectual property rights to all countries eager to be inserted in the global trade. Intellectual property (IP) was mainly introduced in the Uruguay Round because of the pressure of certain economic groups of developed countries (Gervais 2003:8s; Sell 2003:3). The prevailing concern regarding IP regimes in developing countries was the perceived lack of adequate protection. In particular, developed countries with advanced IP protection, and the multinational corporations headquartered in such countries, expressed worries about the adverse effects on trade and investment stemming from inadequate IP right protection and enforcement in developing countries leading to the extensive copying of goods protected by such rights in their home countries (UNCTAD-ICTSD 2005: 727). It does not necessarily mean that IP laws do not exist in developing countries. For several decades in Africa, for example, the African Intellectual Property Organization (OAPI) and African Regional Industrial Property Organization (ARIPO) had set up an expanded framework for the development of IP laws in their member States.[1] But the developed countries remained convinced that those laws were not sufficiently strong to ensure the protection of IP owners.

The introduction of IP in the negotiations was considered a part of the general movement of globalization of trade and exchanges. As counterpart, one of the presumed advantages of such a 'globalization of IP' was that it would boost technology transfer to developing countries. Based on the developed countries' experiences, it was argued that intellectual property remained a powerful tool for development and a major incentive for technology transfer to African countries (Kamil Idriss 2003). Hence, the TRIPS Agreement included a number of provisions on technology transfer. In fact, developing countries see technology transfer as part of the bargain in which they agreed to protect intellectual property rights at WTO.

Unfortunately, Africa is still waiting to see the best side of the globalization of IP. While globalization has encouraged opportunities for economic growth and development in some areas, there has been an increase in the disparities and inequalities experienced, especially in Africa. There is a continuing exclusion of African countries from the benefits of global technology exchanges. Till now IP has neither helped to reduce the technology gap between African countries and developed countries, nor bettered the living conditions of African people.

The situation, therefore, has to be questioned. Developed countries have experienced IP for more than a century. Authors underline that there is good evidence in developed countries that IP is, and has been, an important tool for the promoting invention in some industrial sectors, particularly the pharmaceutical, chemical and petroleum industries. It is also said that IP has proved to be a key determinant for the protection of local commercial and industrial innovation, as well as a major element encouraging technology transfer and foreign investment (Blakeney 2008). These observations are contrary to the African experience. So what is responsible for the gap? Why is the appropriation of a practice of more than a century in developed countries so difficult to reproduce in African countries? Is something lacking in international law or its observance?

This chapter is intended to analyse the relevance of the legal provisions for addressing technology transfer. Considering that the gap may not only be a matter of legislation and the manner of its implementation in the developing world, the chapter first analyses the current architecture and legislations on IP and technology transfer. It also examines to what extent the IP law can be considered a part of trade and industrial policy through the analysis of the necessity to rethink the mechanism of this transfer for the development of Africa.

The Current Architecture of Technology Transfer Regarding International Intellectual Property Legislation

As earlier indicated, technology transfer was enshrined in the TRIPS Agreement of the WTO as a real obligation for developed countries to the developing countries. But the obligation has remained unfulfilled.

The Presumed Advantage Given by International Law for African Countries: The Obligation to Transfer Technologies

Technological innovation is very important for growth and poverty reduction in developing countries. It is widely recognized as one of the major determinants of economic growth, and the idea that the technology transfer from rich countries to poor ones will result in growth and, thereby, reduce poverty is seductive. According to its partisans, IP rights will contribute to make technological developments accessible to people in developing countries, will deeply reduce the technology gap, and level the playing field between countries. Some studies have shown empirically that countries that have imported more from the world's technology leaders have experienced faster growth in total factor productivity (Mayer 2001). However, the technology most needed by the poor is not available to them. It was expected that globalization would offer various vehicles for transfer. To that extent, Foreign Direct Investment (FDI) was considered an even greater opportunity to transfer technology to developing countries. Calls for an accelerated pace of opening up to FDI have intensified, on the assumption that this will bring not only more stable capital inflows but also greater technological know-how, higher-paying jobs, entrepreneurial and workplace skills, and new export opportunities (Prasad and al 2003). FDI can inject new knowledge and technology into African countries, which then have the potential to diffuse widely throughout the local population. Technology transfer in the form of FDI increases the capital stock within a recipient country and produces spillover effects such as the spread of new technical knowledge to other firms and local appropriation or utilization of these technologies.

Conscious of the need for developing countries to acquire technology suitable for their expansion and development for better integration into international trade, the international instruments for the protection of intellectual property rights articulated some provisions in this respect. It should be noted, however, that technology transfer does not dominate most of these instruments, the idea highlighted in the mechanisms is designed to favour, promote and/or facilitate the transfer of technology. This is the case with the Paris Convention for the Protection of Industrial Property (articles 2, 3, 5 quarter, 10bis); the Berne Convention for the Protection of Literary and Artistic Works (article III of the Appendix related to Special Provisions regarding Developing Countries); the International Convention for the Protection of New varieties of plants (UPOV), Act of 1991 (Articles 4, 11, 14-19).[2] At the regional level, some African countries have clearly linked intellectual property with the objective of technology transfer. This is the case in the ARIPO[3] where one of the core objectives is 'to assist [countries] members, as appropriate, in the acquisition and development of technology relating to intellectual property matters'.[4] Thus, Rule 4 of the Regulations for Implementing the Protocol on Patents and Industrial Designs within the Framework of the ARIPO[5] provides that:

> The ARIPO Office shall provide, upon request, patent information services to users of patent information in member and potential Member States of ARIPO for the purpose of facilitating the adaptation, transfer and acquisition of appropriate technology, the development of local research and the creation of indigenous technology.

The objective of the TRIPS Agreement of the WTO is more relevant; it intertwined clearly, at a multilateral level, the relation between IP and technology transfer. In this respect, article 7 entitled *'Objectives'* states that:

> he protection and enforcement of intellectual property rights should contribute to the promotion of technological innovation and to the transfer and dissemination of technology, to the mutual advantage of producers and users of technological knowledge and in a manner conducive to social and economic welfare, and to a balance of rights and obligations.

On the other hand, article 66.2 of the TRIPS Agreement provides that:

> Developed country Members shall provide incentives to enterprises and institutions in their territories for the purpose of promoting and encouraging technology transfer to least-developed country Members in order to enable them to create a sound and viable technological base.

More generally, Article 67 of the same Agreement continues by stating that:

> In order to facilitate the implementation of this Agreement, developed country Members shall provide, on request and on mutually agreed terms and conditions, technical and financial cooperation in favour of developing and least-developed country Members.

It should be noted that about 70 per cent of the least-developed countries are African (see UNCTAD 2007).[6] The text adopted as such in 1994 stands as an obligation for developed countries to take all necessary measures in order to ensure the acquisition of technology by least-developed countries and particularly African countries. The general principle was admitted in the Ministerial Declaration of the WTO adopted on 14 November 2001 (WT/MIN(01)/DEC/1, 20 November 2001):

> We agree to an examination, in a Working Group under the auspices of the General Council, of the relationship between trade and transfer of technology, and of any possible recommendations on steps that might be taken within the mandate of the WTO to increase flows of technology to developing countries.[7] The General Council shall report to the Fifth Session of the Ministerial Conference on progress in the examination (Paragraph 37 of the Doha Ministerial Declaration).

The Decision on Implementation-Related Issues and Concerns, WTO document WT/MIN(01)/17 of 20 November 2001 included a paragraph 11.2 which, in addressing developing countries' preoccupations, provides that:

> Reaffirming that the provisions of Article 66.2 of the TRIPS Agreement are mandatory, it is agreed that the TRIPS Council shall put in place a mechanism for ensuring the monitoring and full implementation of the obligations in question. To this end, developed-country Members shall submit prior to the end of 2002 detailed reports on the functioning in practice of the incentives provided to their enterprises for the transfer of technology in pursuance of their commitments under Article 66.2. These submissions shall be subject to a review in the TRIPS Council and information shall be updated by Members annually.

The principle was clearly reaffirmed in the Doha Declaration on TRIPS and Public Health of 14 November 2001, which insists on 'The commitment of developed-country Members to provide incentives to their enterprises and institutions to promote and encourage technology transfer to least-developed country Members pursuant to Article 66.2' (Paragraph 7 of the Doha Declaration).

In spite of all these provisions, it is necessary to remind member States on the importance of the implementation of article 66.2 of the TRIPS Agreement. A decision of the Council for TRIPS of 2003 requested developed country Members to submit annual reports on actions taken or planned in pursuance of their commitments under Article 66.2. To this end, they are to provide detailed reports every third year and, in the intervening years, provide updates to their most recent reports (Paragraph 1, decision IP/C/28 of the council for TRIPS, 20 February 2003). These reports should specify the type of technology that has been transferred by the enterprises of developed countries and the terms on which it has been transferred as well as the mode of technology transfer.[8]

At least, all these relevant texts are proof of the willingness to facilitate access to and transfer of technologies to developing countries. However, they seem not to have been implemented. More than ten years after the adoption of the WTO treaty, the organization continues rightly to recognize 'the relevance of the relationship between trade and transfer of technology to the development dimension'[9] without taking any measure to implement the agreement.

Implication of Excluding Africa from Technology Transfer

Many developed countries have made efforts to comply with the obligation to transfer technology to developing countries. Those efforts are mostly highlighted through home-country measures (HCMs), i.e., measures in technology-exporting countries that facilitate the transfer of technology to developing countries. HCMs can take different forms: financing of technology transfer; foreign direct investment (FDI); matchmaking and provision of information on technologies; promotion of public-private partnerships; access to venture capital; international alliances and other measures to improve host-country absorptive and technological capacity, such as support for research and development (R&D) activities, transfer of techniques, processes and products (e.g. seeds and animal varieties)[10] to developing countries (UNCTAD 2004). Indeed, UNCTAD (2004: 4) points out that a review of the measures adopted by developed countries show that the incentives provided to private firms mainly fall into two categories: measures encouraging technology transfer through FDI to developing countries; and measures encouraging the participation of home firms in public projects in developing countries.

It may be ambiguous to say that African countries are excluded from technology transfer while, at the same time, there has been a massive increase in the levels of FDI and expansion in international trade with

Africa in recent years. Indeed, as UNCTAD (2005) noted, average annual FDI flows to Africa doubled to US$2.2 billion during the 1980s compared to the 1970s, and further increased significantly to US$6.2 billion and US$13.8 billion, respectively, during the 1990s and between 2000 and 2003. On a per capita basis, this translates into a more than fourfold increase compared to the 1980s. However, compared with flows to other developing countries, it appears clearly that Africa is highly marginalized in the globalization context. The continent accounts for just 2 to 3 per cent of global FDI flows, down from a peak of 6 per cent in the mid-1970s, and for less than 9 per cent of developing-country flows compared to an earlier peak of 28 per cent in 1976 (UNCTAD 2005). FDI is mainly concentrated in Asia and Latin America.

Moreover, FDI as a mechanism for technology transfer, is far from being beneficial to local African industries and, subsequently, cannot successfully achieve sustainable industrialization. Despite the efforts of African governments to comply with the policy by trying to attract FDI, the record of the past two decades with respect to reducing poverty and attracting FDI has been disappointing at best. The technological know-how is generally transferred by northern industries to their parent firms established in African countries. This high incidence of intra-firm technology transfers suggests that spillover effects are not diffused to local firms within the recipient country. Further evidence suggests that when they do occur, the beneficiaries are not competitor firms but other actors within the same value chain (ITDG 2002). Naturally, the result of such a situation is not neutral.

African countries have suffered the loss of competitiveness and opportunities in the international market, particularly as concerns traditional commodity exports. The process of Structural Adjustment Programmes that was supposed to boost competitive share of manufactures did not achieve the desired results (Oyelaran-Oyeyinka 2004:10). Admittedly, recent surges of FDI to some countries have been taken as a sign that opening Africa up to international business can bring about a rapid and region-wide 'economic renaissance'. But in fact, much of the recent improvement in economic performance in Africa is accounted for by a small number of oil-producing countries which have grown at more than double the average for the region. Equatorial Guinea, for example, reached 70 per cent growth in 2001 and 75 per cent growth in 2004 because of oil production, and became one of the biggest receivers of foreign investment in Africa. Also, Angola bolstered by oil fields and mining industries, is one of the fastest-growing economies in the world and the first in Africa in 2009. Improvement in economic performance in Africa is also accounted for by a small group of middle-income economies which enjoyed stronger growth prior to the debt crisis and avoided totally or partially adjustment programmes.[11] With these programmes, African countries run the danger of being locked into traditional low-technology imports, thus limiting any effort of industrialization by the lack of diversification of sectors able to arouse technology transfer.

Particularly, intellectual property rights have not been proved a relevant factor of technology transfer (Tansey 1999:22-24; South Centre 1998: 46). IP rights titles are not gracefully offered to developing countries. They have to pay for it even if it is unaffordable. This contributes to limit potentialities of local industries, which are obliged to respect northern firms' IP rights. African countries have difficulty in accessing and reproducing technology at the local level because of the lack of industrial capability and the high cost of exploitation licences. Moreover, IP rights have been suspected to be a means of undue appropriation of African knowledge, particularly in the domain of agriculture and medicinal plant (Correa 2001a; South Centre 2002:12; Zulu 2003).[12] Some experiences illustrate rather that the abolition of IP was more efficient in bringing technology transfer than the creation of IP laws. As noted by Correa,

> The inconclusiveness of data is also present when particular sectors are considered. FDI in the pharmaceutical industry outpaced FDI in most other sectors in Brazil after patent protection for medicines was abolished in that country. Similarly, FDI in that sector was the largest among all other manufacturing industries with foreign participation in Turkey, which had eliminated pharmaceutical patent protection in 1961 (Correa 2001b:94).

For many people in developing countries, rather than bringing new opportunities in improving innovation process and technology, IP has finally led, as stated by President Thabo Mbeki in other circumstances,[13] to: *'rising inequalities within countries... leads to greater polarisation across countries... and has resulted to greater vulnerability to macro-economic shock that lower growth and employment rates resulting in widening the gap with developed countries'*. There is subsequently a necessity to rethink the mechanisms of globalization and technology transfer in order to achieve African countries' development.

Rethinking Technology Transfer and the Role of Intellectual Property Laws

The mechanisms of technology transfers have to be more adapted to the reality of African countries. As such, the need should be clearly summed up according to some prerequisite that favours a relevant role of IPRs in addressing technology transfer towards Africa in a globalizing world.

Technology transfer is not an end by itself. It should be considered as a means to achieve the economic, social, cultural, and in one word, human development of the region. Hence, the existence of IP laws both at national and international level does not necessarily imply the good or the bad impact on technology transfer. It is difficult to make general statements on the implications that the implementation of the TRIPS Agreement may have on FDI and transfer of technology flows, as well as on the path and rhythm of local innovation in developing countries (Correa 2001b). As noted by Correa,

> The most obvious reason is the great differences in the levels of economic and technological development, as well as their very different position as recipients of FDI and foreign technologies. Another important problem is that IPRs only constitute one of the elements that may influence FDI and technology transfer. It is difficult to isolate their impact from the effects of other factors, such as market size, macro-economic policies, availability of personnel, etc. (Correa 2001b:94).

The livelihoods of the great majority of poor women and men in developing and least-developed African countries depend on micro and small-scale enterprises of one sort or another. They must forge their livelihoods working in their fields, homes and small workshops, and by making vital decisions about the best use of their limited assets in order to survive on the tightest of margins. These populations do not depend on employment in the formal sector, where FDI is directed. Indeed, the formal sector accounts for a minority of the economically active population in most African developing countries. However, this minority has often demonstrated its capability to transfer technological experiences, and to adapt acquired technologies to their context. This is the case, for example, in Benin where some micro and small-scale enterprises have acquired and developed at the local level the needed technology for three kinds of activities: a mechanical workshop (for a foundry where the acquisition of an induction oven was raising difficulties due to financing and capability of the Beninese electrification network); an enterprise for the mechanical conception of rubbery and plastic; and a craft foundry.[14]

The above examples show that the most important in this context is not necessarily to acquire new performing technologies – that will be neither mastered nor controlled – but the one which will effectively help the populations. A non-recent problem in the fight for new technology acquisition is that developing countries often look for higher technologies without verifying if they are able to satisfy the deepest need of their populations (Gilbert 1979:167). An old technology can generate more advantages to an economy than a new one. The publicity surrounding all the northern innovations has to be taken vigilantly by African countries. A certain capability to select, absorb and adapt technologies into local settings and to develop new technologies through local innovation must be present for effective technology transfer, whether at household/enterprise level or national level. Technology diffusion supposes both the imitation and the innovation in the sense of adapting the acquired technology to local realities (Lejosne 2006:260). Technologies should be accessible to marginalized women and men for whom cost is very often the major difficulty for those kinds of transaction (South Centre 2002:12). This does mean not just bringing new technologies to their doorstep, but addressing their organizational, management and the marketing skills' opening new channels of information and knowledge and making credit and markets more accessible. The technology may be capable of reinforcing the local innovative system and be in favour of the promotion of Research and Development (RD) activities.

In a Note by the Secretariat of the WTO Working Group on Trade and Transfer of Technology (WT/WGTTT/W/3, 11 November 2002), it was found that the major barriers to technology transfers to developing countries are: lack of access to information about the full range of technological alternatives; inability to identify the technology best suited to needs; limited access to finances; inadequate level and quality of education and skills;insufficient linkages between universities and research institutes on the one hand and industry on the other; regulatory constraints; market distortions; and, weak and inefficient institutions. The Note also states that the attitude of governments regarding technology transfer might differ to be adapted to national priorities. Thus,

> Technology transfer policy can be classified according to the extent of government intervention in the economy and the preferred mode of technology transfer. It emerges that governments can have a minimal intervention approach, consisting in creating the market environment for successful private-sector-driven technology transfers, or they can have a proactive approach, consisting in promoting government-driven programmes. Moreover, governments can implement an externalisation-oriented policy strategy that aims to build up domestic capacity and favour technology transfers in externalised mode; i.e. a transfer from a multinational enterprise to an entity that is not controlled by that enterprise and can take the form of *licensing, minority joint ventures, technical* cooperation contracts, etc. Alternatively, an internalisation-oriented strategy would favour technology transfers in internalised mode; i.e. technology transfers that occur

between a parent of a multinational enterprise and a foreign affiliate under the ownership and control of that enterprise. Finally, a mixed strategy favours the flow of technology through all mechanisms – trade, FDI and partnership agreements – and simultaneously builds local technological capabilities to enhance absorptive capacity and technology diffusion within the country (WTO Working Group).

Definitely, the exclusion of African countries from international technology transfer practices is not an externally-only-caused problem. Albeit, implementing IP laws may constitute a real advantage if the objectives are clearly defined; meanwhile an unsuited technology may produce a perverse effect on the development of African countries. Hence, the role of IP laws needs also to be rethought.

Analysing the Role of Intellectual Property Laws on Technology Transfer

Of Law and Reality: IP Law as an Instrument of Trade and Industrial Policy

The relation between law and the reality, including development is not always harmonized. Guy Mhone noted in another context that for an African institution *'continues to be the need to recognize its interdisciplinarity and hence the need to be more creative about how it is studied and executed'* (Mhone 2003:4). The *'it'* can be easily applied to technology transfer that needs to be studied in an interdisciplinary approach. In fact, not only an interdisciplinary approach, but also a *'polycentric'* approach (Amin 1993:138). At least two major points can be raised at this level.

First, the law can be an instrument that is used to *'create'* or favour the existence of a situation. Laws are not only objective rules, but also embody the will of governments to orient their policies in a certain way. As it often happens in international negotiations, African countries were not in position of force during the Uruguay Round. The introduction of IP into the process was opposed by many developing countries (Gervais 2003:8-9). The introduction of IP in those negotiations that led to the adoption of the TRIPS Agreement was finally a means to oblige some countries to include into their national laws rules on intellectual property. Sisule Musungu noted that

It is now widely accepted that the adoption and entry into force of the WTO Agreement on Trade-Related Aspects of Intellectual Property Rights (TRIPS) significantly changed the international intellectual property regime in both institu-tional and conceptual terms. By linking the principle of mini-mum intellectual property standards to an effective dispute settlement system, the TRIPS Agreement became the de-facto strategic basis for subsequent multilateral and bilateral intellectual property standard setting. The TRIPS Agreement also ushered in the era where higher standards for intellectual property protection could be directly obtained in exchange for deals in core trade areas such as agriculture (Musungu 2005:6; see also Sell 2003:3).

An example of legal provisions dealing with the appropriation of technology transfer at national level can be found in Nigeria, where there is a law which establishes a regulatory body, the National Office for Technology Transfer and Protection (NOTAP). This institution is established by the National Office of Industrial Property Act, Act No 70 of 1979, as amended by the National Office of Technology Acquisition and Protection Act No 82 of 1992 (see Cap N62, Laws of the Federation, 2004). NOTAP is charged with the responsibility of registering all contracts or agreements having effect in Nigeria for the transfer of foreign technology to Nigerian parties, and all contracts connected with the right to use patented inventions. NOTAP may thus refuse to register any technology transfer agreement which contains undesirable clauses restrictive of technological development. Beyond registration, it also has an obligation to monitor, on a continuous basis, the execution of any such registered agreement, to ensure compliance with the terms of the previously approved contract.[15] These legal provisions, although perfectible, constitute a relevant effort to make technology transfer a reality for African countries.

Globally, in this first scenario, it can happen that the adopted law is very difficult to apply and encounters much reluctance. Also, the law can be so disconnected from the reality that its implementation may lead to produce perverse than positive effects. Often, only the practice or attempts to implement the law will help to discover its inconveniences.

Second, the reality can be prior to the adoption of the law. When there is a concrete situation, very important at a particular moment in a community, very often it becomes urgent to legislate on that situation. Law in this regard shall take into account the positive aspect of the phenomenon to improve it and regulate the negative aspect – often by organising sanctions – in order to make it disappear. Of course, it is always possible – and it is often the case – that the laws could not cover all the situations deriving from the phenomenon.

The borders between the situation when a law has been used to serve as an incentive to the existence of a phenomenon and the situation when a phenomenon has preceded the adoption of a law are not easy to define.

Hence, an intermediate position can be found in the fact that law and reality have to be intertwined to produce the most favourable effect.

If the abolition of IP legislation led to improved technology transfers in some cases, it should be noted also that recent data suggested an increase in FDI in Italy after the introduction of such patent protection for pharmaceutical products in 1978. Subsequently, it is difficult to determine *a priori* the significant impact of IP rights on FDI and technology transfer. Likewise, as it is the case for African countries till now, the introduction of higher standards of IP rights has not proved to have contributed to the significant improvement of technology transfers towards them. As noted by Prof. Correa,

> Evidence on the implications of the levels of IPRs on transfer of technology is as limited and elusive as in the case of FDI. Countries with 'weak' IPRs protection (in terms of the standards adopted by the TRIPS Agreement) have been among the major technology borrowers. The reverse situation can also be found, i.e. countries with high standards of protection but with low performance as technology importers (Correa 2001b).

The developments above suggest that there is neither best nor worst law by itself. A law can be beneficial for one country and not for another. A law initially considered as bad can become very beneficial if conditions are created to ease its implementation. As well, a law considered as good can become very detrimental if conditions for its implementation change. The extent to which the conditions of implementation of a law can change or be reversed are not the object of the present study. Going from the observation that the international IP law, notably under the TRIPS Agreement, has not proved to be as beneficial as it is stated in legal texts, we suggest simply that the conditions of implementation of such a law need to be revisited. Either these laws are unsuited to the African context, or they are suited but African countries have failed to create the conditions to benefit from them. However, there is a wide recognition that the current IP laws can hardly lead to the achievement of the objectives of technological development of African countries. Nwauche notes that *what Africa needs is an African Intellectual Property law* meanwhile *at present there is only intellectual property law applied to Africa* (Nwauche 2005). The issue has to be addressed seriously. This can justify the multiplication of fora where the issue is discussed, including the revision of the TRIPS Agreement of the WTO in 2005,[16] the institution of an Inter-Governmental Working Group (IGWG) at the World Health Organization (WHO)[17] and the introduction of a development Agenda at the World Intellectual Property Organization (WIPO).[18]

Of course, the list of fora and mechanisms is not exhaustive (see, UNCTAD-ICTSD 2005; Biadgleng and Munoz Tellez 2008). Anyway, intellectual property needs to be thought from an African countries' perspective to face effectively and efficiently the issue of technology transfer.

In reality, IP law may be an instrument of trade and industrial policy in the long run. It can be beneficial or detrimental according to the use to which it has been put.. Hence, one has to take into consideration legal aspects but, surely, go beyond that.

Beyond the Law

Opening up to foreign imports and firms can be detrimental for local enterprises. The persistent belief, common in both developed and developing countries and despite the emergence of a few innovative imitators in the South, that developing countries are only 'technology users', importing knowledge embodied in machinery and equipment and/or licensing-in product and process technologies developed elsewhere contributes to the little attention given to building upon indigenous knowledge and exercising creativity in the development of new products or organizational structures that correspond to local conditions and needs (Mytelca 2007:3; Olukoshi 2001:26). As expressed by UNCTAD 2005,

> there is little evidence to suggest that FDI in Africa (or elsewhere in the developing world) plays a leading or catalytic role in the growth process, and while capital formation must be one of the levers of regional recovery, identifying a healthy investment climate with one attractive to FDI is a misleading guide for policy makers.

Africa possesses abundant agricultural and mineral resources. It would be very interesting to promote industrialization based on those resources and diversify economic structures of the continent. Only local industries know better the needs of the populations and can satisfy them (Olukoshi 2001:26). Measures should be taken to promote the private sector and increase new investments by mobilizing both domestic and foreign savings. To this effect, African investors should be encouraged to invest in Africa rather than keeping their wealth outside the continent. Indeed, development almost depends on the mobilization of domestic resources for both public and private sector investment, along with moves towards a more skill- and technology-intensive production profile consistent with high value-added activities and strong productivity growth. Private rather than public financing will eventually be the decisive factor in sustaining growth, while public investment in infrastructure and the social sectors needs to increase rapidly in Africa over the next few years in order to reduce operating costs of private enterprises and increase competitiveness (Economic Commission for Africa 2000). So doing, the capacities of African states may be strengthened, thus resolving at least partially the problem of their permanent dependence vis-à-vis foreign political and economic forces.

Regional trade arrangements have also been raised as a possible response to Africa's poor trade performance and associated development problems. To ensure the success of the strategy to accelerate the pace of Africa's integration into the global economy, Africa needs to mainstream regionalism in a way not done before (ECA 2000). Regionalism may contribute to enlarge and diversify the economic space. Such an integration process within Africa is essential not only to achieve international competitiveness for the continent, but also as a mechanism for diversifying risk and reduce the shocks of an uncertain global and African economic, physical and ethnic environment (Olukoshi 2001).

Even law needs time. The transitional periods accorded by the TRIPS Agreement for the implementation of its provisions was considered very short for developing and least-developed countries. Meanwhile, as stated by Botoy Ituku, there has been more than *'a One-hundred-and-Twelve-Year transitional period for the industrialized countries'* (Elangi Botoy 2004: 115). This period has been extended in the area of pharmaceuticals till 2016. Except for this prolongation, all the other countries have been supposed to implement totally the provision of the TRIPS Agreement since 2005. In fact, a process of *'deindustrialization'* has taken place in many African countries because of globalization, including the globalization of IP. As Joseph Stiglitz, winner of the Nobel Prize for Economics, once said about globalization, *'the rapid pace of change has not allowed countries time for cultural adaptation…'* (Stiglitz 2001). Furthermore, I agree with Professor Amin that a meaningful strategy *'should come within the perspective of a polycentric world bringing together the different regions that make it up, in a flexible way which would make possible the implementation of the specific policies required by the diversity of the objective situations'* (Amin 1993:138).

Conclusion

There is no innocent law. Attention should be paid to how international intellectual property laws are appropriated in African countries in order to create and increase their beneficial effect. Law has to be intertwined with reality; reality can give orientation for the adoption of a subsequent law; also a law can be adopted to create an incentive for the implementation of a policy. But definitely, as part of the trade and industrial policy, the solution goes beyond the simple considerations of law versus the reality. The best approach is neither legal, nor managerial, nor sociological, nor historical etc... (Mhone 2003:4). In fact, an efficient approach shall take into consideration all these aspects; not one of them alone, but all of them together.

It seems that Africa is still far from benefiting from the IP international legislation on technology transfer. However, this paper has demonstrated that the law alone cannot be criticized. It has its part of responsibility, as well as many other factors. The international arena offers a great opportunity to improve Africa's development. There should be attention on an increased representation of African interests in this arena, coupled with a voluntarist approach to development and technology transfer at national levels. The feasibility is hard; meanwhile possibilities exist. The presumption of profit remains; African countries have to and can find their way, with laws, but also beyond.

For that purpose, laws adopted at national levels should be innovative and generate incentive to boost technology transfer towards African countries. The provisions adopted for the NOTAP in Nigeria are very illustrative of the importance of such incentives. African governments could put into place and give effect to organs for the coordination of information and action in the domain of contracts, alliances or other cooperation agreements involving technology transfer. At the same time, partnerships between innovative institutions (including local universities, private enterprises and other actors) abroad and inside African countries should be promoted, always taking into consideration the social, cultural and economic specificities of the African people.

Notes

1. The African Intellectual Property Organization (OAPI) created in 1962 is the organization in charge of the unification of IP rules in its Member States and acting in their name and on their account. It has 16 Member States among the French-speaking nations (headquartered in Cameroon). The African Regional Industrial Property Organization (ARIPO) has 16 member states among the English speaking countries (former British colonies, headquartered in Zimbabwe). It was established by the Lusaka Agreement, adopted at a Diplomatic Conference held in Lusaka (Zambia) on 9 December 1976. It should be noted that these are not the only examples of African countries having at the national level laws on IP.

2. For a general overview of these provisions, see UNCTAD, 2001, *Compendium of International Arrangements on Transfer of Technology: Selected Instruments*, UNCTAD/ITE/IPC/Misc.5, United Nations, pp. 5-15.

3. It should be noted that in the OAPI countries, the Preamble of the Bangui Agreement creating the Organization refers simply to article 7 of the TRIPS Agreement.

4. Article III (h) of the Lusaka Agreement on the Creation of the ARIPO, as amended by the Council of Ministers on 13 August 2004. See note 1 above.

5. As amended by the Council of Ministers on August 13, 2004.

6. Fifty countries are currently designated by the United Nations as «least developed countries» (LDCs): Afghanistan, Angola, Bangladesh, Benin, Bhutan, Burkina Faso, Burundi, Cambodia, Cape Verde, Central African Republic, Chad, Comoros, Democratic Republic of the Congo, Djibouti, Equatorial Guinea, Eritrea, Ethiopia, Gambia, Guinea, Guinea-Bissau, Haiti, Kiribati, Lao People's Democratic Republic, Lesotho, Liberia, Madagascar, Malawi, Maldives, Mali, Mauritania, Mozambique, Myanmar, Nepal, Niger, Rwanda, Samoa, Sao Tome and Principe, Senegal, Sierra Leone, Solomon Islands, Somalia, Sudan, Timor–Leste, Togo, Tuvalu, Uganda, United Republic of Tanzania, Vanuatu, Yemen and Zambia.

7. The Bold is inserted by us.

8. The Ministerial Declaration adopted on 18 December 2005 (WT/MIN(05)/DEC, 22 December 2005) noted in paragraph 43 that: *We take note of the report transmitted by the General Council on the work undertaken and progress made in the examination of the relationship between trade and transfer of technology and on the consideration of any possible recommendations on steps that might be taken within the mandate of the WTO to increase flows of technology to developing countries. Recognizing the relevance of the relationship between trade and transfer of technology to the development dimension of the Doha Work Programme and building on the work carried out to date, we agree that this work shall continue on the basis of the mandate contained in paragraph 37 of the Doha Ministerial Declaration. We instruct the General Council to report further to our next Session.'*

9. See footnote 4 of the Paragraph 43 cited above.

10. For example, the Ministry of Economic Affairs of Netherlands (MINEZ) controls a number of agencies that help and advise Dutch and foreign companies on a range of economic subjects. *Senter International,* one such agency, is involved in a project for the establishment of a safflower oil production plant and production of safflower by farmers in the Arusha region, Northern Tanzania. The project's aims include the development of a safflower oil extraction plant with a capacity of 1,000 tonnes per year. Therefore, personnel training, dissemination and marketing, as well as experiments with new safflower varieties containing high oil content will be the main activities conducted. Local farmers in the region will benefit from production orders of more than 4,000 hectares of safflower and they will receive technical assistance in order to meet production standards. Up to 80 per cent of the safflower is planned to be produced pesticide free and will be exported to Europe, the United States and Japan and is expected to meet internationally acknowledged certifying organization standards. Participants include Quality Food Ltd., DLV Agriconsult, and Pop Vriend Seeds BV as the Dutch investor. *Source:* UNCTAD 2004.

11. This is, for example, the case of Egypt, Libya and Mauritius.
12. That is through biopiracy, the process through which the rights of indigenous cultures to genetic resources and knowledge are erased and replaced for those who have exploited indigenous knowledge and biodiversity.
13. Briefing at the World Economic Forum meeting: Millennium Africa Renaissance Program- Implementation Issues, 28 January 2001.
14. All the details of these examples can be found in N. Lejosne, *Transfert de Technologie : les dimensions oubliées*: A partir de l'étude et la comparaison de trois cas au sein de PME Béninoises, Thèse de Doctorat/Ph.D en Sciences de l'homme et de la société, Ecole Polytechnique et HEC Montréal, 2006, pp. 65-178.
15. In order to avoid the payment for worthless technology, it is specifically provided in the Act that: «*no payment shall be made in Nigeria to the credit of any person outside Nigeria by or on the authority of the Central Bank of Nigeria or any licensed Bank in Nigeria in respect of any payments due under a contract or agreement mentioned in this Act unless a Certificate of Registration issued under the Act is presented by the party or parties concerned together with a copy of the contract or agreement certified by the National Office in that behalf*» (see section 7 of the Act).
16. The TRIPS Agreement was ammended by an Agreement of 6 December 2005 that includes mainly the provisions of the Doha ministerial decision of 30 August 2003.
17. The WHO IGWG was established in 2006 under the mandate of the World Health Assembly Resolution WHA59.24 to draw up a global strategy and plan of action to secure needs-driven, essential health research and development relevant to diseases that disproportionately affect developing countries. This plan includes considerations on technology transfer.
18. The General Assembly of the WIPO created a new Permanent Committee on Development and Intellectual Property (CDIP). The CDIP held its first meeting on 3-7 March 2008.

References

Amin, S., 1993, 'The Challenge of Globalization: Delinking', in South Centre, *Facing the Challenge. Responses to the Report o the South Commission*, London and New Jersey/Geneva: Zed Books and South Centre, pp. 132-138.

Biadgleng, E. T. and Munoz Tellez, V., 2008, 'The Changing Structure and Governance of Intellectual Property Enforcement', *South Centre Research Paper N°15*.

Blakeney, M., 2008, *Guidebook on Enforcement of Intellectual Property Rights*, Queen Mary Intellectual Property Research Institute (QMIPRI), London. Available online at http://www.delpak.cec.eu.int/WHATSNEW/Guidelines.pdf.

Correa, C., 2001a, 'Traditional Knowledge and Intellectual Property – Issues and options surrounding the protection of traditional knowledge', *Discussion Paper, Quaker United Nations Organisation* (QUNO).

Correa, C., 2001b, 'The TRIPS Agreement: how much room for maneuver?', *Journal of Human Development*, Vol. 2, No. 1, pp.79-107.

Economic Commission for Africa (ECA), 2000, *Globalization, regionalism and Africa's development agenda*, Bangkok, Thailand. Available online at http://www.unctad-10.org/pdfs/ux_id_ecapaper.en.pdf.

Elangi Botoy, I., 2004, 'From the Paris Convention to the TRIPS Agreement: A One-Hundred-and-Twelve-Year Ttransitional Period for the Industrialized Countries', *The Journal of World Intellectual Property,*1, 115-130.

Gervais, D., 2003, *The TRIPS Agreement: Drafting History and Analysis*, 2nd Edition, London, Sweet and Maxwell.

Gilbert, H., 1979, 'La commercialisation des inventions non brevetées', in *protection et exploitation de la recherche pharmaceutique*, Journées de Lyon, 5-6 avril, coll. du CEIPI n⁰ 28, Litec 1980, pp.163-168.

ITDG (Intermediate Technology Development Group), 2002, 'How to make technology transfer work for human development', *ITDG*, UK.

Kamil, Idriss, 2003, *Intellectual Property - A Power Tool for Economic Growth*, Geneva: WIPO.

Lejosne, N., 2006, *Transfert de Technologie : les dimensions oubliées*: A partir de l'étude et la comparaison de trois cas au sein de PME Béninoises, Thèse de Doctorat/Ph.D en Sciences de l'homme et de la société, Ecole Polytechnique et HEC Montréal.

Mayer, J., 2001, 'Globalization, technology transfer, and skill accumulation in Low-Income countries', *UNU/WIDER*. Available online at http://www.wider.unu.edu/publications/dps/dp2001-39.pdf.

Mhone, G., 2003, 'The Challenges of Governance, Public Sector Reform and Public Administration in Africa', Cape Town: University of Witwatersrand.

Musungu, S. F., 2005, 'Rethinking innovation, development and intellectual property in the UN : WIPO and beyond', *TRIPS Issues Papers 5*, Ottawa, QIAP (Quaker International Affaire Programme).

Mytelka, L., 2007, *Technology Transfer Issues in Environmental Goods and Services: An Illustrative Analysis of Sectors Relevant to Air-pollution and Renewable Energy,* ICTSD Trade and Environment Series Issue Paper No. 6, International Centre for Trade and Sustainable Development, Geneva.

Nwauche, E. S., 2005, 'A Development Oriented Intellectual Property Regime for Africa', Paper presented at the 11th General Assembly of the Council for the Development of Social Science Research for Africa (CODESRIA), Maputo, 6-10 December.

Olukoshi, A., 2001, *West Africa's Political Economy in the Next Millennium: Retrospect and Prospect*, Dakar/Oxford: CODESRIA and OXFAM/GB I.

Oyelaran-Oyeyinka, B., 2004, 'How can Africa benefit from globalization? Global governance of technology and Africa's global exclusion', *ATPS (African Technology Policy Studies Network) special paper series n° 17.*

Prasad, E., et al, 2003, 'Effects of financial globalization on developing countries: Some empirical evidence', International Monetary Fund (IMF) Occasional Paper 220, Washington, DC.

Sell, Susan K., 2003, *Private Power, Public Law: The Globalization of Intellectual Property Rights,* Cambridge University Press.

South Centre, 1998, *Towards an Economic Platform for the South*, Geneva: South Centre.

South Centre, 2002, *The South and Sustainable Development Conundrum*, Geneva: South Centre.

Stiglitz, J., 2002, *Globalization and its Discontents*, Allen Lane.

Tansey, G., 1999, 'Commerce, propriété intellectuelle, alimentation et diversité biologique',

UNCTAD, 2001, *Compendium of International Arrangements on Transfer of Technology: Selected Instruments*, UNCTAD/ITE/IPC/Misc.5, United Nations.

UNCTAD, 2004, *Facilitating Transfer of Technology to Developing Countries: A Survey of Home-Country Measures*, New York and Geneva: United Nations.

UNCTAD, 2005, *Economic development in Africa, Rethinking the role of Foreign Direct Investment*, New York and Geneva: United Nations.

UNCTAD-ICTSD, 2005, *Resource Book on TRIPS and Development: An authoritative and practical guide to the TRIPS Agreement*, Cambridge University Press.

UNCTAD, 2007, *The Least Developed Countries Report 2007: Knowledge, Technological Learning and Innovation for Development*, Geneva and New York.

Zulu, H., 2003, 'Africa's Stolen Biodiversity – Patenting Life', *African Institute*.

11

The UNESCO Convention for the Protection and Promotion of the Diversity of Cultural Expressions: Implications for African Trade and Culture Policy

E. S. Nwauche

Introduction

On 18 March 2007 the UNESCO Convention for the Protection and Promotion of Diversity of Cultural Expressions[1] became operational, three months after the thirtieth instrument of ratification was deposited. Adopted in 2005 by a vote of 148 to 2,[2] the Convention is steadily growing in importance as the European Union as well as 83 other countries, including 21 African countries, are State parties to the Convention.[3] The UNESCO Convention is the culmination of long-standing efforts to treat culture as a unique category in international trade.[4]

This chapter argues that the UNESCO Convention is a clarion call for Africa to rethink, reformulate, restate, legislate and implement trade and cultural policies at national, regional and continental levels in order to develop and sustain a cultural industry that is able to energize and partake in the global trade in cultural goods and services and form a fundamental plank in the continent's development. To achieve the growth of national and regional cultural capacity, a number of issues that find resonance in the UNESCO Convention must be addressed. These measures include nurturing creativity through a development-oriented copyright regime; an effective policy regime for the protection and promotion of communal intellectual property; and; the nuanced elaboration of the relationship between trade and culture in bilateral and free trade agreements.

It is further argued that the issues focused on in this chapter are peculiar to developing countries and that the aims and objectives of the UNESCO Convention cannot be the same for all countries, a fact that the Convention's history and text recognize. While developed countries conceive of the UNESCO Convention as primarily designed to enhance their cultural industries by recognizing significant protectionist measures, Africa must deal with the promotion of these industries because in many cases it is non-existent and improperly articulated where it exists. Without the proper development of the framework of national cultural industries, the private sector will find it extremely difficult to realise their potential. Gifted cultural practitioners will have a little or no incentive to continue to create and in most cases will look to alternative means of livelihood.

Since a key essence of the UNESCO Convention is that it enables member states to protect and promote the diversity of cultural expressions within their territories, it is not in doubt that the Convention is protectionist because it favours local cultural industries over their foreign counterparts. Most of the UNESCO countries (UNESCO Convention State parties) are also WTO countries. Given WTO's essence of free trade, a fundamental bone of contention is how the protectionist rules of the UNESCO Convention would interface with the free trade rules of the WTO. At a global level the UNESCO Convention could be said to challenge a key process of globalization which is the standardization of markets, products and processes based on the neo-liberal stance that States are equal and the market is the best way for States to maximize their endowments and global wealth. Free trade emphasizes the commercial aspects of cultural goods; and in a globalized world there is a very strong chance that foreign cultural goods marketed by powerful monopolistic multinational companies could swamp local cultural goods and ultimately impose foreign cultural values.

The UNESCO Convention is also a rejection of the idea that free trade is an end in itself, and is more important than non-trade values such as culture. In this way, it can be understood that the inability of the WTO to accommodate national non-trade concerns led countries with a common interest to seek protection outside the system. This chapter does not fully address the legal relationship between the UNESCO Convention and the WTO even as this process is unravelling. No matter how the relationship turns out, the issues discussed in this chapter remain relevant for African countries even in the absence of the Convention. The importance of these issues, as stated above, concerns the development of national cultural industries so that they can become engines of growth through the creation of jobs and foreign exchange earnings.

The UNESCO Convention

This section shall first examine the key features of the UNESCO Convention and then evaluate the Convention.

Key Features of the UNESCO Convention

Article 1 of the UNESCO Convention lists the objectives of the Convention. They are (a) to protect and promote the diversity of cultural expressions; (b) to create the conditions for cultures to flourish and to freely interact in a mutually beneficial manner; (c) to encourage dialogue among cultures with a view to ensuring wider and balanced cultural exchanges in the world in favour of intercultural respect and a culture of peace; (d) to foster interculturality in order to develop cultural interaction in the spirit of building bridges among peoples; (e) to promote respect for the diversity of cultural expressions and raise awareness of its value at the local, national and international levels; (f) to reaffirm the importance of the link between culture and development for all countries, particularly for developing countries, and to support actions undertaken nationally and internationally to secure recognition of the true value of this link; (g) to give recognition to the distinctive nature of cultural activities, goods and services as vehicles of identity, values and meaning; (h) to reaffirm the sovereign rights of States to maintain, adopt and implement policies and measures that they deem appropriate for the protection and promotion of the diversity of cultural expressions on their territory; and (i) to strengthen international cooperation and solidarity in a spirit of partnership with a view, in particular, to enhancing the the Guiding Principles of the Convention are set out in Article 2. They are as follows:

1) *Principle of respect for human rights and fundamental freedoms:* Cultural diversity[5] can be protected and promoted only if human rights and fundamental freedoms, such as freedom of expression, information and communication, as well as the ability of individualsto choose modes of cultural expression,[6] are guaranteed. No one may invoke the provisions of this Convention in order to infringe human rights and fundamental freedoms as enshrined in the Universal Declaration of Human Rights or guaranteed by international law, or to limit the scope thereof. This principle is important because it seeks to ensure that State Parties do not resort to the Convention to deny the fundamental human rights of its citizens by redefining the content of protected human rights on an alleged cultural basis.

2) *Principle of sovereignty:* States have, in accordance with the Charter of the United Nations and the principles of international law, the sovereign right to adopt measures and policies to protect and promote the diversity of cultural expressions within their territory.

3) *Principle of equal dignity of and respect for all cultures:* The protection and promotion of the diversity of cultural expressions presuppose the recognition of equal dignity of and respect for all cultures, including the cultures of persons belonging to minorities and indigenous peoples.

4) *Principle of international solidarity and cooperation:* International cooperation and solidarity should be aimed at enabling countries, especially developing countries, to create and strengthen their means of cultural expression, including their cultural industries, whether nascent or established, at the local, national and international levels.

5) *Principle of the complementarity of economic and cultural aspects of development:* Since culture is one of the mainsprings of development, the cultural aspects of development are as important as its economic aspects, which individuals and peoples have the fundamental right to participate in and enjoy

6) *Principle of sustainable development:* Cultural diversity is a rich asset for individuals and societies. The protection, promotion and maintenance of cultural diversity are an essential requirement for sustainable development for the benefit of present and future generations.

7) *Principle of equitable access:* Equitable access to a rich and diversified range of cultural expression from all over the world and access of cultures to the means of expression and dissemination constitute important elements for enhancing cultural diversity and encouraging mutual understanding.

8) *Principle of openness and balance:* When States adopt measures to support the diversity of cultural expression, they should seek to promote, in an appropriate manner, openness to other cultures of the world and to ensure that these measures are geared to the objectives pursued under the Convention.

The rights and obligations of State Parties elaborated in Article 6 seem ideally contemplated within the framework of a State's cultural policies and measures[7] Each State Party is allowed to adopt measures aimed at protecting and promoting the diversity of cultural expression within its territory. It is important to note that these measures are not restricted to cultural policies but contemplate all measures which may include the following:

(a) regulatory measures aimed at protecting and promoting diversity of cultural expression;

(b) measures that, in an appropriate manner, provide opportunities for domestic cultural activities, goods and services among all those available within the national territory for the creation, production, dissemination, distribution and enjoyment of such domestic cultural activities, goods and services, including provisions relating to the language used for such activities, goods and services; (c) measures aimed at providing domestic independent cultural industries and activities in the informal sector effective access to the means of production, dissemination and distribution of cultural activities, goods and services;

(d) measures aimed at providing public financial assistance;

(e) measures aimed at encouraging non-profit organizations, as well as public and private institutions and artists and other cultural professionals, to develop and promote the free exchange and circulation of ideas, cultural expressions and cultural activities, goods and services, and to stimulate both the creative and entrepreneurial spirit in their activities;

(f) measures aimed at establishing and supporting public institutions, as appropriate;

(g) measures aimed at nurturing and supporting artists and others involved in the creation of cultural expression;

(h) measures aimed at enhancing diversity of the media, including through public service broadcasting.

Article 7 of the Convention permits State Parties to adopt measures to promote forms and modes of cultural expression which should provide an environment in their countries which encourages individuals and social groups to create, produce, disseminate, distribute and have access to their own cultural expression, paying due attention to the special circumstances and needs of women as well as various social groups, including persons belonging to minorities and indigenous people. A related provision of the Convention is Article 13 which encourages State Parties to endeavour to integrate culture in their development policies at all levels for the creation of conditions conducive to sustainable development and, within this framework, foster aspects relating to the protection and promotion of the diversity of cultural expression. Attention must be drawn to Article 8 of the Convention which provides that, in peculiar situations, a State Party may adopt special measures to protect cultural expression in its territory that is at the risk of extinction , under serious threat, or otherwise in need of urgent safeguarding.

The UNESCO Convention recognizes, in Articles 12-18, the need to encourage international cooperation in the promotion of the diversity of cultural expression. Thus in Article 12 the Convention provides that State Parties shall endeavour to strengthen their bilateral, regional and international cooperation for the creation of conditions conducive to the promotion of the diversity of cultural expression. In Article 13 State, Parties agree to endeavour to incorporate culture in their development policies. In Article 14, the Parties agree to endeavour to support cooperation for sustainable development in order to foster a dynamic cultural sector in developing countries through:

(i) creating and strengthening cultural production and distribution capacities in developing countries;

(ii) facilitating wider access to the global market and international distribution networks for their cultural activities, goods and services;

(iii) enabling the emergence of viable local and regional markets;

(iv) adopting, where possible, appropriate measures in developed countries with a view to facilitating access to their territory for the cultural activities, goods and services of developing countries;

(v) providing support for creative work and facilitating the mobility, to the extent possible, of artists from the developing world;

(vi) encouraging appropriate collaboration between developed and developing countries in the areas, *inter alia*, of music and film.

Article 14 also encourages State Parties to engage in capacity-building through the exchange of information, experience and expertise, as well as the training of human resources; technology transfer through incentives and offer financial support through an International Fund for Cultural Diversity which is voluntary by the tenor of Article 18. Article 16 places an obligation on developed countries to facilitate cultural exchanges by granting preferential treatment to artists, cultural goods and services of developing countries. Another obligation on developed countries is found in Article 17 which requires them to provide assistance to developing countries in cases where cultural forms of expression in the latter are at risk of extinction, under serious threat, or otherwise in need of urgent safeguarding.

Articles 20 and 21 regulate the relationship of the Convention with other treaties. Article 20 provides that the Convention is not subordinate to any other treaty and that State Parties shall 'foster mutual supportiveness between the Convention and other treaties'; and 'when interpreting and applying other treaties to which they are parties or entering other international obligations, parties shall take into account the relevant provisions of the Convention' even as the Convention stresses that its provisions do not modify the rights and obligations under other treaties that its members are part of. Article 21 encourages parties to promote the objectives of the Convention in other international forums.

The dispute settlement mechanism of the Convention is found in Article 25 which provides that in the event of dispute the parties shall seek a solution by negotiation and if they cannot reach an agreement they may jointly seek the good offices of or shall request mediation by a third party. Where this fails, the parties may have recourse to conciliation and shall consider the results of the conciliation in good faith. The conciliation is not mandatory as a party may enter reservation about the procedure.

An Assessment of the UNESCO Convention

First, there is no doubt that the Convention is a strong tool for developing countries to develop their national cultural capacity. In this regard, it must be noted that the Convention permits States to deploy 'all' measures to develop their cultural industries and their creative capacity. Thus these measures can be in any sector provided they have an impact on the cultural sector. This is important in Africa so that governments can think of culture not only as a facilitator but a mainstream development pillar. While it is true that the obligations incurred by States are discretionary, it is important that African countries feel obligated to introduce the measures in the Convention if it is to be of any use to them. Secondly, it is important to assess the Convention to determine if it created an exclusive and obligatory legal regime of trade in cultural goods and services. In other words, is the Convention a parallel trade regime to the WTO and other bilateral and multilateral agreements such that members of the latter can rely on the Convention to govern trade in cultural goods and services?

For a number of reasons, the answer must be in the negative. The Convention does not create a compulsory dispute settlement mechanism.

Its members are free to reject the conciliation provided for in Article 25 of the UNESCO Convention. Moreover, State Parties have a wide discretion as to what measures they can adopt in their territories even if the Convention grants them the right to do so. Thus, State Parties are under no obligation to take those measures and there may be nothing much that can be done if a State Party does not take all or any of these measures. This is largely due to the use of the word 'may' in the relevant articles. Furthermore, this discretion is evident in the relevant parts of the Convention that provide for international cooperation. All taken, it is clear that there are no obligations on the Parties to take any capacity building measures and therefore there may be little basis for disputes. Even if there are disputes there is no compulsory dispute settlement mechanism. Clearly, the standards of the UNESCO Convention are lower than those of the WTO. Considering that the Convention stresses that it does not modify existing treaty obligations including the WTO, it may be concluded that it is not a legal substitute to the WTO; and cultural goods and services may not on account of the Convention be out of the reach of the WTO. However, on a deeper reflection the relationship has far-reaching legal significance

The UNESCO Convention and the WTO

To put our discussion in this section in a good context, a brief overview of the WTO is important. The World Trade Organisation became operational on 1 January 1995 following the success of the Uruguay Round Negotiations which resulted in the Marrakech Agreement on the Establishment of the World Trade Organisation signed in April 1994. For almost fifty years before, the General Agreement on Tariffs and Trade (GATT) functioned as the international organization for trade but was concerned largely with the harmonization of tariffs. The WTO was conceived as a more encompassing trade organization and the vehicle of free trade. The principal source of the WTO Law is the Marrakech Agreement which is the basic agreement. There are many other agreements and understandings included as annexes. Annex 1 has three parts. Annex 1A contains thirteen multilateral agreements on trade in goods. Annex 1B contains the General Agreement on Trade in Services (the GATS); while Annex 1C contains the Agreement on Trade Relates Aspects of Intellectual Property Rights (the TRIPS Agreement).

Annex 1A contains agreements such as the General Agreement on Tariffs and Trade 1994 (the 'GATT 1994); the Agreement on Technical Barriers to Trade (the 'TBT Agreement); the Agreement on Implementation of

Article VI of the General Agreement on Tariffs and Trade 1994 ('the Anti-Dumping Agreement) and the Agreement on Subsidies and Countervailing Measures (the SCM Agreement). The WTO dispute settlement mechanism and trade policy review are contained in Annexes 2 and 3 respectively. It is to be noted that agreements in Annexes 1-3 are binding on all WTO members.

There are four key principles and rules that underpin the WTO. They are first the principles of non-discrimination achieved by the obligations of most -favoured nation (MFN) treatment[8] and national treatment.[9] The MFN treatment obligation requires a WTO member that grants favourable treatment to another country to grant that same treatment to all other WTO members. The MFN treatment ensures equal opportunity in export and import to all WTO members. The national treatment obligation requires a State to treat foreign products in the same way it treats local products. Secondly, there are rules on market access including rules on customs duties and quantitative restrictions. The rules on market access seek to ensure that foreign goods are not impeded by tariff barriers like customs duties and non-tariff barriers like quantitative restrictions such as quotas. Thirdly, there are rules on unfair trade which include rules on subsidies; and fourthly, rules embodying general exceptions. These exceptions are recognized to protect other important societal values.[10] In this regard, the most important exception is Article XX(f)[11] of GATT 1994 which provides that nothing in GATT 1994 shall prevent the adoption or enforcement of any measure 'imposed for the protection of national treasures of artistic, historic or archaeological value'. A lot may turn on what this provision really means.

Given the brief overview, there is no doubt that implementing any or all of the measures set out in Articles 6, 7 or 8 of the UNESCO Convention above is sure to warrant allegations of breach of WTO Principles and Rules because many of the measures would appear to be contrary to national treatment obligations, since they discriminate in favour of domestic artists and producers. If these policies contemplate other countries like fellow African artists and producers, then they will also breach the most-favoured-nation treatment obligations. The full legal relationship between the WTO and UNESCO Convention is a complex one and outside the scope of this chapter.[12] What is important for us is a general indication of the possible trajectories for reconciling the two Conventions. First, there is the possibility that because of the UNESCO Convention, much more detailed examination of the procedural and substantive exceptions contained in the WTO will be undertaken. Second, the UNESCO Convention could become an interpretative tool in the WTO Dispute settlement. Third, the UNESCO Convention could be used as a defence in a WTO dispute. Fourth, WTO parties could incorporate the UNESCO Convention into the WTO by influencing the ongoing GATS negotiations on the audio visual services.[13]

The UNESCO Convention and African Countries: Implications for African Trade and Cultural Policy

As stated above, developing countries had a different agenda in the negotiations leading to the UNESCO Convention. They came to the negotiations well aware that they had little or no cultural industries that could engage in the global trade in cultural goods and services. Thus while the developed countries who were in the forefront of the fight for the Convention had an agenda that sought to create an alternative framework for trade in cultural goods and services,[14] developing countries were more concerned with the promotion of cultural industries. Speaking about the negotiations towards the Convention, Nina Obuljien states that:

> Experts also agreed on the need to establish a balance between protection and promotion of cultural diversity, they felt that the convention could not be a narrow *protectionist* instrument. It was also important not to let the Convention become an instrument for the protection of existing cultural industries, their market share and current positions and interests. In order to give an incentive for participation in negotiations to those countries which have less developed cultural industries, experts included in their draft Convention strong measures to assist the development of cultural capacity in the South... [15]

It is important to remember that while Article 6 of the Convention sets out numerous measures which State Parties may take, it appears to be strictly protectionist and, perhaps for the benefit of developing countries, also promotional because in different combinations the measures assist in the development of significant cultural capacity. Even at that, it must be pointed out that the UNESCO Convention does not speak directly to measures designed to stimulate national cultural capacity. Before turning to examine these policies, a review of a number of regional cultural policies to determine how the advocated measures are articulated, if at all, is important. As stated earlier, African countries in a number of documents have articulated cultural policies that had significant trade implications geared towards development before the UNESCO Convention. An appropriate starting point, therefore, is to examine the content of these policies.

An Overview of African Trade and Cultural Policies

The Cultural Charter of Africa and the Draft Charter for the Cultural Renaissance of Africa

The Cultural Charter of Africa was adopted in Port Louis, Mauritius on 5 July 1976 by Heads of State and Government of the Organisation of African Unity in its Thirteenth Ordinary Session.[16] It is important to note the Revised Charter for the Cultural Renaissance of Africa was adopted by the Assembly of Heads of State and Government of the African Union during the Fifth Ordinary Session in Sudan almost three decades later.[17] The key features of the Cultural Charter are its objectives which include:

- to liberate the African peoples from socio-cultural conditions which impede their development in order to recreate and maintain the sense and will for progress, the sense and will for development;

- the rehabilitation, restoration, preservation and promotion of the African cultural heritage;

- the assertion of the dignity of the African and of the popular foundations of his culture;

- the combating and elimination of all forms of alienation and cultural suppression and oppression everywhere in Africa, especially in countries still under colonial and racist domination including apartheid;

- the encouragement of cultural co-operation among the States with a view to the strengthening of African unity;

- the encouragement of international cultural co-operation for a better understanding among peoples within which Africa will make its original and appropriate contribution to human culture;

- promotion in each country of popular knowledge of science and technology;

- a necessary condition for the control of nature;

- development of all dynamic values in the African cultural heritage; and,

- rejection of any element which is an impediment to progress.

In Part 1 of the Charter, African States reaffirmed the link between cultural diversity and national identity and that cultural diversity is the expression of national identity. Accordingly, the assertion of national identity must not be at the cost of impoverishing or subjecting various types of culture within the State.[18] Part 3 deals with National Cultural Development. In Article 6, African States undertook to adopt national cultural policy, with each state setting out its priority which should assist in integrating a cultural development plan in the overall programme for economic and social development. Part 4 stresses the importance of training and life-long education;[19] while part 5 recognizes the importance of African languages.[20] Part 6 obliges African States to encourage the use of the Information and Communication media for cultural development.[21] Part seven of the Charter sets out the role of governments in cultural development. This includes:

(a) assistance to collective and individual artistic creation through competitions and exhibitions; tax rebates; financial assistance and scholarships for training; and the creation of a National Fund for the promotion of culture and the arts;[22]

(b) the preparation of an inter-African convention on copyright, establishment of national copyright offices and encouragement of the establishment of authors associations;[23]

(c) ensuring the legal and practical protection of cultural property.[24]

Finally, Part 8 of the Charter acknowledges the importance of establishing inter-African cultural co-operation.

Even though the Revised Cultural Charter is yet to come into force it is a stronger advocate of the linkage between trade and culture. In addition to the provisions of the Cultural Charter which it incorporates, the Revised Cultural Charter, in its aims and objectives, declares two important points in this regard. The first is the integration of cultural objectives in development strategies and the fact that it provides African peoples the resources to respond to globalization. One key feature of the Revised Cultural Charter is the obligation undertaken by African countries to engage with international cultural treaties. State parties to the Convention undertake therein to ratify the UNESCO Convention, the Convention on the Protection of Cultural Property in the Event of Armed Conflict and the Convention on Intangible Heritage. They also undertake to align their national legislations with these treaties. With respect to copyright, they undertake to modify existing international conventions to meet African interests. Another important feature of the Revised Cultural Charter is an emphasis on the protection afforded by human rights for cultural development. Article 7 links the establishment of an enabling environment for cultural creation and development to the freedom of expression. Unlike the Cultural Charter, Article 9 of the Revised Cultural Charter recognizes the importance of cultural stakeholders in the form of non-institutional actors such as designers, private developers, local associations and the private sector as instrumental to cultural development. Another innovation is found in Article 8 which sets the framework for the role of African

States that are to (i) protect and promote the freedom of artists, intellectuals and men and women of culture on one hand and historical sites on the other; (ii) financially and materially support cultural initiatives in all segments of society; and facilitate access to education and culture for all segments of the population.

An examination of the Cultural Charter and the Revised Cultural Charter shows that they are a modest attempt to link trade and culture generally, and the promotion of cultural capacity in particular, especially at the national level. It is clear that these documents are, in a framework nature, requiring African States to elaborate in more specificity the measures for the development of national cultural capacities. The key issue is whether African States are to proceed by way of national policies or by legislation and/or other strategy in order to domesticate the provisions of these Charters. It is to be remembered that the Cultural Charter recommends the adoption of national cultural policies as a means of domesticating obligations assumed under the treaty. In line with this, a number of African countries have adopted these policies. These include Seychelles[25] Uganda, [26] Botswana,[27] Namibia,[28] Mozambique,[29] and Nigeria. Another strategy that African countries have adopted is to include cultural issues and concerns in Poverty Reduction Strategy Papers (PSRP).[30]

NEPAD and Culture

Given NEPAD's instrumentality in African development, it is important to understand how it treats culture. This is found in paragraphs 140 and 141:

> 140. Culture is an integral part of development efforts on the continent. Consequently, it is essential to protect and effectively utilise indigenous knowledge that represents a major dimension of the continent's culture, and to share this knowledge for the benefit of humankind. The *New Partnership for Africa's Development* will give special attention to the protection and nurturing of indigenous knowledge, which includes tradition-based literacy, artistic and scientific works, inventions, scientific discoveries, designs, marks, names and symbols, undisclosed information and all other tradition-based innovations and creations resulting from intellectual activity in the industrial, scientific, literary or artistic fields. The term also includes genetic resources and associated knowledge.

> 141. The leadership of the *New Partnership for Africa's Development* will take urgent steps to ensure that indigenous knowledge in Africa is protected through appropriate legislation. They will also promote its protection at the international level, by working closely with the World Intellectual Property Organisation (WIPO).

While the protection of indigenous knowledge is a worthy goal, it is doubtful whether NEPAD actually conceives of the linkage between trade and culture in a comprehensive manner. It must therefore be one of the areas of further articulation of the mandate of NEPAD. Perhaps this articulation has already taken place within the context of the Revised Cultural Charter of Africa.

Regional Economic Groupings and Culture

This part examines how Africa's regional economic groupings have grappled with the issue of trade and culture. In this regard, it is the Southern Africa Development Community (SADC) that has bothered to articulate its thinking in this critical area. In 2000 the SADC adopted a Protocol on Culture Information and Sport. [31] This protocol is designed to enable members to cooperate in policy harmonization; training capacity-building and research; resource mobilization and utilization; flow and exchange of information; regional interaction of stakeholders. The cultural objectives of the Protocol are:

(a) co-operation in the formulation and harmonization of cultural policies of Member States;

(b) creation of a socio-cultural environment within which regional integration ideals of SADC can be realised;

(c) promotion of an attitude which takes culture into account in regional development programmes;

(d) identification, promotion and co-ordination of projects in the cultural field, including experience and information exchange between diverse cultures;

(e) ensuring that culture plays a significant role in the economic development of the Region and evaluation of all SADC projects and programmes for their cultural impact;

(f) Development and promotion of institutions of cultural heritage such as libraries, museums and archives in support of the broad and specific objectives of this Protocol; and

(g) promotion of the use of indigenous languages for the promotion of the cultural identity of the region.

While Article 12 deals with language policy formulation, Article 13 obligates members to establish policy guidelines for the preservation and promotion of the region's cultural heritage, Article 14 provides for cultural industries. In this regard, members are to make cultural industries a major cornerstone of their national economies and adopt all measures to nurture, protect and promote their infant cultural industries. Copyright and neighbouring rights are provided for in Article 16 which obligates members to collaborate and harmonise copyright and neighbouring rights legislation; ensure that international obligations regarding the protection of copyright are honoured; accede and ratify international conventions in this area; and, encourage and facilitate the formation of copyright societies.

African State Practice in Cultural Protection and Promotion Measures

In this part a review is undertaken of available evidence of protection and promotion measures that are contemplated by the UNESCO Convention which are deployed by African States to build their national cultural industries. They include:

(i) Subsidies such as the Revised Film and Television Production Incentive 2008 operated by the South Africa's Department of Trade and Industry in order to increase local content generation. This is principally achieved through qualifying rebates. Eligible companies are Special Purpose Corporate Vehicle (SPCV) incorporated in the Republic of South Africa solely for the purpose of the production of the film or television project. The SPCV and parent company must have a majority of South African shareholders of whom at least one shareholder must play an active role in the production and be credited in that role. Another organization that assists South African concerns in film and video development is the National Film and Video Foundation (NFVF). [33]

(ii) Market access restrictions such as local content requirements. This will include screen quotas and television programming limits. For example, the Nigerian Broadcasting Code 1993 provides for a ratio of programming of not more than 40 per cent foreign content for terrestrial programming and not more 80 per cent for cable stations. Satellite stations are to ensure at least 60 per cent Nigerian content and 25 per cent African content. [34] Screen quotas are an exception to national treatment standard found in Article III of GATT 1994 because they are protected in Article IV of GATT 1994. It is to be noted that this exception has been available since GATT became operational in 1947;

(iii) Tax measures; [35] and

(iv) Measures relating to copyright especially collective administration of copyright and use of proceeds from licensing for the development of local artistes.

Other protective measures such as licensing and distribution restrictions; and limitation of foreign investment and ownership do not seem to be favoured.

Some Recommended Measures to Improve African Trade and Cultural Capacity

A number of measures are recommended in this part which can assist in the promotion of national and regional cultural capacities and enable African countries to meaningfully utilize the objectives intendment of the UNESCO Convention.

Nurture a Development Oriented Copyright Regime that seeks a Balance between Public and Private Rights

Even though the UNESCO Convention recognizes the importance of intellectual property rights in its preamble, and in Article 6 provides that a State Party may take different measures to support intellectual property rights including support for artistes, there seems to be an inadequate understanding of the interaction between copyright creativity and culture. While it is clear that the abolition of intellectual property rights cannot be defended on the text or philosophy of the Convention, the *nature* of copyright protection is of fundamental importance to African countries. It is assumed, just like the SADC Protocol on Information Culture and Sport, that merely protecting copyright is enough for African States. It is argued below that unless the copyright regime is socially and developmentally oriented, creativity and cultural renewal are threatened. In many African countries copyright is protected by legislation[37] as part of the pantheon of intellectual property rights. Exclusive rights which are granted to authors and their assignees include reproduction, public performance, communication to the public, adaptation etc. These exclusive rights serve primarily as a means of stimulating creativity and as a means of ensuring that works that may ordinarily not be available to the public are made available. Hence, culture, creativity and copyright are interrelated. As Thiery Desurmont argues:

> [C]ulture is sustained by creativity, which presupposes in turn that creators are protected and can receive adequate remuneration. In the same way, the desire of States to foster their national culture implies that they protect their creators. Thus authors' rights work in favour of cultural diversity and the fight for cultural diversity contributes to the defence of authors' rights.[38]

Copyright also has an instrumental function that enables it to prevent access to information. To understand this point it must be pointed out that copyright is not only about the private interest of the author. It is also about the public interest. This public interest roughly equates to the mechanisms by which the public has access to works that qualify for copyright protection.[39] This is principally achieved through exceptions and limitations which is found in all copyright legislation either in a general form such as fair use or fair dealing[40] or specific provisions entitling the public to certain works. Examples include exceptions and limitations for private use,[41] libraries and educational institutions;[42] parody, pastiche and caricature;[43] and provisions for disabled persons.[44] Without these exceptions and limitations the public would have limited or no access to information contained in copyright works especially if they are unable to purchase these works, a fact which is characteristic of African States. Without information therefore it is difficult to engage in meaningful creative endeavour. The stimulation of knowledge production clearly at the foundation of cultural renewal will be stymied. As argued elsewhere:

> T]he mechanisms of knowledge production involve-in no particular order-construction, deconstruction, criticism, acceptance, review, reexamination and rejection. These mechanisms cannot be efficient if no new information is available. If, for any reason, including copyright protection, information is not forthcoming, a knowledge society cannot take off or stagnates.[45]

Information is at the centre of the control of ideas and without access to copyright works, ideas cannot stimulate further creativity. It is true that copyright protects expressions and not ideas.[46] However, it is often forgotten that the idea is embedded in the expression and without access to the work itself, one may not be able to glean the idea. The effect of denial of access to copyright is felt even more in a digital environment. The advent of this environment has led to an increased threat of copyright infringement. To combat this menace, many countries legislatively permit the use of a technological protection measure (TPM) that bars access to copyright works except with permission. Additionally, these legislations also prohibit the circumvention of these TPMs. These TPMs are, however, potentially non-differentiated between permitted and prohibited uses. Thus, unless specifically configured, the TPM may bar access to use permitted by an exception and limitation. African countries therefore, need to ground their copyright regime on the following fundamentals that are development-oriented, in order to ensure that copyright works for creativity and culture. First, these countries must operationalize the exceptions and limitations that are already in the copyright legislation. For example, if the copyright legislation allows the copying of a limited number of books that are out of print in a country,[47] it may be useful to compile a list of these books for the guidance of libraries. Second, African countries must take advantage of the exceptions and limitations contained in international intellectual property treaties. In this regard, African countries which have not already done so must include the reproduction exception contained in Article 9(2) of the Berne Convention on the Protection of Literary and Artistic Work[48] and generally permitted by the Agreement on Trade Related Aspects of Intellectual Property Rights (TRIPS), the WIPO Copyright Treaty,[49] and the WIPO Performances and Phonograms Treaty.[50]

It must be noted that the prospects of successfully using these treaties to expand the corpus of exceptions and limitations are seriously limited by what is generally known as the 'three step test' which seeks to assess any exception and limitation. This test states that the exceptions and limitations must be limited to special cases that do not conflict with a normal exploitation of the work and do not unreasonably prejudice the legitimate interests of the author. A strict interpretation[51] of this test is likely to strike down many national exceptions and limitations. It is therefore important that the UNESCO Convention be used as a fresh reason to urge a liberal interpretation of exceptions and limitations especially if they are related to trade in cultural goods and services. Third, African countries must ensure that when they synchronize their legislations to deal with the increased threat posed by the digital environment, they should ensure that the technological protection measures used to protect copyright in that environment should be so configured that they are able to allow the public access to works through approved exceptions and limitations. Fourth, the possibility of using guaranteed human rights and the obligations imposed thereby as a basis of ensuring better access to copyright works must be explored especially by African judiciaries. In this regard, the decision of the South African Constitutional Court in *Laugh It Off Promotions v SAB Breweries*[52] must be commended as it shows how the freedom of expression can be used to redefine the limits of an intellectual property right. Fifth, the judiciaries of African countries will do well to adopt the concept of user rights developed by the Canadian Supreme Court in *CCH v Law Society of Upper Canada*.[53] The concept of a user right reinforces the fact that access to copyright works is as important as the protection of an author's rights.

Develop an Effective and Efficient System for the Protection of Communal Intellectual Property

Closely allied to copyright protection is the question of how to deal with the overwhelming communal intellectual property such as folklore and traditional knowledge that the communities of African States produce.

The focus in this section shall be on folklore. There are two broad models of protecting and promoting communal intellectual property in Africa. The first method is the use of *sui generis* regimes. Since most of these communal creations do not ordinarily meet the requirements of conventional intellectual property, most African States devised *sui generis* regimes to protect their communal intellectual property.

With respect to folklore the appropriate legislations require those who want to use these pieces of folklore to seek the consent of the national copyright agency. For example, section 28 (1) of the Nigerian Copyright Act [54] protects expressions of folklore [55] from reproduction, communication to the public by performance, broadcasting, distribution by cable or other means; adaptations, translations and other transformations; when such expressions are made either for commercial purposes or outside their traditional or customary context. The right to authorize consent is vested in the Nigerian State indirectly through the Nigerian Copyright Commission. One of the conditions of the grant is the acknowledgement of the source of the expressions of folklore by indicating the community where the expressions of folklore utilized has been derived. Section 29 of the Act provides that any person who without the consent of the Nigerian Copyright Commission uses an expression of folklore shall be liable in damages injunctions and other remedies. Implied in the grant of consent is the fact that the Nigerian Copyright Commission will impose benefits to be enjoyed by the community. There is little evidence that this system has been utilized in Nigeria even with a massive video film industry that thrives on cultural motifs. It does appear that it is difficult to enforce this provision effectively in Nigeria. So the possibility that many video films in Nigeria have fallen foul of the Copyright Act is a reality that also underscores the impracticability of this provision. Since these expressions of folklore, like other communal intellectual property, is the staple of creativity in many African countries, the dilemma faced in the protection of communal intellectual property is how to ensure that it is not appropriated and/or denigrated and, at the same time, is accessible as a source of creativity. It is clear that the *sui generis* model has not been able to resolve this dilemma.

Another mode which is sought after in South Africa through the Intellectual Property Amendment Bill 2007 [56] intends to employ conventional intellectual property to protect communal intellectual property. This Bill provides that where a commercial benefit is to be derived from a traditional performance, a royalty shall be paid to the National Trust Fund for Traditional Intellectual Property which shall devote its funds to the development of indigenous communities. The Bill also recognizes traditional copyright subject to the interest of the indigenous community where the copyright and trade mark originated. Traditional terms or expression are not permitted to be registered as trade marks by the Bill and only indigenous communities are permitted to register such trade marks. The Bill also recognizes traditional designs and preserves the rights of members of indigenous communities to use the design for their trade. While the final form of the Bill is yet to emerge, it is important to warn of the danger of protecting communal intellectual property by conventional intellectual property. For copyright, it is its exclusionary function that may place communal intellectual property beyond the reach of the public. Ultimately, all African countries must continue to explore how to balance the dilemma of copyright protection and access to these works.

A Social and Development-oriented Collecting Society Regime

A robust trade and cultural policy must embrace a development-oriented collecting society regime since this institutional type is very much in existence in Africa and serves as a more efficient way of collecting royalty for artistes through its licensing activities. Collective licensing activities allow artistes to concentrate on their work while an efficient organization collects royalty for them locally, and internationally through reciprocal agreements with other national collecting societies. Where they exist and are functioning they may be the only credible source of royalties for artistes. Collecting societies assume that there are a lot of copyrighted works within a jurisdiction. If the numbers are not significant as is the case of Africa, there is a strong possibility that these organizations become a conduit for transferring royalties to foreign rights holders. The domination of foreign copyrighted works in African countries poses a considerable challenge to the viability of collecting societies because of the grave reality that they serve as conduits of capital flight to developed countries.[57] A key function of a viable collecting society is to assist the development of their members through devotion of a specific part of their royalties in this regard. This is often referred to as the cultural and social functions of collecting societies. As observed by M. Ficsor,

> The cultural and social functions of collective management organizations are particularly important in developing countries where frequently extra efforts are needed to strengthen creative capacity. In general the same may be said about net importer countries (frequently small ones) where, through an efficient fulfilment of such functions, national collective management organizations may achieve two important objectives: first, they may contribute to the preservation of national cultural identity; and, second, they may improve public acceptance of copyright where the copyright system, unfortunately, is frequently in quite a weak and very defensive 'public relations' situation.[58]

It will be useful to understand the types of collecting societies that exist in Africa. The first type consists of private societies that are created in furtherance of their members' right of association. Examples of these societies are the copyright collecting society of Mozambique known as SOMAS ; the three collecting societies in South Africa – the South African Music Organisation (SAMRO)[59] representing music performing rights, the Dramatic Artistic and Literary Rights Organisation (DALRO)[60] protecting a broad spectrum of copyright in literary dramatic and artistic works, and the South Africa Recording Rights Association (SARRAL)[61] representing rights of composers of musical works. The second category of collecting societies can be described as semi-public societies because though essentially private, they have some form of government participation. Examples include the Copyright Society of Tanzania (COSOTA)[62]; the Copyright Society of Ghana (COSGA); three Nigerian collecting societies – PMRS (Performing and Mechanical Rights Society of Nigeria), MCSN (Musical Copyrights Society of Nigeria), and REPRONIG (Reproductive Rights Organisation of Nigeria).[63] The third type of collecting society is the public collecting societies that also function as the national copyright institutions. Examples include the Copyright Society of Malawi (COSOMA);[64] the Togolese Copyright Bureau (BUTRODA);[65] the Copyright Office of Senegal (BSDA); and the Copyright Office of Benin Republic known as BUBEDRA.

In spite of the wide variety of African collecting societies, it appears that they approach the question of their social and cultural functions as a residual function.[66] It is surprising that the public sector collecting societies are not actively engaged in the social and cultural function. It is therefore gratifying that the Southern Africa Music Rights Organization operates the SAMRO Endowment for the National Arts (SENA) which encourages the development of the arts by combining funding with support and advisory services to individuals and organizations to enable them further their music education and composer careers. Ensuring collecting societies perform their social and cultural function will greatly assist in developing artistes and improve the cultural capacity of their countries.

Develop Critical Multi-Disciplinary Human and Institutional Capacity in International Trade

One major impediment to an effective trade and cultural policy is that the national and regional institutions lack the requisite skills and institutional capacities for effective policy formulation and implementation. Thus, to enhance participation, it is imperative particularly for developing countries to improve skills and the necessary institutional capacity to analyse, follow up, and manage the workings of the agreements, which are regarded as preconditions for designing adequate positions in the follow-up negotiations.[67]

Speaking of the capacity of the Federal Ministry of Trade in Nigeria it is asserted that:

> The trade Ministry which has statutory responsibility for external trade relations lacks the requisite level of skills to effectively engage in the trade policy negotiation process. There seems not to be any standard programme designed for training and skills acquisition in trade negotiations, research and analysis.[68]

If this is true of Nigeria, the situation in many other African countries may be worse.

Ensure the UNESCO Convention is not Rendered Meaningless by Bilateral and Regional Free Trade Agreements

A key part of an African trade and cultural policy should be the realization of the importance of ensuring that the gains of the UNESCO Convention are not eroded by free trade agreements (FTAs) and bilateral trade agreements. It is important to point to Article 20(1)b of UNESCO Convention which advises State Parties to bear the Convention in mind when negotiating bilateral and regional trade agreements. Evidence exists that FTAs concluded between the US & Chile,[69] the US & Singapore;[70] the US & Korea allow existing audio visual restrictions but prohibit digital protectionism. Ivan Bernier concludes that:

> ...[T]he five recent free trade agreements concluded by the United States ...with regard to the cultural sector shows that...they do have a significant impact on the cultural sector and that they are part of a strategy by the United States to ensure that digital networks remain free of cultural protectionism...The new strategy of the United States in the cultural sector rests quite clearly on the view that while measures that do not conform to national treatment, most favoured -nation- treatment and free market access can be tolerated as they presently exist in the audio visual sector because they are bound one way or the other to disappear with time, no such tolerance must be accepted for digitally delivered content which are at the heart of the new com-munication economy and should therefore remain free of cultural protectionism.[71]

African countries should therefore ensure that the potential benefits of the UNESCO Convention are not eroded by an agreement that there should be no protectionism in the digital environment. In negotiating Economic

Partnership Agreements, African countries should examine the recently concluded Economic Partnership Agreement (EPA) between the European Union and CARIFORUM[72] (Caribbean countries who are part of African Caribbean and Pacific Countries (ACP) where a cultural cooperation protocol was annexed to the EPA with the aim of contributing to an increased exchange in cultural goods and services notably by according preferential treatment to artistes. The Protocol relies on Article 14, 15 and 16 of the UNESCO Convention.

Conclusion

There is no doubt that many of the issues discussed in this chapter require a more detailed study from a national and regional perspective. What is critical, however, is for African countries to learn appropriate lessons from the UNESCO Convention. One good lesson is that when a group of States are faced with a problem in the international community, they band together to solve that problem. This attitude must be internalized by African States rather than depending solely on the goodwill of developed countries. It is pertinent that African States should articulate a trade and industrial strategy facilitated by culture through the African Union and regional economic communities. In addition, state practice in ensuring the growth of national cultural industries, along the lines of the recommendations above should be vigorously pursued so that the private sector in culture business will operate in an environment that enhances their competitiveness and survival.

Notes

1. Paris 20 October 2005. Text of the Convention is available at www.unesdoc.unesco.org/images/0014/001429/142919e.pdf (Hereafter *UNESCO Convention*.)
2. Israel and United States voted against the Convention.
3. Benin, Burkina Faso, Cameroon, Cote d' Ivoire, Djibouti, Egypt, Gabon, Guinea, Kenya, Madagascar, Mali, Mauritius, Mozambique Namibia, Niger, Nigeria, Senegal, South Africa, Togo, Tunisia and Zimbabwe.
4. See Article 29 of the *UNESCO Convention*.
5. Article 4 ibid defines 'cultural diversity' as referring «to the manifold ways in which the cultures of groups and societies find expression. These expressions are passed on within and among groups and societies. Cultural diversity is made manifest not only through the varied ways in which the cultural heritage of humanity is expressed, augmented and transmitted through the variety of cultural expressions, but also through diverse modes of artistic creation, production, dissemination, distribution and enjoyment, whatever the means and technologies used.
6. Article 4 ibid defines cultural expressions» are those expressions that result from the creativity of individuals, groups and societies, and that have cultural content.

7. Article 4(6) ibid provides that ' Cultural Policies and Measures' refers to those policies and measures relating to culture, whether at the local, national, regional or international level that are either focused on culture as such or are designed to have a direct effect on cultural expressions of individuals, groups or societies, including on the creation, production, dissemination, distribution of and access to cultural activities, goods and services.

8. See Article 1:1 of GATT 1994.

9. See Article III of GATT 1994.

10. See Article XX GATT 1994.

11. Note also Article XX(d) of GATT 1994.

12. For a more detailed consideration of this relationship, there is ample literature. See T. Voon 'UNESCO and WTO: A Clash of Cultures' *International and Comparative Law Quarterly*, 2006, Vol. 55 No. 3, p. 635; A. Dahrendorf 'Trade meets Culture: The Legal Relationship between WTO Rules and the UNESCO Convention on the Protection and Promotion of the Diversity of Cultural Expressions' *Maastrict Faculty of Law Working Paper* 2006/11; J. Pauwelyn, 'The UNESCO Convention on Cultural Diversity, and the WTO: Diversity in International Law-Making?' in *American Society of International Law Insight*, 15 November 2005; C. Brunner, 'Culture Sovereignty and Hollywood: UNESCO's Convention for the Protection and Promotion of the Diversity of Cultural Expressions and the Future of the Trade In Cultural Products' *New York University Journal of International Law & Politics*, 2007, Vol 40, No.2, p. 351 and P. van de Bossche *Free Trade and Culture: A Study of Relevant WTO Rules and Constraints on National Cultural Policy Measures* Maastrict, University of Maastrict, 2007.

13. See K. Acheson and C. Maule 'Convention on Cultural Diversity' *Journal of Cultural Economies*, 2004, Vol. 28, p. 251.

14. Canada is a good example of such a country. See for example The Cultural Industries Sectoral Advisory Group on International Trade « New Strategies for Culture and Trade; Canadian Culture in a Global World», February 1999. Available at www.international.gc.ca/ trade-agreements-accords-commerciaux/fo/canculture.aspx. 29 April 2010.

15. See N. Obuljen « From Our Creative Diversity to the Convention on Cultural Diversity: Introduction to the Debate» in N. Obuljen & Smiers J (ed) *UNESCO's Convention on the Protection and Promotion of the Diversity of Cultural Expression: Making it Work* Zagreb, Institute for International Relations, 2006 p.32 (Hereafter *UNESCO Convention: Making It Work.*)

16. Available at www.africa-union.org/root/au/Documents/Treaties/Text? Cultural_Charter_ for_Africa.pdf Hereafter *Cultural Charter.*

17. (Assembly/AU/Dec.94(VI). Text of the draft Charter is available at www.ocpa.irmo.hr/ resources/docs/AU_Cultural_Renaissance_Charter_2005-en.pdf. Hereafter *Revised Cultural Charter.*

18. Art 3-5 of the Cultural Charter.

19. Art 12-16 ibid.

20. Art- 17-19 ibid.

21. Art 20-22 ibid.

22. Article 23 ibid.

23. Article 24 ibid.
24. Article 26 ibid.
25. The Cultural Policy of The Republic of Seychelles. Available at www.ocpa.irmo.hr/resources/policy/Seychelles_Cutural_Policy-en.pdf
26. Available at www.ocpa.irmo.hr/resources/policy/Uganda_Cutural_Policy-en.pdf
27. Available at www.ocpa.irmo.hr/resources/policy/Botswana_Cutural_Policy-en.pdf
28. Available at www.ocpa.irmo.hr/resources/policy/Namibia_Cutural_Policy-en.pdf
29. Available at www.ocpa.irmo.hr/resources/policy/Mozambique_Cutural_Policy-en.pdf
30. See B.K Sagnia «Culture and Poverty Alleviation in Africa: A Review of Cultural Effectiveness of Poverty Reduction Strategy Papers in West and Central Africa» A report prepared for the Arterial Conference on Vitalizing African Cultural Assets, Goree Institute Dakar Senegal 5-7 March 2007. Available at www.incd.net.docs.Documets%205%20-%20Sagnia%20paper.pdf 29 April 2010. The author concludes that 'Five countries (Benin, Burkina Faso, Cameroon, The Gambia and the Republic of Congo) incorporate cultural issues and concerns in their poverty reduction strategies mainly as instruments to further the objectives of other development sectors, such as the promotion of cultural tourism or traditional healthcare…[f]our countries (Ghana, Mali, Nigeria and Senegal) integrate culture in their PSRPs as Strategic Pillars or major axes. This gives culture the opportunity to stand out as a major contributor in its own right to poverty reduction rather than being subsumed under other development sectors as instruments to fulfil the objectives of those sectors.'
31. Available at w.w w.sadc.int/english/documents/le g a l/protocols/culture_information_and_ sport.php
32. Details of the programme are available at www.thedti.gov.za/film/SACoGuidelines.pdf
33. The National Film & Video Foundation (NFVF) of South Africa is a statutory body mandated by parliament to spearhead the development of the South African film and video industry. It carries out its mandate with funding for different projects. Funding is for South African Companies. See the National Film & Video Foundation Act 1997.
34. Another example is found in *ICASA South African Television Content Regulations 2002* which requires that at least 20% of music broadcasted from 5am-11pm must be from South Africa. See also *Audiovisual Services: Improving Participation of Developing Countries, Geneva* United Nations Conference on Trade and Development 2002 (Doc. No. TD/B/COM.1/EM.20/2), 8.
35. See section 24F of the South Africa Income Tax Act 1962 (Act 58 of 1962) which enables taxpayers to deduct from taxable income any amount invested by the taxpayer in the production, post-production or international marketing of a South African film. However, if an investment is made on the basis of credit or loans, or is otherwise not paid for in the relevant tax year of assessment, the taxpayer will only be allowed to claim a deduction to the extent that she/he is at risk in respect of future income derived from the exploitation of the film.
36. Africa has a number of collecting societies which are discussed in this section.

37. See for example the Nigerian Copyright Act, Cap C28 Laws of the Federation of Nigeria 2004.

38. See T. Dersumont 'Considerations on the Relationship between the Convention on the Protection and Promotion of the Diversity of Cultural Expressions and the Protection of Authors' Rights' *e-Copyright Bulletin* 2006 October-December. Available at www.unesco.org/culture/en/files/32555/1165586434/dersumont_en.pdf/dersumont_en.pdf . 29 April 2010.

39. See G. Davies *Copyright and Public Interest,* London, Thomson Sweet and Maxwell, 2002.

40. See for example section 12 of the South African Copyright Act. See also paragraph 'a'of the second schedule to the Nigerian Copyright Act.

41. See section 10 of the Copyright Act 1989.

42. See paragraph 's' of the Second Schedule to the Nigerian Copyright Act.

43. See paragraph 'b' ibid.

44. An example can be found in sections 15 & 16 of the Copyright & Neighbouring Rights Act of Botswana 2000.

45. E.S Nwauche 'African Countries Access to Knowledge and the WIPO Digital Treaties' *The Journal of World Intellectual Property,* 2005, Vol. 8, p.363.

46. This is often expressed in copyright legislation by the requirement of the work being in a medium.

47. See paragraph 'q' of the Second Schedule of the Nigerian Copyright Act.

48. 828 United Nations Treaty Series 221. See R.L Okediji The International Copyright System: Limitations, Exceptions and Public Interest Considerations for Developing Countries in the Digital Environment, Geneva, International Centre for Trade and Sustainable Development, 2006.

49. International Legal Materials, 1997, Vol. 36, p.65.

50. International Legal Materials, 1997, Vol. 36, p.76.

51. A WTO Panel interpreting exemptions to exclusive rights contained in section 110(5) of the Copyright Act of the United States as amended by the Fairness in Music Licensing Act of 1998, has interpreted the three step test in such a strict manner that may render all user rights of no practical importance. In the Panel's opinion, 'We believe that an exception or limitation to an exclusive right in domestic legislation rises to the level of normal conflict with a normal exploitation of a work (i.e, the copyright or rather the whole bundle of exclusive rights conferred by the ownership of copyright), if uses, that are in principle are covered by that right but exempted under the exception and limitation, enter into economic competition with the ways in which right holders normally extract economic value from that right to the work (i.e the copyright) and thereby deprive them of significant or tangible commercial gains. In developing a benchmark for defining the normative connotation of normal exploitation, we recall the European Communities' emphasis on the potential impact of an exception rather than on the market at a given point in time, given that, in its view, it is the potential effect that determines the market conditions.' See *United States - Section 110(5)of the US Copyright Act,* WTO Dispute WT/DS/160, Report of the Panel, 15 June 2000, Paras. 6.183 and 6.184.

52. 2006 (1) SA 144 (CC).

53. [2004] 1 S.C.R. 339

54. See also part V of the Copyright Act of Malawi 1989 and section 31 of the Copyright Act of Mozambique 2001.

55. Section 28(5)of the Nigerian Copyright Act defines expressions of folklore as 'a group-oriented and tradition-based creation of groups or individuals'.

56. The Bill is available online at www.info.gov.za/view/DownloadFileAction?id=81111 29 April 2010.

57. See A. Story, 'Study on Intellectual Property Rights, the Internet, and Copyright' Study Paper 5 to the CIPR Report *Integrating Intellectual Property Rights and Development Policy* Available at www.iprcommission.org/papers/word/study_papers/ sp5_story_study.doc He argues that since one of the key functions of national RRO's is to ensure the collection and transmission of copyright fees to foreign right holders and, to facilitate such distributions, national RRO's transfer more money to foreign rights holders and is primarily a royalty collector.

58. *Collective Management of Copyright and Related Rights*, Geneva, World Intellectual Property Organisation, 2002, p.22.

59. See www.samro.org.za

60. See www.dalro.co.za

61. See www.sarral.org.za

62. See sections 46,47 & 48 of the Copyright and Neighbouring Rights Act of Tanzania 1999.

63. The Nigerian Copyright (Collecting Societies) Regulations 1993 provides that a staff of the Nigerian Copyright Commission must be on the Board of Directors of any approved collecting society.

64. 'The Copyright Society of Malawi (COSOMA) is a statutory body established in 1992 with the main aim of promoting creativity and protecting the rights of creators. It functions both as a copyright office responsible for implementing the copyright law of 1989 and as a collective management society for rights owners who have mandated it to administer the rights on their behalf. See www.cosoma.org/about.index.html. See section 42 of the Copyright Laws of Malawi 1989.

65. See Article 73 of the Law on the Protection of Copyright, Folklore and Neighbouring Rights of Togo 1991.

66. Section 42 of the Malawian Copyright Act which provides that the function of the Copyright Society of Malawi is inter alia 'to promote and protect the interests of authors, performers...». Article 3(1)b of the Charter of the Copyright Society of Tanzania empowers the society to ' contribute by all appropriate means to the promotion of national creativity ...'.

67. See I. Briggs 'Nigeria: Mainstreaming Trade Policy into National Development Strategies' Nairobi, *African Trade Policy Centre Work In Progress No. 52*, 2007, p.19. Available at www.uneca.org/atpc/work%20%20progress/52.pdf 29 April 2009.

68. Ibid.

69. Text available at www.ustr.gov/new/fta/Chile/text/index.htm

70. See www.ustr.gov/new/fta/Singapore/consolidated_texts.htm
71. See I. Bernier 'The Recent Free Trade Agreements of the United States as Illustration of their New Strategy Regarding the Audio Visual Sector' Mimeo, 2004 Available at www.mediatrademonitor.org/node/146
72. Text is availab le at www.trade.ec.europa.ec/doclib/docs/2008/Febr uar y/tradoc_137971.pdf

References

Acheson, K., and Maule, C., 2004, 'Convention on Cultural Diversity', *Journal of Cultural Economies*, Vol. 28.

Bernier, I., 2004, 'The Recent Free Trade Agreements of the United States as Illustration of their New Strateg y Regarding the Audio Visual Sector', Mimeo, Available at www.mediatrademonitor.org/node/146

Briggs, I., 2007, 'Nigeria: Mainstreaming Trade Policy into National Development Strategies', *African Trade Policy Centre Work In Progress No. 52*, Nairobi, Available at www.uneca.org/atpc/work%20%20progress/52.pdf=

Brunner, C., 2007, 'Culture Sovereignty and Hollywood: UNESCO's Convention for the Protection and Promotion of the Diversity of Cultural Expressions and the Future of the Trade in Cultural Products', *New York University Journal of International Law & Politics*, Vol. 40, No.2.

Dahrendorf, A., 2006, 'Trade meets Culture; The Legal Relationship between WTO Rules and the UNESCO Convention on the Protection and Promotion of the Diversity of Cultural Expressions', Maastrict Faculty of Law Working Paper 2006/11

Davies, G., 2002, *Copyright and Public Interest,* London: Thomson Sweet and Maxwell. Ficsor, M., 2002, *Collective Management of Copyright and Related Rights*, Geneva: World Intellectual Property Organisation.

Dersumont, T., 2006, 'Considerations on the Relationship between the Convention on the Protection and Promotion of the Diversity of Cultural Expressions and the Protection o f Authors' Rights', *e-Copyright Bulletin,* October-December. Availa ble at www.unesco.org/culture/en/files/32555/1165586434/dersumont_en.pdf/dersumont_en.pdf .

Obuljen, N., 2006, 'From Our Creative Diversity to the Convention on Cultural Diversity: Introduction to the Debate', in N. Obuljen & J. Smiers, eds, *UNESCO's Convention on the Protection and Promotion of the Diversity of Cultural Expression: Making it Work,* Zagreb: Institute for International Relations.

Okediji, R.L., 2006, 'The International Copyright System: Limitations, Exceptions and Public Interest Considerations for Developing Countries in the Digital Environment', Geneva: International Centre for Trade and Sustainable Development. van de Bossche, P., 2007, Free Trade and Culture: A Study of Relevant WTO Rules and Constraints on National Cultural Policy Measures, Maastrict: University of Maastrict. Nwauche, E.S., 2005, 'African Countries Access to Knowledge and the WIPO Digital Treaties', *The Journal of World Intellectual Property,* Vol. 8.

Pauwelyn, J., 2005, 'The UNESCO Convention on Cultural Diversity, and the WTO: Diversity in International Law-Making?', *American Society of International Law Insight*, 15 November.

Sagnia, B. K., 2007, 'Culture and Poverty Alleviation in Africa: A Review of Cultural Effectiveness of Poverty Reduction Strategy Papers in West and Central Africa', A report prepared for the Arterial Conference on Vitalizing African Cultural Assets, Goree Institute Dakar Senegal 5-7 March, Available at www.incd.net.docs.Documets%205%20-%20Sagnia%20paper.pdf

Story, A., 'Study on Intellectual Property Rights, the Internet, and Copyright', Study Paper 5 to the CIPR Report *Integrating Intellectual Property Rights and Development Policy*, Available at www.iprcommission.org/papers/word/study_papers/sp5_story_study.doc

The Cultural Industries Sectoral Advisory Group on International Trade, 1999, 'New Strategies for Culture and Trade; Canadian Culture in a Global World', February, Available at www.international.gc.ca/trade-agreements-accords-commerciaux/fo/canculture.aspx

United Nations Conference on Trade and Development, 2006, *Audiovisual Services: Improving Participation of Developing Countries, Geneva* 2002 (Doc. No. TD/B/COM.1/EM.20/2), 8. UNCTAD, Voon, T., 2006, 'UNESCO and WTO: A Clash of Cultures', *International and Comparative Law Quarterly*, Vol. 55, No. 3.

PART FOUR

Institutional Dimensions of Trade and Industrial Policy

12

Rethinking Industrial Policy in Africa: Toward an Institutional Framework

Howard Stein

Introduction

At the core of the development of Asia is a robust manufacturing sector with a significant export capacity. While there is little doubt that agriculture is important, if the experience of Asia is an indicator, it would seem that manufacturing will need to play a significant role in achieving a path of sustainable development in sub-Saharan Africa (SSA). Yet, the performance to date has been very disappointing partly due to the de-industrializing effect of structural adjustment. Instead of addressing some of the weaknesses of post-independence industrialization, international financial institutions (IFIs) took a battering ram approach; destroying many viable firms with their accumulated knowledge and capacities that could have been used as a base for further expansion. In contrast, Asia actively used industrial policy with great success. Arguably, this will need to be a core component of any new industrialization effort on the African continent. However, still remain largely due to the continued opposition to state forms of support for industry by economists at the Bank and Fund. The chapter will begin with some comparisons between SSA and Southeast Asia (SEA). The middle section looks briefly at the history of industrial efforts in SSA and the de-industrializing impact of adjustment. The final part of the paper generates an institutional theoretical approach to industrial policy focusing on institution-related contrasts between the two regions.

Comparisons between SEA and SSA

The divergence of the trajectories of growth and development between sub-Saharan Africa and Southeast Asia is striking. As indicated in Table 12.1, in 1970 the real per capita GDP was 30 per cent higher in SSA, excluding South Africa, compared to Southeast Asia. By 2006 it had not only fallen below it but had plummeted to 38 per cent of the total. Perhaps the ultimate measure of the divergence of development is the trajectory of life expectancy. In 1977 the gap between the regions was 8 years. By 2007 the gap had risen dramatically to 22 years as life expectancy stagnated and declined in sub-Saharan Africa through the 1980s and 1990s (UNCTAD 2008).

Table 12.1: Development Indicators

Year	1970	1980	1990	2000	2006
R.GDP-SEA	353	565	803	1114	1379
SSA	459	480	471	454	526
L.Exp-SEA	52	58	64	67	69
SSA	45	48	47	46	47
I.Mrt-SEA	105	76	51	34	28
SSA	136	119	111	101	94

Sources: UNCTAD 2008; UN Statistics 2008

RGDP is in per capita figures in 1990 dollars; life expectancy in years and infant mortality is per 1000 (SSA does not include South Africa).

In Table 12.2, we can see the dramatic contrast in growth rates over the decades between the two regions with SEA exceeding SSA in every time period with large decade-long gaps with the exception of the years 2000-05.

Table 12.2: Average Annual GDP Growth Rates SSA and SEA

Time Period	1970-80	1980-89	1992-00	2000-05
SSA	3.3	2.0	3.3	4.8
Southeast Asia	7.2	4.9	4.1	5.1

Source: UNCTAD 2008

On the surface, the latest period appears to have been the first significant growth upturn in Africa in more than two decades. Real GDP growth rates averaged 4.7 per cent between 2001 and 2006, the highest since the 1960s. Per capita income increased significantly although not back to 1980s level. Exports nearly tripled and debt significantly fell due to HIPC and MDRI (multilateral debt relief initiative). So, is SSA on the road to recovery? Unfortunately, this is highly unlikely. The growth is almost entirely explained by the increase in the volume and price of oil exports to a handful of countries which will not be sustained in view of plummeting oil prices. Between 2002 and 2006 fuel exports from SSA increased from 33 to 127 billion dollars or from 51 to 72 per cent of total non-South African SSA exports. Four oil producing countries alone (Equatorial Guinea, Nigeria, Sudan and Angola) which constituted 33 per cent of total SSA GDP (excluding South Africa) in 2002 were responsible for nearly 75 per cent of the GDP growth between 2002 and 2006 (UNCTAD 2008). Real growth rates of oil producers have all been above the average rate and driving the increase. Angola has averaged GDP growth of 11.8 per cent from 2001-06, Equatorial Guinea 21.5 per cent and Nigeria 5.7 per cent (7.3 per cent in 2003-06), Sudan 7.3 per cent, Chad 12.8 per cent etc, compared to an average of 4.7 per cent for all of SSA (World Bank 2008). Tables 12.3 and 12.4 illustrate the growing gap in capital formation, the rising exports relative to GDP in SEA and stagnation in SSA and the growing divergence in the structure of exports. The capital formation statistics are striking. South East Asia was able to sustain levels over 20 per cent and sometimes 30 per cent of GDP which were at times more than double the African rates which hovered in the low to middle teens. Exports relative to GDP grew in line in the two regions through the 1970s and diverged thereafter as SEA exports continued to grow rapidly after 1980 while SSA fell and then stagnated.. By 2006 SSA was merely half the level of SEA.

Table 12.3: Gross Capital Formation and Exports (% GDP)

Year	1970	1980	1990	2000	2006
G.C.F.S.E.Asia	21.4	29	36.5	24.6	23.1
SSA	15.3	16.3	13.8	15.7	18.3
ExportsS.E.Asia	24.4	42.5	49.8	85.4	84
SSA	25.6	43.7	38	38.3	38.1

Source: UNCTAD 2008

Table 12.4: Trade Comparisons between Southeast Asia and SSA 2006

Year	Southeast Asia	SSA (excl. S.A.)
Total (SITC 0 to 9)(Standard International Trade Certification)	774,899,929	177,785,711
All food items (SITC 0+1+22+4)	53,368,811	16,037,322
Agricultural raw materials (SITC 2-22-27-28)	22,622,715	6,213,979
Ores and metal (SITC 27+28+68)	21,812,632	11,037,035
Fuels (SITC 3)	119,000,326 (15%)	127,377,578 (72%)
Chemical products (SITC 5)	55,370,650	1,682,357
Iron and steel (SITC 67)	6,384,598	639,464
Non-ferrous metals (SITC 68)	9,204,275	6,059,427
Machinery and transport equipment (SITC 7)	351,991,328	2,665,873
Other manufactured goods (SITC 6+8 less 68)	132,999,678	11,439,055
Textile fibres, yarn, fabrics and clothing (SITC 26 + 65 + 84)	39,828,311	4,414,106
Primary commodities, including fuels (SITC 0+1+2+3+4+68)	216,804,485	160,665,913
Manufactured goods (SITC 5 to 8 less 68)	540,361,655 (69.7%)	15,787,285 (8.9)

Source: UNCTAD 2008

As indicated by Table 12.4, by 2006 there was also a dramatic difference in the structure of exports. More than 90 per cent of exports from SSA were raw materials (minerals and agricultural). The share of manufacturing goods in SSA exports (excluding South Africa) was merely 8.9 per cent compared to 69.7 per cent for Southeast Asia. Fuels accounted for an overwhelming portion of the primary commodities (72 per cent of total exports) compared to 15 per cent for Southeast Asia. In addition, by 2006 Southeast Asia was able to move up the technological ladder with roughly two-thirds of the massive manufacturing exports focused on machinery and transport equipment compared to a mere 16 per cent in SSA. As discussed below, under structural adjustment SSA has de-industrialized with enormous consequences to the development process. The de-industrializing trends are reflected in Table 12.5. In 1970 both SSA and SEA had similar levels of agriculture and manufacturing in their economies. SSA actually had a more dramatic growth of manufacturing in the 1970s with a similar decline in the role of agriculture by 1980. However, the divergence thereafter was absolutely striking as SSA increased its reliance on unprocessed commodities from agriculture and mining while SEA emphasized structural transformation toward a greater reliance on the manufacturing sector. The developmental consequence of manufacturing versus agriculture or mining is well known in the literature. Manufacturing is subject to increasing returns; is a conduit for the transfer of technology; has higher income elasticity compared to other activities; generates employment; is very tradable; is more heterogeneous; allows for better market segmentation; can stimulate extensive backward, forward and demand linkages; and avoids long-term declines in prices associated with unprocessed resource exports (Prebisch 1950; Singer 1950).

The relationship between higher growth, accumulation and employment generation can be gleaned from Table 12.6 which compares some African countries to Malaysia over the decade of the 1990s. The collapse of manufacturing employment in many SSA countries from very low to ridiculously low levels relative to the population size is quite striking. Why did Africa de-industrialize? A bit of historical background is needed to answer that question.

Table 12.5: Structure of Economy SSA and SEA 1970-2006 (% value added)

Year	1970	1980	1990	2000	2006
Ag-SEA	33.6	22.2	16	11.7	11.8
SSA[1]	35.8	23.9	28.9	28.1	28.1
Mi-SEA	4.3	14.1	7.8	8.5	9.2
SSA	8.8	19.9	15.4	24.0	25.6
Mf-SEA	15.4	18.2	22.8	27.2	27.7
SSA	15.6	24.1	15.1	9.4	7.7

Source: UNCTAD 2008

Table 12.6: Manufacturing, Accumulation and GNP/Capita in Select sub-Saharan African Countries and Malaysia

Country	Year	Man Empl. (,000).	Popu- lation (M)	Man. Empl. Pop.	MVA/* cap ind.	MVA/ GDP %**	Gross Cap. Form.	GNP/ Cap. $
Tanzania	1990	127.3	26.1	.5%	100	9	26	190
	1999	139.6	32.9	.4	94	7	17	270
Senegal	1991	30.2	7.51	.4	100	13	14	720
	2000	21.6	9.53	.2	113	18	20	490
Malawi	1986	37.9	7.4	.5	100	19	23	190
	1998	40.2	10.1	.4	66	13	11	160
Mozambic	1991	70.7	14.4	.5	100	10	16	170
	2000	31.7	17.7	.2	164	12	42	210
Cameroon	1991	63.2	11.8	.5	100	15	18	970
	1999	52.7	14.6	.4	88	11	18	580
Zimbabwe	1991	205.4	10.0	2.5	100	23	17	920
	2001	177.5	12.8	1.4	89	14	8	480
S. Africa	1991	1484.0	35.9	4.1	100	24	20	2890
	2000	1306.8	42.8	3.1	75	19	19	2820
Kenya	1991	188.9	24.3	.8	100	12	20	370
	2000	217.9	30.0	.7	94	13	13	350
Ethiopia	1992	82.6	54.8	.2	100	8	12	160
	2001	93.5	65.8	.1	82	7	18	100
Mauritius	1991	117.4	1.1	10.6	100	25	31	2430
	2000	114.5	1.2	9.5	151	23	24	3830
Botswana	1991	25.8	1.3	2.0	100	5	37	2730
	2000	29.9	1.7	1.8	131	4	22	3100
Malaysia	1990	830.7	17.9	4.6	100	24	32	2320
	2000	2125.0	23.0	9.3	217	31	29	3330

Source: Stein 2004

In 1981, during interviews at TISCO (Tanzania Investment Service and Consulting Company which handled most of Tanzania's appraisals) headquarters in Dar es Salaam, officials could not come up with a single example of a project appraisal recommending the turning down of an industrial project financed through ODA.

History of Manufacturing in SSA

Arguments on the importance of manufacturing were popular and understood in African countries after independence. Between 1963 and 1973, there was a significant commitment to the sector with growth rates exceeding 10 per cent per annum in 12 countries. Another 17 had rates between 5 and 10 per cent, with only one country having a negative growth rate. However, from 1973 to 1979 there were only 13 countries with growth rates above 5 per cent, further falling to only 9 countries between 1979 and 1986 (World Bank 1989). Why the rapid rise and then fall? While there were a number of variations there was a general pattern which included:

i.   An emphasis on first-stage import-substitution often in 'luxury' goods.

ii.   Heavy usage of imported technology, often capital-intensive generating little employment.

iii. High import coefficients with a need for raw materials and spare parts from abroad.

iv.   Lower quality of production compared to imported goods and with capacities that were greater than the quantity of imports replaced.

v.   Heavy reliance on external loans taken with management and ownership by states.

vi.   Many factories were built through bilateral programmes. Often excess equipment from developed countries was dumped through aid.

vii. Project appraisals including those by the Bank, relied on heroic assumptions to justify positive results.[2] In the end, factories were left with high debt burdens and no easy way to service them.

viii. When investment involved FDI, there were often demands for monopoly market access and high protective barriers prior to agreements to invest.

ix.   There was a shortage of engineering and technical capacity to adapt and develop technologies imported from abroad.

The result of this system was that countries in SSA became increasingly reliant on a handful of largely stagnant resource exports to generate the foreign exchange to support the operation of these industries. This made economies susceptible to oil shocks, political instability, downturns in agriculture and sudden declines in terms of trade (see Figure 12.1).

Figure 12.1: Terms of Trade for Africa 1970-1998, 1985=100

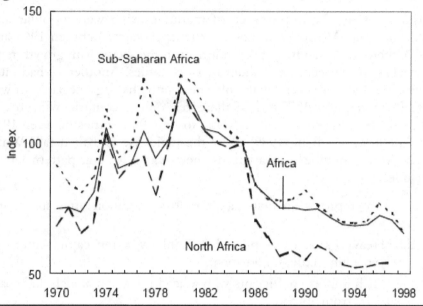

Source: UNCTAD 2001

Many factories were built through bilateral programmes. Often excess equipment from developed countries was dumped through aid. Emphasis was on large-scale operations while small and medium-scale enterprises which used more appropriate technology and were better generators of employment were largely ignored.

As shown in Figure 12.1, there was rapid decline in the terms of trade in the 1977-78 period which pushed many African countries into a balance of payments crisis in the early 80s. Between 1970 and 1980 gold and dollar reserves for SSA countries excluding South Africa and Nigeria fell by 56 per cent with average reserves at 1½ months (Lawrence 2005). This was exacerbated by other factors. In Tanzania, reserves had reached a very comfortable 5 months by the end of 1977. However, the IMF and World Bank in their annual report actually told the government that the reserves were too high for a poor country. They encouraged them to liberalize their imports leading to a flood of non-essential consumer items. By the end of 1978 reserves were down to 10 days of import and Tanzania were in a major balance of payments crisis (Payer 1983). This created a greater dependence on outside agencies for loans and their associated conditionality including structural adjustment policies.

As illustrated in Figure 12.2 and Table 12.7, the terms of trade fell by nearly 50 per cent through 1998 due to the high dependence on commodities and collapsing commodity prices; and this created a serious balance of payments problem with the current account deficit reaching 8.3 per cent of the GDP (World Bank 2005). The recovery in commodity prices and the related rise in the terms of trade have helped exports and economic growth through 2008. However, SSA is now feeling the effect of the global crisis and, once again, there is deterioration in the terms of trade.

Figure 12.2: Terms of Trade for Africa 1980-2009, 2000=100

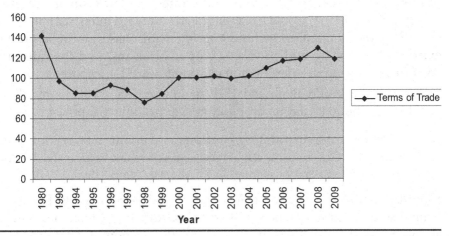

Source: Generated from Table 12.7

Table 12.7: SSA Terms of Trade 1980-2009, 2000=100

Year.	80	90	94	95	96	97	98	99	00	01	02	03	04	05	06	07	08	09
Terms of Trade	142	97	85	85	93	88	76	84	100	100	102	99	101	99	117	119	129	118

Source: IMF 2010; World Bank 2005

After 1980, the new approach, structural adjustment, which was imposed on SSA more than any other region, exacerbated the underlying weaknesses of African economies and actually stunted economic growth on the continent. Its greatest crime was its inherent inability to structurally and institutionally transform African economies and to get them on a path of growth and accumulation. The major reason for this can be found in the economic theory underlying structural adjustment, which is a misplaced emphasis on balancing financial variables in a hypothetical axiomatic world that is largely a-institutional (Stein 2008). It was driven by the assumption that if you simply get a set of prices correct, the economy will grow and develop. Many countries in Southeast Asia, with the exception of the 1997-1998 crisis, were able to chart a much more independent course installing a very different set of strategies and with them developmentally enhanced institutional structures. While there were structural weaknesses in manufacturing, a path-determinant approach (which allows for significant discretionary intervention where the strategy is fairly open but also referenced to the past) would have suggested a state-led industrial approach (as in Malaysia and Singapore lines after their ISI phases) to build on the existing set of state and private sector institutions, and institutional constructs to begin to orient manufacturing toward the export sector.

Instead, the World Bank and IMF hammered SSA with its mindless neoliberal orthodoxy and its prohibition against industrial policy since:

> In promoting exports, governments should not try to pick 'winners'...Governments can best help entrepreneurs discover and develop competitive exports by getting out of the way (World Bank 1994).

From the Bank's perspective, adjustment would help industry. The logic behind adjustment in the industrial arena was that the reduction of tariffs and removal of restrictions on imports, the devaluation of currencies and generation of positive real interest rates would reward industries that are export-oriented and use fewer imports and more local raw materials. The country would then move in line with its comparative advantage while punishing the inefficient industries. The result would be industrial prosperity which would improve balance of payments through the reduction of imports and rise of exports. Policies such as trade, interest, and exchange rate liberalization, thoughtless privatization and large government spending cuts were bound to result in enterprise bankruptcies and markets that are depressed (Stein 1992). Arguably, if state policies had supported rehabilitated problematic enterprises, and industrial policy capacities been sustained and improved, SSAs manufacturing sectors would likely have been able to use twenty years of accumulated learning and experience along path-determinant lines. Industrial policy aimed at institution building was central to the task.

Irrespective of whether a state organizes formal planning systems, the state is the only agent capable of altering the components of the institutional matrix (see below) to set in motion the cumulative process of development. State initiatives in industry have been central to institutional change, structural transformation and development in East and Southeast Asia (Welsh 2002). This is largely indisputable except to the narrowest of neo-liberal ideologues.

Industrial Policy and Institutional Transformation

At the centre of industry is a matrix of institutional constructs that delineate how people interact to produce goods for domestic and international markets. There are five major institutional constructs including capacities, norms, incentives, regulations and organizations which help generate the socially prescribed correlative behaviour or institutions at the centre of a viable manufacturing sector. The diagram below illustrates the interactive nature of the different components through a process of what Gunnar Myrdal (1968) referred to as circular causation (Stein 2008). For development purposes, policy changes should focus on altering institutional constructs to generate new forms of correlative behaviour within industry aimed at augmenting investment, employment, innovation and productivity improvements toward improving the standard of living of the population of a country.

The Institutional Matrix: Circular Causation and Development

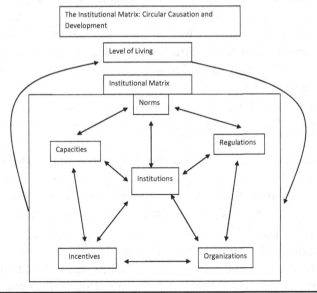

Source: Stein 2008

Norms are habits of thought arising from social sanction and esteem and are generally built up from an established pattern of life and associated ways of thinking. In manufacturing, norms focus on common standards that generate trust that allows business networks to develop effective trading and production networks. Incentives are the rewards and punishments that arise from different behavioural forms. Material conditions are only one of an array of social factors influencing behaviour. Unlike marginally calculating homo-economicus of neo-classical economics, rewards and penalties have more of an effect in reshaping habits of thought including people's ideals and hopes. While policies that improve the profitability of companies to engage in developmentally enhancing industrial activities are important, an institutional approach recognizes a variety of incentives and that the response to incentives is formed slowly and is highly contextualized. What is central is the contingent nature of incentives which will be withdrawn if companies do not perform in line with expectations. Regulations refer to the legal boundaries that constitute the rules of operations. In an industrial context, the focus is to encourage companies to invest in a manner that is developmentally enhancing in terms of employment generation, technological change and increasing value added. Capacities refer to level or abilities of individuals, groups and organizations to operate effectively under rules to reach particular industrial goals. In the industrial context, capacities encompass supply-side dimensions like entrepreneurship, skills and technological capabilities.

Organizations are entities that concatenate the operation of groups of people with narrowly defined common rules and purpose. In an industrial policy context, organizations include new state entities and commercial enterprises involved in manufacturing as well as business and professional groups that both create pressure for change and act as a conduit for information to its constituents.

What is required are industrial policies that put in place a trajectory of institutional change or a continuum of new norms, capacities, incentives, organizations and regulations. The goal is to foster private sector or joint private-state entrepreneurship and accumulation with the aim of enhancing developmental competitiveness – an institutional continuum which generates a dynamic process of accumulation aimed at increasing the market share, diversity, depth and linkages of an economy.

Institutional continuum involves not only private sector change but the alternation of states to better support the process of industrial accumulation. The state is the only agent capable of shifting the components of the institutional matrix to set in motion the cumulative process of development. Many African states are currently poorly equipped to undertake this responsibility particularly in the wake of two and half decades of neo-liberal reforms; donor conditionality has been aimed at emasculating the state's many social and economic functions while distending it in other ways to service donor generated financial targets.

So how does a state begin to build up capacities to successfully implement an industrial policy? Capacities refer to levels of abilities of individuals, groups and organizations to operate effectively under rules to reach particular industrial goals. In the industrial context, capacities encompass supply-side dimensions like entrepreneurship, skills and technological capabilities. This point cannot be over-emphasized. Proper skills are needed for people to be able to interpret and act in a manner which can deal with the multiple challenges of developing and transforming manufacturing capabilities.

States should not be seen as an undifferentiated entity, but as group of connected organizations. Organizations within states can be designed to focus on particular functions. Take the area of firm technological capacities. Gaps in the knowledge and ability of firms in developing countries are especially evident at the level of investment and production. Production capabilities deal with an array of processes, products and industrial engineering skills that are in short supply in many African nations. At the investment level there is a lack of the skills and information to identify viable projects, to locate and buy relevant technology, to design new plants and to manage the commissioning and start of projects. One could think of organizing and concentrating scarce engineering resources into a state agency that that can assess the weaknesses of existing technological capacities of particular industries and come up with strategies to transform these sectors. The sharing of information and the creation of links between the state and private sector should be a central component of the organization of states. A state-private sector framework can be used to identify potential areas of expansion and constraints and strategies needed to support the generation of new industry. In Africa, collaboration between the state and the private sector is quite unusual due partly to the orthodox view that any state intervention impedes the private sector. Industrial policy councils can begin to change this tradition through a transparent process of dialogue and participation. Evans (1995) argues this type of interaction is a key to embedding states in civil society. Any dialogue should focus on choosing strategic industrial needs, and developing programmes to meet those needs.

Among other things, the industrial policy council should identify a minimum of three priority industries capable of enhancing the developmental competitiveness of the country. So how does this framework help us understand the differences in institutions which support industry and trade in SEA versus SSA? This can be explained by a contrasting example of export processing zones in Malaysia and Kenya.

Industrial Policy and Export Processing Zones

Worldwide, there has been a proliferation of export processing zones in recent years. Based on the latest ILO survey in 2006, there were 3,500 zones in 130 countries employing 66 million people. The SSA participation in EPZs has been extremely slow. In 2006 they employed only 2.6 per cent of the global total or just over 1 per cent if you exclude South Africa. In contrast, Southeast Asia which has been much more successful by almost any criteria employed more than 27 per cent of the total (ILO 2007). Zones have the potential to attract significant foreign investment, generate employment, foreign exchange, linkages (demand, forward and backward), capital accumulation, training and technological externalities and significant local spin-offs and co-ownership opportunities. However, the design and operation of zones can lead to dramatically different results where the high expenditures to build and operate the zones are not justified by their economic impact.

The contrast between Malaysia and Kenya is quite dramatic and helps illustrate how different institutional conditions led to contrasting results. In 2006 Kenya exports from their zones were 2 per cent of the level of Malaysia and investment 4.6 per cent. The ratio of the number of firms attracted to the zones in Kenya was only 2.2 per cent of the total for Malaysia (ILO 2007). Malaysia has been able to use the export processing zones to build world class capacity in electronic manufacturing and to attract many of the most advanced firms in the industry (Furby 2005). In 2006, Malaysia employed about 500,000 workers in their zones. Kenya rode the multi-fibre agreement and AGOA to focus on textiles in their zones. Between 2000 and 2004 the number of jobs in the garment sector of the EPZs went from 5,600 to 34,614. The zones were overwhelmingly in garment production and constituted roughly 92 per cent of the total employment in 2004. However, since then the sector has declined by more than 9,000 jobs as Chinese imports have flooded the US market and undercut AGOA-related production in Africa. Between 2004 and 2007, exports to the US from Kenya dropped by nearly 25 per cent before recovering slightly in 2008. By the first quarter of 2009, the situation had deteriorated further with the loss of another 2,300 jobs compared to the first quarter of 2008 (EPZ 2009; a,b).

The key to the success in Malaysia has been through the integration of its EPZ approach into its industrial policy strategy and for government officials to have the professionalism and discipline to ensure that policies are actually implemented. Training of government officials for this purpose should be part of any capacity building strategy.

Over time, Malaysia was able to attract foreign capital and to encourage investors to undertake activities with greater developmental consequences. A central component was to institutionalize linkages with the domestic economy by generating new norms, incentives, capacities, organizations and regulations. Over time, as its policy priorities shifted, so did its EPZ strategies. EPZs were launched in 1970 in line with its attempt to address poverty and inequity. However, the government realized they lacked the technology, manpower and capital to generate jobs through industrialization, and thus created lucrative incentive schemes to attract FDI, focusing on the EPZs. After some attempts to launch heavy industry, the government moved to a new industrial master plan in 1985 focusing on EPZs aimed at technological deepening, exports and encouraging domestic sourcing of inputs by shifting regulations (relaxing foreign equity restrictions) and generating new incentives such as new tax relief measures and subsidized investments loans. The policies were extremely successful leading to a huge inflow of FDI and a large increase of exports by the early 1990s. The government again altered its incentives to attract higher value-added and technology-intense operations through the Action Plan for Industrial Technology Development and Second Industrial Plan. New arrangement like the Malaysian Industry-Government High Technology (MIGHT) in 1993 and the Multimedia Super Corridor (MSC) in 1997 were used to encourage advances in technology. With the shift to technological intensity, the government heavily invested in new capacity in science and engineering. Enrolment increased tenfold between 1995 and 2005 with a proportional shift to science and technology from 40 to 60 per cent of first degree enrolment (Furby 2005).

In the case of Kenya, EPZs were established in 1990. By 2008 there were 38 zones; all but two operated privately. The operational Act (Section 24 a and b) conceptualizes the EPZ largely as an enclave in which all goods arriving from Kenya are 'deemed to have been exported from Kenya' and paid for in convertible currency while all exports from the EPZ into Kenya are 'deemed to be imported'. This extrinsic treatment of the zone creates problems when trying to come up with incentives for utilizing more local products. Along the lines of the World Bank vision of zones, they are simply seen as a second-best solution for free trade beyond the encumbrances of government regulation. Under section 28c of the Act, all currency transactions are exempt from the Exchange Control Act. Under Section 29 of the Act, EPZ enterprises are exempt from all duties payable under the Customs and Excise Act and Value Added Act. Enterprises also receive a variety of other benefits including:

1)   10-year corporate tax holiday after a rate of 25 per cent vs. a general rate of 30 per cent.

2)   There is also a 10-year withholding tax holiday on payment of profits and income to non-residents. Consultants can be brought in tax free. These are good for countries with no tax treaty with Kenya (e.g., avoiding double taxation).

3)   There are stamp duty exemptions (e.g., legal transactions, property purchases (4 per cent rate normally) and banking transactions.

4)   100 per cent investment reduction on tax liabilities which can be spread over a 20-year period (obviously this is for period after 10 years) (Kenya 1990).

What is remarkable is there has been no change in any of these provisions in 20 years; no attempt to design or redesign incentives to change company behaviour to improve developmental outcomes; no efforts to proactively deal with serious gaps in manufacturing and no coordination with industrial policies efforts undertaken in the economy. Athi River Export Processing Zone is the largest publicly-run EPZ in Kenya and is located about 30 km from Nairobi. It is on a 339-acre site developed by the Kenya government for US$30 million with the financial support of the World Bank.

In 2008, they had in place a 40 per cent export tax on hides to encourage local leather processing. Since the EPZ was considered external to the Kenyan economy, hides used by companies in the zone were subject to the same tax. Rather than encouraging the use of local inputs, all the manufacturers used imports from elsewhere to avoid the high tax. Treating the EPZ as an extrinsic zone with no connection to industrial policy efforts in Kenya was creating this perverse result. They have many companies manufacturing garments but not a single weaver in the country or the zone (last one collapsed ten years before). There is a cotton spinning company that uses domestic cotton from ginneries but does not colour or weave. Meanwhile the garment producers only use imported cloth which is absurd given the amount of cotton produced by the country. There has been no attempt to attract or support the cotton weaving industry. The contrast between the two countries is striking. In Malaysia, EPZs were never seen as a second-best solution to free trade but as part of the overall strategic approach to transform the institutions and the structure of the economy for developmental purposes.

Financing Industry

State finance is an essential part of any industrial strategy. At the heart of an industrial policy are state capacities to direct financial flows toward the productive private sector. As Stiglitz (1989, 1994) has argued, within the poorly formed financial markets of developing countries there will be a profound difference between the social value of lending and the private benefits. Banks in developing countries frequently gravitate to finance projects with short turnover, lower working capital, and lower risk (such as financing imports) while avoiding more developmentally-enhancing projects such as manufacturing which has higher working capital requirements, and much greater risk. This has become all the more pressing in view of the growing dominance of foreign banks in developing countries that frequently have even less interest in lending to local private sectors (Stein 2010). States must create incentives including risk sharing to encourage private bankers to support loans which have greater social and economic benefit. State organizations, such as development banks, that have been discouraged and even closed down by the World Bank and IMF, need to be formed or strengthened. Without the socialization of private risk, it is difficult to see how private industrial investment and accumulation can occur. There are many ways of ensuring that the criteria for subsidization or access to funds are being realized and are consistent with industrial policy objectives (Korean-style policy loans, Japanese main bank approach, business-government councils, planning agencies, state ownership of banks, developmental banks, etc). Each of these options implies the creation of particular types of state capacities (Stein et al 2002).

Where do African countries secure the funds to finance industrial policy initiatives? Do aid agencies need to alter their opposition to industrial policy before anything can be organized? Must they provide the funds to support these efforts? There are two components to this question. One relates to political economy and the other to the resource issue. Do governments have the policy space to start to develop new initiatives in case they have access to finance? Second, are resources outside aid channels available to be tapped? Arguably, the World Bank/IMF/bilateral aid cartel of the past twenty-five years is beginning to erode with the arrival of

China and other Asian countries in Africa. Even if they do not directly access Chinese loans or capital, the potential availability of alternative financial sources should allow countries to demand more flexibility from the hard-line neo-liberal conditionality of the past. This creates the possibility of opening up new policy spaces for industrial policy efforts. Second, a number of African countries, particularly oil rich states have accumulated significant reserves by historical standards. The Nigerian foreign exchange reserves hit US$62 billion in April 2008 (compared to about US$4.5 billion in the 94 to 99 period). With a population of 140 million, 70 per cent of them below the poverty line, drawing on some of these reserves to expand manufacturing to generate employment seem vitally important. Yet the manufacturing sector continues to decline. In 2006, manufacturing production volume was 20 per cent below the 1992 level. Over the longer period, manufacturing's contribution to GDP went from 10 per cent of total in 1981 to a tiny 6 per cent in 2003(World Bank 2007; CBN 2008).

Conclusion

This chapter has contrasted the development trajectories of SEA and SSA with a focus on the role of manufacturing. While there were weaknesses with the industry put in place after independence, instead of building on the accumulated knowledge and capacities, structural adjustment took a battering ram approach to industry leaving the countries increasingly reliant on resource exports. As a result, African economies have been subject to the vicissitudes of commodity prices with implications to the terms of trade and the standard of living. The chapter proposes an institutional theoretical framework for understanding the nature of industrial policy and applies it to contrast the experience of the two regions with some examples taken from Kenya and Malaysia. Development is a dynamic process that requires the institutional and structural transformation of economies. Based on the experience of Asia, states need to show flexibility and adaptability when designing trade and industrial policies, while carefully building the institutions that will support industrialization. At every stage, states must carefully engage and closely work with the private sector to understand their transformative needs and to design the kinds of incentive that will encourage expansion into development-enhancing economic activities. The chapter has also tried to point to some analytical tools in an institutional vein that can perhaps begin to put in place the building blocks to reverse the malaise which has been witnessed for far too long in Africa.

Note

1. In 1981, during interviews at TISCO (Tanzania Investment Service and Consulting Company-which handled most of Tanzania's appraisals) headquarters in Dar es Salaam officials could not come up with a single example of a project appraisal recommending the turning down of an industrial project financed through ODA.

References

Central Bank of Nigeria, 2008, *Statistical Bulletin, 2006*, Volume 17.

Evans, P., 1995, *Embedded Autonomy: States and Industrial Transformation*, Princeton: Princeton University Press.

Export Processing Zones Authority of Kenya, 2009a, 'Annual Report, 2008', Nairobi.

Export Processing Zones Authority of Kenya, 2009b, 'Performance of EPZ Enterprise, 1st Quarter', Nairiobi.

Furby, M., 2005, 'Evaluation the Malaysia Export Processing Zones', Thesis, School of Management, Lund University.

International Monetary Fund (IMF), 2010, 'Regional Economic Outlook Sub-Saharan Africa: Back to High Growth?', *World Economic and Financial Outlooks*, April, Washington: IMF.

International Labour Organization (ILO), 2007, 'ILO Database on Export Processing Zones' (Revised), April http://www.ilo.org/public/english/dialogue/sector/themes/epz/epz-db.pdf

Kenya, Government of, 1990, 'Chapter 517, The Export Processing Zones Act, Arrangement of Sections', Nairobi: Government of Kenya.

Lawrence, Peter, 2005, 'Explaining Sub-Saharan Africa's Manufacturing Performance', *Development and Change*, Vol. 36, No. 6.

Myrdal, Jan, 1968, *Asian Drama, An Inquiry into the Poverty of Nations, Volume III*, New York: 20th Century Fund.

Payer, Cheryl, 1983, 'Tanzania and the World Bank', *Third World Quarterly*, Vol. 5, No. 4.

Prebisch, Raul, 1950, 'The Economic Development of Latin America and its Principle Problem', UN ECLA.

Singer, Hans, 1950, 'The Distribution of Gains between Investing and Borrowing Countries', *American Economic Review*, No. 40.

Stein, Howard, 1992, 'Deindustrialization, Adjustment, the World Bank and the IMF in Africa', *World Development*, Vol. 20 No.1.

Stein, Howard, 2003, 'Rethinking African Development', in Ha-Joon Chang, ed., *Rethinking Development Economics*, London: Anthem Press.

Stein, Howard, 2004, 'Fighting Poverty in Africa: Poverty Reduction Strategies, Employment and Accumulation', Occasional Paper, Centre for African Studies, University of Copenhagen.

Stein, Howard, 2008, *Beyond the World Bank Agenda: An Institutional Approach to Development*, Chicago: University of Chicago Press.

Stein, Howard, 2010, 'Financial Liberalization, Institutional Transformation and Credit Allocation in Developing Countries: The World Bank and the Internationalization of Banking', *Cambridge Journal of Economics*, Vol. 34, No. 2, March.

Stein, Howard and Ajakaiye, Olu, 2009, 'Industry-Led Development in Africa: Toward a Policy Framework', in Diery Seck and Sylvain Boko, *Sector-Led Growth in Africa and Implications to Development*, Trenton, NJ: Africa World Press, forthcoming.

Stein, Howard, Ajakaiye, Olu and Lewis, Peter, eds, 2002, *Deregulation and the Banking Crisis in Nigeria: A Comparative Study*, Basingstoke: Palgrave.

Stiglitz, J., 1989, 'Financial Markets and Development', *Oxford Review of Economic Policy*, 5, 4.

Stiglitz, J., 1994, 'The Role of the State in Financial Markets', Proceedings of the World Bank Annual Conference on Development Economics, 1993, Washington,DC.:World Bank.

UNCTAD, 2001, *Economic Development in Africa: Performance, Prospects, and Policy Issues*, Geneva.

UNCTAD, http://www.unctad.org/en/docs/pogdsafricad1.en.pdf

UNCTAD, 2008, *On-Line Handbook of Statistics* http://stats.unctad.org/handbook/

United Nations Statistical Division, 2008, *National Accounts On-Line*, http://unstats.un.org/unsd/snaama/selectionbasicFast.asp

Welsh, Bridget, 2002, 'Globalization, Weak States and the Death Toll in East Asia', in K. Worcester et al, eds, *Violence and Politics: Globalization's Paradox*, London: Routledge.

World Bank, 1989, *From Crisis to Sustainable Growth: A Long Term PerspectiveStudy*, Washington, D.C.: World Bank.

World Bank, 1994, *Adjustment in Africa: Reforms, Results and the Road Ahead*, Washington, DC: World Bank.

World Bank, 2005, *African Development Indicators*, Washington: World Bank.

World Bank, 2007, *African Development Indicators*, Washington: World Bank.

World Bank, 2008, *World Development Indicators 2008*, on-line.

13

Institutional Foundation of Trade and Industrial Policies in Africa

Adewole Musiliu Adeolu

Introduction

The problem of Africa's underdevelopment has attracted the attention of scholars worldwide in the last few decades. The vast literature on the development crisis has identified a number of constraints confronting Africa. They range from geography, demography, wrong policy choices, bad governance, ethnic diversity, Dutch disease and inappropriate institutional structure. This chapter attempts to establish the fact that much of Africa's development problems have strong institutional roots. Other identified factors, including the issue of pareto-inferior trade and industrial policies, might be mere reflection of the faulty institutional foundation of most African states. This is a follow-up on the recent attempts by Acemoglu et al (2003) and Witold (2004) at studying macroeconomic problems of growth, revenue and expenditure volatility, high levels of unemployment and inflation, and exchange rate instability, which has plagued many LDCs in the recent past as being basically due to existing institutional matrix in these countries. A recent paper by Olayiwola and Busari (2008) found volatility in real GDP growth rate, fiscal deficit, inflation rate, real exchange rate and terms of trade have negative impact on growth in Africa. They also found out in another econometric model that institutional parameters such as political stability, government effectiveness and regulatory quality equally have significant and positive impact on economic growth. Since their study did not use a single econometric framework, they could not establish the medium via which volatility translates to lower growth. Acemoglu et al and Witold took account of this. Thus, they were able to establish the fact that the measures of volatility become insignificant when institutional measures are duly accounted for.

Esfahani and Ramirez (2003), like many other researchers (Aschauer 1989a, b; Easterly and Rebello 1993; Canning et al 1994; Sanchez-Robles 1998) found significant impact of infrastructure on growth. But beyond that they equally found that government credibility (a measure of the tendency of government to repudiate legally binding contracts) and private ownership of infrastructure have significant impact on infrastructural investment. This implies that institution will matter also a great deal in determining the quantum of infrastructure provided in any given society. It is therefore, not a mere coincidence that societies with high-quality institutions also have significantly higher investment in infrastructure.

This background information is important because the search for optimal trade and industrial policies for Africa, or indeed any developing country, will not yield any significant results if we do not understand the institutional structure that drives the policy choices in the first instance. The issue for Africa should be more than a switch from import-substitution strategies to out-ward oriented strategies. There is the need to understand the institutional undercurrent of the continent policy regime. What should strike a chord is that the establishment of civil rule in Africa for nearly two decades has not yielded the expected growth dividends because the institutional structure that undermines development efforts was barely unaltered by the wave of democratization which swept through Africa. It is for the same reason that decades of economic reforms in Africa have produced few success stories, and in many instances, have produced disappointing results. But we must bear in mind that numerous stylized facts are inconsistent with the claims that policy effects have had significant impact on growth (Easterly 2004). In spite of this, Sach (2005) believes there is a set of big bang policies that can fast-track economic development in poor countries and eliminate poverty.

This chapter provides a model of inefficient institution which seeks to explain important features of underdevelopment, including growth-inhibiting trade and industrial policies, which have limited opportunities for economic development of Africa. With respect to trade and industrial policies, the model explains the low level of *industrialization* in spite of the post-independent industrialization drive, lack of visible *success in skill-intensive export markets*, the rapidly *rising informal sector of Africa*,[1] macroeconomic volatility in the terms of trade, inability to diversify the export base, and general underdevelopment of productive entrepreneurship.

State apparatus and state policies are used to redistribute national resources to members of the ruling elites. It explains the state-engineered sub-optimal investment in human capital, R & D, and physical capital. Both costly redistributive strategies and severe under-investment in public infrastructure, for example human capital, further worsen income inequality.

This model therefore argues that there is need for restraint, just like Rodriguez and Rodrik (2001) did, in the near-universal conclusion that openness is one sure way to accelerate development. But beyond rejecting the several theoretical and empirical studies that have elevated the geography and demography into theories of economic determinism, it also modifies in important ways existing theories of inefficient institution as summarized in Acemoglu, Johnson and Robinson (2005, henceforth to be called AJR). It incorporates psychology into the political economy of inefficient institution, making it less reliant on the more popular rational choice theory of social science. By including the ruling elite's penchant for control, it draws the conclusion that industrial and trade policies that achieve structural transformation of the economy and generate widespread prosperity will be resisted if political control of the ruling elites will be undermined. We characterize loss of political control as the transformation of ruling elites from *de facto* political leadership to *de jure* leadership. The equivalent in private market is when increased entry in a particular industry reduces the power of the pioneer monopoly firm to influence price and other important market variables. Increased competition does not necessarily imply profits decline, more so because other factors are not constant. Attached to *de facto* leadership is what we call *power salience,*[2] which may be strong enough to impede institutional transformation and account for the patterns of trade and industrial policies which has characterized Africa. Power salience declines as the share of the total wealth in possession of the ruling elites reduces. Restraining massive industrialization is, therefore, at the core of the ruling class strategies in sustaining power salience.

While the ruling elites would want to maximize their total wealth, what is more important to them is the maximization of their relative share of the total pie. State policies, including trade and industrial policies, have been used to maximize the ruling class fraction of national wealth. This is subject to the fact that other fragmented groups would not be able to overcome the costs of collective action. The sub-optimal underdevelopment equilibrium would be at the point where many other groups outside the ruling class would be thinking of organizing a revolt against the ruling class.

Though the ruling elites in our model cannot credibly commit to policies that facilitate investment and industrialization, the political Coase theorem does not have much relevance in our model. In other words, the reason why the ruling elites resist institutional change has nothing to do with the absence of credible commitments that can guarantee their compensation from the social surplus generated by the transition itself. This is because the transition process undermines power salience. Our model neither anticipates loss of wealth nor political power for the ruling class. In fact absolute wealth can rise, but as long as their relative share of wealth declines, political power would now be exercised on behalf of the people whose relative share of national wealth has risen. Prospect theory is incorporated by treating the transition from inefficient to efficient institution as a combination of two separate events. One manifests concave gains as the ruling elites maximize their wealth. Second, the process that leads to wealth maximization reduces their share of wealth and undermines their control. This produces convex losses in control.

The ruling elite's losses are in terms of the fall in relative share of total wealth as that of other larger non-ruling groups rises. The idea that people's well-being is less dependent on their wealth level but more on their wealth relative to others in their neighbourhood is not new. Kahneman (2006) reports that surveys conducted over decades have shown that people assessment of their well-being has hardly changed in spite of significant rise in real income per capita. Duesenberry (1949), Easterlin (2003) and Frank (1999) argue that relative income has greater salience in determining well-being than absolute income.

The rest of the paper is organized as follows. The second section reviews literature on institution-trade-industrialization nexus. Section three provides a simple model of inefficient institution which optimizes neither the absolute wealth of the ruling elite nor that of the society. The model equally shows the equilibrium public good provision when the intention is either to maximize absolute wealth or relative wealth. Section four analyses the ruling elite policy strategies when the intention is to optimize relative wealth. These include using growth-inhibiting redistributive policies that undermine industrialization and limit gain from trade and under-supplying vital public goods required for optimal social welfare. In section five, we summarize our work and draw relevant conclusions.

Literature Review

In this section, we will examine how institutions explain industrialization and trade. The institutional structure provides the underlying incentives for industrial and trade development, and consequently explains economic performance. Institutions do in fact have great implications for long-run economic development. According to North (1991), the expansion of trade beyond the village level brought about fundamental changes in the nature of trading. Personal and repeated trading interactions within the village was replaced by impersonal and non-repeated trading between people dispersed across the region of the world. As distance grew longer, there arose the twin problems of agency losses as well as contract negotiation and enforcement. To overcome agency losses, merchants that did not keep agreements were ostracised. This allowed long-distance trade to flourish.

The argument here suggests that the right kind of institution will always arise as the situation demands. Though there could be initial problems of getting the right set of institutions, continuous interaction will eventually help to correct the initial errors made. The implication here is that every society will eventually be able to entrench the most efficient institution that maximizes social welfare. Therefore, we can conveniently ignore the role of institutions in explaining inter-country variation in output levels. In social, economic and political bargaining among individuals or within a group, we can expect efficient outcome as long as property rights are well established and there are zero transaction costs (Coase 1960 and Stigler 1966). If the growth rate differs across countries, we should be looking at factor accumulation, level of savings, and technology as possible reasons for this observed phenomenon.

The reality we confront today is that societies choose institutions that do not maximize the welfare of their people. Even countries with relatively strong institutions today were once bedevilled by the problem of weak institutions. One question scholars who have studied institutions have asked is: why do some societies choose efficient institutions while others do not; or why does a society first grapple with an inefficient institutional structure before transiting to an efficient one?

Apart from the views of those who believe that inefficient institutions are temporary deviations caused by lack of information (North 1994) and could be corrected by informational feedback as people continuously interact, others have argued that inefficient institutions may become a permanent and pervasive feature of any society. Several decades of under-development in about half of the world's population, and more specifically for Africa, implies that we can jettison the argument that inefficient institutions are temporary deviations which can be corrected after some time.

The argument posited by Engerman and Sokoloff (2000 and 2002) shows that inefficient institutions are not temporary situations that are capable of self-correction. While conditions at the start of colonization by the West may have informed the choice of production techniques and initial institutions, the initial institutions persisted when there was obvious need for change. Thus, the initial institutional matrix created a dependence path of some sort, unyielding to change needed to optimise social welfare. In the language of Przeworski (2005),

> Institutions were reproducing the conditions which originally gave rise to them and, in turn, were reproducing themselves under these conditions. Not only were certain fundamental characteristics of the New World economies and factor endowments difficult to change, but government policies and other institutions tended to reproduce the conditions that give rise to them (p.3).

Under this institutional inertia, it was difficult to transform from the basically agrarian economy exporting sugar (with considerable initial income inequality) to an industrial nation exporting essentially high value-added manufactures. Though the ruling elites, using the existing institutions, blocked industrialization which has the added advantage of making use of new technologies and spreading mass prosperity, the papers of Acemoglu et al (2002) and Engerman and Sokoloff (2000, 2002) have not given convincing explanation as to why this was the case. Stranger still is the fact that producers of sugar crops did not move into other more profitable activities, particularly industries. Though there was an acknowledgment of the fact that the transition to industrialization would facilitate the access of the poor to productive assets via the establishment of political, educational and legal institutions, it is hard to see the link between institutional change and loss of political power in their papers. In any case, why would a government that has brought mass prosperity to its people lose political power when political business cycle theorizes the very opposite?[3]

More recently, some economists have proposed a modern variant of the social conflict view of inefficient institution (Acemoglu 2003; Acemoglu, Johnson and Robinson 2005). Not only did their models recognize the endogenous nature of institutions; it equally placed class conflict at the heart of the debate as far as the origin and persistence of inefficient institutions is concerned. Institutions from the social conflict perspective are a deliberate creation of politically powerful groups and may not necessarily coincide with institutions that maximize social welfare. According to Acemoglu (2003) and AJR (2005:36):

> Institutions are not always chosen by the whole society (and not for benefit of the whole society), but by the groups that control political power at the time (perhaps as a result of conflict with other groups). These groups will choose the economic institutions that maximize their own rents, and the economic institutions that result may not coincide with those that maximize total surplus, wealth or income.

We could traditionally separate the issues of efficiency and equity in many spheres of human interaction, but at the level of the state, commitment problems make the two almost inseparable. In the absence of any credible commitment as to how political power will be employed in the future, efficiency and equity issues cannot be separated. Thus, factors that maximize the social pie cannot be divorced from those that impinge on the distribution of the pie among competing groups. Individuals who willingly enter into a contract often do so because they believe a state exists that can act as an impartial arbiter in resolving breaches if they occur. In the case of a group of persons and the state, no impartial arbiter exists that can force the state to honour its contract. This is the origin of commitment problems in politics. Absence of credible commitments must therefore limit welfare-promoting trade and industrialization activities. Because political rents are the exclusive source of wealth in these societies, the best of talented and educated men are drawn into the rent-seeking activities with adverse consequences for growth.

Having sketched the idea of social conflict view of inefficient institution, it is important we note the theory emphasizes that political power is deployed to create and sustain economic rents. There is the need to protect political power because it is the source of incomes, rents and privileges for those who wield political power. Any institutional change that will accelerate economic growth will equally raise rival political groups that will contest political power in the future. Thus, economic growth which will be beneficial to all will however jeopardize the future economic rents of ruling elites if any positive institutional change were to take place (Acemoglu and Robinson 2000). The possibility of the loss of political power and economic rents is, therefore, a reason for blocking institutional change.

The mere fact that the industrial revolution which took place in Britain spread at differential rate across Europe is an ample testimony to this particular theory of inefficient institutions. For instance, in Russia, only one railway line was constructed between 1825 and 1855 for limited travel between Moscow and St. Petersburg. The fear of social and political changes which would result into a loss of future economic rents and privileges was the main reason why Nikolai 1 and the ruling elites in Russia blocked institutional change that would lead to accelerated economic growth (Mosse 1992 and Gregory 1991).

The rise of Western Europe between 1500 and 1850 was facilitated by access to the Atlantic, particularly for countries involved in colonialism and transoceanic trade. However, varying economic performance by these Atlantic trading nations is explained by whether the initial political system was absolutist (where power salience was high) or not (Acemoglu, Johnson and Robinson 2003b). For nations with initial non-absolutist political institution (low power salience), their economic performance exceeded those with an absolutist system. These initial political institutions in non-absolutist countries allowed further checks to be secured by trading merchants against monarchies for the protection of property rights. Thus, the initial political institutions influenced subsequent political institutions, and the long-run development. Where the initial system was more absolutist, Atlantic trade was controlled by the crown and loyal groups. Thus, a strong constituency to push for growth-promoting institutions was not formed. The strength of internal political institutions has significant implications for industrialization and trade performance. The evolution of institutions making collective decisions was central to the emergence of the industrial revolution and the foreign trade successes of England.

Yet the social conflict theory of institutional inefficiency suffers from obvious weaknesses. One of the conclusions to be drawn from the social conflict view of institutional inefficiency is that once the problem of credible commitment is solved the appropriate institution can be established. The social conflict view seems to have ignored the fact that optimal institutional structure creates equal opportunities for all members of the society to raise their stock of wealth through production. By unduly emphasizing economic rents as the only avenue for personal enrichment, it has foreclosed the possibility that the ruling elite could enhance their economic power or wealth by exploiting one of several opportunities available in institutionally efficient societies.

Similarly, alternative model offered by Acemoglu et al, failed to answer the important question of why only predatory, and not developmental institutions, would better serve the interest of the colonial masters and the local ruling elites that succeeded them. The simple logic is that developmental institutions in all colonies will promote even development across the world, reduce migration across borders, significantly decrease the probability of civil or external wars, encourage greater international trade and ensure widespread global prosperity. The established fact that there is greater level of trade among rich nations is enough reason why colonial powers should have planted developmental institutions in their colonies if the main objective for engaging in international trade was the maximization of their trade value. At least one lesson to draw from gravity models is that trade value is significantly and positively related to the combined magnitude of national output (GDP) of trading nations. Thus, if one country attempts to reduce the national output of the other by planting extractive institutions, it should expect to trade less and not more with this nation. Her own volume of gains from trade should be less, not more. The mere fact that institutionally strong societies trade more with each other is an ample testimony to this observation. The level of output and employment in countries which plant developmental institutions in other countries, and then trade with them should be higher, other things being equal, than countries which plant extractive institutions.

Because the social conflict viewpoint employs conventional approach of rational choice, it has found it difficult to acknowledge the fact that there could be other motives for holding political power than instituting a system that would maximize the ruling elites' revenue base. The possibility that the political power could afford ruling elites the avenue for both economic rent and control over the larger society had been ignored by social conflict theory. Yet it is a possibility that the ruling elites derive some intrinsic utility from wielding enormous political power, not only as an avenue for creating and sustaining economic rents, but as a means of dictating the outcomes of political, economic and social bargaining processes. If the argument here is correct, a new and efficient institution that decreases significantly political and economic inequality may result into a loss of intrinsic utility attached to wielding power by the ruling elites but not necessarily the loss of material wealth, or even *de jure* political power. In fact the new institutional structure will increase the absolute wealth base of the ruling elites. However, the transformation process reduces *de facto* political leaders to mere *de jure* political leaders. This represents huge loss of intrinsic utility attached to wielding political power. Thus, the power to dictate outcomes in the bargaining process, between the ruling elites and the larger society, is significantly reduced.

Therefore, an inefficient institution may not be the one that maximizes the absolute wealth level of the ruling elites as the social conflict viewpoint will make us believe, but the type which generates some rents and ensures absolute control over the larger society. An inefficient institution may be seen as one which maximizes the relative share of the national income that accrues to the ruling elites, subject to the probability of civil revolt and intra-group conflict. The choice here is between an efficient system where the ruling elites can enjoy both the highest level of absolute wealth and *de jure* political power and an inefficient system which guarantees a lower level of absolute wealth (but highest percentage of total income) as well as *de facto* political power.

A recent study by Lizzeri and Persico (2004) did assert that at the outset of the nineteenth century, a tiny group of powerful elites had considerable influence on public affairs in most countries and that the extension of voting rights to all adults helped to dilute elites' power to influence public policy which resulted in a loss to the elite group. The change which took place in Britain can be described as a transition from an inefficient to an efficient institutional state. The aftermath of the institutional transformation did not result into the direct transfer of wealth to the newly enfranchised poor people. According to Lizzeri and Persico (2004), welfare spending actually decreased from the peak two per cent in 1820 to less than one per cent for the rest of the century. The same thing happened to taxation. Only spending on public goods, which is beneficial to both the ruling elites and the general public increased rapidly after the change.

It does not appear that the social conflict viewpoint can produce evidence of economic losers after the transition to efficient institution. Historical evidence points to scores of absolute monarchies transformed into powerless kings. But they are no less economically successful than their ancient contemporaries who wielded enormous absolute powers. What was lost through the transition is termed in this study salience of power[4] (see Akerlof 1991 for the economic analysis of salience, a popular concept in cognitive psychology). The new political institutions significantly reduced their share of total wealth as they raised investment, productivity, schooling attainment and prosperity among other groups.

The evolution of new institutions governing public choice in seventh-century England did obtain for the winners security of property right, protection of their wealth and elimination of confiscatory government (North and Weingast 1989) but did not produce poorer monarchies. What was lost can be described as power salience, because arbitrary powers of monarchies were significantly curtailed. High power salience before the institutional change in England was characterized by wealth confiscation, arbitrary sale of monopolies, a public expenditure process that was not subject to any form of control, land appropriation by the crown, repudiation of public debt and arbitrary tax increases (in this case, high custom rates). But the aftermath of the institutional change resulted in a richer government still led by monarchies but with severely reduced powers. To appreciate the significance of the change which took place, let us pick directly the words of North and Weingast (1989):

> To see the dramatic results of the fiscal revolution, we turn to the public finances during the period... On the eve of the revolution governmental expenditures were about $1.8 million, reflecting a slow but steady increase over two decades. Government debt was limited to about $1million or between 2 and 3 per cent GNP (estimated to be $41million). Moreover, at a time when Holland was borrowing $5million long term at 4per cent per year, the English Crown could only borrow small amounts at short term paying between 6 and 30 per cent per year. The Revolution radically altered

this pattern. In 1697, just nine years later, governmental expenditures had grown fourfold, to $7.9 million. The immediate reason for the rise was the new war with the France. But importantly, the government's ability to tap the resources of the society increased. This is evidenced by the increased in the size of government debt, which grew during the nine years of war from $1million to nearly $17million.

More wealth was made available to the crown than before the change but power to spend had largely been curtailed. If the argument put forward here is accepted, at least tentatively, the lack of political Coase theorem cannot be a hindrance to institutional change.

Equally important for mass industrialization and foreign trade is the issue of geography. Geographical locations of countries could determine people's attitude to work. When climate is unfavourable, it could induce laziness, sap the body of energy and kill curiosity and the spirit of entrepreneurship. In attempting to understand underdevelopment, Myrdal (1968) asserts that we should study the impact of climate on soil, vegetation, physical assets and humans. More recently, Sach (2000) raised the issue of disease burden that is prevalent in the tropics and its impact on growth. Bloom and Sach (1998) estimated that the prevalence of malaria in SSA reduces growth annually by 1.3 per cent. Though health conditions and disease environments have considerable impact on economic performance, but like Acemoglu et al (2003b) assert, they do so indirectly via institutions. The disease environments determine whether the Europeans will settle or not and perhaps whether they will be able to take complete or partial control. This shapes the kind of institutions that emerge.

Other studies on the geography-development nexus emphasised the difficulty in applying technologies developed in temperate countries in tropics, though it failed to explain why these tropical countries could not adapt these technologies to their local conditions as some countries (South Korea and Taiwan) have done. The gravity models, incorporating important geographical determinants of trade, have explained why nations trade more or less (see Anderson and Wincoop 2004 for a recent review of the literature). The general conclusion from these studies is that being landlocked and being located far from major markets will significantly reduce trade with other nations. In spite of being landlocked, Botswana has made remarkable progress in growth and export of diamonds because of her strong institutions. While geographical environments may impose considerable limitations on trade and industrial development, every society can create institutions to overcome these limitations.

The model proposed here captures the political economy of policy-making in Africa and other less developed countries. When power salience is high among ruling elites, policies generally, and trade and industry policies in particular, are meant to institute or reinforce an inequitable resource allocation system. When this is overlooked, mere policy switch might not produce the expected results. Even when appropriate policies are put in place, institutional impediments limit their implementation and reduce expected gains.

The Model

The proposed model is based on a ruling group utility function which depends on the amount of public goods (x_1), and the intrinsic value of controlling the larger society(c). Thus, utility function for the ruling elites can be written as

$$U_E = u (G_1 \text{ è})$$

To achieve its objectives, it can employ either of these two strategies. It can provide small amount of G_1 to the public and worse still, it can geographically localize it provision to exclude the larger society from benefiting from its provision and exercise a great deal of control over the larger society because its percentage share of national income is enormous. It exercises both *de jure* and *de facto* powers and or at least, *de facto* power.

It can also build a developmental state by making higher amounts of x_1 available which can help the increased production of private goods and spread mass prosperity. This is a sharp contrast to the first case where few public goods are produced. However, optimal production of public goods reduces power salience, turning elites into agents exercising political power on behalf of the people. To illustrate power salience in our theory, let us use three vertical bars. If the group has high power salience, stage 2 would be the preferred institutional choice, a result inconsistent with rational choice theory where high levels of absolute wealth (represented by efficient institution) would have been chosen. Thus, by incorporating salience in the utility function of ruling elites, we can derive an institutional structure that maximizes their relative share of the national income of the ruling elites (i.e. 60 % or 28.57 % where their absolute wealth base is at maximum with limited provision of public goods.

The model shows how the ruling class preferences shape the quantity of public goods provided in a particular society. The first part of the model proves that the marginal increase in the ruling elite' absolute wealth stock (Y_e) as a result of a rise in national wealth stock (Y_n) is higher than the marginal rise in their relative wealth stock when national wealth stock increases. If the ruling class therefore decides to maximize their relative wealth, it would not conform to the strict definition of rationality in economics. Our central argument remains that if the rise in the absolute wealth level of the ruling elite (Y_e) will reduce their relative share of the overall pie $[Y_e/ Y_n]$, the incentives do not exist to raise both societal and their absolute wealth level. The reduction in their relative also implies a decline in their ability to exercise discretionary and arbitrary powers over the larger society. Note also that attempting to raise their relative share of wealth above a particular level could provoke civil unrest or revolution. Most of revolutions which have taken place are essentially on account of extreme wealth inequality. Thus, the relative share of the larger non-ruling group of the total wealth is an important binding constraint in ruling elite ability to continuously raise their relative share of wealth.

Figure 13.1: Power Salience

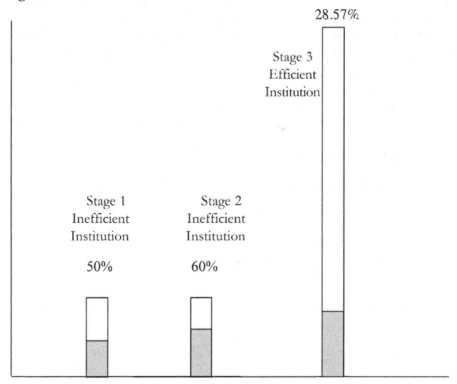

Vertical Bars represent national income

Keys:

☐ Relative shares of the non-elite group out of the National Income

▨ Relative shares of the ruling elite group out of the National Income

The second part of the model attempts to demonstrate the level of public goods provided under two important conditions. One is the optimal public good that maximizes the social wealth. Two, is the quantity of public goods that maximises the relative wealth of the ruling elites. To start with, let national wealth be a combination of the wealth stock of both the ruling elites (Y_e) and the larger society (Y_s). Y_e is a combination of rent appropriation (nNA) and other income from productive activities (Y_p). This distinction will become important later in this model when we focus rent appropriated. Thus,

$$(Y_n) = (Y_e) + (Y_s) \qquad (2)$$

If we assume that all the savings of these groups are invested, then

$$I = S \qquad (3)$$

Where I is investment and S represents savings. If α represents the fraction of the elites' wealth stock that is saved and invested and á represents the fraction of the non-ruling elite wealth stock that is saved and invested, total investment can be represent by the equation below;

$$I = \alpha\,(Y_e) + á(Y_s) \qquad (4)$$

Given that $(Y_s) = (Y_n) - (Y_e)$ equation can be rewritten as

$$I = {}_e(Y_e) + \alpha_s\,(Y_n - Y_e) \qquad (5)$$

And can be rewritten as

$$I = \alpha\,(Y_e) + áY_n - áY_e$$
$$I = \alpha\,(Y_e) - ÜY_e + áY_n \qquad (6)$$
$$I = Y_e\,(\alpha - á) + áY_n$$

If both sides of the equation are divided by Y_n we have

$$\frac{I}{Y_n} = \frac{Y_e\,(\alpha_e - \alpha_s)}{Y_n} + \frac{\alpha_s}{Y_n} \qquad (7)$$

Taking the relative elite share to the left-hand side of the equation, we now have

$$\frac{Y_e}{Y_n} = \frac{I}{(\alpha_e - \alpha_s)\,Y_n} - \alpha_s \qquad (8)$$

From equation 8, we can now see that increase in national wealth diminishes the relative share of the ruling elites and undermines their control over the larger society. If members of the ruling class are unproductive, so that

(α_s - α_e) is small or even negative, then we expect the relative share of the ruling elites to rise and increase their control over the larger society. Because political power is equally concentrated in the hands of the ruling elites, they can effectively block the emergence of an alternative productive political or entrepreneurial class. The more unproductive members of the ruling elites are, the higher their share of national wealth and the greater their control over the society and the more they are differentiated from the rest of the society. The rapid rise in Y_n reduces the elites' relative share and, by extension, their control coefficient (è). This is what Olson (1965) referred to as the destabilizing force of rapid economic growth.

Differentiating the relative wealth stock of the ruling elites ($Y_e / Y_n = \alpha_1$) with respect to change in national wealth Y_n from equation 8, we derive the equation 9 below:

$$\frac{d\alpha_1}{dY_n} = -I/(\alpha_e - \alpha_s)Y^2_n - \alpha_s/(\alpha_e - \alpha_s) \qquad (9)$$

From equation 9, it is quite clear that elites' relative share of total wealth drops as investment increases and the fraction of the income saved by the non-ruling group rises. Thus, increasing investment must be raising both the absolute and relative wealth stock of the larger non-ruling society. As the relative share of total wealth declines, so does the power of the ruling elites.

Their absolute stock of wealth will rise as national income rises, and as you would soon see, both rents appropriated as a fraction of their wealth portfolio and their relative share of total wealth will decline. Thus, if raising institutional capacity will raise national income, it probably would reduce opportunities for unearned rents. Rise in absolute wealth of the ruling elites must then come from productive wealth-creating activities. Murphy, Shleifer and Vishny (1991) record people who made fortunes in institutionally weak societies from rent-seeking but made greater fortunes when they relocated to institutionally strong countries. Though not specified, it would be practically impossible for them to exact as much influence on economic, political and social activities as they would in institutionally weak countries. Public policy tends towards optimal social welfare policy as power salience declines. Collective decisions therefore approximate collective will as power salience declines. The transition from discretionary or arbitrary society governed at the whims and caprices of the ruling elites to a ruled-based is only possible as this power salience sharply declines. Institutional structure erected to prevent this transition is at the heart of developmental challenges in LDCs. Societies with strong and efficient institutions are those that have managed to break this power salience.

From equation 10^5, the rise in national income also increases the absolute wealth level of the ruling elites since $I./(\alpha_e - \alpha_s) > .\alpha_s /(\alpha_e - \alpha_s)$. If the sole objective of the political class is the maximization of their absolute wealth stock, they can do so by increasing national wealth stock. But by doing this, they equally raise the absolute and relative share of the non-ruling group. The emergence of mass middle-class that pushes for reforms and asks for greater participation in the ruling of the state is inevitable when elites attempt to maximize their relative share of national income.

$$\frac{Y_e = I}{(\alpha_e - \alpha_s)} \quad - \quad \frac{Y_n.\alpha_e}{(\alpha_e - \alpha_s)} \tag{10}$$

There are two optimal quantities of public goods that can be produced depending on the whether the ruling class wants to maximize the absolute wealth or relative share of social wealth. As we would soon see, optimal public goods produced when the aim is to maximize relative share of total wealth are substantially less than when they desire to maximize absolute wealth. From the model it would then be easy to see that relative share of total wealth is higher when less public goods are supplied than when more public goods are made available. The under-supply of public goods does more than raise rents for the ruling elites, it increases power salience. It is within this context that state policies could be analysed, including policies that inhibit entrepreneurship and those that limit the implementation of welfare-improving trade and industrial policies. The model here explains why growth-inhibiting redistributive policies which characterise states in LDCs, particularly in SSA, are borne out of the need to raise power salience. Niskanen's (1997) model is a useful starting point. The model was used to show what tax rates, quantity of government services and output are possible under autocratic, democratic and optimal governments. For our purpose, we ignore what the tax rates under these alternative forms of governments would be, but rather concentrate on public goods and national output levels are under alternative objective functions of the ruling elites. Thus, we consider only institutional arrangements framed by the preferences of the ruling elites and the quantity of public goods that would be produced these different arrangements.

In the modified Niskanen framework, government revenues are derived from two main sources. This includes taxes levied on productive sector and the other is tax derived from appropriated natural resources.

$$y = a(1+G)^{b}(1-R)^{c} \tag{11}$$

$$T = Ry = {}^{b}R^{c} \tag{12}$$

$$nT = Ry =)^{b}Rn^{c} \tag{13}$$

$$Y_{n} = nT + R_{N} =)^{b}Rn^{c} + R_{N} \tag{14}$$

Equation 11 represents common function any government may have to confront. For equation 11, y is output per person, G is per person government expenditure on public goods and R is government choice of tax rate and T is tax collected per working person. Output per person multiplied by R yields the total tax paid (T) per member of the non-ruling working group (equation 12). Government collects a total of nT (equation 13) from the n-members of the working society. We can further simplify our model by assuming that the total income of the country (Y_n) is a combination of taxes (nT) paid by members of the working group as well as revenues derived from natural endowments (R_N). This yields equation 14. For all these four functions, a is the level of output per worker when G and R are zero, while parameters b and c represent elasticities of output and tax revenues with respect to government expenditure and after-tax rate.

For government to carry out its functions efficiently and effectively, it exercises the right to tax and spend. Depending on existing institutional structure or the preference of the ruling elite, there might be a small or big gap between revenues collected by government and what is spent on public good. If NA represents what the ruling elites can appropriate per person from revenues collected from workers and natural endowments after expenditure on public good (nG), then

$$nNA = nT - nG + nr_{n} \tag{15}$$

Substituting equation 13 into 15, we obtain

$$nNA = a(1+G)^{b}Rn(1-R)^{c} - nG + nr_{n} \tag{16}$$

Benevolent ruling elites will choose not to appropriate state resources ($nNA=0$)

If the ruling elite choose to maximize their rents (nNA), the optimal public good ($1 +G$) provided is

$$(1+G) = [abR(1-R)^{c}]^{1/1-b} \tag{17}$$

Before now, we asserted that the general problem of underdevelopment is not due to the fact the elites want to maximize their total wealth stock as is common in the political economy literature but because they want to maximize their relative share of the total wealth. If they maximize their total wealth base as depicted by equation 17, the level of public good made available will raise both the relative share and absolute wealth stock of the larger society. This will diminish the status value of wealth they have acquired and reduce their ability to unilaterally decide the fate of the society in which they are resident.

With equation 16 as the numerator and 14 as the denominator, we can obtain another equation (equation 18) indicating the elite relative share of total wealth («).

$$\infty = \frac{a(1+G)^b Rn\,(1-R)^c - nG + nr_n}{a(1+G)^b Rn\,(1-R)^c + R_N} \cdot \tag{18}$$

The optimal public good when the elites want to maximize their relative of total wealth is

$$(1+G) = \left[\,abR(1-R)^c \frac{Y_n - Y_e}{Y_n}\,\right]^{1/1-b} \tag{19}$$

Since $Y_n - Y_e / Y_n$ cannot be equal to one, given that the ruling elites will always use state apparatus and policies to redistribute resources towards themselves, public goods supplied will be consistently smaller than if the elites want to maximize the total wealth base. Equation 19 is also very informative, showing that as the relative share of total wealth declines for members of the working group, the public goods provided by the ruling class falls. The general trend here is that optimal public goods made available if relative share of wealth stock is maximized is less than what is provided when the elites want to maximize their wealth stock. However, there is no unique equilibrium for every society. *Country-specific characteristics, particularly the possibility of civil unrests, bloody revolution, probability of external invasion, existing social values, ethnic and religious composition, extent of natural resource endowments, among many others, will determine the extent to which the rulers can reduce the relative share of the working group.* Obvious from equation 19, is that $Y_n - Y_e / Y_n$ values range between 0 and 1. In fact $Y_n - Y_e / Y_n$ is our measure of power salience (è), which was an important part of the rulers' utility function in equation 1. Lower values indicate high power salience, where rulers' share of total wealth is very high and high values depict low power salience.

The history of nations, including the developed countries of the world, often shows that they start with high power salience. Over time, both internal and external factors help to undermine power salience, compelling the elites to increase the supply of public goods and create conditions for prosperity. Going into the details will take us further afield, but the literature on this is considerable. For the present purpose, it is important to understand that those with access to power deliberately construct an institutional arrangement to maintain high power salience, where person, rather than the system, matters in the allocation of scarce resources.[6] The words of Acemoglu et al (2004) help to bring out the sharp contrast between societies with high power salience and those with low or zero power salience,

> Indeed the qualitative nature of politics appears to differ markedly between strongly and weakly institutionalized politics: when institutions are strong, citizens punish politicians by voting them out of power; when institutions are weak, politicians punish citizens who fail to support them. When institutions are strong, politicians vie for the support and endorsement of interest groups; when institutions are weak politicians create and control interest groups. When institutions are strong, citizens demand rights; when institutions are weak, citizens beg for favours (p.163).

One important implication of the model sketched here is that Mobutu or anybody of his kind could make far greater wealth under institutionally strong society and still retain power for many years like the Lee Kwan Yew of Singapore, but the power to unilaterally dictate outcomes would be permanently lost. Efficient institutions are unattractive to the ruling class because they destroy state-citizen dependency. In the absence of real and significant threat to both their wealth and *de facto* political power, the society might be trapped in the long-run underdevelopment equilibrium. When the transition eventually occurs, what is lost is power salience, measured quantitatively as è, but qualitatively it can be seen as the move from *de facto* to *de jure* political leadership. Thus, institution building in itself is a form of mechanism design.

Figure 13.2

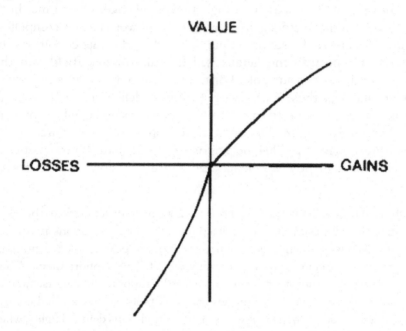

Productive entrepreneurship, developmental trade and industrial policies, which one would expect in institutionally strong societies, will yield monetary gains to the ruling elites by raising the absolute stock of wealth. However, they will suffer psychological loss because reduction in relative share of wealth reduces power salience. This is why the simple model presented is very well illustrated by prospect theory (Kahneman and Tversky 1979). For Figure 13.2, the increase in elite absolute is concave in gains while the reduction in relative share, equivalent of power salience loss in our model, is convex. Thus, losses loom larger than gains. There is therefore a special utility derived from wielding power and exercising it arbitrarily. Except there is a significant threat to elite entire wealth, which looms even larger than the possible loss of power salience, the statuesque will remain, leaving the society in underdevelopment equilibrium state.

The analysis of trade and industrial policies, we believe, can be better understood by the model presented here. We can understand how the trade and industrial policies of the old era undermined development and why the new era of open trade and outward-orientation strategies has not succeeded in fast-tracking development. In the public good context, the model allows us to appreciate why the ruling elites support sub-optimal provision of human capital, massive under-investment in research and development and inadequate provision of physical infrastructure.

Implications of the Model

Our simple model yields interesting implications. It explains why the polity in societies with high power salience is characterized by growth-inhibiting redistributions. It also explains why growth-enhancing redistribution is sub-optimal or non-existent and why public good investment is grossly inadequate. Within the framework provided by the model, we could ask what the old industrial and trade policies constituted, and whether the new policies in respect of industrialization and trade could in any way raise or decrease the values taken by è, our measure of power salience. Logically, redistribution towards the ruling elites, sub-optimal investment in human capital,[7] under-investment in research and development activities, preventing the introduction of new innovations and technologies and significant under-investment in physical infrastructure are all strategies geared towards raising and sustaining high power salience.

With this model, it is not difficult to see why neither the old nor the new industrial and trade policies, given the institutional operating environment, have impacted positively on development. The old policies have raised power salience, and the new policies have not succeeded in lowering it. They have in fact exacerbated it. This is probably because the new democratic order in many African countries has not altered the power configuration in a way that would drastically reduce power salience. In the four sub-sections of this particular section, we discussed the trade and industrial policies and economic performances of LDCs, particularly SSA. The remaining three sub-sections are devoted to discussing under-investment in human capital, R & D, and physical infrastructure. These sub-optimal investments are regarded as core strategies of the ruling elites in raising or sustaining control over the larger society. We must not lose sight of the fact that the problem is basically institutional in nature. The issues discussed in these sub-sections are reflections of the quality of institutions available.

Trade and Industrial Policies and Economic Performance

The post-independent challenge of African countries was to chart the pathway to rapid development. Having inherited weak and extractive institutions from colonial authorities, early political leaders did not seek to improve political and economic institutions, but made policy choices that exploited the institutional weakness of the country they sought to lead. Industrial and trade policies, either in form of import substitutions, high tariffs, quota restrictions or outright ban on importation reflect the institutional framework constructed to maintain and increase high power salience. As the ruling elites transited from the much larger group of autocratic democracies to essentially military oligarchies, power salience rose across the continent. Since all African countries were essentially agrarian in nature in the immediate post-independent years, and in fact many are still at that state, it would be interesting to see how government treated the pricing of agricultural exports as major sources of state revenue. Bates' (1981) classic is a useful starting point. According to him,

> Most African states possess publicly sanctioned monopolies for the purchase and export of agricultural goods ... These agencies, bequeathed to the governments of the independent states by their colonial predecessors, purchase cash crops for export at administratively determined domestic prices. By using their power to keep the price paid to the farmer below the price set by the world market, they accumulate funds from the agricultural sector (Bates 1981:12).

Thus, the difference between the world market price and what they paid became an important source of tax revenue to the government. For a benevolent government confronted with a huge informal economy, which is difficult, if not impossible to tax, that policy choice was understandable. Though taxing the farmers' incomes would have produced lesser distortions, what is important from the viewpoint of our model is what the ruling elites did with the tax revenues made from peasant farmers. Given the absence of institutions to curb predatory tendencies, a significant part of these revenues found their ways into private pockets. Though Bates argued that the nature of agricultural pricing policy was responsible for the growth tragedy that befell Africa, we argue from the standpoint of this model that the collapse of Africa's growth is only partially connected to the size of rent appropriated, but more importantly, is related to what the ruling elites did with the rents they appropriated.

This seems a logical way to look at it. We should expect different economic performance depending on whether the ruling elites spent their share of the loot on conspicuous consumption or invested it. If they invested their loot in the economy, the positive externalities generated will spill over to a wider category of persons. They seek the evolution of political and economic institutions that would protect private rights. The difference between the economic performances of SSA and those countries in East Asian is not so much the absence of corruption and pervasive rent-seeking in one part and the presence in the other; it is a question of what was done with the rents. We argue here that *conspicuous consumption* undermines the possibility of evolving an industrial nation or the use of trade policies to foster development. According to Mkandawire (2001):

In addition, rents can be both 'productive' and 'unproductive' in their incentive impact. In most models, it is assumed that rents are exogenous to the individual firm. They are out there, and the firm allocates resources to get them. It follows from this assumption that such an allocation will leave fewer resources for productive investments. However, once the assumption of exogeneity is dropped, and once we assume instead that the level of rents a firm gets depends on the size of the firm's activities, the story changes, and we get an entirely different dynamics in which rent is a function of firm's performance. The pursuit of rents can lead to expansion of productive activity. In such cases, rent-seeking becomes a spur to growth as rent seekers attempt to capture as much of the rents as possible (Mkandawire 2001:301).

The character of the rent-seeking class in East Asia and Africa must be different in terms of what its ruling elites do with rents obtained from public office, and so the same applies to the business interest they interact with. Why it differs is a topic for another day. However, the investments of rents across different sectors would make continuous rent extraction hurt established business interests. From the second part of our model, higher provision of public good will reduce rents (nNA), but the mere fact that the absolute value of their wealth will rise over time implies that more wealth will have to be generated from productive activities. Since this East Asian experience is not replicated in Africa, mass industrialization has not been possible for many African countries. Mass export of manufactures is therefore not possible. Yet in nearly all countries which experienced rapid growth and high living standards, industrialization had been the main medium for achieving this (Murphy, Shleifer and Vishny 1989a).

In Africa, rents appropriated are either expended on status goods[8] or invested abroad. This undermines the need to produce an optimal number of productive entrepreneurs required for accelerated growth and development. The mere fact that the ruling elites have a disproportionately large fraction of the national wealth in their possession also creates a very small domestic market size, further limiting the opportunities of massive industrialization (Murphy et al 1989a). Both small domestic market size and lack of critical mass of entrepreneurs conspire to limit the possibility of building an industrial nation in Africa. Because the small domestic market size is an equilibrium outcome of ruling elite-society interaction, it will be difficult to break out of low-level-industrializsation trap except when power salience is sufficiently lowered to a level that industrialization will become self-sustaining. Exports offer an alternative route if domestic demand is small, but the institutional environment can hardly generate the volume of exports required to increase local demand sufficiently to make mass-industrialization self-sustaining.

If farmers sold their produce directly to international markets and paid tax out of their foreign exchange earnings, they would have constituted the critical mass of entrepreneurs required to initiate industrialization. They naturally would have transited into large-scale industrial entrepreneurship as structural transformation of the economy makes increasing returns technologies more applicable to industries. This would have led to the creation of large middle-class required to create domestic market for sustained industrialization. Thus, if rents represent the only medium via which other firms could be affected, then the industrialized equilibrium cannot co-exist with the unindustrialized equilibrium (Murphy et al 1989a). If it affects all sectors or firms by raising the wages of workers induced to work in factories, it can support mass industrialization by boosting domestic demand capacity.

Ultimately, under-developed productive entrepreneurship, lean domestic market and constrained export capacity limit industrialization in Africa. The institutional environment contrived to maintain high power salience is essentially responsible for these growth-inhibiting features of African landscape. Lack of local investment of rents by the ruling elites makes productive entrepreneurship less rewarding, leading to sub-optimal supply of entrepreneurs required to drive industrialization and high value-added foreign trade. Positive externalities that the investment of rents could have created by increasing the number of industries that can apply increasing returns techniques and raising the wages of workers are lost. This keeps domestic demand at a low level. With inadequate investment in human and physical capital, exports success is limited, and in fact confined to low-value-added primary commodities. If exports could record considerable success, there is every chance industrialization could be prompted by increased domestic demand (Murphy et al 1989b). The limited gains from the export of agricultural commodities were captured by the ruling elites via their marketing boards. Therefore, the local farmers were in no position to make large-scale demands for products of industries because they made little profits from farming.[9] It is not a natural outcome; it is a contrived bad equilibrium outcome resulting from the use of political power to create extreme economic inequality. As political power is used to raise the elite relative share of total wealth, power salience rises. This creates an effective barrier against industrialization, because wealth is not widespread to create effective large-scale demand for manufactures. The creation of a critical mass of middle-class as a result of relatively even distribution of national wealth is the impetus required to drive rapid industrialization (Murphy et al 1989b). Since the new market-driven trade and industrial policies have left this institutional structure essentially unaltered, the possibility of growing an industrial Africa is limited and large-scale exports of manufactures near impossible.

In spite of political rhetoric, leaders of post-independent Africa feared that industrialization could lead to the diffusion of political power across many groups. Beyond the agricultural policy that adversely affected the possibility of mass industrialization, there was a more direct attempt at impeding local industrial growth in immediate post-independent years in Africa. With respect to Ghana, Killick (1978:37) had this to say:

> Even had there been the possibility of creating an indigenous entrepreneurial class, it is doubtful that Nkrumah would have wanted to create such as class, for reasons of ideology and political power. He was very explicit about this saying 'we would be hampering our advance to socialism if we were to encourage the growth of Ghanaian private capitalism in our midst'. There is evidence that he also feared the threat that a wealthy class of Ghanaian businessmen might pose to his political power.

Acemoglu et al (2005) said Nkrumah limited the size of businesses Ghanaians could own to maintain political power. In the context of our model, he did that to sustain the influence he had on public policy. Promoting industrialization would have turned him into a *de jure* leader holding power in trust for the non-ruling group. Rising prosperity that accompanies industrialization would have raised the participation rates of many groups in the larger society in governance and collective decision-making. It is inconceivable that a government that brought about mass prosperity would be voted out of office. When institutional transformation takes place, productive activities outside politics become even more rewarding. The issue of possible loss of rents does not arise. In fact, it takes greater efforts and time to access and sustain rents than to compete in the market place.

The endowments of natural resources, such as crude oil, created further bottlenecks for industrialization beyond the Dutch disease syndrome usually discussed in the literature. While the old agricultural pricing policy may have led to the collapse of national output as farmers responded to incentives by quitting farming, the presence of oil offers government the opportunity to take over the production process and appropriate the greater part of the rents. The oil economy further worsens economic inequality, and via the channel described earlier, limits industrialization. Thus, an oil sector isolated from the remaining sectors of the economy cannot generate substantial spill-over effect.

The inability to diversify foreign exchange earnings, which could have been brought about by rapid industrialization, is a necessary outcome of our model. Diversification creates many wealth-generating groups across the country. This will compel the evolution of institutions to protect property rights and reduce power salience. In fact, diversification allows vested interests across several sectors to evolve, creating opportunities for positive cooperative and coordinating equilibrium among competing groups likely to be hurt by the absence of institutions that protect property rights. When institutional structure limits opportunities for industrialization, and allow for fewer economic opportunities for the rural populace, the ensuing rural-urban migration leads to the expansion of the informal sector. Numerous informal sector entrepreneurs are too weakly organized and coordinated to become an alternative power source. These entrepreneurs cannot overcome the huge costs of collective action and cannot constitute a threat to the political power of the ruling elite. Growing informal sector in Africa is also a bad equilibrium, resulting from the frustrated attempt at industrialization.

The old trade and industrial policies[10] could have created huge rents for the ruling elites, but it would be difficult to say that Africa's poor performance in terms of industrialization and trade is because of these policies. If it were so, the policy switch in the last two decades would have produced better results. Under the new trade and industrial policy regimes, Africa has been steadily de-industrializing. As governments withdraw from the direct ownership of businesses via privatization, it will be strategic to contain the emerging business and working-class elite by exposing them to unfair competition and sustaining an institutional environment that raises transaction costs. While East Asia adopted outward-oriented strategy to boost exports, it is not true that import-substitution strategies and protective tariffs were not employed. Reflecting on the general experience of East Asian countries, Lall (2000) had this to say concerning Korea,

> Asia offers lessons in liberalization as well as intervention. Korea, for instance, started to liberalise in the 1980s in a gradual manner, retaining considerable control over resource allocation during the process. It accompanied opening up with a strategy of restructuring and upgrading, rather than a rapid, indiscriminate and sweeping exposure to international market forces. The speed of liberalisation was based on a realistic, detailed and differentiated assessment of which activities were viable in the medium term, with the process geared to the learning and 'relearning' needs of various activities. At the same time, there were strong pressures on industries to invest in building up new capabilities to face import competition within a limited

period. It was designed to overcome market failures, not to ignore them. It involved the close monitoring of the progress of liberalisation, and it requires that the government is able to address the supply side needs of the industries along with allowing a phased process of liberalisation.

In the 1980s, Korea already had well-developed physical infrastructure and had made significant progress in human capital investment. She would probably be able to compete better than Africa with far less impressive records. Given its diversified export economy and it huge endowment of quality human capital, it should be better able to cope with trade shocks or should at least be far less vulnerable to them. Yet it never exposed itself to fierce international competition. New policies on industrialization and trade will indeed create economic losers among the ruling elites and the bureaucracy. However, the important question is whether institutional environments in Africa will spur efforts in wealth-creating activities. If they do, economic losers will take advantage of new wealth-creating opportunities. Because fundamental institutional change is yet to occur, losers have only relocated to other kinds of growth-inhibiting activities.[11] The absence of vast natural resources and the fear of communism spreading are factors that lowered power salience over time in East Asia. They prompted the evolution of an inclusive society and massive investment in human and physical capital. Thus, East Asia's rapid economic progress is due largely to institutional transformation with the added advantage that the initial economic inequality condition was low. Institutions created the right incentives for government to provide infrastructure required for industrialization and trade[12] and forced rents to be invested in productive activities. These institutions also supported productive entrepreneurship. Sobel's (2008) cross-country empirical study reveals that areas with better institutions have more productive entrepreneurship, and also less unproductive entrepreneurship. The net effect of this is rapid growth and development. In the next section, we would argue the absence of strong institutions translated to significant shortfall in infrastructure required to promote rapid industrialization and foreign trade. The infrastructure includes quality human capital in the right amount, research and development activities with significant externality component, and physical infrastructure.

Infrastructure and Industrialization

Human Capital and Industrialization

Human capital via education has become so fundamental that the last century has been termed the human capital century (Golden 2001). United States which led other nations in mass secondary education also rose to be the most productive society or country ever known to mankind. The practice among industrial giants even before the beginning of the twentieth century was to watch each other closely and send delegations to discover the source of each other's greatness. At first, most of the delegations before the twentieth century were interested in studying 'capital and technology' as driving forces of economic greatness. At the outset of the 20th century, delegations sent to understudy other countries were in fact sent to study people and training (Sawyer 1954). From 1910 to 1940 in the US, secondary school enrolment and graduation rates had risen dramatically, with the rise more dramatic for non-southern states between 1920 and 1935 (Goldin 1998).

According to Denison (1985), 28 per cent of economic growth could be attributed to rise in the years and quality of formal schooling for every American worker. But human capital contribution to economic growth might, of course, be greater than 28 per cent, if the unaccounted fraction of the residuals could be traced to knowledge-driven technological change and its diffusion (Goldin 1998). Barrow (2001) said higher human to physical capital stock translates to growth via two channels. First advanced technologies are much more readily accepted and absorbed into the labour force when human capital is high. Second, high initial human to physical capital promotes growth by increasing the stock of physical capital required to match up, given that human capital cannot be readily adjusted. The absence of this high level stock of human capital in many less developed countries (LDCs) partly accounts for inadequate inflow of foreign investment and technology which should complement human capital (Mankiw 1995). Most of the jobs that drive growth require high level of education, the type of education that adapts people to the changing dynamics of rapidly evolving technology (Nelson and Philip 1966).

In 1960, 13 South Korean workers would produce what 2 American workers could make. Forty years down the line, 3.5 South Korean workers will produce the equivalent of what 2 American workers can produce. Within the same period, it would take 50 Nigerian workers to produce what 2 American workers would produce from initial ratio of 12: 2. The sharp decline in output per worker in Nigeria, and the dramatic rise in that of South Korea, has its human capital dimension. According to a World Bank publication,

> In nearly all the rapidly growing East Asian economies, the growth and transformation of systems of education and training during the past 3 decades has been dramatic. The quality of schooling ... and training in the home has markedly improved. Today, the cognitive skill level of secondary school graduates in some East Asian countries is comparable to or higher than those of graduates in high income economies.

The dramatic economic growth of East Asian countries within a relatively short period of time is not unconnected with a massive investment in human capital. According to Krugman (1994),

> Consider in particular the case of Singapore between 1966 and 1990 the Singaporean economy grew a remarkable 8.5 per cent per annum, 3 times as fast as the United States: Per capita income grew at a 6.6 per cent rate roughly every decade. This achievement seems to be a kind of economic miracle but the miracle turns out to be based on perspiration rather than inspiration. Singapore grew through a mobilization of resources that would have done Stalin proud. The employed share of the population surged from 27 to 51per cent. The educational standards of the work force were dramatically upgraded. While in 1966, more than half of that work force had no formal education at all, by 1990, two thirds had completed secondary education.

If human capital can accelerate growth via industrialization and success in global knowledge-driven trade, then it remains a threat to the ruling elites. It does this by lowering income inequality. Significant reduction in income inequality will reduce the ruling elites' relative share of total wealth. Arbitrary exercise of power is curtailed, leading to the emergence of a rule-based society. To prevent this possibility, an elitist educational system is institutionalized. This system skews public resource in educating the children of the ruling elites. Where some form of free education is extended to the poor, the quality leaves much to be desired. Recent estimates of returns to primary education have been very low while higher education has had considerably higher returns. Thus, the elites' relative share of national wealth will rise if their children benefit more from state-supported higher education while the credit-constrained members of the larger society benefit less. The result is the same if the non-ruling members of the society benefit only from lower level education with poor returns. The need to sustain *de facto* power will lead to sub-optimal human capital investment. Massive industrialization and success in knowledge-based global trade will be impossible. Wood and Mayer's (2001) empirical study confirms that Africa exports basically unprocessed primary products because of her low level of education and abundant natural resources.

According to King (1991), African governments have only made minor adjustment to the educational structure they inherited from colonial masters. From the perspective of Oyelaran and Barclay (2003), there is an inappropriate mix of skills. Higher institutions of learning in Africa enrol 60 per cent of her students into the arts and the humanities, and 40 per cent into science and engineering disciplines. While Africa enrolled about

0.04 per cent of her population into technical subjects such as engineering and mathematics, it was 1.34 per cent for the four Asian tigers (Hall 2001). Using Harbison-Mayer technical enrolment index, Norway is first with 73.52, South Africa has 23.61 and Nigeria a paltry 5.85 (Oyelaran and Barclay 2003). Technological development which can support industrialization and trade is unlikely with this kind of skill-mix. In fact, Murphy el al (1991) established that this skill-mix is significant for achieving rapid growth. In their growth regression, they showed that societies with high engineer/ lawyer ratio are more productive than those with less. This is because lawyers are prone to rent-seeking activities while engineers are more involved in production. Sub-optimal investment in human capital and the inappropriate skill-mix of African human capital portfolio are not inadvertent policy mistakes, they are deliberately contrived to sustain a desired institutional structure. If we start with equal distribution of wealth among individuals, 'reversal of fortune' or symmetry-breaking occurs as political power is used to redistribute resources towards the ruling class.

Due to lack of complementary investment in physical capital, Africans with higher education have migrated to richer countries for better rewards. According to World Health Organisation (2006), an increasing number of health professionals are migrating to richer countries for better jobs though there is substantial shortfall in the number required to provide proper healthcare. Migration rates of skilled professionals exceed 50 per cent in countries such as Cape Verde, Gambia, Seychelles, Mauritius and Sierra Leone (World Bank 2006). It is in fact sad that there are more African scientists and engineers in the USA than in the entire continent as whole (Oyelere 2007). But this situation has arisen because political power has been used to alter the returns to different kinds of endowments. By under-supplying infrastructure required for industrialization, returns to human capital investment are reduced substantially. As trained professional workers migrate to richer climes, resistance against dictatorship tends to wane and institutions of state are further weakened. Thus, industrialization possibilities are diminished and mass exports of manufactures are highly unlikely. This should be understood as part of strategies required to sustain the under-development equilibrium described in our model.

Research and Development (R & D), Industrialization and Trade Performance

High standards of living experienced in selected parts of the world would be impossible to achieve without technology. Whether it is from outside as the conventional Solow model would emphasise or is learnt, absorbed, adapted and improved upon as the endogenous theories say, technologies do play critical roles in promoting economic development. The Industrial Revolution was preceded by a number of technological revolutions. By extension, positive institutional change equally preceded both technological and industrial revolutions.

Curiously, despite the vast opportunity for radical improvements in living standards via technology, ruling elites operating under different institutional environments do not have the same incentives to promote technology via R & D activities. Sometimes, they block the introduction of welfare-improving technologies (Parente and Prescott 1994; 1999). The barriers against the introduction of new techniques account for significant differences in the per capita income of many countries. But it is not sheer coincidence that the barriers against technology are strongest in societies which are institutionally weak or, to use our phrase, in societies with high 'power salience' (Hall and Jones 1999). Forward-looking ruling elites anticipate that the introduction of new techniques will alter existing power configuration by raising new political power contenders. It does not matter whether their absolute wealth stock will rise. What is important is that the emergence of a vibrant middle-class will impose constraints on the exercise of power, making the outcomes of all forms of interactions more predictable. Becoming trustees of power constitutes a huge loss to members of the ruling class. Gonzalez (2005) argues that superior technologies when property rights are insecure occur when entrepreneurs expect conflict over distribution. When wealth created by new technologies can be appropriated by ruling elites, the strategic response comes in the form of introducing inferior technologies. Since this will not alter existing political and economic inequality, societies with weak institutions will be characterized by inferior technologies. Massive indus-trialization and large-scale external trade (particularly manufactures and capital goods exports) are near impossible. Development is therefore stunted.

Apart from direct blockage of new technologies, the ruling class has limited the spread of modern technology by restricting public provision of schooling. Since modern technologies are readily learnt and adopted by the educated, limiting schooling attainment will restrict the adoption of life-changing technology. Unlike the experience of Asian Tigers such South Korea, Taiwan, Hong Kong and Singapore, public schooling has been generally poor in developing countries (Tooley 2006). If schooling is the main source of modern scientific knowledge (Eisemon 1989), poor quality schooling translates to poor economic growth. Though some of the literature emphasized the problem of introducing new technologies to the hostile climate of the tropics, that argument is difficult to sustain, because countries such as South Korea and Singapore, which are located in the tropics, have been able to successfully adapt Western technologies to local geographic conditions. Israeli located in an even harsher environment of the desert has been able to do the same. These countries have not only adapted the acquired technologies, they have also been able to improve on them.

The public and private expenditure patterns on R & D activities allow us to determine to a large extent how much technology is valued in a particular society. Lall (2000) provides valuable data (see Table 4 of Lall 2000) to that effect. For the list of developing countries presented in the tabulated data, South Korea and Taiwan lead, with the government spending 2.7 and 1.00 per cent of GDP on Research and Development activities. For two of Africa's most successful stories in industrialization and export of manufactures, South Africa and Mauritius, public expenditure as percentage of GDP is 1.00 and 0.4 respectively. Oil-rich Nigeria only spends about 0.1 of GDP on R & D. Lall (2000) gave a comprehensive list of measures undertaken by the East Asian countries. These include direct support for private R & D activities, tax incentives offered for the importation of new technologies, giving grants and long-term loans to firms participating in 'National Projects' and the provision of technology finance. South Korea is underscored by the fact that she has been able to stimulate the private sector to spend 2.27 per cent of GDP on R & D activities, while the corresponding percentage for Nigeria is 0.00 per cent. Private sector spending as a percentage of GDP is 25 times more than that of Mexico though they have the same manufacturing value-added, but the later country is more dependent on foreign technology.

The sub-optimal expenditure on R and D is a natural outcome of our model because *de facto* political power needs to be sustained. Since optimal expenditure on R & D activities and on human capital will reduce economic inequality and reduce elite share of total wealth, keeping expenditures at a low level is a key strategy in sustaining political power.

Physical Capital, Industrialisation and Trade Performance

Public investments in physical infrastructure provide incentives to private investors to establish industries and help in achieving success in the export of manufactures. The role of infrastructure in raising productivity, reducing transaction costs and accelerating economic growth has been well established in the literature (Gramlich 1994; Lynde and Richmond 1993; Ferreira and Isser 1995). It equally spurs investment in complementary human capital investments. It encourages specialization in production (Bougheas and Demetriades 1995) and balanced growth across all sectors. It boosts international trade by reducing transport costs (Bougheas, Demetriades and Morgenroth 1999).

Infrastructural deficiencies raise the costs of production, making firms lack competitiveness in both domestic and international markets. A government whose de facto political power is threatened by industrialization and trade will limit growth by under-supplying public infrastructure. Even more important is the fact that physical infrastructure does not only accelerate growth, but also reduces economic inequality (Calderson and Serven 2005). Even for the proponents of trade liberalization, investment in physical infrastructure is required to enhance efficient resource reallocation and export growth.

When physical infrastructure is made available by the ruling elite, it is usually regional or local public goods, so that national integration via internal trade is impossible to establish. When this obtains, it is possible for entrepreneurs of hatred to effectively divide numerous small groups (Glaeser et al 2005) which require cooperation to constitute an alternative political power. When local or regional goods are supplied, comparative advantage may be exploited in one region and left unexploited in others. Balanced growth is therefore impossible and evenly distributed interest groups do not exist. These groups are required if one sectional group is not to grow into a monopoly that adversely affects growth.

White elephants supplied as regional goods do not allow the benefiting region to exploit its comparative advantage, making the net impact on growth negative, except that it transfers public resources to members or supporters of the ruling elites. Regional public goods or worse still white elephants are virtually the hallmarks of ruling elite strategy of sustaining political power. This limits competitiveness of primary product exports, but more importantly, makes diversification into products that promote rapid growth impossible.

Those who are promoting open trade as a way to rapid growth are yet to tell us how it would cure infrastructural deficiency. Except when it can be established that greater level of openness would naturally lead to increased supply of public goods, it is most unlikely rapid development will take place without institutional restructuring of the state. Appropriate institutional change will prompt the formulation and implementation of proper industrial policy and optimal supply of infrastructure required to accelerate growth via industrialization and trade.

Summary and Conclusion

In this chapter, an attempt has been made to examine trade and industrial development challenges of Africa from an institutional perspective. By developing a model of institutions where ruling elites' objective function is the maximization of the relative share of total wealth, and by extension control over the larger society, the sub-optimal supply of public goods required to facilitate the process of large-scale industrial development and significant success in growth-promoting exports of manufactures and capital goods is predicted. The important public goods under-supplied include human and physical capital as well as investment in R & D activities. We therefore conclude that the mere switch from the protectionist policies of the 1960s through the 1980s to the more open and outward-oriented strategies of the 1990s have not produced the expect results because the underlying institutional cause of underdevelopment is yet to be addressed.

If the third wave of democratization in Africa has not broken this power salience, it would be foolhardy to think that a mere switch from import-substitution industrialization to export-led strategies would do so, in the short or long run. In fact, by failing to appreciate the institutional roots of underdevelopment in Africa, we tend to be dismissive of import-substitution industrialization generally. Yet historical account reveals that import-substitution strategies, properly implemented, have produced significantly positive results for general well-being elsewhere (see Sanjaya 2000 for a review). To accelerate development and mass prosperity in Africa, there is need to improve the political leadership selection process to exclude as much as possible the ruling elites described in this piece. Fundamental changes that transfer *de facto* political power to the majority need to institutionalize to ensure the production of optimal public goods that can support industrialization.

Notes

1. This is a misnomer when viewed against the backdrop of the historical growth patterns of Western nations and the more recent experiences of the East Asian tigers.
2. It is the measure of degree to which the ruling elites exclusively determine the eventual choice of collective decision or public policy. It is measured by the elite proportional share of national wealth. The higher it is, the more they are able to unilaterally influence outcome of public policy.
3. Botswana and Singapore are good examples.
4. Akerlof (1991) said this about salience, 'A central principle of modern cognitive psychology is that individuals attach too much weight to salient or vivid events and little weight to nonsalient events.' Applied to power, it implies that the ruling elites cherish the vivid picture of people looking for patronage, the thousands of people who kowtow to leadership, unquestioned rights to exercise arbitrary powers, the coterie of security personnel around them, the troop of praise singers who daily surround around them, the joy of issuing commands to other men etc.
5. This is derived from equation 8.
6. Acemoglu et al (2004) gave extreme examples such as Mobutu Sese Seko of Democratic Republic Congo, Rafael Trujillo of Dominican Republic, Duvaliers of Haiti, Idi Amin

of Uganda, Charles Taylor of Liberia, and Ferdinand Marcos of Philippines. In respect to Mobutu, Acemoglu et al said, 'He was a true kleptocrat. In the 1970s, 15-20% of the operating budget of the state went directly to Mobutu. In 1977, Mobutu's family took $71 million from the National Bank for personal use and by the early 1980s his personal fortune was estimated at $5 billion.'

7. This is an important way of redistributing towards the credit-constrained poor which could have beneficial impact on growth and development. Egalitarian educational policies pursue by some countries is toward this end.

8. This aspect of behaviour could be phrased as a rat race problem (Akerlof 1981) where competition for top position or status fuel unnecessary dissipation of energy or resources in specially branded goods valued for price rather than actually utility or value.

9. A large number of works posit a strong and positive correlation between domestic demand capacity and the level of industrialization — Rosenstein-Rodan (1943), Nurkse (1953), Lewis (1953 1954), Ranis-Fei (1961), Thorbecke (1979) and Ranis (1979). The key development approach advocated by Lewis (1953) is based on raising farm productivity and crop exports to boost domestic demand in order to bring about industrialization in Ghana.

10. Import substitution, quota restriction, import licensing, ban, over-valued exchange rate etc

11. The corruption ratings of many African countries are an ample testimony to this.

12. Haggard S. and Chung-In Moon (1990) provide comprehensive description of the Korean experience.

References

Acemoglu, Daron, Johnson, S. Robinson, J. and Thaicharoen, Y., 2003, 'Institutional Causes, Macroeconomic Symptoms: Volatility, Crises and Growth', *Journal of Monetary Economics*, Vol. 50 (January), pp. 49-123.

Acemoglu, Daron, Johnson, S., and Robinson, J., 2003b, 'The Rise of Europe: Atlantic Trade, Institutional Change and Economic Growth', Unpublished mimeo, MIT.

Acemoglu, D. et al, 2003c, 'Disease and Development in Historical Perspective', *Journal of the European Economic Association Papers and Proceedings*, V.1, pp.397-405.

Acemoglu, D., Robinson, J.A. and Verdier, T., 2004, 'Kleptocracy and Divide-And-Rule: A Model of Personal Rule', *Journal of European Economic Association*, Vol. 2 (2-3), pp. 162-192.

Akerlof, 1976, 'The Economics of Caste and of the Rat Race and Other Woeful Tales', *American Economic Review*, Vol.90 (1976) No. 4, pp. 599-617.

Anderson, J.E. and Wincoop, E., 2004, 'Trade Costs', *Journal of Economic Literature*, Vol.42, No.3, pp. 691-751.

Antonny, Manos and Pangs, Tsakloglou 2002, 'Who Benefits From Public Education? Evidence and Policy Implication', Working Paper 99-02, Department of International and European Economic Studies, Athen University of Economics and Business.

Aschauer, D.A. 1989a, 'Is Public Expenditure Productive', *Journal of Monetary Economics*, Vol. 23, pp. 177-200.

Aschauer, D.A. 1989b, 'Does Public Capital Crowd Out Private?', *Journal of Monetary Economics*, Vol. 24, pp. 171-188.

Barrow, Lisa and Rouse, Cecilia E., 2005, 'Do Returns to Schooling Differ by Race and Ethnicity?', Unpublished mimeo.

Bates, Robert 1981, *Markets and States in Tropical Africa*, University of California Press, Berkeley, CA.

Bloom, D. E. and Sach, J.D. 1998, *Geography, Demography, and Economic Growth*, Brookings Papers on Economic Activity, 2, pp. 207-295.

Bougheas, S. and Demetriades, P. O., 1995, 'Infrastructure, Specialisation and Economic Growth', Keele University Working Paper No. 95/15, Paper Presented at the Royal Economic Society Conference, Swansea, April 1996.

Bougheas, S., Demetriades, P.O., Morgenroth, L.W., 1999, 'Infrastructure, Transport Costs and Trade', *Journal of International Economics*, Vol. 47, pp. 169-189.

Calderson, C. and Serven, L. 2005, 'The Effects of Infrastructure Development on Growth and Income Distribution', Unpublished mimeo.

Canning, D., Fay, M., Perotti, R., 1994. 'Infrastructure and growth', in M. Bsaldassarri, M. Paganetto, E.S. Phelps, eds, *International Differences in Growth Rates*, New York: St. Martins Press, pp. 285– 310.

Connolly, Michelle 2003, 'Human Capital and Growth in the Post-Bellum South: A Separate But Unequal Story', Working Paper Department of Economics, Duke University.

Dennison, Edward, 1985, *Trends in American Economic Growth, 1929-1982*, Washington DC: The Brookings Institution, 1985.

Duesenberry, J., 1949, *Income, Saving and the Theory of Consumer Behavior*, Cambridge, MA: Harvard University Press.

Easterlin, R. 2003, 'Building a Better Theory of Well-Being', Discussion Paper No. 742, Bonn: IZA.

Easterly, W., 2004, 'National Policies and Economic Growth: An Appraisal', *Handbook of Economic Growth*, Vol. A1, Philippe Aghion and Steven N. Durlauf, eds.

Easterly, W. and Rebello, 1993, 'Fiscal Policy and Economic Growth: An Empirical Investigation', *Journal of Monetary Economics*, Vol. 32, pp. 417-458.

Eisemon, O. T., 1989, 'Schooling, Cognition and Creating Capacity for Technological Innovation in Africa', *International Review of Education*, Vol. 35, No. 3, pp. 329-348.

Esfahani, Hadi Salehi and Ramý´rez, Marý´a Teresa, 2003, 'Institutions, infrastructure, and economic growth', *Journal of Development Economics,* 70 (2003), pp. 443– 477.

Ferreira, P. C and Isser, J. V., 1995, 'Growth, Increasing Returns, and Public Infrastructure: Time-Series Evidence', Gatulio Vargas Foundation, Mimeo. (Paper Presented at the Econometrics Society World Congress, Tokyo, August 1995).

Frank, R., 1999, *Luxury Fever*, Princeton, NJ: Princeton University Press.

Glaeser, E. et al, 2005, 'Political Economy of Hatred', *Quarterly Journal of Economics*, Vol. 120, No., pp. 45-86.

Gramlich, E. M., 1994, 'Infrastructure Investment: A Review Essay', *Journal of Economic Literature* Vol. 32, pp. 1176-1196.

Goldin, Claudia, 1998, 'America's Graduation from High School: The Evolution and Spread of Secondary Schooling in the Twentieth Century', *Journal of Economic History*, Vol. 58, No. 2, pp. 354-374.

Goldin, Claudia, 2001, 'The Human Capital and American Leadership! Virtues of the Past', *Journal of Economic History*, 61, pp.263-91.

Hall, R. E and Jones, C. I., 1999, 'Why do some countries Produce So Much Output than Others?', *Quarterly Journal of Economics*, Vol. 114, No. 1, pp. 83-116.

Kahneman, D. and Tversky, A., 1979, 'Prospect Theory: An Analysis of Decisions Under Risk', *Econometrica*, Vol. 47, No. 2, pp. 263-292.

Killick, 1978, *Development Economics in Action: A Study of Economic Policies in Ghana*, Heinemann, London.

King, K, 1991, 'Education and Training in Africa. The Research to Control the Agenda for their Development', in D. Rimmer, ed., *Africa 30 years on*, Royal African Society, London and Portsmouth, New Hampshire: James Currey,pp. 103-144.

Krugman, Paul, 1994, 'The Myth of Asia's Miracle', *Foreign Affairs*, 73(6), pp. 62-78.

Lynde, C. and Richmond, J. 1993, 'Public Capital and Long-Run Costs in UK Manufacturing', *Economic Journal*, Vol. 103, pp. 880-893.

Lewis, W. A.,1953, *Report on the Industrialization of Gold Coast*, Accra: Government Printing Office of the Gold Coast.

Lewis, W.A. 1953, *Economic Development with Unlimited Supplies of Labour*, Manchester School, XXII, 139-91.

Mankiw, Gregory, 1995, 'The Growth of Nations', *Brookings Papers on Economic Activity* 1, pp .275-326.

Mkandawire, Thandika, 2001, 'Thinking about Developmental States in Africa', *Cambridge Journal of Economics*, Vol. 25: 289-313.

Murphy, K.M,, Shleifer, A., and Vishny, R.W. 1991, 'The Allocation of Talent: Implications for Growth', *Quarterly Journal of Economics*,Vol.106, No.2, pp. 503-30.

Murphy, K, Shleifer A., and Vishny, R.W., 1989a, 'Industrialisation and the Big Push', *Journal of Political Economy*, Vol. 97, No.5,pp. 1003-1026.

Murphy, K, Shleifer, A. and Vishny R.W., 1989b, 'Income Distribution, Market Size and Industrialisation', *Quarterly Journal of Economics*, Vol. 104, No.3, pp. 537-564.

Myrdal, G. 1968, *Asian Drama: An Inquiry into the Poverty of Nations*, 3 Volumes, Twentieth Century Fund, New York.

Nelson, Richard and Edmund, Philip, 1966, 'Investment in Humans, Technological Diffusion and Economic Growth', *American Economic Review*, 56, No.2, pp. 69-75

Niskanen, Williams, 1997, 'Autocratic, Democratic, and Optimal Government', *Economic Inquiry*, Vol. XXXV, July, pp. 464-479.

Nurkse, Ragnar, 1953, *Problems of Capital Formation in Underdeveloped Countries*, Oxford: Basil Blackwell.

Olayiwola, Kolawole and Dipo, Busari, 2008, 'Macroeconomic Stability or Good Institutions of Governance: What is Africa Getting Wrong?', Covenant University College Seminar.

Oyelaran-Oyeyinka, B. and Barclay, Lou Anne, 2004, 'Systems of Innovation and Human Capital in African Development' *African Development Review*, Vol 16, No 1, pp 115-138.

Oyelere, U. R. 2007, 'Brain Drain, Waste or Gain? What We Know about the Kenyan Case', Unpublished mimeo, School of Economics, Georgia Institute of Technology.

Parente, S. L and Prescott, E. C., 1994, 'Barriers to Technology and Development', *Journal of Political Economy*, Vol. 102, No. 2, pp. 298-321.

Parente, S. L. and Prescott, E. C., 1999, 'Monopoly Rights: A Barrier to Riches', *American Economic Review*, Vol. 89, No. 5, pp. 1216-1233.

Przeworski, Adam, 2005, 'Geography vs. Institutions Revisited: Were Fortunes Reversed?' Unpublished mimeo, New York University.

Ranis, G. and Fei J. H. H., 1961, 'A Theory of Economic Development', *American Economic Review*, LI, pp. 533-65.

Ranis, G., 1979, 'Industrial Development', in *Economic Growth and Structural Change in Taiwan*, Walter Galenson, ed., Ithaca and London: Cornell University Press.

Rosenstein-Rodan, Paul 1943, 'The Problems of Industrialization of Eastern and South-Eastern Europe, *Economic Journal*, 53, pp. 202-211.

Sobel, R.S., 2008, 'Testing Baumol: Institutional Quality and the Productivity of Entrepreneurship', *Journal of Business Venturing*, Vol. 23, No 6, pp.641-655.

Sach, J. D., 2000, 'Notes on the New Sociology of Economic Development', in Lawrence E. Harrison and Samuel P. Huntington' eds, *Culture Matters: How Values Shape Human Progress*, New York: Basic Books.

Sachs, Jeffrey, 2005, *The End of Poverty: Economic Possibilities for Our Time*, New York: Penguin Press.

Sanchez-Robles, B., 1998, 'Infrastructure investment and growth: some empirical evidence', *Contemporary Economic Policy*, 16, pp. 98–108.

Lall, Sanjaya, 2000, 'Selective Industrial and Trade Policies in Developing Countries: Theoretical and Empirical Issues', QEH Working Paper Number 48.

Sawyer, John E. 1954, 'The Social of the American System of Manufacturing, *Journal of Economic History*, 14, pp. 361-79.

Thorbecke, E., 1979, 'Agricultural Development', in *Economic Growth and Structural Change in Taiwan*», Walter Galenson, ed., Ithaca and London: Cornell University Press.

Tooley, J., 2006, 'Educating Amaretch: Private Schools for the poor and the new frontier for investors' , IFC and the *Financial Times* First Annual Essay Competition, Business and Development: Private Path to Prosperity.

Witold, Henisz, 2004, 'Political Institutions and Policy Volatility', *Economics and Politics*, Vol. 16, No.1: 1-27.

Wood, A. and Mayer, J. 2001, 'Africa's Export Structure in a Comparative Perspective', *Cambridge Journal of Economics*, Vol. 25, pp. 369-394.

World Bank, 2006, *Global Economic Prospects: Economic Implications of Remittances and Migration* Washington: World Bank.

World Health Organisation, 2006, *Working Together for Health. World Health Report*, Publication of the World Health Organization.

Wright, G. 1986, *Old South New South: Revolutions in the Southern Economy since the Civil War*, New York: Basic Books.

Young, Alwyn, 1995, 'The Tyranny of Numbers: Confronting the Statistical Realities of the East Asian Growth Experience', *Quarterly Journal of Economics*, 110(3), pp. 641-80.

14

Conclusion and Recommendations

Theresa Moyo and Aderibigbe S. Olomola

Introduction

The central theme of the book is the re-thinking of Africa's trade and industrial policy so that it promotes development. This arises from the recognition that, although trade and industry have a potential to increase economic growth and contribute significantly towards social, economic and human development, this has not been the case for many African countries despite the continent's rich endowment with natural and human resources. Data from UNIDO, UNCTAD and the African Development Bank, among other sources, show clearly that although there have been some improvements in the last 10 years, these sectors are not as developed as they could be. Except for a few countries such as South Africa, Mauritius, Morocco, Egypt and Tunisia, industrial development in most of Africa is limited. This is evident in the smaller share of Africa's Manufacturing Value Added (MVA) in global MVA. The share of manufacturing exports in total exports has also remained small. In addition, intra-African trade flows are still small compared to trade with the Northern or advanced countries.

Summary of Key Issues

Several issues are raised in relation to trade and industrial policy in Africa. These are summarized as follows:

Stagnation of African Industry and Dominance of Primary Commodities in Trade

A fundamental issue of concern relates to the continued domination of primary commodities in exports, a pattern of specialization which has been dictated by an out-dated, neo-liberal and neo-classical notion of 'comparative advantage'. The so-called 'comparative advantage' continues to disadvantage the African continent because of the inherent inequality which characterizes any pattern of trade where a developing country exports primary commodities (with lower prices) and imports manufactured goods (which fetch higher prices than unprocessed goods). Alternative strategies and policies must therefore seek to find solutions to build and develop the productive capacity which is critical for enhancing the MVA and therefore transforming the structure of African trade. In essence, African states should be seeking new and dynamic comparative advantages which are only feasible if a strong industrial base is developed.

The new Global Trading and Finance Environment Restricts use of Trade and Industrial Policies

As argued by Moyo and Olomola, the new global trading and finance environment has ushered in new rules which seek to promote a more market-driven or free market system. At the political level, the unequal power relations between Africa and the advanced countries continues to dictate a pattern of specialization in production and exchange which disadvantages the continent. The emergence of the WTO, with its rules-based international trading and financial system, has ushered in a shift in trade policy from state-led or controlled trade and industrial development towards more market-based, free trade approaches. It is a system which advocates trade liberalization on an unprecedented scale. The challenge for African countries hinges on the asymmetrical nature of the implementation of the WTO rules, that, whereas they are forced to open up their economies, a number of the advanced countries continue to protect their markets, thereby making it difficult for African countries to access those markets. As Olomola argues in Chapter 6, Northern countries continue to subsidize their farmers, making imported agricultural products into Africa much cheaper than local products. He argues that the situation is making it difficult for many African farmers to compete and survive. It is driving farmers off the land and has created poverty. Greater reliance of African countries on cheap food imports is also undermining food security as local agriculture stagnates in the face of subsidized Northern agriculture. Re-thinking Africa's trade and industrial policies is fundamentally linked to the quest for a just and equitable global trading and finance system in which trade rules are applied fairly and also take into account the historical realities and contexts within which countries exist. Since negotiations on WTO agreements are still on-going, African states need to continue to lobby for rules/agreements which will enhance the developmental aspirations of the continent. Specific recommendations are made under section 14.3.

Trade Liberalization Versus Africa's Limited Productive Capacity

The pursuit of trade liberalization policies at a time when the fundamental requirements are not in place (as reflected, for example, in the low productivity levels of industry and the consequent low level of competitiveness, the inadequate human and technological base, among other factors), has retarded rather than facilitated industrial development and trade expansion. Liberalization of African economies has opened them up to stiff external competition. As a consequence, in a number of countries, trade liberalization has led to de-industrialization rather than enhancing local industrial capacity. De-industrialization, in turn, has led to stagnation of the growth of manufactured exports. Describing Zambia's experience with the IMF-World Bank supported Structural Adjustment Programmes, Chiputa demonstrates how trade liberalization actually destroyed Zambia's industrialization base. Sunday Khan explains how, although local industry has benefited from trading with China in terms of access to cheap consumer and durable goods, the net effect of that trade has not been beneficial to Cameroun because, he argues, the cheap imports have made local industries uncompetitive, with a number actually closing. In the case of Botswana, Kapunda argues that the flood of cheap Chinese imports led to the closure of some local textile industries. In the case of Tanzania, he observes, trade liberalization did not lead to a significant transformation of the industrial sector because most of the private investment was channelled into consumer and light goods industries instead of the intermediate and capital goods sector which are the cornerstone of a country's industrial base. Emina-Monye, writing about Nigeria's experiences with SAPs, concludes that trade liberalization failed largely due to the inadequate capacity of the local industrial sector and the absence of mechanisms for greater intra-industry and inter-sectoral linkages.

At the structural level, African trade and industrial growth are constrained by weak productive capacities at national and regional levels. This is due to lack of technical skills and technology which are critical for building an industrial base.

As argued by Memfih in Chapter 7, high transportation costs, poor access to market information and lack of reliable and efficient services such as telecommunications, electricity and water, have also constrained the growth of trade and industry. Consequently, intra-African trade constitutes a relatively smaller proportion of the continent's trade and financial flows in relation to that with industrialized countries and other least developed nations in Asia and Latin America.

Institutional Weaknesses

Weak governance and lack of accountability has also contributed to the failure to implement many of the industrial development strategies which have been developed in the past. For example, the Lagos Plan of Action, the UN Industrial Development Decade for Africa (IDDA), the AU Africa Productive Capacity Initiative (APCI), among others. Furthermore, even where there are potential benefits to be reaped from WTO agreements, for example the potential for technology transfer from the industrialised to least developed countries.

Recommendations: Towards Alternative Strategies and Policies for Trade and Industrial Development in Africa

A number of strategies and policies are proposed in response to the many challenges which are presented in the book.

A Fundamental Paradigm Shift: A Developmental Framework for Trade and Industry

The case for a developmental trade and industrial policy for Africa is cast within the broader framework of what is the meaning of development in an African context. Moyo, in Chapter 2 evokes development as a multi-dimensional and complex process which seeks to enhance the human, social, economic and cultural welfare of people. As shown in the work of Sen (1998), development is about enhancing the capability of the people to function, to have the freedom of choice and to realise their full potential. A developmental trade and industrial policy must therefore aim to advance human development as contextualized by Sen. It should promote economic growth, create decent jobs, and promote value-addition which enhances Africa's competitiveness internationally.

It must also be an approach which is based on the mutual interdependence of nations as equal partners. It must deepen Africa's productive capacity and promote the exchange of goods and services on terms which are mutually beneficial between North and South as well as among Southern countries. Thus, the quest for alternative trade and industry strategies and policies essentially calls for a fundamental paradigm shift from a neo-liberal, wholesale 'free-trade'/market-liberalization model towards a more transformational, developmental, dynamic, innovative and pro-poor oriented approach. Such a paradigm shift also implies that, even while promoting the role of the private sector in trade and industrial development, there is still room for the creative use of appropriate policies as may be necessary in specific country contexts and situations.

Structural Transformation of African Economies

A structural transformation of African economies is inevitable in order to achieve the shift from the dominant paradigm of primary production and exports – a model which has been dictated by historical, colonial, neo-colonial and neo-liberal comparative advantage theories. There must be a shift towards seeking new comparative advantages which enhance Africa's productive capacities so that they can produce more manufactured goods and ultimately improve their share in MVA in global output. To achieve such transformation requires active participation by the state.

UNCTAD (2006) emphasizes that the Least Developed Countries have to develop and enhance their productive capacities. It argues that:

> Developing productive capacities is the key to achieving sustained economic growth in the LDCs. It is through developing their productive capacities that the LDCs will be able to rely increasingly on domestic resource mobilisation to finance economic growth, to reduce dependence and to attract private capital inflows of a type that can support their development process. It is also through developing their productive capacities that the LDCs will be able to compete in international markets in goods and services which go beyond primary commodities and which are not dependent on special market access preferences.

In essence, it means that even if African nations were able to gain increasing access to markets in Northern countries and through South-South cooperation, without developing their domestic productive capacities, they will not be able to gain much through trade. Substantive gains through trade will arise largely through improving domestic manufacturing of goods and services.

A developmental trade and industrial policy should therefore formulate and implement strategies which support domestic producers in agro-processing, mineral processing and other related manufacturing activities which tap on the continent's natural resource base. Developing productive capacity calls for African states to invest in technology development, skills development, entrepreneurial skills, support to the small-to-medium-scale enterprise sector, promoting linkages between the public and private sectors through Private Public Partnerships (PPPs).

The state has an important role to play in all this. As argued by North (1990) and Chang and Rowthorn (1995), and also demonstrated by successful industrialisers in East and South Asia, 'there is no industrialized country in which the government has not played a central role in promoting and supporting change'. This is not to advocate any form of government intervention, particularly in view of the failure of some of the forms of state intervention in the 1960s and 1970s. Rather, it is to define specific strategies where the state can play a role, for example, development and financing of industrial infrastructure, cluster formation, partnership development, an appropriate policy environment to attract local and foreign firms into local manufacturing.

The UN ECA (2010) proposes practical strategies to achieve structural transformation. It postulates that:

> Long-term strategies involve investment that will transform the structure of African economies from reliance on low-employment-generation natural resource extraction to high-employment labour-intensive manufacturing, agro-industry and service provision. In addition to changing the pattern of investment and production, it will also require not only an increase in the quantity of human capital, but a change n the type of human capital that will be provided. Factor markets will have to be reformed to encourage the use of labour-intensive production techniques, in contrast to current policies which favour capital-intensive techniques.

The Commission also identifies potential sources of financing to promote structural transformation. These include investing the rents from commodity exports in labour-intensive non-resource sectors to expand output and increase productivity in these sectors; making resources (e.g., financing) available to priority sectors at reasonable rates. It also suggests aggressive efforts to attract FDI in non-resource-extraction sectors, especially in the areas of service exports, agro-industry and 'green' industries, such as renewable energy, where Africa may have a comparative advantage; and creating an enabling environment for the private sector to invest and create jobs.

The emphasis on labour-intensive manufacturing is important because of the high unemployment in most African countries. However, emphasis must also be on ensuring that there are investments in human capital development in order to improve the quality and skills levels of that labour.

Because women and other vulnerable groups tend to be marginalized from industry and trade, the UN ECA also emphasizes the need to pay special attention to vulnerable groups, such as women and young people, with special targeted employment interventions.

A More Flexible, Dynamic and Innovative Approach

Sub-Saharan African countries should draw some lessons from the experiences of the East and South-Asian countries which embarked on their industrialization through export promotion based on an aggressive strategy of industrial development. Contrary to the prescriptions of the SAP model, in the early stages of their industrialization effort, they used state intervention (infrastructural support, tariff and non-tariff protection, linkages between Transnational Corporations and local enterprises, export incentives, for example) to promote the growth of domestic industry. The major recommendation is that a more developmental trade and industry agenda must be driven by the state as was the case with some countries in East and South Asia; that industrial policy must advocate a more selective and targeted approach to providing state support and incentives to emerging industry, that a phased approach within a short, medium to long-term framework would be more ideal than a strategy which embraces wholesale opening up of African markets to external competition when domestic industries are ill-prepared, as was the case with the World Bank and IMF- determined SAP model. The structural adjustment policy was expenditure-reducing, trade liberalizing and outward-looking, with emphasis on export promotion. The adjustment policy was desirable to address the macroeconomic disturbances that emerged in the wake of a slump in the world market in the early 1980s. The adopted trade and industrial policy, however, failed to yield the desired result.

Dialogue with Industrialized Countries over the WTO

It will be necessary for Africa to enter into extensive dialogue with Northern countries in the context of the Doha Development Round and to try to influence the developmental agenda of the WTO so that it is more favourable to Africa. In addition to the provision of better market access and reduction in subsidies for products competing with African exports, external resources are required to compensate for losses and to fill the resource gap in order to ensure adequate investment in the development of human and physical infrastructure, institution building and diversification. There is a need to promote South-South cooperation and encourage effective regional integration within the continent through deliberate African efforts and initiative. This is not to say African countries should not trade with the North; but the trading arrangements with the developed world should be more gradual and only entered into after careful and informed negotiation.

Moreover, Africa should seek a more unified approach to dealing with the World Trade Organisation (WTO) some of whose trading rules have been criticized for further marginalizing rather than developing Africa. Africa should have a common agenda in negotiating the Economic Partnership Agreements (EPAs) with the European Union instead of what the continent has witnessed as many African nations, through their regional groupings (SADC, COMESA, EAC, ECOWAS) or even as individuals (e.g. South Africa). Furthermore, non-tariff measures such as sanitary and phyto-sanitary technical barriers to trade, requirements and other contingency trade-protection measures should be applied in a manner that does not necessarily hinder the exports of African countries. Such a process would be facilitated by greater liberalization of OECD domestic agricultural markets through a significant reduction, and finally elimination, of massive agricultural subsidies and support for commodities such as cotton, groundnuts and sugar, which are of export interest to Africa.

Build on and implement Past Initiatives Developed to Promote Industrial Development

African governments should take advantage of the many innovations which have been developed in the past but have not yet been implemented. For example, the African Productive Capacity Initiative (APCI) which was developed under the auspices of the AU-Council of African Ministers of Industry (CAMI) and with support from UNIDO, should be the basis of developing a more comprehensive continental industrialization strategy. Since one of the reasons for the failure to implement the initiative was the lack of financing, African governments should embark on a massive resource mobilization strategy to finance the programme. Priority should be to use their own national resources such as revenues from mining royalties, land taxes and budgetary resources. They should also explore funding sources within the framework of South-South Cooperation. Joint ventures with companies from the BRICS countries (Brazil, Russia, India, China and South Africa), should be established within the context of a comprehensive framework for South-South Cooperation which African governments should develop in order to ensure that there is no replication of the unequal and, in some instances, exploitative relationship which has characterized North-South trade relationships.

Industrial development should also be integrated into National Development Plans or Strategies. The experiences of the successful industrializers in East Asia show the important role which was played by carefully designed long-term plans for national development which also included industrial development. Some African countries have already embarked on such processes; for example, South Africa (under IPAP I and II), Morocco, Botswana and Mauritius. These plans may be in their infancy but at least they demonstrate a commitment towards diversification of their economies.

Firstly, African governments should take advantage of existing rules within WTO where there is still room for manoeuvre in terms of the possibility of using protectionism to grow the local industrial base. For example, WTO allows for a phased approach to tariff reduction and provision of subsidies to certain sectors or sub-sectors. These provisions should be used intensively to support the emergence and growth of African industry.

Human Capital Development

It is also necessary for African governments to invest massive sums of money into human resource development, particularly in terms of skills in science and engineering and other technical fields. National budget policies should prioritize and increase allocations towards the education sector in the fields alluded to above and also promote vocational education. Government policies should also be used to create an environment which can promote the creation of joint ventures between local firms and those from other countries of the South, BRICs and others where the continent can benefit in terms of access to technology and skills.

Investment into Trade and Industry Infrastructure

Secondly, African governments should develop comprehensive strategies for industry and trade infrastructure which Memfih has shown to be a major obstacle to intra-African trade. Investments to improve infrastructure will improve such trade. According to UN ECA (2010), the second global review of the Aid for Trade (AfT) initiative concluded that progress had been made. By 2007, commitments to Africa had risen by 62 per cent to US$ 8.3 billion. Economic infrastructure (60 %) and productive capacity (36 per cent) accounted for the bulk of these commitments. The review indicated areas of emphasis on future AfT commitments, including the honouring of pledges. African governments should follow through on those pledges and channel the resources into building and strengthening productive capacity and exchange institutions, infrastructure and processes.

Invest into Strengthening of RECs

Furthermore, the need for regional approaches and strategic partnerships to complement national measures must be stressed, since international trade involves the use of infrastructure and services of at least two countries. This is especially true for landlocked countries with key transit facilities lying outside their territorial boundaries. A regional approach can be an efficient means of coordinating actions, setting priorities, reviewing progress, mobilizing resources, allocating funds, and monitoring contribution levels, with regard to solving common problems. It is important to stress that despite significant reductions in tariff and non-tariff barriers in many African countries in recent times, government policies, including restrictive trade and poor customs regulations and administration – all related issues of trade facilitation – still continue to discourage exporting from the continent. Significant improvements in infrastructure, well- functioning institutions, and e-business usages may expand trade; whereas regulatory barriers and the perception of corruption in a country will deter trade in Africa. Governments in different African countries will need to emulate the drive towards best practices in investment climate and well- functioning institutions, which seem to be driving the success of APEC regional member countries in trade and industrial expansion in the global value chain.

Development of a Comprehensive Framework for South-South Cooperation

African states should also explore the opportunities offered by South-South cooperation. It must be recognized, however, that there is a danger that unless there is a clear strategic framework to ensure that such cooperation serves Africa's development agenda, it may also end up replicating the traditional trading relations between Africa and the industrialized Northern countries. The African Union, in particular, should take the initiative to develop a framework for Africa's cooperation with countries of the South – a framework which does not replicate the traditional North-South trading and financial relationships. Africa's cooperation with emerging economies such as China, India and Brazil, among others, must lead to diversification of its production base instead of perpetuating the production and sale of commodities and raw materials. African states should be negotiating for trade and investment agreements which promote joint ventures with companies from emerging economies as well as any other companies from the industrialized world (as long as they are willing to enter into the kind of agreements which are herein proposed). Such ventures, among other things, should also increase investment in infrastructure development, technology transfer and human capital development in order to enhance Africa's productive capacity.

South-South Cooperation should be a vehicle that enables Africa to shift from primary to manufactured goods production and exports. It should lead to a shift where Africa moves from being a net importer of consumer goods towards a situation where it imports more capital goods which can enable it to develop local productive capacities. Appropriate trade policies to achieve that goal should be explored.

Resource Mobilization for Financing Trade and Industry development

UN ECA advocates a more inward-looking approach to resource mobilization. According to its 2010 report, it says:

> Finally, Africa cannot continue to rely on the international community to finance its development agenda. It is therefore important for African countries to boost their efforts to increase the mobilization of domestic resources to finance African development through innovative programmes. Increasing the savings rate to the levels attained by East Asian countries, will generate substantial revenue to finance development in Africa. Financing development from domestic resources will not only reduce the volatility inherent in African development, but will also make Africans 'masters of their destinies'.

Trade and Industrial Policy: International and Regional Context

The configuration of trade between Africa and major international trading partners has been changing considerably in recent times. This is an issue because goods imported from China pose more of a competitive threat to locally manufactured goods than those from Europe, which are generally more expensive and allow some market space for local industry. Trade with China is providing cheap and diverse consumption and capital goods, though issues of quality abound. These imports pose a great challenge for Africa's competitiveness not only in the domestic market, but also in sub-regional export markets. Wages and employment are also likely to be affected. Specialization in the export of primary commodities (due to rising global prices) and import of cheap manufactures from China risk undermining the industrial sector and locking Africa in primary activities. Trade with China presents both opportunities and challenges, and it is advisable for African countries to systematically and regularly assess the nature and impact on their economies with a view to maximizing the benefits and reducing the risks.

With regard to other trading partners, especially the EU, the emerging trade policies tend to have deleterious consequences for industrial development in Africa. For instance, the implications of the Economic Partnership Agreements (EPAs) under which the EU's trade with African countries is to be negotiated appear to pose even greater challenges. In agriculture, which is the largest sector in many African countries in terms of contribution to gross domestic output and employment, free trade agreements with the EU often emphasize the promise that all farmers will find prosperity by increasing their export market shares. To the contrary, however, the free trade model in agriculture is flawed and has been regarded as one of the major causes of hunger and poverty around the world. The potential benefit appears to be limited in view of the liberalization policies already put in place in many countries. Evidence suggests that both LDCs and non-LDC African ACP countries will face considerable challenges if they comply with the so-called WTO compatible reciprocal liberalization policies inherent in the EPAs. A review of the potential impact of African regional EPAs with the EU shows that there may be a decline in welfare levels, as the losses in tariff revenues exceed any gains from trade through lower import prices, and that unilateral trade liberalization by African ACP countries would be better for sustained economic growth and development. Thus, it is expected that changes in current form of the EPAs will be required in several areas, especially in terms of (i) doing away with arbitrary timeframes and setting realistic time that reflects the pace of development in Africa, (ii) reviewing the rules of origin and the demand for reciprocity, (iii) providing concrete assurance to address resulting revenue losses by African countries, (iv) supporting regional initiatives aimed at developing African agriculture, and (v) ensuring that African countries are not constrained in attaining the MDGs. The agricultural sector should be regarded as a sensitive sector and should be exempted from any rule of reciprocity. On the domestic scene, African governments must ensure that appropriate policies are put in place to transform the agricultural sector from being exporter of raw materials to exporter of value-added commodities that enhance their revenue generation potential and guarantee sustainable livelihood for the masses of the people that depend largely on agriculture.

Dealing with Climate Change

Industrial development in Africa must be pursued within the context of emerging discourse and negotiations on climate change. There is a need for increased awareness around the Kyoto Protocol (KP) and post-KP carbon trade facilitation in Africa. The continent must see itself performing an increasing and irreversible, pro-active, pro-participatory role regarding the post-KP trade mechanisms. In order to reap the benefits of fair trade mechanisms within the new KP, emphasis must be on: the use of CDM project quota system; the need for capacity building and sustained awareness raising programme; mobilization of more local financial resources; the role of national GHG mitigation and adaptation policies and legislation; the call to prioritize climate change adaptation rather than mitigation; the call for climate justice, right to economic growth and co-leadership in climate change.

Intellectual Property Rights, Technology Transfer and Culture Policy

The fact that innocent law is not easy to come by implies that attention should be paid on how international intellectual property laws are appropriated in African countries in order to create and increase their beneficial effect. Law has to be intertwined with reality; reality can give orientation for the adoption of a subsequent law; also a law can be adopted to create an incentive for the implementation of a policy. But definitely, as part of the trade and industrial policy, the solution goes beyond the simple considerations of law versus the reality. The best approach is neither legal, nor managerial, nor sociological, nor historical, etc... (Mhone, 2003:4). In fact, an efficient approach shall take into consideration all these aspects; none of them alone, but all of them together. It seems that Africa is still far from benefiting from the IP international legislation on technology transfer. However, law cannot be the only culprit. It has its part of responsibility, as well as many other factors. The international arena offers a great opportunity to improve Africa's development. There should be attention on an increased representation of African interests in this arena, coupled with a voluntarist approach to development and technology transfer at national levels. The feasibility is hard; meanwhile possibilities exist. The presumption of profit remains; African countries have to and can find their way, with laws, but also beyond.

Institutional Dimensions of Trade and Industry Policy

The low level of industrial development in Africa after decades of political independence of many countries warrants a rethinking of the industrial policy within an appropriate institutional framework. In developing the framework, an effort is made to contrast the development trajectories of SEA and SSA with a focus on the role of manufacturing. Although there were weaknesses with the industry put in place after independence, instead of building on the accumulated knowledge and capacities, the structural adjustment programmes of the 1980s worsened the situation and virtually laid the foundation for the collapse of the industrial sector leaving the countries increasingly reliant on resource exports. As a result, African economies have been subjected to the vicissitudes of commodity prices, with adverse consequences for the terms of trade and the standard of living of the people. The SAP approach failed to realize that development is a dynamic process that requires the institutional and structural transformation of economies. As shown by the experience of Asia - there is no alternative to a state-led approach to transforming economies through industrial policy interventions.

A further analysis of the trade and industrial development challenges of Africa reveals a sub-optimal supply of public goods required to facilitate the process of large-scale industrial development and significant success in growth-promoting exports of manufactures and capital goods. The important public goods under-supplied include human and physical capital as well as investment in R & D activities. As a corollary, the mere switch from the protectionist policies of the 1960s through the 1980s to the more open and outward-oriented strategies of the 1990s have not produced the expected results because the underlying institutional cause of underdevelopment is yet to be addressed. In this connection, the lack of good governance, as well as weak and corrupt leadership, has to be resolved. Otherwise, a mere policy switch from import-substitution industrialization to export-led strategies cannot be expected to significantly promote industrialization in Africa in the short or long run. Historical account reveals that import-substitution strategies, properly implemented, have produced significantly positive results for general well-being elsewhere. To accelerate development and mass prosperity in Africa there is need to improve the political leadership selection process to exclude as much as possible the ruling elites described in this piece. Fundamental changes that transfer *de facto* political power to the majority need to be institutionalized in order to ensure the production of optimal public goods that can support industrialization.

Finally, Africa must pursue industrialization on the basis of the available natural resource endowment. Following the local resource-based approach, the process of industrialization can begin with semi-processing of such natural resources and over time develop them into a fully processed products. This development should depend largely on local engineering and industrial technology which must be encouraged to evolve for the purpose. While regional integration is being promoted, it is important that individual countries rise up to the challenge of designing and implementing appropriate harmonization industrial policies while maintaining national industrial policies and interest and accommodating other global trade agreements. African countries should take advantage of the opportunities arising from regional industrial policy harmonization. Furthermore, they should take advantage of international opportunities like those implied in AGOA, EPA and others, while not compromising their national interest.